"Peniel Joseph, the preeminent scholar of Black Power studies, has written the definitive biography of Stokely Carmichael, one of the most important figures of the post-World War II era. Exhaustively researched and beautifully written, Joseph's nuanced biography reveals the crucial interconnections between militants and moderates, nationalists and integrationists, with Stokely emerging as an essential leader of the civil rights movement."

—John Stauffer, author of *Giants:*
The Parallel Lives of Frederick Douglass and Abraham Lincoln

"*Stokely: A Life* is a magisterial biography of one of the most important figures in the history of the black freedom struggle in America. Peniel Joseph paints a vibrant and sweeping portrait of the times that shaped Stokely Carmichael, and in turn, portrays how Carmichael impacted his age with imaginative social activism and provocative ideas. By tracing Carmichael's ascent through the ranks of black resistance to the front ranks of the struggle for "Black Power"—the slogan he immortalized—Joseph wields his poetic pen to tell a riveting story of a generation hungry for affirmation and influence beyond the outlines of nonviolent protest. If Martin was the King of civil disobedience, then Carmichael was the Prince of black revolution, and *Stokely* is the brilliant chronicle of his complicated and remarkable reign during tempestuous times."

—Michael Eric Dyson, author of *April 4, 1968:*
Martin Luther King, Jr.'s Death and How it Changed America

"Stokely Carmichael made his name with a two word proclamation: 'Black Power.' In this compelling narrative, Peniel Joseph, the leading historian of the black power movement, reconstructs Stokely Carmichael's influential life from his childhood in Trinidad to his involvement in the Freedom Rides and SNCC to his role in the rise of the Black Panthers to his last days as a radical internationalist in Guinea, grappling with the politics of race and resistance, the promise and limits of black radicalism, and the temptations of celebrity. This book belongs on a short shelf of must-read biographies of the era."

—Thomas J. Sugrue, author of *Sweet Land of Liberty:*
The Forgotten Struggle for Civil Rights in the North

"When Kwame Ture died in 1998, the *New York Times* obituary identified him as the 'Rights Leader Who Coined "Black Power,"' effectively reducing the most revolutionary voice in the Civil Rights movement to slogan. Peniel Joseph changes all that with this richly documented political and intellectual biography. Without polemics or apologetics, Joseph brings Ture's radical ideas into clear focus—from his Pan-African socialist vision and his critique of empire to his unwavering commitment to mass-based revolution."

—Robin D. G. Kelley, author of *Thelonious Monk:*
The Life and Times of an American Original

"Peniel Joseph has delivered a masterwork for generations to come. Without making the rough edges smooth, Joseph captures the essence of why Stokely Carmichael was the voice who aroused a voiceless generation, the wretched of the earth. We who knew the real Stokely in the many phases of his life always loved him, learned from him, laughed at his wisecracks, and were awed by his risk-taking and courage. He opened our dying culture to new possibilities of freedom."

—Tom Hayden, Director, Peace and Justice Resource Center

"By tracing the life and work of a brilliant and charismatic soldier for racial change, this beautifully realized biography opens windows into the complex and often vexed ideas, strategies, and contributions of Black Power. As a result, we now possess a richer understanding of how leadership and movement insurgency helped remake modern America under conditions of deep racism and wartime violence, and of how American insurgencies came to possess a global imagination."

—Ira Katznelson, author of *Fear Itself:*
The New Deal and the Origins of Our Time

"Peniel Joseph has succeeded in bringing Stokely Carmichael back to life. *Stokely* transports the reader on an insightful and entertaining journey through postwar New York City, the Civil Rights Movement, and the late Cold War years in the United States and Africa. This is the history of a remarkable individual who embodied many of the tumultuous changes occurring around him. The powerful accomplishments and lingering disappointments of racial reform are elucidated in this beautifully written and deeply researched biography. Anyone interested in recent history should read this path-breaking book."

—Jeremi Suri, Mack Brown Distinguished Chair for Leadership in Global Affairs, University of Texas at Austin, and author of *Liberty's Surest Guardian:*
American Nation-Building from the Founders to Obama

"Peniel Joseph long has been acknowledged as our premier interpreter of Black Power. And now with the publication of this magisterial book—this exceedingly thoughtful and beautifully written study—Peniel Joseph has been catapulted into the front ranks of historians of Black America."

—Gerald Horne, John J. and Rebecca Moores Chair of History and African American Studies, University of Houston

STOKELY

A Life

ALSO BY PENIEL E. JOSEPH

Dark Days, Bright Nights

Waiting 'Til the Midnight Hour

STOKELY

A Life

By **Peniel E. Joseph**

BASIC *CIVITAS*

A Member of the Perseus Books Group

New York

Designed by Pauline Brown
Typeset in 11-point Minion Pro by the Perseus Books Group

Library of Congress Cataloging-in-Publication Data

Joseph, Peniel E.
Stokely : a life / Peniel E. Joseph.
    pages cm
Includes bibliographical references and index.
ISBN 978-0-465-01363-0 (hardback)—ISBN 978-0-465-08048-9 (epub)
1. Carmichael, Stokely. 2. African American civil rights workers—Biography. 3. Civil rights workers—United States—Biography. 4. Black power—United States—History—20th century. 5. African Americans—Civil rights—History—20th century. 6. Civil rights movements—United States—History—20th century. 7. United States—Race relations—History—20th century. I. Title.
E185.97.C27J63 2014
323.092—dc23

[B]

2013032408

For Astrid

Contents

Preface

STOKELY CARMICHAEL IS A TROUBLING ICON OF AMERICA'S CIVIL RIGHTS years. His Black Power call became a national Rorschach test: whereas many blacks viewed it as righteous, many whites saw violent foreboding. Newspapers brooded over Carmichael's words, quickly forming a consensus that judged the slogan to be at best intemperate and, at worst, a blatant call for anti-white violence and reverse racism. In 1966, Black Power reverberated around the world, galvanizing blacks, outraging whites, and inspiring a cross-section of ethnic and racial minorities. In 1969, Carmichael left the United States for Conakry, Guinea, where he reinvented himself as a roving Pan-Africanist organizer and professional revolutionary. For the next thirty years, he remained an energetic dissident, a throwback to the heady years of the 1960s. Carmichael turned the quest for black political power into his life's work. His faith in a style of politics many considered anachronistic came out of the same tenacity and stubbornness that once made him the most effective and controversial activist of his generation. These same qualities, however, limited Carmichael's efforts as a Pan-Africanist political mobilizer.

Before leaving America, Stokely reigned as Black Power's glamorous *enfant terrible:* telegenic, brash, equal parts angry and gregarious. Whether dressed in three-piece suits, leather jackets, sharecropper's overalls, or African dashikis, Carmichael came to represent the era's multifaceted identity: a "hipster hero" whose easy grace allowed him to consort effortlessly with both the dignified and the damned.[1]

The name Stokely Carmichael first came into my consciousness when I was a young boy coming of age in New York City. As the proud son of a Haitian mother who belonged to Local 1199 Hospital Workers union (a part of the Service Employees International Union), I grew up hearing stories of how civil rights activists, Black Power revolutionaries, Pan-Africanist freedom fighters, and trade unionists helped to shape a new world in America and beyond. By the time I was in elementary school I was on my first picket line, accompanying my mother in support of an 1199 strike. Malcolm X, Martin Luther King Jr., and Stokely Carmichael supported 1199 during the 1960s. Stokely's political importance came into sharper focus when I was in junior high, after the premiere of the landmark PBS documentary series *Eyes on the Prize,* which featured the twenty-four-year-old Carmichael's fiery "Black Power" speech and rightly characterized Stokely as his generation's heir to Malcolm X. Over the course of a decade of research on Carmichael, I would come to understand him as that and much more.

Carmichael's youth, casual dress, and charisma made him an easily identifiable hero, one whose quick smile and passionate speeches left an indelible impression. An adopted son of the South by way of Trinidad, the Bronx, and Harlem, Stokely adapted to while transforming whatever environment he encountered. As a native New Yorker growing up in the city's tense racial climate of the 1980s, I found Carmichael's survival instincts appealing. As a young graduate student in Philadelphia, I had the opportunity to hear him speak and briefly met him afterward. He encouraged me to stay committed to the black freedom movement, a struggle he defined as infinite. With his flowing African robes, gray hair, and white beard he looked like a prince. And he had changed his name. He was no longer Stokely Carmichael. As Malcolm Little had become Malcolm X and later, El Hajj Malik El Shabazz, Stokely had become Kwame Ture. It was a name that paid homage to his two African heroes: men who had been the first presidents of their countries: Ghana's Kwame Nkrumah and Guinea's Sékou Touré. Kwame Ture spelled the Guinean's name not as the French did, as white Europeans did, but as Arabs and Muslims did: Seku Ture.

As a college student, Carmichael helped transform America by organizing sit-ins, demonstrations, and voter registration during the civil rights movement's heroic years, a period that roughly encompasses the decade between the 1954 *Brown* Supreme Court desegregation decision and the 1965 Voting Rights Act, and has become enshrined in public memory through national holidays, films, commemorations, and monuments. Carmichael's deep sense of justice contributed to his evolution into Kwame Ture, the Pan-Africanist revolutionary and anti-capitalist organizer who moved to West Africa and remained tenacious in the face of searing political setbacks.

Carmichael ultimately judged America incapable of creating the free and just world he had struggled for as a young man. But despite living in Africa for the final thirty years of his life, Carmichael's legendary stature as a Black Power activist lingered even if many ignored his lasting contributions to civil rights struggles that included a bruising quest for the vote in the deep South.

Although today largely forgotten, Stokely Carmichael remains one of the protean figures of the twentieth century: a revolutionary who passionately believed in self-defense and armed rebellion even as he revered the nation's greatest practitioner of nonviolence; a gifted intellectual who dealt in emotions as well as words and ideas; and an activist whose radical political vision remained anchored by a deep sense of history. In a very real sense, Carmichael remains the last icon of the racial and political revolutions that have come to be associated with the 1960s.

In Mississippi and Alabama, Carmichael pursued a vision of radical democracy that he defined as more than ending racial segregation in public accommodations and gaining the right to vote, although he vigorously pursued both of these objectives. Carmichael's vision of democracy placed rural black sharecroppers and the urban poor as leaders in a new society freed from racial inequality and economic injustice.

As a young man, Carmichael dreamed of becoming a college professor, and his rapid-fire speeches offered a partial fulfillment of these youthful aspirations. Carmichael's ascendancy to national leadership deepened his friendship with Martin Luther King. Both men took pains to publicly speak well of each other, and Carmichael's antiwar speeches offered creative space for King to speak out against Vietnam. Their joint antiwar declarations led critics to argue that Carmichael and King represented two sides of the same coin. Carmichael's words of fire have overshadowed the depth and breadth of his antiwar crusade, which made him, for a time, the nation's most outspoken critic of the Vietnam War.

By 1966, Stokely Carmichael the civil rights militant had become a Black Power revolutionary. The pace of his political evolution from this point forward seemed to accelerate at breakneck speed; in short order he became a Black Panther; the leader of a Black United Front in Washington, DC; and then a Pan-Africanist revolutionary who made Conakry, Guinea, his new home.

As Kwame Ture, the leader of a new group, the All-African People's Revolutionary Party (AAPRP), he launched rhetorical broadsides against

American capitalism. He described the nation that he struggled for in his youth as an empire willing to wage war in the name of peace and kill innocents to preserve a vision of democracy that did not benefit African Americans.

Ture would not be surprised by the Supreme Court's 2013 *Shelby County v. Holder* decision, which stripped the Voting Rights Act he had fought for of much of its strength. This latest setback would confirm Ture's belief that nothing short of global Pan-African revolution could secure justice and human rights for black Americans and those African descendants living across the entire world.

Yet his organizer's instincts made him a relentless optimist. He believed, until his last breath, in the ultimate victory of the masses of humanity over an enemy whose face he had first encountered in the Deep South. Ture came to believe that the contorted visages expressing hate against sit-in activists and sharecroppers were merely instruments of a larger, more dangerous, imperial mindset and system that wreaked havoc on the world.

But ultimately, Stokely Carmichael's story, from his childhood to his political evolution into Kwame Ture, is that of an organizer. Indeed, this was the aspect of Ture's personality that drew me to write a critical biography. The fact that the young Stokely more readily admitted to confusion and political errors than the seasoned Ture made him an all the more fascinating and complex political figure. His story, with its many successes and failures, victories and defeats, reminds us, in the Age of Obama, how past struggles for racial justice shape the present. His story reminds us of roads not traveled and outcomes that might have been.

The sheer range of people whom Stokely Carmichael influenced is vast. They include figures as different as Mumia Abu-Jamal, the imprisoned former Black Panther, journalist, and revolutionary, for decades on death row, and Brian Lamb, the founder of C-SPAN. Years after Ture's death, Abu-Jamal vividly recalled Carmichael's impact on his generation, and the experience of seeing him in person: "There, standing tall, lean, and black as a Masai warrior, stood Stokely Carmichael, spitting fire and rage, lightly seasoned with his Trinidadian clip of the English tongue."[2]

Brian Lamb's image of Stokely remained indelible for different reasons. After listening to Carmichael speak at a black church during the 1960s, Lamb was shocked to discover how a thirty-minute presentation was distorted by the nightly news. "Well, of a thirty-minute speech, probably, . . . maybe two minutes was incendiary," remembered Lamb. "The rest of it was thoughtful and intelligent and very well stated." But the only part of Carmichael's speech deemed newsworthy by the mainstream media "was the fire and brimstone." This surreal experience, which Lamb quickly observed to be the norm, inspired him to found a cable channel "where everybody gets to see everything from start to finish."[3]

For novelist John Edgar Wideman, Stokely represented a truth seeker and myth buster, one who revealed the contradictions of American democracy to a global audience:

> Kwame Ture's dreaming was visionary, a countervision, counterreality, to the reigning myths. He shouted, *The emperor is naked*. Pointed at the emperor with a finger attached to a black hand, stepped forward, stepped away with a black foot. *Black* not because of their color, but because Stokely Carmichael was an African-descended man, and, yes, it's his voice, his finger-pointing, his foot, so they're *black* and thus negative in the eyes of lots of folks, then here comes Stokely challenging the obscene spectacle of Empire, uh-uh; and call his anger, his critique, his truth, black if you want to, in fact he's also calling it black, but with a difference—*black* equals pride, fierce militancy, a determination to pursue the dream of freedom on his terms, *black* terms if you please, but really a new dream replacing an old one, so try to wrap your mind and heart around that too, recognize the legitimacy of his vision, not its color, acknowledge its applicability, the seeds of clarity, its promise to seek change, to move all willing Americans to a more equitable, fulfilling social order, more freedom for so-called *whites* and so-called *blacks* than Stokely found when he arrived here.[4]

While the entire world commemorates Martin Luther King's dream, few people know that Stokely Carmichael even had one. Carmichael did indeed have a dream, one deeply rooted in a global vision of human rights. From its initial groundings in black social-democratic traditions and Pan-Africanism through its evolution into revolutionary anti-imperialism and anti-capitalism, Carmichael remained convinced that indigenous people deserved self-rule and that empires could be toppled by political organizing.

This biography, then, represents an act of recovery. Carmichael helped to organize and participate in every major civil rights demonstration and development in America between 1960 and 1965, the second half of the movement's heroic period. Stokely's DNA is as much a part of the civil rights struggle as it is of Black Power. His erasure from America's collective memory is tragic in that it impoverishes our understanding of the most important movement in our national history. For Stokely Carmichael's story, which took him to African kingdoms, Caribbean ports, European capitals, and assorted global travails is, at its core, also a uniquely American one.

Prologue

STOKELY CARMICHAEL'S VOICE BROKE THROUGH THE HUMID MISSISSIPPI night. He thrived in the heat—especially in the Delta, an area he considered to be a second home.

It was Thursday, June 16, 1966. Less than a year before, President Lyndon Johnson had signed the Voting Rights Act into law, and thirteen months before that had ushered in the Civil Rights Act. They were watershed laws designed to conclude the nation's unfinished work begun after the Civil War. Carmichael was now in Mississippi to ensure that the federal laws passed with pomp and circumstance in Washington would apply to black sharecroppers living in plantation communities that harkened back to the antebellum South's bullwhip days. Released from his latest stay in jail, Carmichael immediately returned to Greenwood, where he had first cut his teeth as an organizer. Carmichael intuitively possessed an orator's gift of speech and a showman's sense of timing, with inflections of his West Indian heritage, New York upbringing, and recent years in the South. His most obvious asset was his good looks—proverbially tall, dark, and handsome, with wide eyes that conveyed mischief. His long arms sliced through the muggy air to punctuate his words. Carmichael's mannerisms resembled the loose-limbed energy of Malcolm X, a speaker he had studied up close while still in college.

Stokely Carmichael brought an outsider's perspective to America's racial landscape. He was born in 1941 on the Caribbean island of Trinidad and spent his first ten years there. In 1952, he moved to the Bronx to join his family. He had graduated from Howard University in Washington, DC, but it was in rural Mississippi that he found his calling as an organizer. He fell in love with the South's impoverished black community. Friends noticed he began speaking with more than a hint of a southern accent.

That June night in 1966, as the twenty-four-year-old Carmichael gazed upon the sweat-soaked crowd gathered under the night sky, he spoke out of frustration, anxiety, even anger. But most of all, he spoke from a sense of combative hope. His latest arrest, which took place shortly after the fifth anniversary of his first, completed a circle that had begun in Mississippi.

"This is the twenty-seventh time that I've been arrested," he shouted, "and I ain't going to jail no more!" With words that echoed through the night, Carmichael urged the crowd to take control of their destiny. "We want black power!" he shouted. A thunderous reply of "Black Power!" emanated from the crowd, sparking a call-and-response chant that gave the event the feel of an outdoor religious revival.[1]

Like a prosecutor before a surging jury of six hundred, Carmichael made a case for political revolution. "We have begged the president. We've begged the federal government—that's all we've been doing, begging and begging." Racial and economic oppression in the South required something more: "Every courthouse in Mississippi ought to be burned down tomorrow to get rid of the dirt and the mess. From now on, when they ask you what you want, you know what to tell 'em."

"Black Power," was the response. "Black Power!"

The speech that night introduced Stokely Carmichael not just to the six hundred people before him but also to the nation and the world. His life changed that night, and so did America's civil rights movement. Black Power provoked a national reckoning on questions of civil rights, race, and democracy. Carmichael, whose charisma was matched by his ambition, stood at the center of this storm deploying boldly provocative rhetoric with passion and eloquence. He instantly commanded the space previously occupied by Malcolm X, assassinated sixteen months earlier.

———————

IN THE PUBLIC'S IMAGINATION, Stokely Carmichael stood distant from civil rights. But in fact, that very movement had shaped and nurtured him. Martin Luther King, as much as Malcolm X, influenced Carmichael's political vision. He cultivated a well-earned reputation as a radical but counted King as a personal friend and a professional mentor. Although he greatly admired Malcolm X, Carmichael spent far more personal time with King, whom he credited with teaching him to confront racial violence with grace and dignity. The two survived disagreements over strategies and tactics to find common ground in connecting black protest to antiwar and anti-poverty campaigns.

If King's regal bearing and biblical rhetoric drew comparisons to Moses, Carmichael's pugnacious energy resembled that of John the Baptist, an itinerant evangelist whose teachings challenged received wisdom.

Like many in his generation, Carmichael found himself drawn to the power and charisma of Malcolm X. He watched Malcolm speak at Howard University and occasionally bumped into him when he visited Washington. After Malcolm's assassination in February 1965, Carmichael, both consciously and unconsciously, followed aspects of his political trajectory. Beyond superficial physical similarities in height, weight, and speaking style, Carmichael and Malcolm shared reputations as troublemakers who hid boundless political and intellectual ambitions. Both men took life-altering pilgrimages to Africa, adopted revolutionary Pan-African politics, and changed their names.

In the 1960s, the now largely forgotten name of Stokely Carmichael easily rolled off of the tongues of American presidents, the head and agents of the FBI, college students, ministers, and soldiers. National magazine profiles, television appearances, and hundreds of speeches around the country made Carmichael a revolutionary icon. But three years after unleashing Black Power upon an unsuspecting nation and world, Carmichael seemed to vanish. Considered the heir to Malcolm X at twenty-five, he became by the age of thirty a political nomad operating out of the tiny West African country of Guinea.

By the time an undergraduate named Barack Obama, who would become a community organizer in Chicago a few short years later, heard him speak at Columbia University in the early 1980s, Kwame Ture was promoting plans "to establish economic ties between Africa and Harlem that would circumvent white capitalist imperialism." Ture's unabashed critiques of Reagan-era capitalism and embrace of a style of black radicalism out of vogue since the 1960s perplexed Obama, who found more comforting inspiration in the Student Non-Violent Coordinating Committee (SNCC, pronounced "snick"), the group of which Carmichael had been elected chairman just before chanting Black Power into the Mississippi night. "His eyes glowed inward as he spoke," wrote Obama in his memoir *Dreams from My Father*, "the eyes of a madman or a saint."[2]

CHAPTER ONE

The Chocolate Fred Astaire

June 29, 1941–February 1960

ON JUNE 29, 1941, STOKELY STANDIFORD CHURCHILL CARMICHAEL WAS born in the family home at 54 Oxford Street in Port of Spain, the capital of the island of Trinidad. The centrally located house in Port of Spain's Belmont neighborhood rested at the bottom of a set of forty-two government-built steps that were a local landmark. The intricately designed house dazzled Stokely's young imagination. The porch and roof rested on five levels that gave the entire structure an imposing heft that belied the inhabitants' working-class origins. Adults were impressed, too, especially by the series of movable walls that, properly shifted, turned several rooms into one large space perfect for hosting the kinds of fêtes that native Trinidadians enjoy. Stokely was the middle child, bookended by sisters Umilta and Lynette, of master carpenter Adolphus Carmichael and the former Mabel Florence Charles, known by all as May Charles. A jewel of the British West Indies, Port of Spain, like Stokely's ancestry, reflected the diasporic nature of African migration to the New World. May Charles was born in the US Canal Zone in Panama; her mother and father came from Montserrat and Antigua, respectively. Adolphus traced his paternal roots to Barbados; his mother, Cecilia Harris, was born in Tobago. Stokely inherited his father's bronze color and his mother's fiery temperament. As a child of the English-speaking Caribbean, he claimed a heritage marked by both voluntary and forced relocation. This pan-Caribbean background made him a citizen of the world who, for the rest of his life, would feel equally at home in Port of Spain, the Bronx and Harlem, Washington, DC, Mississippi, and Conakry.

Living in a home crowded with in-laws proved to be suffocating for May Charles. She left Trinidad bound for relatives in the Bronx when Stokely was three. Adolphus followed, arriving in New York in 1946. Stokely would not see either of his parents again until he was almost eleven. His extended family became surrogate parents to him, and Stokely pragmatically adapted to these less than ideal circumstances. In his parents' absence, he cultivated an independent streak that he would carry with him for the rest of his life.[1]

His earliest childhood memories centered on the elegant family home that Adolphus had meticulously built but scarcely enjoyed. The relatively idyllic environment included a local steel band, Casa Blanca, which practiced at the top of the forty-two steps. Cecilia Harris Carmichael, Stokely's paternal grandmother, became the dominant maternal force during his early years, aided by three willful daughters—dubbed Tante Elaine, Tante Louise, and Mummy Olga—whose clashes with May Charles had accelerated her departure.

Grandma Carmichael doted on Stokely, who suffered from childhood asthma. Tante Elaine was the disciplinarian that the more carefree Mummy Olga could never be. Stokely and his older cousin Austin, Elaine's son, were inseparable, two small boys in a house dominated by strong women. Weekend trips to Point Fortin, twenty miles from Belmont, exposed Stokely to Trinidad's lush beauty, with its tropical forests, deep blue seas, and vast sugarcane fields. As an adult, he would call the Botanic Gardens he traipsed through as a child "perhaps the only completely unambiguous good produced by colonialism." Such bucolic sights coexisted uneasily against Port of Spain's wartime landscape. American military personnel stationed in nearby Chaguaramas filled the bustling city, as did European sailors whose merchant ships docked in the harbor. Yankee dollars flowed into Port of Spain through means legal and illegal, setting up a short-lived boomtown. Calypso songs surged through the downtown's thriving nightlife interrupted periodically by blackouts in anticipation of enemy air raids. Eastern Boys School, a British colonial entity free to locals, facilitated Stokely's unambiguous admiration for Western civilization, European history, and Anglophone culture. The form, if not substance, of this colonial education would prove critical to his future.[2]

Stokely's relatively privileged childhood shielded him from the harsh living conditions faced by the typical Trinidadian family. The Carmichaels owned their own home, and their lifestyle was supplemented by incomes from Stokely's three gainfully employed aunts. They also received regular care packages from the States in the form of clothes and American dollars courtesy of

May Charles and Adolphus. Stokely was a precocious student, and his encounters with fellow classmates who trekked to school barefoot reinforced his natural sympathy for underdogs. This inclination dovetailed into his early religious training, where Sundays included visits to Anglican, Presbyterian, and Methodist services. On such occasions, Stokely donned a wide-lapelled suit, accented by a bowtie and handkerchief that earned him the nickname "Little Man" from neighbors who delighted in his dapper attire.[3]

Stokely came of age in a colonial port city, a dominion of the once sprawling British empire whose darker citizens proudly retained vestiges of their unique Anglophone heritage as exhibited by Carmichael's middle name Churchill. Port of Spain was, like many parts of the British Caribbean, a place where a hybrid culture flourished, with a predominantly black population cultivating an appreciation for both African and Anglophone roots. Trinidad's annual Empire Day introduced Stokely to anthems such as "Rule Britannia" and "God Save the Queen" and the pageantry of a decaying empire. In such rare instances, fleeting images of whites penetrated Stokely's largely all-black community. Empire Day made for a bracing juxtaposition—a world where the white heroes of history books and poetry contrasted with the black teachers, bus drivers, nurses, and laborers who populated Stokely's neighborhood. Stokely was reared in a majority black city, which made him comfortable from an early age with the idea of black power.

When Princess Margaret paid a visit to the island, ten-year-old Stokely, armed like hundreds of others with tiny Union Jack flags, lined the procession route and waited for hours for an unrequited glimpse of Her Royal Highness. By this time, Stokely was enrolled at Tranquillity Boys' Intermediate School, where, in addition to his academic studies, he enjoyed playing cricket and soccer. In Trinidad, Calypso songs, steel bands, and carnivals existed comfortably alongside colonial schools, British literature, and Empire Day. But the comfort of this existence soon vanished for Stokely.[4]

Stokely's paternal grandmother, Cecilia, died on January 16, 1952, setting off a chain of events that would reunite him with his parents. Adolphus Carmichael returned soon after his mother's funeral for a brief reunion with the son he had not seen in six years. By the time Adolphus departed back to America, it had been decided that his children would permanently relocate to New York to live with their parents. Adolphus and May Charles had settled into a cramped three-bedroom apartment on Stebbins Avenue in the South Bronx. It was, as she later described it, a "mixed neighborhood kind of on the run-down side." They identified themselves as forward-thinking West Indian pioneers determined to claim a piece of the American Dream. On May 26, 1952, Stokely applied for an immigration visa at the American Consulate General in Port of Spain, a request granted that very day. His visa application listed his height at four feet, seven inches, his complexion as "dark" with no distinguishing marks, and his occupation as "student." Stokely, Mummy Olga, Umilta, and Lynette now joined May Charles, Adolphus, and two new siblings, Janeth and Judith, born in the States, swelling the American wing of the Carmichael clan to eight.[5]

On June 15, 1952, two weeks before his eleventh birthday, Carmichael arrived in New York City. The entire trip to the United States mesmerized Stokely, who, in short order, experienced his first airplane trip, took in the sights and sounds of New York City, and wondered if the speeding cars hurtling down expressways like missiles would arrive home safely. He spent that first summer getting reacquainted with his parents. May Charles would prove to be a diminutive firecracker of a woman in contrast to the more idealistic Adolphus, with his immigrant faith in the possibilities of New York City and America. Adolphus toiled at multiple jobs, including driving a cab, to provide for his growing family. Life as a West Indian carpenter meant seasonal work, "two weeks on and four weeks off," stretches exacerbated by racial discrimination in the city's trade unions. Life in New York meant readjusting to parents he loved but hardly remembered. Stokely immediately gravitated toward the outspoken and chatty May Charles over a father whom he remembered as "submissive, quiet, and obedient," traits that he found more puzzling than endearing. May Charles, on the other hand, projected an air of combative assertiveness, humor, and passion, characteristics that were amplified in her only son.[6]

Stokely's arrival in New York City began the process of becoming African-American. The Bronx introduced Carmichael to black America's cultural rhythms and idioms. There were technological wonders as well, including a black-and-white television unlike anything he had seen in Port of Spain. By mid-August, Stokely found temperatures cold enough to wear a winter coat, a practice he continued despite ridicule from neighbors. Carmichael enrolled in PS 39 in Longwood that September, anticipating, as his parents had assured him, that America's educational system would prove more advanced than Trinidad's. Instead, the school turned out to be socially chaotic and absent the academic rigor of his schools in Port of Spain. The new boy

from Trinidad easily outshone his fellow fifth graders with an academic focus distinguished by his love for reading and a pronounced writing ability.
He befriended the black students, but their scholastic ineptitude made a bad
first impression, leading him to privately conclude that "American kids were
stupid." In New York, Stokely fell in love with his mother for the second time.
"Mabel Charles Carmichael would become—and remains—a major influence in the lives of me and my sisters," he would much later write. "This little
dynamo of a woman was the stable moral presence, the fixed center around
which the domestic life of this migrant African family revolved."[7]

The Carmichaels soon departed their overcrowded South Bronx apartment for a house in the predominantly white Morris Park neighborhood.
They were the first black family to move into a part of the Bronx still dominated by Italian immigrants. Irish and Jewish neighbors added to the community's ethnic stew. It was January 1953, the middle of the school year,
which forced Stokely to get acclimated to a new school and new neighborhood for the second time in less than a year. Adolphus immediately began
renovations on the run-down house on 1810 Amethyst Street, a process that
would continue over the next decade in the form of small and large construction projects. Adolphus and May Charles' thirst for better opportunities for
their children marked Carmichael's entrée into a world that would be filled
with interracial contact.

Stokely's enrollment at PS 34 to finish the fifth grade made him the school's
second black student. He quickly befriended the Italian kids in the neighborhood and traipsed around the surrounding blocks with his best friend, John
DiMilio. A self-described miniature "*paisano* in blackface," Stokely came to
appreciate Italian cooking and the culture's dramatic flair for self-expression.
His friends called him "Sichie," a play on the word "Siciliano" to describe
their new dark-skinned playmate. For a time, Carmichael's friendship with
the local kids drifted into small acts of petty theft and juvenile delinquency.
He ran with a neighborhood gang, the Morris Park Dukes, but quit after a
half-hearted participation in a minor burglary. The most important event
that happened to Stokely that first year came courtesy of his father. On April
27, 1953, Adolphus, who had entered the United States illegally on July 15,
1946, became a naturalized citizen. Thus ended legal proceedings that had
threatened to split the Carmichael family apart. Adolphus had secured the
intervention of a government immigration agent sympathetic to his plea that
his deportation would economically harm May Charles. That Monday, under

the provisions of the Immigration and Nationality Act and most likely while attending classes at PS 34, Stokely Carmichael became an American citizen.[8]

Carmichael's citizenship arrived on the cusp of revolutionary transformations on America's civil rights front. In the fall of 1954, less than four months after the Supreme Court's historic May 17th *Brown v. Board of Education* desegregation decision, Stokely enrolled at PS 83, a school for junior high school students that drew a relatively diverse mix of ethnic students (although he was one of only two blacks in the entire school). Placed on the high-achieving academic track with white classmates who excelled in their studies, Stokely thrived. In the eighth grade, he was elected vice president of the student council. Despite his popularity among local neighborhood toughs, ease in acclimating to his academic surroundings, and acceptance by his peers as a chocolate-hued *paisano*, Stokely's family stood apart from his predominantly Italian neighborhood. Black Methodists from Trinidad living in a largely Italian Catholic community, the Carmichaels kept to themselves, rarely socializing with neighbors. Stokely's process of assimilation proved more complete than his parents'. He attended Sunday school nearby at Westchester Methodist Church in the Bronx, where he played piano and became a Boy Scout.[9]

Harlem, where Stokely accompanied his father to a barbershop on 145th Street, became a personal sanctuary and political classroom. From 1953, until departing for college seven years later, Stokely traveled to Harlem to get a haircut every few weeks. It was a world away from his Amethyst Street home. It was a world where black culture flourished in the routine activities of passersby, in barbershop conversations (sometime political, sometimes humorous, and always interesting), and in the photos of black heroes that lined the walls of restaurants and businesses. Two subjects of political debate made their way inside the barbershop during Stokely's junior high years. The *Brown* decision triggered fierce discussions about the probability of integrating public schools in the South and whether or not the reverberations, both good and ill, would reach north.

And then a terrible event reminded everyone how dangerous racism was. Emmett Till was the same age as Stokely, fourteen. He was from Chicago and visiting relatives in Mississippi, when his summer vacation turned tragic. He had talked to a local white woman, and that simple act suddenly snowballed. Some white men seized and tortured him, shot him fatally in the head, and threw his body in the Tallahatchie River. *Jet* magazine placed Till's mutilated corpse on its cover, instantly turning the murdered teenager into a civil rights martyr for Stokely's generation and beyond.[10]

Stokely was coming of age in a world where race shaped hope and opportunity, and where life chances made the ability to adapt a necessary survival skill. His charisma and intuitive gift for observation augmented a keen intelligence. For Stokely, the worlds of Morris Park and Harlem became social and political laboratories where he fashioned distinct identities for separate audiences. He did more than just blend into the black and white worlds he inhabited; he became among their most popular representatives.

This talent served him well upon enrolling at one of New York's best public schools. Stokely entered the prestigious Bronx High School of Science in September 1956, joining a small group of black students at the academically intensive school. Stokely's acceptance into Science kept pace with Adolphus' dream of his son becoming a physician and returning to Port of Spain to work in a family-run medical clinic.

Bronx Science's promise of intellectual excellence and educational rigor, however, masked political and racial minefields. On the surface, the student body accepted the few black students without complaint. Some liberal students went out of their way to openly embrace their darker classmates, who reveled in the attention, invitations, and friendships crafted along the way. But social acceptance carried a steep cost. Assimilation into the school's politically liberal social and intellectual culture cast the precocious Stokely as an exceptional Negro, talented enough to consort with the scions of liberal Jewish New Yorkers, but, however remarkable, an outlier destined to be one of the few brown faces at Bronx Science and its surrounding political and social milieu. A short-lived romance with a white classmate hastened the discovery of this paradox. Stokely overcame his initial reluctance to ask her to a school dance only to be overwhelmed by the harsh stares on the subway they received and disappointed by the response of Bronx Science's liberal faculty to the budding interracial romance. The disapproving "looks of my teachers" coupled with his self-consciousness about violating "this real taboo" led to the relationship's abrupt end. Stokely's closest friends at school were Jewish students, although he had cordial relations with several black and Puerto Rican students.[11]

Initially, Bronx Science's competitively rigorous intellectual environment knocked the preternaturally confident Stokely off balance. His new classmates were already well versed in the works of William Faulkner, Ernest

Hemingway, and John Steinbeck while Stokely had been poring over detective mysteries and *Reader's Digest*. When on his first day of classes, a teacher asked about their summer reading, one student confidently announced he was reading Karl Marx's *Capital*, a book Stokely added to an ad hoc reading list that he would use to catch up to his peers. Gene Dennis, who on the first day of school claimed to be reading both Steinbeck and Marx, became one of Stokely's best friends. Gene's reading list was no accident. Eugene Dennis Sr. served as a high-ranking Communist Party official, and young Gene belonged to the Young Communist League. Stokely and Gene bonded as soccer teammates and over a love of books and intellectual debates. Shared subway rides to soccer practice cemented a deep friendship, and Gene became a frequent dinner guest at the Carmichaels'. Gene soon invited Stokely to a party at his house in Harlem, where the sight of interracial revelers surprised Stokely, by now used to being the lone Negro at the soirées hosted by liberal classmates. Stokely, Gene, and several other scholar-athletes formed a social club, Kokista, to discuss personal and political issues, organize parties, and provide self-defense against neighborhood bullies.[12]

Gene Dennis introduced Stokely to New York City's left-wing political subculture. As their relationship grew, Stokely discovered Gene's political background, which included Eugene Sr.'s political affiliation. The revelation made Carmichael's parents nervous, but the friendship remained intact. The Dennises' apartment on West 151st Street in Harlem became a second home for Stokely, where he witnessed the interracial bonhomie between high-ranking Communist Party officials, freelance radicals, and independent agitators gathered to discuss politics, plan demonstrations, and debate the prospect for revolution. The discovery that Gene's father was a communist drew Carmichael deeper into the orbit of New York's left-wing Jewish intellectual culture—a community steeped in the struggle for social justice and dripping with Ivy League–credentialed doctors, lawyers, and professors. Emboldened by Adolphus and May Charles yet slightly intimidated in comparison to his new peers, Stokely set out to "beat everybody" at Bronx Science.[13]

In short order, he began attending Young Communist League meetings, study sessions that grappled with the economic roots of social and political oppression, and rallies. In essence, association with Gene offered the intellectually curious Stokely an opportunity to develop a more systematic political worldview. But while these new relationships broadened Stokely's political vision, he remained firmly rooted in the black experience, especially on religious matters. The casual atheism of his friends initially shocked him and over time, even as his own personal religious beliefs waned, struck him as counterproductive to the black community, which regarded the church as its personal and political headquarters. "I did not want to be alienated from my people," Stokely ruefully noted, "because of Marxist atheism." Carmichael would spend much of the next several years negotiating what he perceived to be a tension between the religious faith that enveloped the black community and more secular Marxist strivings.[14]

As a student at Bronx Science, Stokely became a fixture at radical meetings, youth marches, and rallies sponsored by groups whose various campaigns revolved around issues of poverty, nuclear proliferation, civil liberties, education, and civil rights. Bronx Science's rich intellectual milieu of socially conscious students and precocious young activists provided a model of active engagement. Carmichael studiously explored a parallel curriculum that took place at suburban political camps, Harlem rallies, and New York City house parties. Long days of discussion turned into parties, which ended in "singing 'Hava Nagila' and dancing the hora." After Carmichael's youthful support for Israel switched to an unbending advocacy for Palestinian rights, these episodes would provide defensive comfort against charges of anti-Semitism that critics routinely hurled at him.[15]

Carmichael quickly discovered that leftist politics was not merely the terrain of white radicals; he became immersed in the rich tradition of black socialism. Bayard Rustin, perhaps the nation's most well-known black socialist, stood out as a leading figure of New York City's Left. A former disciple of the white pacifist A.J. Muste, Rustin briefly joined the Young Communist League in the 1930s before hitting his stride in the Fellowship of Reconciliation (FOR) and the Congress of Racial Equality (CORE)—two groundbreaking civil rights organizations that combined nonviolent activism and civil disobedience during the Second World War. As a young organizer, Rustin worked with A. Philip Randolph, the legendary labor leader (and former socialist) whose March on Washington Movement (MOWM) leveraged the threat of massive disruption in the nation's capital to compel President Franklin Roosevelt into signing an executive order banning racial discrimination in the nation's wartime plants and factories. Rustin was born in West Chester, Pennsylvania in 1912, and grew up there, but his elegant style of speech led people to believe he was from the Caribbean, an erroneous assumption he chose to cultivate rather than correct. He continually reinvented aspects of his biography to friends, reporters, and the general public, giving him an air of mystery that only added to his gifts as an organizer, political strategist, and raconteur. A talented student at Wilberforce University in Ohio, Rustin left school in 1934 in the wake of what would prove to be the first of many scandals related to his homosexuality. After a brief membership in the Communist Party, Rustin aligned himself with Randolph's MOWM and then Muste's FOR. He served a three-year prison sentence for refusing to register for the Selective Service in the mid-1940s. After his release in 1946, he spent the next five years as an increasingly well-known peace activist. He accepted invitations to speak in India, where he worked with Prime Minister Jawaharlal Nehru. He also visited West Africa, where he tutored Kwame Nkrumah and Nnamdi Azikiwe (who would become in the early 1960s the first presidents of, respectively, Ghana and Nigeria) on the finer points of nonviolent resistance to British colonial rule. Publicity surrounding Rustin's 1953 arrest for lewd conduct found him struggling to separate his personal life from his political ambitions. By 1956, Rustin had refashioned himself again, this time as a middle-aged adviser who swooped in clandestinely to school a young Martin Luther King in nonviolence at a pivotal moment of the Montgomery, Alabama, bus boycott.[16]

Stokely was blissfully unaware of Rustin's biography when he first heard him speak at a Young People's Socialist League meeting. Rustin's typically masterful and highly theatrical speaking style was on display, including his pinched, vaguely British accent, which lent him an air of sophistication. Mesmerized as much by Rustin's showmanship as his political manner, Stokely asked Gene Dennis who the speaker was. Informed that it was "Bayard Rustin, the socialist," Stokely replied, "That's what I'm gonna be when I grow up." Rustin's race impressed Stokely as much as his politics. Memories of predominantly black Trinidad still stirred within Stokely, despite his increasing forays into the overwhelmingly white cultural and political milieu of New York's radical circles. Carmichael encountered the tiny coterie of high-ranking black communists at Gene's house, but none struck him as politically engaged and attuned to the everyday rhythms of black life as Rustin, whom he befriended while in high school. Their relationship drew Stokely closer to Rustin's social-democratic politics and gave him access to one of the most brilliant organizing minds of the era.[17]

Carmichael imbibed black America's customs, traditions, and rhythms through popular culture. A naturally gifted mimic and perceptive observer, he absorbed black language, idiom, and vernacular through a set of personal experiences that shaped his political outlook. Through his family's shortwave radio, which he commandeered, Stokely enjoyed gospel, rhythm and blues, jazz, classical, and African music. Adolphus' prodigious personal collection of Caribbean calypso records supplemented his growing musical appetite. He noticed the difference between white disc jockey Symphony Sid's sophisticated music editorials and black deejay Jocko's entertaining, but intellectually unsatisfying, raps.

Sid's biggest impact on Stokely came through the introduction of South African singer Miriam Makeba, whose voice Carmichael fell in love with while still in high school. Makeba's African name, "Zenzi," was a play on the word "Uzenzile," which roughly translated into "This is your own stubborn fault." Makeba's maternal grandmother had repeated this word during her daughter's difficult, almost fatal, delivery of Miriam. Zenzi's outwardly calm demeanor masked a stubborn and independent will that matched Stokely's.[18]

The South African singer had burst onto the American music scene in 1959. A chance meeting in London with Harry Belafonte had set her on course to becoming an international star. Her appearance on national television, on *The Steve Allen Show,* announced her as a beguiling new musical sensation. When Makeba played the legendary Village Vanguard jazz club in New York City, Belafonte arranged for a line-up of special guests in the audience—Miles Davis, Nina Simone, Duke Ellington, Diahann Carroll, and Sidney Poitier—that left her almost speechless. The enamored teen-aged Stokely predicted (correctly) to his sister Janeth that he would one day marry the singer. Meanwhile, summers spent running his Uncle Stephen's Atlantic City record store turned Stokely into an amateur sociologist. He observed the growth of a burgeoning youth market aided by the increasing popularity of 45 rpm singles, which he convinced his uncle to play on Friday and Saturday nights as a successful marketing tool.[19]

On visits to his cousin Inez in Harlem, Carmichael encountered the neighborhood's radical street-speaking tradition. It dated back to Hubert Harrison, the intellectual powerhouse who helped facilitate the rise of Marcus Garvey—the Jamaica-born Pan-Africanist whose Back-to-Africa movement galvanized millions of blacks in the years after World War I. They were New Negroes, proudly defiant and visionary black leaders who promised to usher in a new era of militant intellectual, political, and social struggle. On Harlem's famous 125th Street corridor, Stokely encountered Richard Moore,

Lewis Michaux, and Eddie "Porkchop" Davis, all of whom offered rich historical insights not found among young communists or at dinner parties hosted
by Gene Dennis' family. These griots rejected a "scientific" solution to black
misery. Instead, like intellectual and political provocateurs, they highlighted
revolutions taking place throughout Africa, the Caribbean, and the larger
Third World. In a remarkable burst of freedom twenty-five African nations
had declared independence between 1957 and 1962. On stepladders draped
with the black nationalist colors of red, black, and green on one side and the
American flag on the other, speakers introduced Carmichael to contemporary African revolutionaries. Improbably, two of the leaders most often mentioned, Ghana's Kwame Nkrumah and Guinea's Sékou Touré, would become
Carmichael's political mentors within a decade.[20]

In Harlem, racial matters anchored political affairs, and activists reveled
in exposing American lies. They substituted narratives of forward national
progress with a starker political reality that portrayed America as a modern-
day empire whose foreign and domestic policies imperiled dreams of black
liberation at home and abroad. The political revolution that Carmichael's
white friends discussed frequently relegated blacks to a supporting, rather
than a central, role. Practically, he recognized that their talk of interracial
class solidarity failed to acknowledge the entrenched racism in labor unions
that he overheard his father privately rail against.

Carmichael's activism progressed to include attending youth marches
organized by Rustin, where he first heard Martin Luther King speak. Socialism shaped Carmichael's political and organizing sensibilities, and for a
time he organized black paint-factory workers on Rustin's behalf. Through
the eyes of the teenaged Stokely, Rustin managed the improbable feat of connecting radical theory to practice in service of civil rights agitation. He never
formally joined any particular group, preferring instead to rally with black
nationalists, socialists, and young communists as an independent political
activist. Conversations with Benjamin Davis, a black communist and former
New York City councilman imprisoned for over three years for his political
beliefs, exposed Carmichael to the political cost associated with radical politics. Stokely idolized Paul Robeson, the black Marxist singer-actor-activist
who, during the 1940s, could bring tens of thousands of Americans together
for concerts that were as much about politics as art. Robeson's defiant support of the Soviet Union had turned him, virtually overnight, from an American hero to a pariah. The State Department stripped him of his passport

and, in the process, curtailed his financial opportunities and almost broke his spirit. The 1958 publication of his autobiography, *Here I Stand*, marked a small comeback for Robeson, who mentored a generation of black cultural activists, including the playwright Lorraine Hansberry and Harry Belafonte. In a few short years, Stokely would embrace what Robeson, "one of my early heroes," had characterized as "Negro power," the collective and unified political strength of black Americans, in a fashion that would thrust him onto the world stage.[21]

Frequent visits to Lewis Michaux's African National Memorial Bookstore opened up new intellectual worlds. Diminutive, agile, and outspoken, Michaux was a mentor to Malcolm X, the dynamic Nation of Islam national spokesman who frequently held large rallies outside the bookstore. Nicknamed the "House of Common Sense and the Home of Proper Propaganda," African National Memorial served as a headquarters for black radicals during the 1950s and 1960s, a living testament to Garvey's legacy and the New Negro. Michaux introduced Stokely to a classic text, *Pan-Africanism or Communism?*, written by George Padmore, a writer, organizer, and adviser to African revolutionaries and a principal founder of postwar Pan-Africanism. Though Padmore was dismissed as a traitor in Marxist circles for his embrace of African nationalism, Carmichael came to admire him as a fellow Trinidadian who had grown up near his old neighborhood. Padmore was not the only black radical conspicuously absent from the reading lists of Carmichael's study groups. C.L.R. James, another Trinidadian, remained marginalized as a Trotskyite, despite his renown as one of the most important and innovative radical thinkers of his generation. James' *The Black Jacobins*, an eloquent and moving history of the Haitian Revolution, would lead Carmichael to a further exploration of black history at one of Harlem's most famous institutions, the Schomburg Center, perhaps the most important repository of black history in the country.[22]

Carmichael's intellectual curiosity made him aware of the significance of global events that paralleled domestic civil rights struggles. In Harlem, the name Kwame Nkrumah rolled off the tongues of street speakers and newspapers announcing Ghanaian independence in 1957. Carmichael found himself transformed that summer, following his freshman year at Bronx Science. "Sichie," the honorary black Italian, part-time neighborhood tough, and exotic became Stokely, the cosmopolitan black teenager who played tennis and enjoyed swimming with friends from Bronx Science. Carmichael's old crowd responded by calling him a "fag," but by his sophomore year he had severed old neighborhood ties for good. Handsome, intelligent, and charismatic, Stokely became the most popular student at Bronx Science, and teachers and students predicted great things for his future. "I thought I was going to be brilliant, I was going to solve the race problem," Carmichael recalled years later.[23]

He increasingly occupied dual social worlds, careening between Bronx Science's formal parties and Harlem's grittier pleasures. These divergent realities seemed to converge in Greenwich Village, where white beatniks adopted black vernacular, listened to jazz, and romanticized ghetto life in hopes of "becoming completely Negrofied." The racial complexities of class politics momentarily jarred the senses of the sixteen-year-old Carmichael, who offended black sensibilities each time he lapsed into the Lindy Hop in Harlem and sparked enthusiasm by dancing the Slop around whites. During his sophomore year, he found himself "being ashamed of being a Negro" and temporarily stopped listening to gospel music. The white kids at Bronx Science considered Carmichael their "chocolate Fred Astaire." Already a budding maverick, he simply decided against choosing sides. "I resolved the problem by just going wherever I wanted to go," he recalled. "If I felt like going to Harlem, I'd go to Harlem, if I felt like going down to the Village, I'd go down to do whatever I wanted to do." This decision proved an important turning point for Stokely, one that allowed him to shed whatever anxieties remained over his immigrant background, intellectual sophistication, racial identity, and comfort around whites. Carmichael adamantly resisted narrowly focusing on a singular part of his multifaceted personality. His outward exterior of cool repose hid his ambition to make a political mark on the world, one that events in North Carolina would soon make possible.[24]

CHAPTER TWO

Howard and NAG

February 1960–June 1961

STOKELY CARMICHAEL'S GENERATION CAME OF AGE IN THE WINTER OF 1960. A Monday afternoon sit-in at a segregated lunch counter on February 1 by four black students in downtown Greensboro, North Carolina, triggered rolling waves of similar protests that, in a matter of weeks, shook much of the South. The decision by Joseph McNeil, Ezell Blair, Franklin McCain, and David Richmond, students at the local black college, North Carolina A & T, to sit in at a Woolworth's lunch counter reserved for white customers turned that Monday afternoon into a watershed historical moment. Refused service, they returned the next day with more than two dozen allies and sat in for two hours in quiet protest that attracted local media. They returned each day in more numbers, and one week later, demonstrations broke out in five more cities in North Carolina, and by the end of the month sit-ins had burst out in Baltimore, Lexington, Richmond, Chattanooga, and Montgomery. By the early spring, an estimated fifty thousand people in more than seven states had engaged in the movement. The sit-ins provided the nation with a unique experiment in moral theater, where black protesters (at times with white allies) nonviolently withstood verbal and physical abuse. The movement did not simply give young people inspiration to participate in protests that were now bubbling around the nation; it galvanized them to action.[1]

On March 5, nine veterans of the sit-in demonstrations held a press conference at the 125th Street headquarters of the Brotherhood of Sleeping Car Porters in New York City. That same day, pickets gathered outside of Woolworth's Seventh Avenue Harlem store in a CORE-sponsored demonstration.

Three of the southern students followed their press conference with an appearance at Abyssinian Baptist Church on 138th Street, where pastor and Congressman Adam Clayton Powell Jr. called for a national boycott of Woolworth's and of the Kresge and W.T. Grant chain stores by citizens of all races. The sit-in movement transcended the racial fault lines that separated the two political worlds Stokely Carmichael operated in. The same day that black students rallied in Harlem, three hundred white students picketed outside Woolworth's Herald Square store on 34th Street. Sponsored by the predominantly white National Student Association, the sympathy demonstration confirmed earlier comments by the southern black students touring Harlem that whites were providing vital moral and financial support.[2]

By March 16, President Dwight Eisenhower, whose public discomfort addressing racial matters remained a hallmark of his presidency, called for "biracial conferences in every city and every community of the South" during a press conference. Eisenhower's comments, which made *The New York Times* front page, reinforced the view from the White House that race remained, even during times of national crisis, a regional matter best left in the hands of local political and civic groups. Yet the president admitted that the sit-ins, as long as they remained nonviolent, were a constitutional form of protest that had "been recognized in our country" since the nation's founding. The sit-in movement altered the nation's political and racial equilibrium, forcing a reticent sitting president to address the matter, despite his lame-duck status. That summer, John F. Kennedy, the dashing forty-three-year-old Massachusetts senator and presumptive Democratic presidential nominee, positively referenced the sit-ins during a meeting with African diplomats: "It is in the American tradition to stand up for one's rights—even if the new way to stand up for one's rights is to sit down."[3]

That fall of 1960, Stokely enrolled at Howard University. It was the start of four intense years of civil rights activism that events in Greensboro made possible. Carmichael's keen intelligence and voracious reading made him both a budding scholar and activist who recognized Washington's political contradictions, where black poverty coexisted alongside the wealth of power brokers and politicians. He crammed in a lifetime's worth of experience during his time in college. Time spent in Washington taught him to recognize the depth and breadth of political power. Beyond the city's obvious symbols and monuments to American power lay an undiscovered country, one populated by African and Caribbean embassies, the collective will of university students, and the heroic example of ordinary black people that Carmichael would claim as his own.

Armed with little more than a sharp mind and endless reserves of confidence, Carmichael formally began the political journey that would make him an icon. He soon found himself captivated by Malcolm X's revelatory speeches, yet increasingly drawn to Martin Luther King's deep and abiding love of black culture. Guided by an expansive vision of democracy, heavily influenced by Bayard Rustin's social-democratic teachings and his own personal empathy for downtrodden southern Negroes, Stokely became an outlier: a militant civil rights organizer whose allegiance to nonviolence rested more on practical than on moral considerations. An unexpected trip to Mississippi, where he endured his first arrest for civil rights activism, transformed Carmichael, beginning the journey that would turn him into a full-time organizer.

Carmichael initially greeted the news coming out of Greensboro with skepticism. "Niggers will do anything to get their names in the paper," he grumbled to himself at the time, using a word that whites frequently deployed as a racial slur but many black folks used among themselves as a term of endearment. The demonstrations' apparent spontaneity rankled Stokely, who believed that such protests required organization in order to be effective. But he would soon change his mind. "Negroes, like the spring, are breaking out all over," he told himself.[4]

Newspaper reports that characterized the sit-in movement as spontaneous were true but missed important nuances. Greensboro anticipated a nationwide surge in nonviolent direct action. The movement's unofficial architect would be James Lawson, a Vanderbilt University divinity student who led nonviolent training workshops in Nashville, Tennessee. He was a colleague of Martin Luther King, and his gentle demeanor hid a burning resolve to dismantle Jim Crow. By the end of February, Nashville students organized parallel demonstrations that resulted in their arrests and, after they refused to pay fines on moral grounds, their incarceration. Diane Nash, James Bevel, and John Lewis were three of the most impressive young leaders, all destined to become legends of the movement's early days. The crush of publicity surrounding the sit-ins created new activist networks at once attuned to local politics and mindful of national implications. Atlanta, Nashville, and Washington, DC, emerged as distinctive centers of student activism and future SNCC strongholds.[5]

Martin Luther King tried to bridge the divide between two generations of civil rights activists. He cautiously supported the movement and huddled with advisers on how best to harness the power of the young demonstrators. During the week of March 7, 1960, Ella Baker, the outgoing executive director of the Southern Christian Leadership Conference (SCLC), the civil rights group founded after the Montgomery Bus Boycott and a political ally of King and Rustin, began making plans for an April conference at Shaw University in Raleigh (her alma mater) that would organize student protests. Behind the scenes, Baker insisted that the SCLC underwrite an Easter weekend meeting of student activists at Shaw. Born in Norfolk, Virginia, in 1903 and reared in tiny Littleton, North Carolina, Baker received an unusually rich and well-rounded education for someone whose maternal and paternal grandparents had been slaves. In 1927, she graduated from Shaw as valedictorian and immediately made her way to New York City to begin a lifetime of civil rights activism. She was director of branches for the National Association for the Advancement of Colored People (NAACP) in the 1940s, and her activism flourished into the next decade. Her political acumen inspired Rosa Parks, who would become an effective local activist in her own right before fate stepped in and cast her as the unassuming heroine of the Montgomery Bus Boycott in 1955. Baker would prove a savvy mentor, brilliant strategist, and outspoken proponent of collective action and leadership for Stokely's generation. Her time in Harlem during the Great Depression and war years made her a reservoir of living history: she had organized alongside the activist Pauli Murray (who would go on to be one of the founders of the National Organization for Women), Garveyites, and socialists. In short, Ella Baker was a pioneering radical black feminist.[6]

The April 15–17 gathering in Raleigh, North Carolina, followed fast on the heels of a conference at the Highlander Folk School, in Monteagle, Tennessee, with almost one hundred student activists. Highlander's gathering leaned heavily on radical political energies that could be traced back to the Depression and were reflected in their newly acquired protest songs, some of which would become major anthems of the movement.[7]

Baker proved to be Raleigh's most important organizer. She mentored students during closed-door strategy sessions and encouraged them to organize as equal partners in the civil rights struggle. Her affinity for frank talk and firmness in dealing with Dr. King impressed students in the process of forming impressions about the very nature of leadership. Baker's plainspoken brilliance irritated some of her colleagues, but younger activists recognized the presence of genius. Baker's speech, titled "More Than a Hamburger," characterized the sit-in demonstrators as advance troops in a battle over the meaning of American democracy. Baker's poise could be traced back to a stellar background as a professional civil rights organizer and trade unionist whose past ties to the NAACP and SCLC made her a kind of political sage capable of imparting wisdom to even the most recalcitrant. Baker's experience as an organizer made her wary of charismatic leadership. She objectively recognized Martin Luther King's enormous political talents yet inspired student activists to become independent thinkers capable of existing outside of King's large shadow. Baker's ideal of radical democracy emanating from ordinary people instead of famous political leaders would capture the imagination of an entire generation of student activists.[8]

The name they chose for themselves, the Student Nonviolent Coordinating Committee (SNCC), reflected a commitment to nonviolence, their generational role as the movement's youthful face, and a pragmatic understanding of the sacrifices that lay ahead. In a display of the precocious political gifts that would lead him to become, in 1979, mayor of Washington, DC, Fisk University student Marion Barry claimed the chairmanship of the new group while King and Lawson became advisers.[9]

SNCC's activism would inspire key white student radicals. Tom Hayden, a University of Michigan junior, found himself drawn to the romantic and pragmatic sides of unfolding events. Determined to be both a participant and an observer, the twenty-year-old Hayden penned editorials for the *Michigan Daily*, networked with other activists, and made plans to attend the Democratic National Convention in Los Angeles, where he met with a delegation of SNCC activists. Hayden would serve, in 1962 and 1963, as president of the largely white Students for a Democratic Society (SDS), a group whose antiwar and civil rights activism would place it at the center of left-wing struggles as the decade progressed. Over time, Hayden's outspoken political radicalism made some characterize him as the white Stokely Carmichael.[10]

That spring, Stokely encountered a group that would change his life. As civil rights demonstrations gripped the national imagination, he met the Nonviolent Action Group (NAG) during a trip to Washington organized by Bronx Science's Young Communists to protest the House Un-American Activities Committee (HUAC). Noticing a very energetic group of black picketers, he asked them whether they were socialists or communists. They belonged to neither group, they said, but were students at Howard University affiliated with SNCC; they struck Stokely as "smart, serious, political, sassy—and they were black." Carmichael hopped into line and decided, in that instant, to attend Howard University.[11]

Carmichael graduated from Bronx Science in June, one of sixteen blacks in a class of almost four hundred seniors. His yearbook photo, which noted his appointment as soccer team captain and student council representative, failed to mention the laundry list of off-campus activities that made him one of the school's most popular and visible students, a political and intellectual prodigy who seemed destined for professional success. Carmichael spent the summer after high school graduation making frequent weekend trips to Washington and joining sit-in demonstrations in Virginia. Ultimately, the opportunity to engage in civil rights activity overcame his initial hesitation about enrolling at "an all Negro school," psychological residue from a young lifetime of messages that suggested the inferiority of black institutions.[12]

As Carmichael later wrote, Howard "opened vast new horizons" for him. Howard's student body hailed primarily from the South, as did most of its staff, and the university's cafeteria served the black southern cuisine known as "soul food." A born sociologist, natural anthropologist, and budding philosopher, Stokely observed the cultural variations between blacks in Harlem and Washington, from the superficial differences in accents to more remarkable behavioral contrasts. He found black southerners to be for the most part "relaxed, friendly, and courteous, not at all as hard-edged and in-your-face as in Harlem."[13]

Howard is located in the predominantly black neighborhood off of Georgia Avenue in the city's Northwest section. Its sprawling campus extends toward a hill that houses the Founders Library and assorted other buildings where liberal arts classes were held. As a pre-med major, Stokely found himself in "the valley," the lower campus that headquartered the natural sciences.

By 1960, Howard enjoyed a rich history of civil rights advocacy and racial uplift dating back to the nineteenth century. Founded in 1867 as a national university open to all, it was named after Oliver O. Howard, a general in the Union army during the Civil War. After the war, Howard headed the Freedmen's Bureau, the government agency charged with integrating former slaves into American society, and helped found the university. It quickly became the most comprehensive institution of higher education open to blacks in America.

A new Howard president, James Nabrit Jr., was installed a few months before Stokely's arrival. Small, neatly dressed, and outwardly unimposing, Nabrit possessed a quiet fire and intellectual integrity that cautiously embraced an era of academic freedom and institutional reforms undreamed of under his predecessor, the imposing and fiercely dictatorial Mordecai Johnson.[14]

In a sense, Howard was a darker-hued version of Harvard. At Howard, the black sons and daughters of the Talented Tenth attended dances and balls, joined fraternities and sororities, and planned lucrative professional futures. Sports, drinking, beauty pageants, and popularity formed the core of Howard's social life as did long-standing traditions of "class and color snobbery" that made the university stand apart from the lives of ordinary black Washingtonians.[15]

Howard's contingent of international students provided tangible cultural and diplomatic links with newly emerging African and Caribbean nations. Carmichael's freshman roommate, for example, hailed from Jamaica. Directed to orientation for foreign students because of his Trinidadian birthplace, Stokely listened to a campus representative warn about the crime-ridden black community that surrounded Howard and of the cultural distance between West Indians and black Americans. Carmichael "resolved then and there" to nurture relationships with African students in what would be a lifelong effort to bridge real and imagined political and cultural divides between black America and the Third World. Trinidad and Jamaica achieved independence within two years of Carmichael's arrival at Howard as did various African countries, none as prominently or as poignantly as the Congo, whose prime minister, Patrice Lumumba, would become a symbol of anticolonial resistance following his assassination on January 17, 1961. The initial success of African and Caribbean independence movements buoyed Carmichael's optimism about the world's political future, and living in Washington afforded him the opportunity to consort with African and Caribbean nationals, diplomats, and political activists.[16]

Howard's faculty impressed Carmichael as both brilliant scholars and politically engaged intellectuals. The Howard tradition was luminous and included Alain Locke, the leading philosopher of the New Negro and Harlem Renaissance era; Charles Hamilton Houston, the architect behind the NAACP's successful legal challenge against Jim Crow; and Ralph Bunche, former chair of the political science department, United Nations diplomat, and winner of the Nobel Peace Prize in 1950. E. Franklin Frazier, the towering black sociologist and author of the classic work *The Black Bourgeoisie,* was one of the school's most beloved professors. Frazier's expertise in black history and culture were widely covered in the university's student newspaper, *The Hilltop.* Frazier's unusual combination of erudition and humor made him a favorite among students, including Stokely. But he disagreed with the professor's contention that American blacks no longer possessed enduring African roots. Carmichael sympathized with the work of one of Frazier's intellectual combatants, the white scholar Melville Herskovits, of Northwestern University, whose writing on African American's cultural retentions broke new historical and anthropological ground.[17]

Conversations with historian Rayford Logan opened up new ways of imagining slavery and antebellum America's impact on contemporary race relations. The presence of William Leo Hansberry (uncle of Lorraine Hansberry), Frank Snowden, and Chancellor Williams offered creative students the chance to study Africa from antiquity to the age of decolonization. African artifacts on display in the university's art gallery set Stokely's mind ablaze with questions about black people's racial and ethnic origins, while plays at the Ira Aldridge Theater gave dramatic expression to black literary productions that, for Carmichael, reached the level of Greek tragedy.

Sterling Brown, the scholar, poet, and critic, took a special interest in Carmichael. Brown counted as friends and acquaintances the musicians Paul Robeson, Huddie Ledbetter (Lead Belly), and Duke Ellington, and the pioneering Pan-Africanist W.E.B. Du Bois. His earthy demeanor and razor-sharp wit instantly endeared him to undergraduates. Brown frequently invited Carmichael to his office for chatty reminiscences about literary and historical figures. Stokely and fellow students Mike Thelwell, Courtland Cox, Butch Conn, Ed Brown, and Tom Kahn eagerly accepted invitations to Brown's home on occasional weekends, when they listened to jazz and indulged in his rare book library. Brown urged them to pay careful attention to the voices of not just the dignified but also the damned: the poor, rural and urban, grassroots and street-corner inhabitants. He would credit Brown "for first showing me how to really appreciate and love our people's culture."[18]

At fifty-nine, Brown was old enough to be Carmichael's grandfather, but Howard's younger faculty also provided inspiration. Toni Morrison, who would later win the Pulitzer and Nobel Prizes, taught Stokely's freshman English class. If Howard's internal contradictions proved disorienting they also produced a new sense of intellectual balance for Carmichael, whose professors combined scholarly erudition with a progressive black intellectual orientation. Although Howard lacked a formal Black Studies program during his undergraduate years, Carmichael dove into curriculum choices beyond his designated major, which changed from pre-medicine to philosophy, and included a deep interest in black history, politics, and culture.[19]

Beyond the mentorship of some of Howard's best professors, Carmichael's most important association came by joining the Nonviolent Action Group. Composed of some fifty core members, less than half of whom were women and eight white, NAG was propelled by "the conviction that youth could change the world" and set out in a determined fashion to do so. Most members were Howard students, but some, like Paul Dietrich, a white socialist who owned a jazz club that served as a NAG hangout, were local activists. By the time Stokely arrived, the older students Thelwell, Cox, Brown, Kahn, Bill Mahoney, Dion Diamond, and Hank Thomas were already NAG veterans.

NAG members were considered racial and political mavericks. Ed Brown had enrolled in Howard after expulsion from Southern University in Louisiana for organizing sit-ins and wound up living across the hall from Stokely and became a trusted ally. Hank Thomas was a native of St. Augustine, Florida. His parents sent him to Howard to escape the state's racial problems. The six-foot-five-inch Thomas had been offered a football scholarship from the University of Wisconsin. He chose Howard out of a commitment to the movement that he traced back to his high school years in segregated schools, where his teachers nurtured an appreciation of black history and contemporary African independence movements. Mahoney combined striking physical features—high cheekbones, olive skin, and almond-shaped eyes that gave him the look of a Native American—with a casual penchant for discussing obscure philosophical issues. Tall, light-skinned, articulate, and sternly handsome, Thelwell stood out as the group's most talented literary propagandist and a future novelist. Born in Jamaica to a politically minded family, Thelwell grew up discussing independence movements flourishing all over the Caribbean and took particular interest in the Cuban Revolution. Thelwell's stylish goatee, pipe smoking, and confidence lent him an aura of cosmopolitan insouciance. With his thick Jamaican accent, encyclopedic literary knowledge, and serious demeanor, he could be easily mistaken for one of Howard's young professors, and his habit of delivering pro-Cuban lectures to fellow students earned him the nickname "Castro." As a sophomore Thelwell roomed in the same dormitory as Stokely. Carmichael's engaging demeanor, wicked sense of humor, and charisma marked him as a unique personality—both larger than life and down to earth. "He was," Thelwell would recall, "just a very spirited young man."[20]

Carmichael's fellow Trinidadian and New Yorker Courtland Cox exuded intellectual energy and inner calm. Prone to offering ingenious bits of philosophical wisdom ("Blackness is necessary," he once remarked, "but it is not sufficient"), Cox cultivated a reputation for maintaining grace under pressure. The trio of Stokely, Brown, and Cox functioned as a rump group within NAG. Some, like Carmichael, traced their activism back to high school or earlier, while others had found inspiration in the lunch counter sit-ins that had set the nation on fire the previous spring.[21]

At his first NAG meeting, the sophisticated level of discussion exhilarated Stokely. Members talked about how to organize Howard's campus and challenge Jim Crow in Washington and the neighboring states of Maryland and Virginia. Concerned with the intellectual and theoretical matters that lay at the core of the practical struggle for civil rights, members quoted Martin Luther King and linked individual civic action to a larger vision of collective social justice.[22]

NAG members read Bayard Rustin's 1942 essay "The Negro and Non-violence" as part of their training. Citing Gandhi's observation that "freedom does not drop from the sky," Rustin argued that nonviolent direct action could tap into existing black church networks and assist in dismantling racial segregation. He dared American pacifists to extend their antiwar activism to the struggle to end racism. "This demands being so integral a part of the Negro community in its day-to-day struggle, so close to it in similarity of work, so near its standard of living," observed Rustin, "that when problems arise he who stands forth to judge, to plan, to suggest, or to lead is really at one with the Negro masses."[23]

Carmichael read Rustin's words with pride that turned into astonishment. Racial violence, fear, and racial resentment had grown worse since Rustin's essay. Rustin's prophetic words raised his stature in Carmichael's eyes, as did another essay, "Nonviolence vs. Jim Crow," a moving account of Rustin's refusal to obey segregation laws during a bus trip from Louisville to Nashville. Carmichael's admiration for Rustin grew into a kind of reverence after reading these essays, a feeling that gripped many in NAG.

Armed with Rustin's words, Carmichael spent his freshman year attending classes (armed also with stethoscope, thermometer, and rubber hammer

supplied by Mummy Olga for the future physician), NAG meetings, and following news from the national civil rights front. In an era where Reserve
Officers' Training Corps (ROTC) drills were compulsory, Carmichael staged
fainting spells that earned him a permanent stay from such activity. Impatient to earn his stripes in southern civil rights demonstrations like some
of NAG's veterans, Carmichael settled for attending local demonstrations,
planning future organizing drives, and studying the nuances of nonviolence, sometimes under the direction of Julius Hobson, an outspoken local
CORE leader.[24]

In a remarkably short time, Stokely became a leader among equals. His
knack for turning competitors into friends made him an effortless politician,
one whose gift for mimicry could soothe a wounded ego and whose words
could alternately flatter, tease, cajole, and admonish. Carmichael's ability
to simultaneously project an aura of bold confidence, reckless nerve, and
laid-back cool made him something of a phenomenon on campus. Six years
before he would become a national political leader, Carmichael began, as
natural leaders often do, to transform his environment. Howard University
would, in many ways, never be the same. Stokely's activist legacy would impact future generations of students long after his time as an undergraduate
had concluded.

Carmichael's leadership qualities, which were cultivated in NAG, would
be tested as a Freedom Rider. In the spring of 1961, an interracial group of
civil rights activists, a mixture of student leaders and veteran organizers,
launched Freedom Rides throughout the South in defiance of Jim Crow. The
plan grew out of the 1947 Journey of Reconciliation, a project co-sponsored by
CORE and FOR, whose architects included Rustin, Ella Baker, and African-
American journalist William Worthy. Ironically, although the initiative
contained his fingerprints, Rustin observed the proceedings from London,
having been temporarily excluded, once again, from advisory capacities because of sexual and political indiscretions.[25]

Designed to test the recent Supreme Court ruling that banned Jim Crow
at interstate bus terminals, "Project Freedom Ride 1961" sparked a national
crisis through benign provocation. Riders were instructed to enter southern
bus and train terminals and simply defy segregated spaces. Black volunteers
would sit in waiting areas and enter bathrooms reserved for whites. Hank
Thomas' decision to volunteer as a Freedom Rider, following a typically
charged NAG debate, drew Carmichael closer to joining the mission. CORE's

Washington headquarters became the staging point to train twelve volunteers who would travel down south, accompanied by national director James Farmer. Carmichael met John Lewis at a dinner, remembered as the Last Supper (because of the twelve) honoring volunteers. The soft-spoken, impeccably dressed Lewis impressed Stokely as calm and courageous. A devout Christian who had practice-preached to chickens as a boy growing up in Alabama, Lewis patterned his humble manner after Martin Luther King. Within two years he would become SNCC chairman and emerge as the youngest nationally recognized civil rights leader of the era.

The next day, May 4, Carmichael and a group from Howard and CORE activists escorted the volunteers to the bus station. He watched the group of thirteen board two buses (one Trailways, one Greyhound) with a mixture of admiration and apprehension. There were good reasons to be concerned. Spectacular waves of violence would confront Freedom Riders ten days later in Anniston, Alabama, where a mob set fire to the Greyhound bus and injured several riders, including Hank Thomas. A photo of the burning bus accompanied evening newspaper coverage and catapulted the Freedom Rides into global significance. In Birmingham, violent ambush—coordinated between the local branch of the Ku Klux Klan and Birmingham's commissioner of public safety, Eugene "Bull" Connor, and tacitly abetted by FBI agents aware of the impending attack—greeted the Trailways bus.[26]

Carmichael followed these developments from Howard with a sense of horror that grew into rage. From Nashville, the hot-tempered Diane Nash drifted into cool precision. After Farmer succumbed to White House pressure for a moratorium on future rides, Nash organized a new contingent of riders. No sooner had the Freedom Riders hopped a prearranged flight to New Orleans than word leaked that a fresh wave of volunteers were heading to Alabama. NAG responded to Nash's plea for volunteers with fresh recruits, including a past skeptic, the white club owner and socialist Paul Dietrich. Stokely, Bill Mahoney, and fellow students Travis Britt and John Moody rescheduled finals so they could join soon after.[27]

On June 7, NAG volunteers prepared to go south. Stokely was embarking on a dangerous mission, so he called his mother from the Washington airport. "May Charles, this is for real now. Something I gotta do. I only ask one thing. If the press should contact you, just tell them you're proud of me." May Charles rebuked him for "chatting nonsense" and putting his life on the line "for people who don't care about you," but Stokely held firm. He made the call just as he and other volunteers prepared to board a night flight to New Orleans. Julius Hobson, NAG member Travis Britt, and the Greene sisters, Connie and Gwen, whom Carmichael knew from Baltimore-area demonstrations, joined him. Dispatched with strict instructions from Hobson, they boarded the plane with carry-on luggage and quickly deplaned in New Orleans for a prearranged rendezvous with two CORE workers. At New Orleans, this group would be the first to test restrictions at a train station bound for Jackson, Mississippi. Carmichael alleviated his own fear of dying by philosophically reasoning that "somebody will die, but it won't be me, it will be the guy next to me." As the years passed, this personal mantra would hold true.[28]

Carmichael's Freedom Riders arrived in New Orleans at three in the morning. They hoped their middle-of-the-night arrival would throw off suspicion of civil rights activity. The plan worked and a CORE escort drove them to the city. Stokely marveled at the warm air and inhaled sweet smells that reminded him of his childhood. As the group drove to the edge of town to spend a fitful night's sleep, Carmichael noted the sight of strange trees glittering with Spanish moss, a picture that evoked images of a gothic South teeming with lynch mobs. Billie Holiday's "Strange Fruit" might have come to mind. The sense of poverty was overwhelming. Well acquainted with housing projects in Harlem, Carmichael considered the ghettoes in New Orleans to be "absolutely appalling." It was the furthest south in the United States he had ever been.[29]

In the morning, a large mob convened outside the New Orleans train station, forcing Carmichael's group to scurry onto the train for Jackson through a blur of concentrated violence. Once safely on the train, they were too relieved to dwell on cuts and bruises sustained during the frantic boarding. The image of an elderly white woman shaking a cane in rage would remain with Stokely for the rest of his life.[30]

On June 8, Stokely and eight volunteers entered a white waiting room in Jackson, Mississippi, and were quickly arrested and put in Hinds County Jail. Seven of the nine were NAG members. The group's interracial makeup, which included several white women, caused one officer to snap as they spilled out of the paddy wagon: "We got nine: five black niggers and four white niggers." Prisoner 20978 stared into the camera pensively, his remarkably expressive eyes fixed straight ahead as if contemplating a future too distant to fully comprehend. Carmichael's profile betrayed youthful acne and a slightly oversized suit jacket. The trip marked his first visit to "the enemy's stronghold," Mississippi, a place he would soon call home. While being processed, he discussed Henry David Thoreau's ideas on civil disobedience, insulted racist police officers and prison guards, and adopted a general tone of open defiance. Hinds County Jail housed notable movement figures: the devout Nashville contingent led by Jim Lawson and the seminarians James Bevel, John Lewis, and Bernard Lafayette; Reverend C.T. Vivian, who managed to retain his defiant eloquence even amidst repeated beatings at the hands of authorities; and a group from NAG that included Hank Thomas, Dion Diamond, John Moody, and Nashville student Freddy Leonard. Joan Trumpauer, a white Southerner from Georgia who had transferred from Duke University to historically black Tougaloo Southern Christian College, near Jackson, after accepting the movement as her calling, was also on hand. She kept a diary of her time in jail, where riders were segregated by race and sex. The devoutly Christian Trumpauer longed to be housed with the black women who shared her love of spirituals. "I think all the girls in here are gems but I feel more in common with the Negro girls & wish I was locked with them instead of these atheist Yankees—particularly when they sing," she wrote. "The boys have devotions twice a day. Sigh!"[31]

In New York, May Charles listened to the radio for news of her son. To neighbors who asked, "Is that your boy Stokely they've got down there?" she responded as her son had instructed. "Yes, that's my boy and I'm so proud of him I don't know what to do!" Adolphus Carmichael frowned upon his son's activism but took Stokely at his word that he would earn a college degree before devoting his life to the movement. His parents learned early on to compromise with Stokely, who proved more willful, mischievous, and political than his four sisters. If May Charles identified with her son's independent streak, Adolphus retained a stubborn faith in God, hard work, and a hope in the promise of America's immigrant roots that conflicted with Stokely's ingrained skepticism.[32]

While May Charles put on a good public face, Carmichael remained in jail. In the middle of the night on June 15, Carmichael and forty-four other male prisoners were transferred by bus to Parchman Farm, Mississippi's notorious prison. They sped across Highway 49. Bill Mahoney remembered seeing two children who were walking through a cotton field stop in their tracks at the sight of the speeding convoy. Parchman's tower and concrete buildings formed tiny specks against the Delta's stark landscape, where flatlands stretched as far and wide as the eye could see. Barbed-wire fences and shotgun-toting sentries made entrance into Parchman memorable, as did the warden's threat to unleash the prison's "bad niggers" on the Freedom Riders. Herded to the maximum-security wing, the bleary-eyed group listened to a profanity-filled tirade from Deputy Tyson, whom Carmichael later described as "a massive, red-faced, cigar-smoking cracker in cowboy boots and a Stetson who strutted and stomped about blustering out orders and 'promises.'" Tyson fit the stereotype of southern law enforcement as a grotesque caricature complete with an incongruously high-pitched voice that contrasted with his extra-large size.[33]

Parchman's legendary brutality had reached Carmichael in Greenwich Village, through the heartbreaking laments of guitar-strumming folk singers. Carmichael and his cellmate, Nashville's Freddy Leonard, were the two youngest riders, and in the next cell was the forty-one-year-old James Farmer, chastened, but relieved to be in the thick of things after his absence from Anniston. In his rich baritone, Farmer shared war stories and tall tales and debated Stokely over the nuances of nonviolence. They found a collective bravado in freedom songs they sang from their concrete windowless cells. A "moral stubbornness" united the strong group of personalities who stayed in twenty-four-hour lockdown relieved by twice weekly showers. Hank Thomas led an exercise routine after breakfast each day and doubled as music conductor for songs the men sang to pass the time and raise their spirits.[34]

The singing tested the patience of guards, who ordered it halted. When the Freedom Riders refused, the guards removed their mattresses, leaving them to sleep on the floor or on steel box springs. Guards and inmate trusties snatched Stokely's mattress and, after a brutal effort, Freddy Leonard's. The brutality inspired Carmichael to join in song later that day in a religious service that would be interrupted by water hosing. The more spiritually inclined strove to imbue their suffering with a sense of higher purpose. James Bevel refuted complaints over prison garb with a line that he spoke as if delivering a newsflash: "Gandhi wrapped a rag around his balls and brought the whole British Empire to its knees!" Hank Thomas evoked the biblical examples of Paul and Silas "bound in jail" as a salve against depression.[35]

A hunger strike was the next tactic. Carmichael initially resisted the idea. He preferred to take turns with Freddy taunting guards with backtalk that earned them time in "wrist breakers," vise-like handcuffs that caused even the toughest convicts to double over in pain. During one particularly grueling session with the wrist breakers, Carmichael chanted to Deputy Tyson from a blues song, "I'm going to tell God how you treat me one of these days." The song was soon taken up by the entire cellblock. After he finally joined the hunger strike, Carmichael remained on it for eight days, two days longer than the majority of the group, and one day longer than Farmer. Afterward, he gave a short speech to his fellow Freedom Riders, humorously referring to the ordeal of going without food for so long:

> Friends, most of you don't know me. My name is Stokely Carmichael. I'm in with Freddy Leonard. You may have heard of us. We're the youngest in here. Myself, I'm a very young man but I intend to be fighting the rest of my life so I'll probably be in jail again. So probably will some of you. So this may not be the last time we are together in prison. That's why I want you to remember my name. Because if we are ever in jail again and any of you mention the words hunger and strike, I'm gonna denounce you properly. I will be the first to denounce you. You tell everybody that. That if they are ever in jail with Stokely Carmichael never ever mention anything about a hunger strike.

John Lewis noted Stokely's special "knack for starting an argument and for winning it." Lewis, who appreciated Carmichael's assertiveness, quick wit, and unpretentious manner, decided on the spot that he liked him.[36]

CHAPTER THREE

Finding a Way in New Worlds

June 29, 1961–January 1962

ON JUNE 29, 1961, STOKELY CARMICHAEL CELEBRATED HIS TWENTIETH birthday in his tiny cell. He came to interpret his arrest as a rite of passage. "It would be the first of many I was to spend in Southern jails," he would remember. SNCC workers made jokes about his habit of being incarcerated during his birthday. "It got so that people would say, 'Hey, it's Carmichael's birthday. Keep your distance from him today unless you want to be arrested too.'"[1]

While some chose bail as it became available, a few riders remained incarcerated. After forty days in jail, the final remaining Freedom Riders were released on bond. CORE had arranged his release, a deal that Carmichael found distasteful but was powerless to refuse. From Parchman, the riders arrived in Jackson, where they were fêted at Tougaloo College's gymnasium. "Welcome Freedom Riders," proclaimed a large banner that gave the occasion the feel of a pep rally, albeit one complete with heaping tables of soul food, loud music, and energetic dancing.[2]

That evening, Carmichael flew to New York and hopped a subway train home to the Bronx. The sight of her emaciated son prompted May Charles to spend the next few weeks nursing him back to good health. Meanwhile, Carmichael's exploits made him a minor celebrity in movement circles. There were now speaking requests for fundraisers in well-appointed homes where white liberals eagerly listened to his account of Parchman's harsh conditions and responded with the cash that served as the movement's lifeblood. At times, these encounters produced a discomfort in Carmichael, who chafed at the slightest whiff of liberal condescension by white allies. His speaking schedule brought him into the orbit of Harry Belafonte, the singer and movie star whose peerless commitment to civil rights made him the rare entertainer who transcended artificial divides between art and politics. Belafonte's friendship with Martin Luther King and SNCC placed him in the unique position of being held in equally high esteem by movement power brokers and radicals. Carmichael and Belafonte shared a passion for civil rights activism and more. Belafonte's mother hailed from Jamaica, and the Harlem-born singer had spent part of his childhood there before returning to New York, where he found unparalleled success by turning Jamaican calypso songs into mainstream American music.

The similarity of the Caribbean backgrounds of Belafonte and Carmichael, their physical confidence and their personal egos made their relationship crackle with an unspoken competitive tension. At least some of this revolved around a woman. Belafonte introduced Carmichael to the South African singer Miriam Makeba, whom Stokely would marry in 1968. Makeba had of course served as the teenaged Stokely's romantic dream. In fact, in Carmichael's telling, he wore a "silky Harry Belafonte shirt," complete "with flared collars, a deep V neck, and billowing sleeves" the first time he met Makeba, but she took no special interest in the young man when they finally met after her concert. It would have been nearly impossible for Stokely to compete with Harry Belafonte, especially in Miriam's eyes. In her memoir, she vividly recalled her first meeting with Belafonte, whose international fame preceded him. "This man is so handsome he could make a god jealous!" Belafonte had surprised Miriam that first evening by expressing genuine interest in the racial politics of South Africa in a manner that made her curious and admiring all at once. Now, as Belafonte introduced Stokely to Makeba at a concert in Queens, the two men perhaps briefly imagined trading places, with the singer earning the chance to engage in the dangerous and gritty world he supported financially and the young activist dreaming of the opportunity to consort with international celebrities as a peer instead of a fan. Less than five years later, Carmichael would join the rarified world where politics and celebrity collided, drawing comparisons to Belafonte's good looks on the road to finding time to turn his romantic fantasies about Makeba into reality.[3]

Stokely went from consorting with celebrities to attending a SNCC-sponsored seminar in Nashville that began on July 30. It was the first time he had attended such a meeting. Ella Baker, Martin Luther King, and Jim Lawson joined some of the major intellectuals of the era, including L.D. Reddick,

C. Eric Lincoln (whose trailblazing study *Black Muslims in America* was published that year), August Meier, Kenneth Clark, and Howard University professors Rayford Logan and E. Franklin Frazier. Tim Jenkins, a former Howard student-body president who had graduated a year before Stokely's arrival on campus, attended the conference. Jenkins' political acumen and ability to knit innovative political alliances made him the rare black leader who could be vice president of the domestic affairs section of the predominantly white (and surreptitiously CIA-infiltrated) National Student Association (NSA), serve on the executive committee of SDS, and maintain a strong relationship with SNCC. John Lewis and Diane Nash, two veterans of the Nashville sit-in movement with close ties to the SCLC, were on hand, as were NAG members Dion Diamond and John Moody. The idea for the seminar originated with Jenkins, who informed Carmichael of his determination to leverage the momentum from the summer's Freedom Rides. The pragmatic Jenkins sought to outline areas of mutual interest between the student movement and the federal government. In late-night bull sessions, they grappled with a range of questions, including whether to shift energies from sit-ins to voter registration. "For me those sessions were important," Carmichael would remember. "I think that was when we began to bond into 'a band of brothers.' I know that I certainly started to feel the strong respect and love for these brothers and sisters, which has lingered all my life."[4]

In Nashville, Carmichael encountered Julian Bond, the light-skinned, boyishly handsome son of Dr. Horace Mann Bond, the first black president of Lincoln University in Pennsylvania. Poised and elegant, Bond was destined to be a key figure in the Atlanta student movement. A founding member of SNCC who also served as a student leader at Atlanta's black, all-male Morehouse College, Bond wed a Brahmin pedigree to an acute sense of social justice. Creeping doubt rested beneath a raffish grin and unflappable surface, marking the anxiety-prone Bond as more suited for public relations than the hazards of the field. Also passing through was James Forman, soon to be SNCC's first full-time executive secretary. He had the stout physique of a bulldog and a fiery temperament, and his administrative abilities would shortly transform the fledgling group.[5]

Ruby Doris Smith, a Spelman College co-ed who had already served two stints in prison (in Rock Hill, South Carolina, and Parchman Farm as a Freedom Rider), was among the most vocal and eloquent attendees. Of all the young black women inspired by the sit-in movement, Smith possessed

the most irrepressible combination of youthful idealism, iron-willed determination, and outspoken assertiveness. Ten months younger than Stokely,
Smith would, after short stints in the field organizing, become one of SNCC's
most valuable administrators.[6]

Perhaps the most important SNCC activist who would have an enduring
impact on Stokely was also its most unassuming member. A high school math
teacher and budding philosopher from New York named Bob Moses joined
the group after Bayard Rustin sent him to Atlanta to work for Martin Luther
King and the SCLC. After an awkward meeting with King, who warned Moses about associating with suspected communists, Moses accepted Baker's
offer to tour the South. He immediately plunged into a recruiting effort for
SNCC's planned October conference (where the group formally structured
itself) that would seem quixotic had it not been so successful. In the unassuming town of Cleveland, Mississippi, Moses developed a fast friendship
with Amzie Moore, a local black businessman and World War II veteran.
Moses left Mississippi to resume his teaching job but offered to return to
assist Moore in voter registration efforts destined to change the very face of
American democracy.[7]

In September 1961, Stokely returned to Howard from Nashville a campus
celebrity. The fall semester was marked by other changes as well. His infatuation with Mary Lovelace, who joined NAG his sophomore year, now
bloomed into love. On Wednesday afternoons the smitten Stokely assisted
Mary, a talented visual artist, by handing her paintbrushes. It was a romantic
pairing doomed as much by their egos as by the unpredictability of the movement and competing schedules, but the two would date on and off throughout Stokely's time at Howard. Key patterns emerged that semester, including
Carmichael's tendency to get arrested. He would earn his second trip to jail
for sitting in at a Baltimore restaurant.[8]

The Hilltop, under managing editor Mike Thelwell, dedicated the fall
semester's first issue to the subject of nonviolence. "In doing so," the editorial reasoned, "we pay homage not only to a revolutionary ideal struggling
to be heard in a world hell-bent on suicide, but, with special warmth, to
seven Howard Freedom Riders who forayed into the Deep South to redeem
a moral wasteland." In the same issue, Stokely recounted the details of his

post-Parchman encounters with police while demonstrating in Nashville. His account played up the Sisyphean nature of nonviolent struggle; a group of eight students protesting outside a department store withstood eggs, chunks of ice, tomatoes, and bricks hurled by an angry mob that, in quick order, began throwing punches at demonstrators and lit cigarettes down their backs. He vowed to return to the Delta the next year and challenged Howard students to join him.[9]

Charlie Cobb, a freshman born in Washington, DC, but transplanted to Springfield, Massachusetts, would answer Carmichael's challenge. Cobb's personal aversion to attending group meetings made him a more frequent presence at protests than at campus strategy sessions, but his infectious smile, easy humor, and good-natured personality made him a well-liked colleague who quickly became one of Carmichael's good friends. The son of a radical Congregationalist minister open-minded enough to form political alliances with Black Muslims, Cobb met Malcolm X in the 1950s when the latter stopped by his father's house to discuss politics.[10]

Malcolm X, whom Cobb knew as a family friend, came to Howard in October as the most controversial speaker ever to visit the university. That year, Malcolm had become one of the most sought-after public speakers in America, delivering well-received lectures at Harvard, Yale, Brown, Temple, Michigan State, and Berkeley. He was born Malcolm Little, in Omaha, Nebraska, on May 19, 1925. Black radical activism was a part of Malcolm's birthright. His parents, Earl and Louise Little, were followers of Marcus Garvey. Earl's willingness to plant the seeds of black nationalism in the midwest city of Lansing, Michigan, carried a high cost. Malcolm remembered his father's death as a lynching, although authorities claimed a streetcar accident had practically severed Earl Little in two. The death of the family patriarch sent the Little family into decline, with Louise Little suffering from mental and emotional scars that prevented her from taking care of Malcolm and his seven brothers and sisters.[11]

During the 1940s, Malcolm lived in Boston, New York, and Detroit, where he cultivated a reputation as a slick-talking petty criminal. Malcolm's arrest in Boston in 1946 on burglary charges drew him closer to his activist roots. In prison between 1946 and 1952, when he was paroled, Malcolm Little transformed himself through reading, a strict diet, and embracing the teachings of the Nation of Islam (NOI). The Nation stressed personal responsibility, discipline, and race pride in a manner that mirrored Marcus Garvey's ideas. But the NOI replaced Garvey's worldly dreams of revitalizing Africa with religious prophecy that predicted the white man's doom. The group's leader, Elijah Muhammad, was a former sharecropper from Georgia whose frail health only strengthened his devout followers' belief in his divinity. Malcolm Little left prison as Malcolm X, the new surname reflecting the NOI's belief that blacks were a lost tribe wandering in America's racial wilderness, blindly clinging to a culture and tradition (including last names) rooted in slavery and oppression rather than to their actual history.

Malcolm X emerged during the 1950s as a political phenomenon who transformed the NOI. It went from a small, obscure religious group into a sprawling and financially secure organization capable of injecting itself into the national debate over civil rights and race relations. Malcolm's brilliant mind, voracious reading, and supple debate skills made him the group's most politically motivated spokesman. He became the group's national representative in 1957, and soon the NOI was as much political as it was religious. His minimalist style, dark suit, tie, and glasses, became as legendary as his biting sermons, which combined humor, politics, and autobiography in an effort to convince blacks that they were important and intelligent enough to choose their own fate and design their own futures. Malcolm's advocacy, following the teachings of Muhammad, of self-defense elevated him as the primary rhetorical opponent of Martin Luther King. The two men would meet only briefly once. King assumed the role of a defense attorney, extolling the inherent humanity of blacks and whites to each other. Malcolm, in contrast, relished his ability to serve as black America's district attorney based in Harlem's Temple No. 7. From there, he publicly condemned white racism for creating urban ghettos, condoning lynching, and maintaining a society that was so bankrupt that African Americans were forced to organize, protest, and march in order to gain citizenship rights that were supposedly guaranteed. For Stokely's generation, Malcolm X became the avatar of a new movement for black liberation, one anchored in the quest for self-determination epitomized by Garveyism and its many variations that would come to be known as Black Power.[12]

Upon hearing news of Malcolm's visit to campus, Carmichael promised to lick envelopes and sweep floors so long as he garnered a front-row seat. The October 30th event was a debate between Malcolm X and Bayard Rustin, and it would become an instant legend. Carmichael did indeed make it to the front row of the debate; dressed in a suit and tie, he gazed intently at the proceedings. In a few short years, after Malcolm's assassination, supporters and critics would practically anoint Carmichael as the slain leader's official political heir. But at the great debate, Carmichael could only watch in awe, along with his classmates, at the power of Malcolm X. Here was a man who at thirty-six years old had transcended a life scarred by childhood tragedy, juvenile crime, and almost seven years in prison to emerge as the most authentic working-class black leader of the twentieth century. NAG hosted Malcolm's visit through Project Awareness, a forum designed to present opposing views of hot-button issues. E. Franklin Frazier helped to negotiate the terms of Malcolm's appearance in the kind of behind-the-scenes maneuver that endeared him to campus radicals. Rustin had personally approached Malcolm with the idea after university administrators objected to the Nation of Islam minister delivering an unopposed lecture. "You'll present your views," said Rustin, "and then I'll attack you as someone having no political, social, or economic program for dealing with the problems of blacks." This last line represented a vintage Rustin provocation, one that Malcolm responded to accordingly: "I'll take you up on that."[13]

Project Awareness politicized Howard's campus. President James Nabrit's approval of the program signaled a breakthrough for a university whose most outspoken students decried its claustrophobic definition of academic freedom. Malcolm's impending arrival set the campus abuzz, especially as it came on the heels of Queens College canceling a planned appearance. Project Awareness cultivated the era's leading black cultural and political figures, including Harry Belafonte, novelists James Baldwin and John Oliver Killens, and actors Sidney Poitier and Ossie Davis. The project sought to expose middle-class students to radical figures who routinely made headlines yet rarely visited black colleges. Tom Kahn, a white, openly homosexual Howard student and Rustin disciple, led the student committee that crafted the speakers' forum. Mike Thelwell's friendship with Kahn helped him better appreciate Rustin's political wisdom. Howard's most politically radical and intellectually astute student activists became, in quick order, "Bayard Rustin people." On the eve of Malcolm's visit to campus, Stokely remained in Rustin's thrall.[14]

In person, Malcolm proved better than advertised. A capacity crowd of fifteen hundred jammed into the newly built Cramton Auditorium, while five hundred more listened outside over loudspeakers. Malcolm and Rustin each spoke for about thirty minutes, followed by a ten-minute rebuttal for each. Moderator E. Franklin Frazier lent intellectual gravitas to the event's deliberately straightforward title, "Integration or Separation." At Howard, Malcolm extolled the value of economic self-determination as a sacred corollary to political empowerment. "When the Jews were discriminated against in Miami," he quipped, "they bought Miami Beach." The audience laughed at Malcolm's well-placed verbal jabs and exploded in applause throughout his talk. While Rustin criticized Malcolm's dreams of a separate black economy as vague and impractical, the minister contended that African Americans were "being used as political footballs in the token integration farce" designed to thwart a black revolution.[15]

Malcolm spoke in the biting parables of a working-class prophet. Blacks would never be equal citizens, he insisted, as long as they remained intent on occupying the white man's house, a place where they were neither wanted nor welcomed. "I don't believe the Freedom Ride on Route 40 is going to solve anything," he said defiantly. "I wouldn't want to tell my child someday that I had to beg a white man to let me eat in a restaurant." With the audience primed to erupt, he continued. "I would rather build a restaurant and say to him, 'Here's your restaurant.'" This last line unleashed furious applause that shook Cramton. "It was from this point that it can be dated," Carmichael recalled over a quarter-century later, "when nationalism took its firm root and became dominant" in NAG.[16]

Malcolm's lecture galvanized racial pride at Howard. He planted seeds of political conversion that would turn many in the audience, over time, into ardent black nationalists, committed Pan-Africanists, and lifelong political radicals. Carmichael took as much pleasure in Malcolm's physical presence as in the words he spoke. Thirty-five years later, he possessed instant visual recall of Malcolm striding onto the stage: a singular silhouette tracking him from above by spotlight as if he was a featured performer in the theater piece that was the debate. If Malcolm's physical swagger and intellectual bravado made a lasting impression on Carmichael, it evoked similar feelings campus wide. James Nabrit spoke for many when he described the entire affair as a "very thrilling evening" that contributed to Howard's intellectual mission of creating a new generation of critical thinkers. Nationally, black newspapers such as the *Baltimore Afro-American* and *Chicago Defender* covered the debate. Their reporters agreed that, despite their differences, Malcolm and Rustin spoke eloquently against the brutal effects of racial and economic injustice. *The Hilltop* offered a respectful assessment of Rustin as a stalwart foe overwhelmed by Malcolm's rhetorical genius. Over time, the debate would grow in reputation and significance. Although Malcolm won the hearts of the student body on that late fall evening, Rustin would, for at least a while longer, retain the allegiance of its young organizers.[17]

Stokely dove into the kind of organizing that Malcolm scorned during his appearance. Still buzzing from Malcolm's lecture, Carmichael helped lead a contingent of two hundred Howard students as they launched a campaign to desegregate restaurants and public facilities along Route 40, the main drag out of Washington through Maryland. By this time, the local black leader Julius Hobson routinely called on him to organize troops to support CORE's latest plans for sit-ins and racial demonstrations. Carmichael's wide range of networks made him an effective organizer; with his intimate understanding of Howard's campus culture, he was able to entice recruits with promises of parties after their political work ended.[18]

As Carmichel and NAG led the organizing arm of the Route 40 protests, by November more than a thousand volunteers had joined the effort. On Saturday, November 11, carloads of Howard students staged sit-ins at fifty Baltimore-area restaurants. Volunteers from area colleges and universities fanned out in demonstrations to publicize the city's racial segregation. Stokely and Mary Lovelace were among seven Howard students arrested for picketing. Courtland Cox and Tom Kahn led a team of protesters through Baltimore's "Little Italy" waterfront. They drove through narrow streets teeming with neighborhood thugs and belligerent teenagers. Amidst the smell of pizza and the sounds of heavily accented immigrants screaming racial slurs at picketers, some school-age black kids in the crowd watched the commotion. Released from jail after one day, Carmichael announced that the demonstrations would resume the following Saturday.[19]

Malcolm X's appearance and the Route 40 demonstrations competed with news of Bob Moses' travails in McComb, Mississippi. In that small town, Moses was directing SNCC's first project in the Deep South. He recruited two others to head up a voter registration project, including Reggie Robinson, whom Stokely knew from Baltimore's SNCC affiliate. Within a month of arriving in McComb, Moses and Travis Britt were beaten, local black teenagers and movement supporters arrested, and, most tragically, Herbert Lee of Amite County was murdered by a pro-segregation legislator in Mississippi's House of Representatives. In the long term, Lee's death remains one of the major unpunished crimes of the civil rights era. In the short run, it galvanized SNCC. Reinforcements trickled into McComb in the form of new

SNCC chairman Chuck McDew, former chairman Marion Barry, and Bob Zellner, an Alabama native and the group's only white field secretary. NAG's Dion Diamond, now a full-time SNCC field secretary, helped to organize ad hoc classes for striking high school students, and SDS president Tom Hayden lobbied the Justice Department for protection for civil rights workers after he had been beaten in McComb while posing as a credentialed reporter in early October.[20]

Later that month, *The New York Times* characterized the "Camellia City of America" as a "hard-core segregationist city." The story was accompanied by a map that highlighted tiny McComb's location as if both to satisfy reader curiosity and to offer proof that Mississippi remained part of the United States. By November, voter registration efforts in McComb ground to a halt, slowed by the arrests of Moses and McDew and the mass incarceration of 119 student supporters charged with disturbing the peace. From a Magnolia, Mississippi, jail, Moses smuggled out a letter that drew an incisive portrait of quiet determination in the face of racial injustice. In it, he described Mississippi as "the middle of the iceberg," where the sentencing judge extolled McComb's racial harmony, prisoners ate rice and gravy without forks and spoons, and local activist Hollis Watkins led the group in freedom songs that carried the predictive clarity of Old Testament prophets. SNCC's efforts in McComb offered a rough outline of the cost of grassroots direct action in the Magnolia State and would set the stage for the ambitious and era-defining Summer Project that Carmichael would help lead three years later.[21]

Compared to Moses' dramatic exploits in Mississippi, Carmichael regarded his own work as part of a secondary line of attack in a civil rights struggle whose main front raged in the South. News of Moses' courage under fire earned him Stokely's lasting respect and even a tinge of envy for Bob's having successfully tested his mettle under difficult circumstances. More than once that semester Carmichael asked himself, "Shouldn't we all be heading south to reinforce Bob's hard-pressed troops?"[22]

Chapter Four

"The Movement Was My Fate"

January 1962–August 1963

At the end of the semester, Carmichael made his usual pilgrimage back to New York to spend the holidays with his family in the Bronx. Sporadic trips home, often accompanied by Mary Lovelace, provided welcome relief from his now established routine of attending classes and NAG meetings, intensive studying and cramming for exams, and demonstrations.

On January 21, 1962, shortly after returning to Howard, May Charles telephoned Stokely with the news that his father had died suddenly of a heart attack that afternoon. He was only forty. For the rest of his life, Stokely would blame Adolphus' death on America's toxic racial environment. "My father literally worked himself to death providing for us," he recalled. Adolphus' passing elicited a jumble of emotions in his son. Stokely alternately remembered Adolphus as an unsung working-class hero and a foolhardy believer in the American Dream. He felt ashamed of Adolphus' laid-back reticence in the face of institutional racism, feelings that occasionally burst forth in public interviews over the years before maturity allowed him to better understand his father's sacrifices. Stokely would carry the unfulfilled dream of his devoutly religious, taxicab-driving, carpenter father as a kind of bitter inheritance. Adolphus' death left him starkly aware of the fate that awaited too many black men who toiled within the hidden bowels of Jim Crow America. Like many young black men of his generation, Stokely revered his father even as he self-consciously patterned his own behavior on a model of masculinity that hewed closer to Malcolm X than to Adolphus Carmichael. Thirty-five years later, he would remember Adolphus as "a wiry, industrious man full of energy and life," but at the time he privately anguished over his father's resigned acceptance of a fate he vowed would never be his own.[1]

Adolphus' death left May Charles as the family's chief breadwinner. It was a role she would assume with characteristic fortitude. After the funeral, she informed Stokely that completing his university studies was no longer subject to debate and insisted he graduate from Howard since "that's what your father wanted." May Charles proved as good as her word. Over the next two and half years, Carmichael's tuition would be paid for through a combination of work-study grants, a college fund set up by May Charles' own labor, and an unexpected inheritance from a relative.

Stokely worked through his grief by pouring his energies into the movement. On February 1, 1962, on the second anniversary of the Greensboro sit-ins, SNCC field secretary Dion Diamond returned to Southern University to give an invited talk, only to be arrested under Louisiana sedition laws. Carmichael led a seventeen-person contingent of SNCC's Committee to Free Dion Diamond to the Justice Department on March 13 and staged a sit-in to garner publicity for the case in hopes of meeting with Attorney General Robert Kennedy. Bill Mahoney insisted on talking to Kennedy personally but had to settle for Burke Marshall, assistant attorney general for civil rights. Marshall claimed the Justice Department lacked jurisdiction to intervene in Diamond's case but promised a future meeting with Kennedy. Mahoney and the group left, but not before delivering a statement that questioned the White House's determination to protect the constitutional rights of victims of southern injustice. "If the Attorney-General has not drafted such legislation," Mahoney explained, "then we want to know why not. If he has drafted it, we want to know why the President has not acted upon it." Three days later, Stokely, Tom Kahn, and Courtland Cox sat-in at the attorney general's office. This time they refused to leave, eventually being forced out of the building in three wheelchairs just after nine at night.[2]

Carmichael weighed in on the entire affair in one of his occasional articles for *The Hilltop*. He described the protests as "the ageless inseparability of intellectual ferment and social ferment, of thought and action." He noted how rumors of a university crackdown on the campus's most militant students in the days following the protest seemed to be confirmed after officials confiscated the key to Project Awareness offices for suspected collaboration with protest organizers. What would officials do next, he wondered: close down the student council or newspaper? Quoting the old American protest song, he characterized the student-activists as leaders of a new generation "whose answer to injustice and intimidation is 'We Shall Not Be Moved!'" Diamond's release on bond after two months in solitary confinement highlighted the movement's strength while exposing the limits of the sit-ins, its favorite tactic.[3]

E. Franklin Frazier's unexpected death cast a pall over the end of the semester. Carmichael had admired the legendary sociologist. After final exams, he returned home to spend time with his family. On the last Sunday in June, shortly before his twenty-first birthday, Carmichael was arrested during a demonstration at Beth Israel Hospital sponsored by the Local 1199 hospital employees union. The arrest, his third, for "loud and boisterous" behavior came, as he made plans to spend his second consecutive summer in Mississippi.[4]

STOKELY CARMICHAEL FELL IN LOVE with the Mississippi Delta that summer. The rhythms, the food, the essence of the place reminded him of Trinidad. In Mississippi, Carmichael found his *métier*: "I had discovered what I was—an organizer—and that the movement was my fate." Later that June, Carmichael reported to Greenwood in Leflore County, where Bob Moses had retreated after fleeing McComb. Eager to meet the organizer he had been hearing about for so long, Carmichael asked an unassuming man in overalls how he could be introduced to Moses. Of course, it was Moses himself he was asking. Dressed in those overalls and a white shirt, and sporting his trademark black horn-rimmed glasses, he chatted with Carmichael about philosophy and a shared admiration for Albert Camus's *The Rebel: An Essay on Man in Revolt*. Moses struck him as a kindred spirit whose contrasting personal style disguised a creative and disciplined mind. Their discussions influenced Carmichael's decision to change his major from pre-med to philosophy. Moses' cool "example of clarity and rationality" proved soothing for Carmichael, whose emotions tended to run hot. Stokely was a budding organizer in the Delta, and Moses became his hero.[5]

Stokely became fast friends with June Johnson, a fourteen-year-old high school student whose family would host him. Located four blocks from Broad Street Regular High School, SNCC's Greenwood office attracted June and other students interested in the new arrivals. Carmichael asked pointed questions about Broad Street's curriculum, chided the young girls for straightening their hair, and organized classes and study sessions that drew them further into the movement. If June initially found Stokely to be a handful, he charmed her mother, Lulabelle, a pattern that he repeated throughout his years in the Delta. Mrs. Johnson adopted Stokely as her thirteenth child, cooked him hot meals, and gave him the run of her house.[6]

Carmichael recognized the Delta's endless stretches of flat land, cotton fields, shotgun shacks, and soybean plantations as the culmination of a small miracle. He marveled at the region's landscape, stood in awe of its environmental wonders, and found himself drawn to the land's rich colors, black soil, red clay, and earth tones, seemingly created on an artist's palette. "Working on voter registration, I would meet some black folk who did not exist" for lack of birth certificates. Many had never ventured beyond the plantation they worked and lived on. Formal education proved a distant dream, with children settling for a sharecropper's education of seasonal schooling in between cotton harvests. Black life in rural Mississippi bore an unsettling resemblance to what it had been in America's antebellum era, where slaves had virtually no control over their lives.[7]

Carmichael encountered great poverty in the Delta but also witnessed even greater courage. Local people loved him, and he returned their trust and admiration with an affection that soon turned to reverence. Blacks in Mississippi, Carmichael observed, carried themselves with an unassuming dignity and grace that he found remarkable. Poor, unlettered sharecroppers made the well-educated young activist proud to be black. Their determination to pursue citizenship and democracy in the face of violence and terror offered profound lessons that he would carry with him for the rest of his life. Living, working, and struggling in Mississippi obliterated Carmichael's preconceived notions of the Delta. He recognized himself as less a missionary on a holy crusade to save wayward souls and more an explorer who had stumbled upon lifelong teachers. "I met heroes," Stokely remembered. "Humble folk, of slight formal education and modest income, who managed to be both generous and wise, who took us in, fed us, instructed and protected us, and ultimately civilized, educated, and inspired the smart-assed college students."[8]

Women formed the backbone of the Mississippi movement. They attended mass meetings in great numbers, demonstrated for voting rights, provided food and shelter for civil rights workers, and faced jail, and at times, violent reprisals. Fannie Lou Hamer led this cohort. A sharecropper from Ruleville, Mississippi, Mrs. Hamer became an SNCC activist and the face of Mississippi's voting rights efforts. Stokely worked with her in Mississippi and came to recognize her as one of the movement's most important and inspiring figures. He fashioned similar bonds with Victoria Gray, Susie Ruffin, Annie Devine, and Mama Quinn, all strong black Delta women who came to view him as extended family.[9]

Failure in McComb informed SNCC's Greenwood project. Carmichael's warm relationship with locals drew from Moses' experiences in Amite and Pike Counties. Greenwood's success built on defeat in McComb but took more concrete form in meetings held earlier in the year that mapped out strategies and tactics based on a careful assessment of Mississippi's race relations, politics, and demography. Moses and CORE activist Tom Gaither wrote a memo in January 1962 that proposed voter registration as a motivating tool to spur political involvement in cities and rural areas. Rather than viewing SNCC as some kind of civil rights cavalry of college-educated missionaries, Moses proposed that field workers exert only as much leadership as a situation required. Ideally, local adults and young people would lead grassroots struggles. The Council of Federated Organizations (COFO), an umbrella organization composed of all the major civil rights groups, grew out of this memo. SNCC dominated COFO's Mississippi identity, with CORE providing support in the southeast and the NAACP maintaining a strong statewide presence of local chapters under the leadership of the indomitable Medgar Evers.[10]

For Stokely, Mississippi offered new lessons. These came sometimes through conversation but more often by witnessing local people's responses to a confrontation with the police or to his latest arrest. Polite, calm, and unassuming around Greenwood's black citizens, he turned into a firebrand when police officers called him "boy" or if whites disrespected him. Carmichael enjoyed a reputation as an indefatigable worker who showed proper deference to local ministers and elders and played the role of big brother to kids of all ages.[11]

He left Mississippi at the end of the summer grateful for new friends and contacts, but burning to return to the Delta full-time. Building on the work of the summer, Greenwood's local movement flourished over the next year, turning the city into a major hub of civil rights protest and, briefly, a national focal point. The summer left Carmichael exhausted, exhilarated, and transformed. The Delta's speech patterns and inflections found their way into his soul, and he came away with a deeper appreciation of the richness and complexity of rural black folkways, where a mask of servitude could fade into stone-faced determination in an instant. Mississippi offered a unique education where Carmichael and other activists underwent a process of "unlearning" the internal prejudices against race, age, skin color, and region ingrained in them. Mississippi found Carmichael in a state of grace.[12]

Stokely returned to Howard for his junior year still grieving over his father's death but with a renewed sense of purpose. For politically minded students, Carmichael's swelling reputation made him a popular attraction. Cleveland Sellers recognized Carmichael's social and political charms immediately. Serious and unflappable, Cleve Sellers entered Howard in 1962 as an oddity, an intellectual from tiny Denmark, South Carolina, more comfortable in jeans, t-shirts, and army fatigues than the more formal clothes worn by Howard students. Attracted to Carmichael's outsized personality and aware of his matching ego, Sellers also sensed something more. He correctly identified Carmichael's arrogance as the protective shell of a sensitive core. By the winter, Sellers would join NAG and begin a close friendship with Carmichael.[13]

Stokely and Cleve would come to regard each other more as brothers than friends. The twenty-one-year-old Stokely adopted Cleve as a little brother, and they spent long hours in Stokely's Euclid Street apartment plotting strategy and debating politics. Sellers came to establish close relationships with Mary Lovelace, Stokely's girlfriend, and the Carmichael family, and his penchant for diplomacy made him a trusted adviser and gentle critic. Their political and personal friendship lacked the competitive fires that inevitably touched Stokely's relationships, especially with fellow activists.[14]

Carmichael's political networks helped galvanize Howard in the spring of 1963, when NAG reported a bombshell story. Howard's new men's gymnasium was being built with segregated labor. *The Hilltop* highlighted Jim Crow labor practices aided by a maze of federal agencies that made racial integration irrelevant in the granting of government contracts. A constant flow of press releases, news stories, and *Hilltop* editorials turned the subject of employment discrimination into a campus-wide sensation, one that triggered broader political ramifications.[15]

On March 1, Stokely testified in support of NAG's complaint before the subcommittee on equal employment opportunity of the Commission on Civil Rights. It was the first time, but not the last, he would address an official government body investigating domestic race relations. He reasserted

NAG's charges that trade unions representing plumbers, sheet metal workers, electricians, and steamfitters engaged in employment discrimination. "The students at Howard would like to think that at least in the confines of our university, if nowhere else, racial discrimination is banned," he said. "This is unfortunately not the case." He offered a list of suggestions that included strict enforcement of presidential orders barring discrimination in government contracts. His testimony brought to mind "bitter conversations I'd listen to between my father and his friends about the building trades in New York."[16]

The combination of Carmichael's testimony, *The Hilltop*'s outrage, and threats of campus demonstrations and White House pickets caught the Kennedy administration's attention. Attorney General Robert Kennedy obliquely addressed this issue during a March speech on "international understanding" at Howard. Kennedy identified civil rights as "the greatest internal problem facing" the nation and lamented the damaging global consequences of domestic racial unrest on America's worldwide reputation. Restoring America's once pristine global image would require bridging the chasm between democracy's lofty rhetoric and its sobering reality. Afterward, one student asked Kennedy what he was doing about the segregated union locals that Carmichael had recently testified about. "The situation will be remedied," promised Kennedy.[17]

On March 22, President Nabrit summoned Carmichael and Mike Thelwell to his office. They sighed with nervous relief as Nabrit shook their hands and handed them a letter from the Labor Department requiring full compliance by Howard's contractors with anti-discrimination laws under threat of Justice Department intervention. A planned campus demonstration turned into a massive victory celebration. "This is a victory for democracy," declared Carmichael, before wryly observing the irony of the Justice Department's belated enforcement of a two-year-old executive order. "It took a great deal to entice the government to put teeth into the executive order." Carmichael ultimately reasoned, "While it is true that in this case it was the unions that were guilty of discrimination, it is the responsibility of the government, which represents all the people, and to whom Negroes pay taxes also, to see that discrimination is kept out of federal projects."[18]

Stokely's brief remarks embodied his personal credo. He believed that civil rights struggles formed the basis of establishing genuine democracy in America and that the federal government, more than labor unions that

practiced discrimination, bore primary responsibility for enforcing constitutional principles. Governments did not always live up to their responsibilities
unless there was corresponding political pressure from below. At this point in
his political development, Stokely still believed that political coalitions could
be leveraged on behalf of racial and economic justice. But his vision of radical
democracy contrasted dramatically with the rhetoric of President Kennedy's
New Frontier. Organizing with trade unionists and radical pacifists in New
York City, dialoguing with street speakers in Harlem, and participating in sit-
ins along Route 40 offered unique perspectives about America's racial crisis.
His experience as a Freedom Rider, his time in Parchman Farm, and subsequent visits to Mississippi made Stokely adopt a vision of radical democracy
that placed the fate of the nation far outside the corridors of Washington
power brokers. The rough hands of Delta sharecroppers, the gentle prodding
of Ella Baker, and the heroic example of Fannie Lou Hamer shaped this portrait of democracy, where poor, unlettered, and semi-literate black folk living
in a 20th-century version of bondage would usher in a new era of citizenship
and racial justice. If the Kennedy administration deployed the rhetoric of
democracy as a shield from criticism from the backdrop of the Cold War's
global and domestic political theater, Stokely adopted the term as a sword to
combat the enemies of racial justice and economic equality.

Democracy, for Stokely, required a political commitment to social justice.
His organic intellectual leanings and political affiliations made him skeptical of the way in which Cold War notions of democracy cheerfully existed
alongside of Jim Crow, as well as of America's politically expedient ties to
colonial regimes still occupying large swaths of Africa and the Caribbean.
Racial terror simmered beneath popular national bromides extolling individual liberty and achievement. Stokely's personal introduction to democracy's
soft underbelly began in New York but continued via a life-changing stint in
two Mississippi jails during the late spring and early summer of 1961. But if
political experience exposed dark shadows of American democracy, organizing among NAG and SNCC workers offered an alternative and combatively
hopeful vision. Sit-in demonstrations, freedom songs in Parchman Farm,
conversations with Ella Baker, James Baldwin, and Malcolm X, and personal relationships with civil rights workers and local people from Baltimore
to Mississippi emboldened Stokely in the belief that ordinary citizens could
reshape America's social and political landscape. Bayard Rustin's eloquent
speeches, writings, and organizing abilities shaped Stokely's views on democ-

racy during the early 1960s, as did his relationship with Tom Kahn, who served as Rustin's political surrogate at Howard University. While Stokely admired Malcolm X deeply, at this point, Rustin's social-democratic politics exerted far more influence on his political organizing. But in a very real sense, the debate between Malcolm and Rustin at Howard challenged the political sensibilities of Stokely and NAG. Malcolm's appeal, most often considered emotional, contained important political and philosophical critiques about race and democracy. For Malcolm, civil rights organizing required a leap of faith that, because of America's tortured racial history, defied logic. Rustin combated Malcolm's pessimism with an appeal to the strengths of political coalitions, especially labor, which he regarded as the pivotal building block of a new society. For Rustin, strategic alliances could heal ancient racial wounds by introducing a new era of economic prosperity. Stokely's active role in Washington-area civil rights politics placed him squarely on the side of Rustin, while his militant posture made him an unacknowledged disciple of Malcolm X.

NAG's political organizing not only successfully publicized racial discrimination in federal construction projects; it forced the Kennedy administration into the role of reluctant ally, a pattern that would continue. The focus on racial discrimination in the building trades anticipated similar difficulties in Philadelphia, Pennsylvania, where efforts to integrate the building trades culminated in bruising protests near City Hall. Fearing that cascading waves of racial unrest in the North over jobs would parallel roiling racial disturbances in Cambridge, Maryland, Danville, Virginia, and Birmingham, Alabama, the Kennedy administration banned discrimination against minorities in federal construction projects via executive order, less than four months after Carmichael's testimony before the Commission on Civil Rights.[19]

The victory over Jim Crow labor practices emboldened Carmichael to organize outside of Washington. Carmichael spent weekends traveling to Maryland's Eastern Shore that spring to assist the Cambridge Nonviolent Action Committee (CNAC), a border-state SNCC affiliate led by Howard alumna Gloria Richardson. Richardson and CNAC battled to desegregate the small city of Cambridge, an effort that turned Maryland's sleepy Eastern Shore into a national site of civil rights unrest. Cambridge was a segregated city of less than 15,000, a third of whom were black, and its African-American community suffered under the constraints of high unemployment, poor housing, and segregated schools. Violence in Cambridge during the summer of 1963 drew national headlines and the attention of the Kennedy administration. Richardson's political determination and no-nonsense personal style led to her being characterized as the "Lady General" of the civil rights movement. After Bobby Kennedy personally helped to broker a desegregation agreement at the Justice Department between CNAC and Cambridge city officials, in exchange for ending street demonstrations, he asked Richardson, "Do you know how to smile?" She responded with what SNCC chairman John Lewis remembered as "a weak one." Richardson reserved her enthusiasm for black political radicals, especially Malcolm X, whom she heard speak in Detroit in November 1963. Malcolm's electrifying "Message to the Grassroots" speech in the Motor City brought him new admirers, among them one of the movement's rare female leaders of national repute. Perhaps Cambridge's biggest historical resonance would be its apparent effect on Bobby Kennedy, who, after reading CNAC's in-depth reports explaining how racial discrimination and poverty impacted the city's African-American community in a way as powerful as Jim Crow, made a startling confession to John Lewis. "John," said Bobby, pulling Lewis in close to confer, "the people, the young people of SNCC, have educated me. You have changed me. Now I understand."[20]

Carmichael's junior year came to a close as racial tensions in Cambridge drew him into a simmering local conflict with national implications. For Carmichael, trips to Cambridge made 1963 less about the much-talked-about March on Washington than about spending time in a "nondescript, hard-bitten, little town some fifty miles or so from the nation's capital." The city also provided Stokely with one of his most unusual experiences in the movement, when "Eddie Dickerson, from Cambridge, Maryland, a white fellow, two years ago, dragged me off a stool, and kicked me in the stomach about seven, eight, nine times," Carmichael remembered. "One of the roughest times I've ever had was at the mercy of his hand. The same night he came to the church, apologized, said he was sorry, and started working in the movement." The entire episode remained forever etched in Stokely's memory as an example of nonviolence's power to transform individuals. "It does in certain cases, I'm not going to deny this," he admitted.[21]

Racial violence in Cambridge was part of a wave of national civil rights upheavals that inspired President John Kennedy to act. On Tuesday, June 11, Kennedy delivered his first nationally televised civil rights speech. Raw politics shaped Kennedy's decision as racial violence in Danville made national headlines, eliciting a telegram to the president from Martin Luther King, whose public announcement of plans for a March on Washington included a direct plea for presidential support for a proposed civil rights bill. Kennedy began his speech by describing events that had transpired earlier in the day, when Assistant Attorney General Nicholas Katzenbach successfully enrolled two black students at the University of Alabama over the vociferous objection of segregationist Governor George Wallace. Black soldiers "sent to Vietnam or West Berlin," said Kennedy, answered a call to duty that transcended skin color. Black students should be allowed to enroll in public universities "without having to be backed up by troops." Kennedy touched upon racial disparities that faced African-American babies in education, employment, life expectancy, and income. "This is not a sectional issue," he argued, brushing aside the widespread myth that race remained a regional crisis. "Difficulties over segregation and discrimination exist, in every city, in every state of the union, producing in many cities a rising tide of discontent that threatens the public safety." Kennedy spoke with an urgency that civil rights leaders had dreamed of since his inauguration, and Martin Luther King and Roy Wilkins, head of the NAACP, responded positively as did the baseball great Jackie Robinson, who had, up until that moment, remained largely immune to the young president's charm. Medgar Evers' shocking assassination early the next morning in Mississippi illustrated the tragic depths of the racial crisis that Kennedy eloquently outlined. Upon hearing news of Evers' murder, Kennedy privately said that civil rights "has become everything."[22]

Kennedy's speech and Evers' assassination gave added weight to the March on Washington for Jobs and Freedom planned for August. Carmichael's initial support for the march's proposal to shut down Washington faded as the idea turned into what he called a "spectacular media event" expertly "choreographed entirely for the television audience." He channeled disappointment into action, assisting Rustin's organizing efforts in Washington, which attracted Cleve Sellers, Bill Mahoney, and Mike Thelwell. When Rustin complained about "young SNCC Negroes" who preferred "ambulance chasing" to office work, Carmichael could only marvel at his mentor's gift for passionate and well-timed displays of agitation. "That was one of the reasons," he observed, "that working with him was never dull."[23]

As Rustin planned the March on Washington, Carmichael spent his second consecutive summer in Greenwood and third straight year of traveling to Mississippi. White students arrived in the Delta for the first time that summer.

The subject of white participation in the Deep South underwent dramatic transformations, partially the result of a conversation between the black Bob Moses and the white Allard Lowenstein, a resourceful and at times overbearing Democratic Party activist and organizer with extensive contacts to white liberals on college campuses. Carmichael's complex relationship with white activists could be traced back to political relationships and personal friendships forged at Bronx Science. He embraced white volunteers who risked violence on Freedom Rides and Route 40 demonstrations, yet remained wary of paternalism and sensitive to even the slightest hint of condescension. Carmichael teased SDS members into mock submission over the issue of organizing poor whites, a suggestion that the group took to heart in Chicago. At the National Student Association convention in Indiana, Carmichael passionately implored the overwhelmingly white delegates to support the March on Washington, even as he privately characterized the event as a "middle-class picnic." He never embraced the racial separatism of the Nation of Islam, however, even during his Black Power years. Carmichael instead came to judge white participation in civil rights struggles as good or bad depending on tactical considerations. His personal relationship with whites was friendly, cordial, and intimate. Carmichael scoffed at the argument of black militants within SNCC who, in later years, identified the mere presence of whites as stoking fear and self-loathing among African Americans. He based his objections to white participation in Black Power on politics rather than racial animus.[24]

In Mississippi, Carmichael reunited with Tim Jenkins, fresh from his second year at Yale Law School. Jenkins supplied eager law school volunteers and a fresh take on SNCC's organizing efforts in the Delta through the casting of mock ballots called Freedom Ballots in local primaries permitted by state law but intended to highlight the state's racism. The influx of white volunteers would strengthen and energize SNCC even as it partially laid the groundwork for burgeoning controversy over interracial organizing, white power, and black identity that would grip the organization in later years.[25]

Violence, meanwhile, hovered over the entire summer. Civil rights workers Fannie Lou Hamer, Annelle Ponder, and June Johnson were brutally beaten during the second week in June in the town of Winona. Hamer suffered permanent injuries from her ordeal.[26]

Sam Block and Willie Peacock, Mississippi locals working with SNCC, found an eager student in Carmichael, whose canvassing skills, knowledge of rural roads and folkways, and rapport with elders continued to impress.

Meanwhile, Carmichael quietly seethed with rage over the fate of black youth. "The more time I spent with the young people of Greenwood," he recalled, "the angrier I became." Carmichael's relationship with Greenwood's students made him acutely sensitive to Jim Crow's greatest casualties: black youth across the country whose enormous potential remained untapped.[27]

If sending carloads of aspiring voters to the local courthouse for voter registration remained the movement's main local strategy, recruiting black sharecroppers on surrounding plantations proved the most difficult task. Not surprisingly, plantation organizing, which Delta authorities regarded as a crime, became Carmichael's passion. Walking past large "NO TRESPASS" signs, he sneaked onto plantations, paying careful attention to the where-abouts of a "bossman" armed with a gun and charged with keeping "voter registration workers off the property." The danger of this kind of organizing appealed to Carmichael's daredevil instinct just as schmoozing with locals tapped into his natural affability in social settings. He developed a knack for fleeing "a plantation at speeds averaging 110 M.P.H."[28]

By late summer, SNCC embraced the moral force of mass organizing in the face of the official denial of voting rights. On August 6, the date of the state's gubernatorial primary, over seven hundred black Mississippians, including four hundred Greenwood residents, voted by affidavit as a way of making a claim of illegal voter disfranchisement. Carmichael led dozens of residents past hostile whites positioned as a human barricade at the court-house. Undeterred, the nervous Carmichael "directed the group courteously through the middle of them" while ignoring a volley of threats and epithets. In Mississippi, where the stakes of black voting rights were measured in dead bodies, such a scene represented progress. "Two years ago," he confessed in his post-election report, "we would have been shot for a stunt like this." Ten days later, Carmichael welcomed SNCC workers released after two months in Parchman Farm for civil rights organizing. He teased the large, bearish Law-rence Guyot that his unintended weight loss represented an improvement and traded war stories with Curtis Hayes over his time in Parchman two years earlier. More than 25,000 Mississippi blacks staged a statewide protest vote on August 25, two days before the gubernatorial runoff between dueling segregationist candidates. Carmichael, who helped to organize Greenwood's turnout, viewed the vote as a prelude to a looming crisis, one recently examined by his friend James Baldwin in his book *The Fire Next Time*. "Given the test that one has to take in order to become registered and given the dissatisfaction of black people in the states and given the federal government's inactivity who knows," observed Carmichael, "maybe Baldwin is right—it may be the fire next time."[29]

Carmichael returned to Washington with a contingent of Mississippi SNCC workers. On August 27, the day before the March on Washington, he stood at the Mall, awed by the beehive of activity between civil rights workers, volunteer staff, and Washington police. "I guess Bayard really done made the revolution," remarked a grinning Carmichael. The March on Washington was a part of the revolution that he would miss. Stokely would explain his absence in his autobiography with a story about accompanying Bob Moses to an SDS meeting in Virginia, but Moses was conspicuously present at the March. Stokely's exact whereabouts that day remain a mystery. Perhaps his youthful ego made him miss one of the watershed events in American history (since he was not a speaker) or he simply preferred to remain a contented behind-the-scenes soldier.[30]

On the day before the march, Malcolm X spoke to reporters at the Statler-Hilton Hotel in Washington. Malcolm was there at the request of Bayard Rustin, who had invited him to spend the afternoon at the march's unofficial headquarters. Malcolm's sharp sense of humor and quick smile made him a disarming adversary. He revealed several sides of his personality in the course of a single conversation: the black revolutionary who thundered about social inequality and the impossibility of racial justice; the statesman who admired the courage of SNCC activists; the good-humored combatant of Bayard Rustin who insisted that only the Nation of Islam possessed the formula for black liberation in America. As Malcolm spoke to reporters about the merits of the next day's events, word reached him that SNCC chairman John Lewis' proposed speech had triggered controversy for its characterization of Kennedy's civil rights bill as "too little too late." This was all Malcolm needed to hear. He reiterated to reporters how the entire demonstration amounted to a made-for-television production artfully orchestrated by the Kennedy administration, what he would later call a "Farce on Washington," at the expense of black self-determination. Ten days earlier, in Boston, Malcolm had characterized the march as "ridiculous" and spoke of "Southern foxes" and "Northern wolves" united in a common pursuit of racial subjugation, since "the government doesn't endorse anything it doesn't control."[31]

The March on Washington, in combining a plea for racial equality with a demand for economic opportunity, offered a bold vision for racial and economic justice that defied Malcolm's predictions. On the morning of the march, a slight panic gripped Courtland Cox as he toured the Lincoln Memorial with Bayard Rustin and counted "fifty people out there," but within two hours "a sea of humanity" abated these fears. The demonstration rallied a quarter million Americans for freedom's cause and turned the civil rights struggle into part of a larger narrative of national progress. The speakers included United Auto Workers president Walter Reuther; Rabbi Joachim Prinz of the American Jewish Congress; and John Lewis, whose placid demeanor hid intense emotions that surfaced whenever he spoke of the need to end Jim Crow. Bayard Rustin, the march's main logistical and tactical organizer, re-emerged as a credible leader and social activist. The conspicuous presence of a Hollywood contingent organized by Harry Belafonte added further star power. Paul Newman, Marlon Brando, Diahann Carroll, James Garner, and Charlton Heston lent glamour to the proceedings. Leading entertainers crowded the stage at the Washington Monument just after 10:00 A.M. Joan Baez sang "Oh Freedom," and Odetta gave a powerful rendition of "I'm on My Way." Bob Dylan joined Peter, Paul, and Mary to sing his hit song "Blowin' in the Wind." The historic performance then reached for the transcendent by inviting SNCC Freedom Singers, including Bernice Johnson, who would later found the group Sweet Honey in the Rock, on stage. Collectively, these artists defied Jim Crow by their very presence.[32]

A. Philip Randolph and John Lewis were the march's oldest and youngest speakers. For Randolph, the event represented the culmination of four decades of political activism. After cutting his teeth as a young socialist organizer in Harlem during the 1920s, Randolph abandoned radical politics to emerge as the stately leader of the Brotherhood of Sleeping Car Porters during the Depression, a position that made him black America's most powerful labor leader. The mere threat of a march on Washington in 1941 convinced President Franklin Delano Roosevelt to sign an executive order banning discrimination in the military. Tall, courtly, and elegant, Randolph spoke with the conviction of a man whose political travails had led to this day:

> We are gathered here in the largest demonstration in the history of this nation. Let the nation and the world know the meaning of our numbers. We are not a pressure group, we are not an organization or a group of organizations, we are not a mob. We are the advanced guard of a massive moral revolution for jobs and freedom. This

revolution reverberates throughout the land touching every city, every town, every village where black men are segregated, oppressed and exploited. But this civil rights revolution is not confined to the Negroes; nor is it confined to civil rights. Our white allies know that they cannot be free while we are not.[33]

John Lewis' speech, drafted with the assistance of Tom Kahn, Jim Forman, and Courtland Cox, retained a combative edge. Lewis had grudgingly abandoned parts of his speech objectionable to Washington's Roman Catholic Archbishop, Patrick O'Boyle, who delivered the convocation. Lewis, who in a few short years would be judged too moderate to lead SNCC, spoke from the podium with an edge of defiance in his voice:

> We will not stop. If we do not get meaningful legislation of this Congress, the time will come when we will not confine our marching to Washington. We will march through the South, through the streets of Jackson, through the streets of Cambridge, through the streets of Birmingham. But we will march with the spirit of love and with the spirit of dignity that we have shown here today. By the force of our demands, our determination and our numbers, we shall splinter the desegregated South into a thousand pieces and put them back together in the image of God and democracy. We must say, "Wake up America. Wake up!!!" For we cannot stop, and we will not be patient.[34]

News that W.E.B. Du Bois had died in Ghana moved Roy Wilkins, his one-time nemesis, to praise him from the podium as "the voice" of an earlier generation "that was calling to you to gather here today in this cause."

While black liberation was the topic of the day, women's liberation took a back seat. Organizers insisted that the leaders' wives, such as Coretta Scott King, march separate from their husbands. Randolph, however, did introduce a roll call of women, including Rosa Parks; Daisy Bates, who had helped desegregate Little Rock Central High School in 1957; Gloria Richardson, the Cambridge, Maryland, leader; and Diane Nash. Daisy Bates, who hadn't initially been scheduled to speak on the program, made a few remarks that emphasized women's supportive roles:

The women of this country, Mr. Randolph, pledge to you . . . and all of you fighting for civil liberties, that we will join hands with you as women of this country. We will kneel-in, we will sit-in, until we can eat in any counter in the United States. We will walk until we are free, until we can walk to any school and take our children to any school in the United States. And we will sit-in and we will kneel-in and we will lie-in until every Negro can vote. This we pledge you, the women of America.[35]

Martin Luther King's speech inspired an enduring and national conversation about race and democracy in America. His brilliant extemporaneous conclusion, with its refrain of "I Have a Dream," elevated him into the sacred space of the nation's Founding Architects:

I still have a dream that one day on the red hills of Georgia the sons of former slaves and the sons of former slave-owners will be able to sit down together at the table of brotherhood. I have a dream that one day even the state of Mississippi, a state sweltering with the heat of injustice, sweltering with the heat of oppression, will be transformed into an oasis of freedom and justice.[36]

King's final words sent this hope, the hard-earned faith in radical democracy and racial and economic justice, resounding through the entire National Mall:

And when this happens, when we allow freedom to ring, when we let it ring from every village and every hamlet, from every state and every city, we will be able to speed up that day when all of God's children, black men and white men, Jews and Gentiles, Protestants and Catholics, will be able to join hands and sing in the words of the old Negro spiritual, "Free at last! free at last! thank God Almighty, we are free at last!"[37]

If Martin Luther King arrived in Washington as the nation's moral political leader, this speech made him enter the ranks of American and world history as a genuine prophet whose transcendent voice seemed capable of transporting an entire nation from one epoch toward a new one.

CHAPTER FIVE

The Local Organizer

September 1963–August 1964

MORE THAN ANY OTHER EVENT IN HISTORY, THE MARCH ON WASHINGTON focused the nation's attention on civil rights. It was against this backdrop of growing national recognition of the civil rights movement and of SNCC that Stokely Carmichael began his senior year at Howard University. Despite his tendency toward cynicism, Stokely remained a relatively idealistic activist, and he spent his final year of college exploring his vocation as an organizer. The Democratic Party's betrayal of black sharecroppers forever changed Carmichael's approach to politics. He remained committed to democracy, but he considered both major parties hopelessly bankrupt. Protracted voting rights campaigns in Mississippi and Alabama afforded a kind of postgraduate education in civil rights organizing along with bitter lessons about the limits of democracy in parts of America. Mississippi, as usual, offered the most painful lesson.[1]

Although it was unspoken at the time, Carmichael now embarked on a quest for black political power. He traveled a lifetime in one remarkable eighteen-month span. He went from being a college student in Washington to running two major civil rights campaigns and rubbing shoulders with Martin Luther King. Full-time organizing changed him. He became, simultaneously, an unlikely diplomat, a wily administrator, and a respected leader in the Deep South. Time in school had mediated past experiences on the front lines, providing a respite from the stress of movement work. Life as an organizer extracted a higher personal cost, which included periodic bouts of nervous exhaustion, sleep deprivation, poor eating habits, and stress associated with the constant risk of violence and even death. The nitty-gritty work of organizing forced him to re-examine his own views about self-defense, racial integration, and personal longevity. But in the face of ever increasing danger, he adopted a mask of cool defiance.

HOWARD'S DEEPENING RELATIONSHIP with the civil rights movement took center stage on November 5 and 6, 1963, during a two-day conference on Youth, Nonviolence, and Social Change. Martin Luther King headlined a speaking lineup that included Gloria Richardson, James Farmer, John Lewis, James Baldwin, and James Meredith, who had integrated the University of Mississippi the previous year. Local speakers included Carmichael and Jean Wheeler, who was fresh from a tour of duty in the Mississippi Delta. Activists representing the clergy, the NAACP, and the SCLC also participated. The conference's stated purpose of analyzing the impact of nonviolence organizing on youth made public debates about self-defense that had been privately occurring within the movement.

The conference opened with a paper on the "Psycho-Social Implications of Non-Violence." Its author, Dr. Jerome D. Frank, a Johns Hopkins University psychiatry professor, examined the way that nonviolent activists could reject "enemy politics" by sympathizing with their opponents. He concluded with two questions that were already haunting Stokely: "How long will the nonviolent movement last in the face of strengthened violence?" and "What does the nonviolent participant do with repressed feelings?" During a morning panel featuring Baldwin, Farmer, and Yale University chaplain William Sloane Coffin, Jr., Baldwin questioned student activists' perseverance in the face of continued violence and government ineffectiveness. "At what point," he asked, "will they despair when the government fails to protect them and says it cannot do anything?"[2]

During the next day's session, Carmichael responded to Frank's and Baldwin's existential questions about nonviolence. First, he demolished the popular belief that blacks embraced nonviolence out of a love for whites, since, Carmichael argued, "Negroes don't even love all Negroes." Blacks, he insisted, understood nonviolence as a strategy rather than a political religion. In fact, adherents of nonviolence had cleaved off into separate wings almost from the birth of the sit-in movement, with its most pious followers embracing the teachings of Gandhi, King, and James Lawson, while more political strategists were at home in NAG. The symbolic presence of John Lewis, SNCC's humble public face and chairman, obscured these differences in the public's imagination.[3]

Dr. King's evening address closed the proceedings. Delivered before a standing-room-only audience at Cramton Auditorium, it amounted to an implicit response to Carmichael's words. "Violence might bring about temporary victory but never permanent peace," King warned. He characterized the civil rights struggle as a "long night of oppression" that could be met by acquiescence, violence, or nonviolence. While submission proved to be the "easy way out" and violence impractical, nonviolence remained "the most potent weapon of freedom." *The Hilltop*'s coverage featured a photo of King speaking in Cramton above a caption that referred to him as "De Lawd"—a term of both affection and derision used by SNCC—and the paper subsequently apologized for printing it. At Howard, the contrast between Carmichael's "outspoken militancy" and King's "mystic idealism" remained part of an internal debate among movement insiders.[4]

Carmichael participated in the conference amid preparations for SNCC's annual retreat scheduled to take place on Howard's campus from November 29 to December 1. Bill Mahoney and Courtland Cox organized the retreat, which would include leading trade unionists and received generous contributions from organized labor. Mahoney's interest in the links between racial poverty and economic development led to the opening of a Washington SNCC office. The event marked an important turning point for the group, as questions of race and class came to the fore.[5]

The retreat opened a week after the November 22nd assassination of President Kennedy. Delegates arrived from all parts of the South on Thanksgiving, the day after President Lyndon Johnson announced his support for civil rights legislation in a speech to Congress. The leadership conference, "On Food and Jobs," attracted four hundred participants and took place amid the raw emotion surrounding Kennedy's assassination. The program was organized as a series of workshops to train SNCC workers on the nuances of black life in the South. Kennedy's death haunted the proceedings with the slain president's image providing the face of a hastily printed conference program. The president's death undoubtedly left a mark on Carmichael, especially as it came only months after Kennedy's June 11th nationally televised speech, which characterized civil rights as a moral issue. Carmichael had found himself pleasantly surprised by a speech that was "accurate, clear and truthful." It was, for many, Kennedy's finest moment as president.[6]

Bob Moses spoke about SNCC's efforts in Mississippi in bold terms. He described the group's main objective as the "political overthrow of the South as we know it." He spoke about the Summer Project, for which SNCC planned to recruit hundreds of white volunteers to secure national attention and federal intervention. The Summer Project embodied SNCC's pragmatic efforts to topple the nation's existing racial order. "It is true," Moses noted, "the Negroes are blackmailing the Federal Government to force other elements in the power structure to accept a compromise; our job is to change the power structure."[7]

During the discussion, a kind of symbiosis developed between the movement participants and the federal government. Washington officials described the wide range of federal resources available to aid southern blacks and ways in which SNCC workers could make them more effective. Representatives from a variety of federal agencies overseeing job training, area redevelopment, funds for rural areas, and education and health answered tough questions from field staff about employment discrimination and local corruption. Federal officials pointed to their minimal ties with local people as an area where SNCC could act as a conduit between rural communities and Washington. For SNCC, contact with Washington bureaucrats now proved to be a necessity, since southern officials frequently deployed economic reprisals that blocked federal dollars from reaching poor blacks. Yet SNCC's relationship to the federal government would remain fraught, burdened by the fact that field staff and Washington officials possessed contrasting visions of what democracy in the South would look like.[8]

In the spring of 1964, Carmichael turned his personal vision of democracy into a political crusade for civil rights justice in Cambridge, Maryland. Chronic unemployment, poor housing, and unequal education that NAG protested against in Washington plagued Cambridge. Gloria Richardson's advocacy of self-defense made her a self-described "radical revolutionary" and a political ally of Malcolm X. She impressed Cleve Sellers as "one of the most outstanding leaders in the civil rights movement." Carmichael based his admiration for Richardson on local people's obvious affection for her. Cambridge's stark color line and racial hostility reminded him of Mississippi, with the glaring exception that the city's black population were able to exercise their voting rights.[9]

When Stokely returned to Cambridge on May 11, he found a city under siege. Alabama Governor George Wallace was visiting Cambridge to kick off his campaign in Maryland's Democratic presidential primary, and Carmichael was infuriated by the seemingly permanent presence of the National Guard, which was there as the result of more than a year of intense local civil rights demonstrations. Over six hundred people gathered to protest Wallace's presence. Gloria Richardson led a march down Race Street only to be met by a wall of guardsmen. As members of the National Guard arrested Richardson and two bodyguards, SNCC workers sat in the middle of the street, bringing a temporary halt to any other arrests. Sellers wrestled with a guardsman to a standoff and barely escaped arrest after dozens of demonstrators formed a human shield by piling on top of him. Carmichael desperately held onto the ankle of SNCC photographer Cliff Vaughs, whose arms were being pulled with greater force by gas-masked guardsmen. One of the first volleys of gas canisters hit Stokely in the face. Taken to the CNAC offices, he drifted in and out of consciousness and awoke the next day in a hospital, only to depart over a nurse's objections that he had been placed under arrest.

In June, as his classmates prepared for graduation, Carmichael flew to Greenwood, Mississippi, to become a full-time activist. That summer, after graduation, Carmichael emerged not simply as a deft organizer and eloquent movement spokesperson but as a leader, diplomat, and cheerleader who inspired interracial groups of activists to brave some of America's most dangerous territory in pursuit of democracy. On June 17, Carmichael addressed the first wave of volunteers at the Western College for Women in Oxford, Ohio. During a workshop on nonviolence, he countered Reverend Jim Lawson's contention that they were engaged in a moral struggle. It was a struggle for power, he contended. In these orientation sessions, however, Carmichael listened more than he talked. He instantly sized up volunteers and, like a military recruiter seeking talented soldiers for an upcoming battle, set out to lure those who confirmed his first impression. "Ask for the Delta," he would say. "We can use you in the Delta."[10]

Stokely's attention was diverted from the training sessions by a tragic turn of events on June 21. Three civil rights workers—Andrew Goodman, James Chaney, Michael Schwerner—had disappeared, and everyone expected the worst. A widespread search began. Three days into it, Stokely and Charlie Cobb traveled from Greenville to Batesville with plans to head toward Meridian, where Goodman, Chaney, and Schwerner had last been seen.[11]

In the late afternoon on Thursday, June 25, Carmichael, Cobb, and a white summer volunteer met with the mayor of tiny Hollandale to dispute a local order prohibiting white volunteers from living with blacks. Pressed by Carmichael to explain the questionable statute, the local officials threatened to arrest the three, who promptly departed. Later that night, Carmichael and Cobb drove toward Neshoba County with one hundred dollars hidden in the automobile's floorboards. Police detained them en route to Meridian after their car broke down in Durant, a rude little town with a reputation for racial violence. When the police found movement literature in the car, they arrested Carmichael but released Cobb. Sensing that separation might trigger the exact kind of crisis they were investigating, Cobb parked the car outside the jail for the night, his eyes ever alert to the armed sentries who were going in and out. Early the next morning, with bail money secured from their car's secret compartment, Carmichael and Cobb headed toward Meridian, where nervous SNCC workers greeted their return with relief.[12]

Over the next three nights, Carmichael, Cobb, and Cleve Sellers searched Neshoba County for Chaney, Goodman, and Schwerner. Guided by maps of the area's unforgiving terrain, they made their way through swamps, woods, and hilly land, but came up empty. Carmichael would describe the whole ordeal as "surreal" and said that it offered up a lesson in "loyalty and what real courage" were.[13]

Chaney, Goodman, and Schwerner were shot and killed on the night between June 21 and 22. Their bodies were discovered six weeks later. The tragedy did not deter Carmichael from the mission of Freedom Summer. As the project director for Mississippi's Second Congressional District, Stokely returned to Greenwood from the futile search near the end of June to orient thirty summer volunteers. He would work with Bob Zellner, a white Alabamian whose ties to Mississippi dated back to SNCC's early work in McComb. Colleagues since 1961, Carmichael considered Zellner a friend whose solid temperament and good nature positively reflected the complexity of white southerners. Ivanhoe Donaldson, a whippet-thin SNCC activist from New York who had made a name for himself in Danville, Virginia, a year earlier, was also in Mississippi, leading a project in Moss Point. Donaldson was brilliant and volatile, with a habit of yelling at SNCC's white female staff. Like his friend Stokely, Ivanhoe developed a reputation as a skilled, sometimes reckless, driver. Donaldson assured a colleague that summer who fretted over the danger of local authorities, "We ain't going to be stopped. They going to have to catch us. At a hundred and twenty miles an hour, more if the car will do it."[14]

Moses and Carmichael had agreed to an additional sixteen mostly black volunteers from Howard, and they were on hand. There was an irony in NAG's robust presence in Mississippi, since its membership had initially opposed the Summer Project on the grounds that it would hinder the development of local organizing efforts. Carmichael and NAG regrouped and vowed to outwork the project's organizers. Debate around the Summer Project also showcased organizational tensions within SNCC, as NAG increasingly took on the role of a loyal, but militant, opposition to forces drawn to Bob Moses.[15]

Volunteers sprawled across Greenwood Library's lawn in stifling heat as Carmichael introduced himself and recounted his recent visit to Philadelphia, Mississippi. "All the whites are out on the corners with their guns," he said. Carmichael suspected the townspeople knew the fate of the three missing workers but remained cowered in silence. "Sheriff [Lawrence] Rainey of Neshoba County got elected on his record as nigger-killer," Carmichael remarked matter-of-factly. "It's certain about two; some say the number's nearer eight."[16]

Like a professor delivering a freshman seminar, Carmichael outlined the group's duties and responsibilities. Freedom Schools, organized to teach civics, black history, and citizenship lessons, served as hubs of political and educational energy throughout Mississippi. Stokely warned the Freedom School teachers against conventional student-teacher hierarchies, noting that in the Delta both sides would learn from each other. In proposing the establishment of such schools the previous winter, Charlie Cobb had imagined them as sites of black political power. "Education in Mississippi," wrote Cobb, "is an institution which must be reconstructed from the ground up." Carmichael took Cobb's words to heart, offering classes whose Socratic nature impressed colleagues. Carmichael's English classes during and after the Summer Project coaxed participants into a larger dialogue that went beyond issues of grammar. His simple, unhurried erudition encouraged learning over lectures and challenged students to question society's rules and makeup.[17]

Carmichael's years of experience in the Delta made him particularly well-suited to planning clandestine organizing in the rural South. White volunteers, too conspicuous for stealth missions to plantations, would stay in town. The dangerous work of trespassing to recruit locals would be left to blacks. "SNCC policy is to work the areas where there is violence," Carmichael informed volunteers. "Any time they shoot one of us, ten of us go back next time. Then if they shoot ten, we take a hundred." Carmichael also discussed the cultural folkways that shaped local organizing in the South. Philosophical arguments over religion were taboo. "None of them has ever heard of atheism," he noted wryly. The church provided the ultimate vehicle for black self-determination and in doing so offered an avenue to organize diffuse energies. "We are doing the Lord's work," Carmichael reminded them. "Don't forget that. The movement developed largely out of the churches, and if God can start a movement, hooray for God." Carmichael warned against profanity, excessive drinking, and overt interracial dating. For those arrested and then released, he cautioned against ever departing jail at night. He advised against women wearing pants so as not to offend locals, and he set a 5:00 P.M. standard curfew for returning to their living quarters.[18]

"We've got a lot to do this summer," Carmichael told a mass meeting in Greenwood shortly after. Surrounded by an interracial group of locals and summer volunteers, Carmichael proclaimed the key to racial justice lay in exploiting one of the more hideous but little-discussed aspects of Jim Crow. "While these people are here, national attention is here. The FBI isn't going to let anything happen to them. They let the murderers of Negroes off, but already men have been arrested in Itta Bena just for *threatening* white lives." Then he issued a call for action. "What do we have to do?" asked Carmichael. "REGISTER!" was the enthusiastic response. Freedom Days, a series of elaborate rituals designed to show the federal government that blacks were prepared to vote if given the opportunity, regularly took place in counties throughout Mississippi. Freedom Days were more than just dramatic political theater complete with threats of arrest and more often beatings and jail time; they also served as practical forms of mobilization a notch above regularly scheduled mass meetings.[19]

Stokely soon became the poster boy for the Freedom Summer, his handsome face appearing in national coverage of the Summer Project. The national weekly magazine *The Saturday Evening Post* ran a long article on Mississippi, with a photo of Carmichael casually leaning against a rural porch—a relatively obscure local organizer, yet every inch a star, canvassing in the little town of Itta Bena. After his release from his latest arrest in July, Carmichael sauntered into the SNCC office more concerned about the arrival of the latest care package from the Friends and Admirers of Stokely Carmichael (FASC, an ad hoc group of supporters around the nation) than his own safety. Care packages filled with baby powder (for prickly heat), soap, tooth-paste, and candy became a vehicle for Carmichael's famous humor: "Young man tell FASC what you want and FASC will see to it—FASC is generous and fair." Carmichael's cool pose in the face of risk marked his identity as an activist and organizer, and his habit of calling everyone "Sweets" endeared him to volunteers and locals.[20]

Carmichael worked closely with the MFDP (Mississippi Freedom Democratic Party), an independent organization led by Fannie Lou Hamer, in its effort to gain official recognition from the Democratic Party. On July 15, Carmichael spoke at a community meeting in Greenwood. Referring to James Eastland, Mississippi's segregationist senator, Stokely said, "Eastland made a statement yesterday about everyone in the movement being a communist. All we want is the right to vote. If that's being a communist, then we're communist." Over a loud chorus of "Amens!" he continued: "Eastland also says that Negroes are happy, Negroes love to pick cotton, Negroes love to eat watermelon, Negroes love making three dollars a day, being illiterate, not voting. Eastland is a liar, and that's all there is to it."[21]

Six days later, on July 21, Martin Luther King arrived in Greenwood. It was the first stop in a five-day campaign swing to promote both the MFDP and Lyndon Johnson's election. While King stumped for Johnson, an anxious trio of Washington power brokers—Attorney General Kennedy, FBI Director J. Edgar Hoover, and President Johnson—burned up phone lines to offer him protection against assassination threats. Hoover's personal antipathy toward King had poisoned the bureau's ability to effectively handle civil rights cases, but, in this case, he was persuaded to assign King a discreet FBI security detail.[22]

King arrived in Greenwood as the movement's symbolic leader, but he recognized Carmichael's talent. Under the codename Greenwood Sweets, Carmichael shuttled King around the city in a caravan of cars. According to Stokely, the cars were "filled with guns," including the one he carried for protection. During this visit, Carmichael and King cultivated a friendly professional relationship that formed the basis of their future dealings. For Stokely, the episode offered another opportunity to personally interact with "De Lawd." But unlike some of his SNCC colleagues, Carmichael displayed signs of neither competitive envy nor fawning mimicry.[23]

King was a man of the South, and his deep rapport with poor black southerners genuinely touched Carmichael. King's calming steadiness in the face of the hurricane that surrounded his life impressed the younger man. And Carmichael appreciated aspects of King's speech—his inflection, cadence, and rhythm—in a way that only a fellow orator could.

King's visit temporarily relieved the everyday pressures of the Freedom Summer volunteers. But they quickly resumed after his departure. On August 4, Carmichael led a group of fifty blacks who tried to register to vote in the small town of Cleveland, Mississippi. The registrar admitted one person every forty-five minutes. Summer Project volunteers distributed registration literature without incident in front of the courthouse, but when they ventured across the street to continue leafleting, they were arrested and charged with violating an anti-littering ordinance. Police asked Carmichael, who had been refused entrance to the courthouse by deputies earlier, if he was the leader of the demonstration. Carmichael replied affirmatively and was immediately taken into custody. While the volunteers stayed in Cleveland's city jail, Carmichael posted $300 bond and returned to Greenwood.[24]

That evening, at a mass meeting in Greenwood, there was an air of mournful apprehension. The bodies of Michael Schwerner, James Chaney, and Andrew Goodman had been discovered. The news sparked conflicting feelings of shame, anger, and frustration. Carmichael publicly denounced unnamed black locals he accused of betraying the movement by leaking information to authorities. "I talk a lot of nonviolence to the white folks, but let me catch a black man doin' us wrong!" he cried. "You tell them to keep their mouths shut. 'Cause just as soon as I'd tell a white man to go to hell, I'd shoot a black man. I'm goin' to loudmouth everyone in this town ain't doing right. . . . We are not goin' to stick with this nonviolence forever."[25]

Stokely was grappling with a fundamental dilemma that profoundly altered the shape of the civil rights movement: how to stay nonviolent in a fatally violent atmosphere. During a late-night staff meeting, he paced the floor mulling over participation in a local demonstration planned the next day that COFO organizers feared would turn violent. He told Greenwood's locals that testing public accommodations posed an unnecessary risk. But he privately chafed at his own strategic pragmatism and nearly cried after giving advice that went against the grain of his own temperament. "Our lives are on the line now," Carmichael blurted out before explaining that he could not single-handedly prevent violence since "Negroes have always carried guns in Mississippi." Concluding that SNCC could only calm the march by joining it, Carmichael excused himself to gain permission from Bob Moses to join a march where locals might be armed. He came back from his conversation with Moses chastened (and abandoning plans to march) but recommitted to tactical nonviolence. "What I think we ought to do," announced Carmichael, once again turning from a militant to a sage, "is work harder on freedom registration forms." In that moment, recalled one volunteer, Carmichael appeared as "calm and thoughtful as Moses himself."[26]

Chapter Six

A Struggle for Democracy

August 1964–March 1965

In Atlantic City, New Jersey, the Democratic Party was to hold its national convention from August 24 to 27. The Democrats would nominate Lyndon Johnson as president. Although the presidential nomination was a fait accompli, numerous bits of palace intrigue abounded, including who would be named as Johnson's running mate. Robert Kennedy's mournful speech eulogizing his slain brother proved cathartic and served as a symbolic passing of the torch. By the New Year, Bobby Kennedy would be elected senator from New York, swept into office by sheer star power and the national Johnson presidential landslide. Racial politics hovered over the entire convention, punctuated by press speculation about how Johnson would defuse the MFDP's rogue presence.

Stokely and dozens of SNCC activists traveled to Atlantic City to challenge Mississippi's segregated delegation to the convention. It was a historic mission, but one destined to crush his faith in mainstream American politics and begin his journey toward independent political organizing. The movement's political strategy rolled along two lines, with some civil rights workers lobbying various state delegates on behalf of the unseated Mississippi Freedom Democratic Party delegation while others camped outside the convention to bear witness to the coming week's events. Demonstrators carrying massive posters with photos of Michael Schwerner, James Chaney, and Andrew Goodman lined the city's famous boardwalk. The certainty of Lyndon Johnson's nomination made the Freedom Democratic Party challenge a wild card that received considerable press. Fannie Lou Hamer's televised afternoon

testimony to the convention's credentials committee described the horrors of
Mississippi racism in poignant enough detail to compensate for being cut off
when television channels switched to a hastily organized news conference by
President Johnson. Hamer's plainspoken sincerity would serve as a testament
to SNCC and Carmichael's belief that poor, unlettered sharecroppers could
be not only citizens but political leaders.[1]

Armed with a walkie-talkie, Carmichael joined one hundred activists
who surrounded the Convention Center for a Sunday night vigil of freedom
songs that would triple in size the next day. Carmichael helped coordinate a
silent vigil between the Convention Center boardwalk and Temple Baptist
Church, where demonstrators crafted large picket signs. High drama played
out inside the Convention Center over the next few days as Freedom delegates milled around courtesy of spectator tickets provided by party officials.
The official all-white Mississippi delegation mulled over a compromise offer
of two nonvoting seats for Freedom Party delegates coupled with a promise
of an integrated state delegation by 1968. Martin Luther King, Bayard Rustin,
Roy Wilkins, and Minnesota Senator Hubert Humphrey (whose nomination
as vice president purportedly depended on brokering a deal with the MFDP
that would not embarrass Johnson or alienate the white regulars) alternated
between passive advice, gentle scolding, and behind-the-scenes arm twisting
in an effort to negotiate a deal.[2]

At stake in Atlantic City were two competing but equally critical issues: whether black Mississippians were full-fledged American citizens and
whether the Democratic Party was willing, once and for all, to become the
party of civil rights. Emissaries from the Johnson administration, national
civil rights leaders, and MFDP delegates met in secret on Wednesday morning to debate a compromise. Bayard Rustin's passionate insistence that the
"difference between protest and politics" necessitated accepting the compromise anticipated his evolution from socialist dissident to liberal power broker. His speech elicited groans from his former Howard disciples and at least
one outburst. "You're a traitor, Bayard, a traitor!" screamed Mendy Samstein,
a Brandeis graduate and one of Carmichael's favorites in SNCC. Samstein
voiced the thoughts of those, including Stokely, Courtland Cox, and others
who vocally opposed the idea of dishonorable compromise. Jim Forman would
remember the entire spectacle as producing an epiphany among Rustin's
former acolytes. "They had seen the light," Forman observed. Carmichael's

anger over Rustin's words overcame the heartbreak of watching the demise of someone he now considered a false prophet.[3]

Stokely was one of a handful of organizers trusted by the MFDP delegation. Shell-shocked activists peppered him with questions and sought out his advice before ultimately rejecting the offer. Carmichael took special pride in the fact that some of the most resolute voices opposing the compromise were black women from the Delta. For Carmichael, the political outcome in Atlantic City followed a familiar pattern. He privately hoped that the entire process would strengthen the MFDP's political independence through the invaluable, if dispiriting, experience in the bruising world of major-party politics. MFDP supporters, however, would remain committed to changing Mississippi's Democratic Party from within rather than building an independent political base.[4]

The summer of 1964 transformed Stokely Carmichael. "I felt, after the pressure and intense discipline all summer," he would confess, "a kind of deflation." Carmichael's ennui mirrored that of SNCC, which experienced the departure of some Summer Project volunteers and the unexpected offer by many others to stay. The influx of new members, many of whom had participated in civil rights activism for the first time, changed SNCC, transforming a tight-knit unit into a sprawling and diffuse entity. Meanwhile, Carmichael continued as project director for the Second Congressional District, which in the fall directed precious energies to supporting the MFDP in the November elections. Photos of Lyndon Johnson and his running mate, Hubert Humphrey, appeared on top of SNCC posters for the MFDP just above pictures of the congressional candidates in the Second, Fourth, and Fifth Districts, Fannie Lou Hamer, Annie Devine, and Victoria Gray.[5]

Freedom Summer's chaotic conclusion in Atlantic City overshadowed the project's remarkable achievements. On August 29, SNCC issued a press release that summarized the Summer Project's official results. The drive, which began on June 21 and ended that week, recruited hundreds of students, doctors, lawyers, preachers, and ministers to Mississippi to coordinate efforts that centered on Freedom Schools, voter registration, and political action. One hundred and seventy-five Freedom School teachers taught over two thousand students enrolled in forty-one Freedom Schools spread through twenty different communities. Project workers organized an additional thirteen community centers that established libraries, literacy programs, and health and child care programs. In the towns of Mileston and Harmony, civil rights workers and local people were building two new centers from the ground up. More than 55,000 African Americans successfully filled out Freedom Registration forms symbolically proving that democracy remained in the hearts and on the minds of Mississippi blacks if it was not yet a political reality.[6]

In September, a contingent of SNCC activists took a life-changing journey to Africa. The group, including Ruby Doris Smith Robinson (now married to Clifford Robinson, the mechanic for SNCC's Sojourner Truth Motor Fleet) and Fannie Lou Hamer, would spend three weeks in the west African country of Guinea. Harry Belafonte had arranged the journey, which would have lasting consequences on Stokely, even though he did not accompany the others on the trip. Belafonte counted the dashing Guinean leader Sékou Touré as a personal friend and arranged for SNCC to have full access to the president. Touré's insistence that Guinea, a former French colony, remain independent of French assistance had come at the high cost of economic hardship but made him a hero to black Americans who connected their own struggles at home to anti-colonial struggles in the Third World. A country the size of Oregon, Guinea, despite its own travails, offered generous assistance to other embattled African nations. Robinson would name her son Kenneth Touré in honor of the Guinean revolutionary, and Fannie Lou Hamer cried after meeting the president, overwhelmed at being afforded courtesies undreamed of back home. Jim Forman, Bob Moses, and John Lewis also came back with stories extolling the wonders of visiting a country whose entire government was led by blacks. Forman returned with gifts from Touré, including an African robe that he gave to Stokely.[7]

On October 3, Stokely was a featured speaker at the Mississippi Report Dinner in Chicago. It was the first organized tribute to the Freedom Summer, destined to register in the national conscience as a mean season of historical reckoning. Fannie Lou Hamer spoke about "A New Politics for the South" and Bob Moses about "Mississippi: Future Prospectives for Change." Hamer presented the summer's highs and lows as a one-woman performance: she sang and shouted her story so enthusiastically that attendees clasped hands and offered "amens" as if in a Baptist church. Guest-of-honor field workers regaled the audience with tales of racist terror that garnered immediate donations totaling $2,500. Carmichael delivered a memorial to the civil rights workers martyred during the Summer Project. The Chicago dinner turned out to be more than a commemoration of the Summer Project; it served as an unwitting memorial to the spirit of trust that had allowed young organizers to almost singlehandedly implement an "operation as diverse and complicated, as radical in intent and operation, and as dangerous" as Freedom Summer.[8]

During that summer, SNCC had come as close as it ever would to being a cohesive organization. If SNCC began its early period as a loose confederation of independent campus-based groups, after 1964 it functioned as a collection of autonomous local projects bound together by mutual political objectives. The odds were huge. Mississippi was the battleground for America's soul. During the event, SNCC activist David Llorens asked a poignant question that would haunt Carmichael well into the next year: "Will Mississippi become a part of America or will America become Mississippi?"[9]

But after the Chicago dinner, political tensions in SNCC grew. In November, a week-long SNCC staff retreat highlighted divisions. It was held at Waveland, Mississippi, a resort on the Gulf of Mexico, a relaxed setting for increasingly fierce debates over the group's political direction and organizational structure.

The role of women, increasingly discussed in the country at large, took center stage at Waveland. Mary King and Casey Hayden (the wife of SDS leader Tom Hayden) had written a paper, "Sex and Caste," which challenged SNCC to confront sexism within its own ranks. The authors compared discrimination against women to that suffered by blacks. "Sex and Caste" would come to be recognized as a watershed document of second-wave feminism, but at Waveland, not only the men but some of the women dismissed it as an unnecessary intrusion into what many activists still erroneously viewed as primarily a racial struggle. SNCC's most powerful female member, Ruby Doris Smith Robinson, disagreed with "Sex and Caste." She believed that its arguments were based on the frustrations of white female staff who had tired of administrative work but whose presence in the field was considered too dangerous. Confident and tough, Robinson considered herself the equal of any man in the organization and commanded their respect.[10]

After a long day of haggling over the fate of the world, Carmichael once again offered comic relief. Carmichael's natural charisma lent a patina of celebrity and showmanship to everything he did. At the conclusion of one of his patented monologues that made fun of a wide range of targets, he turned to a discussion of position papers. "What is the position of women in SNCC?" he asked rhetorically. "The position of women in SNCC is prone!" he impishly

answered. Carmichael and his audience, men and women included, laughed
for a long time. Retrospectively, this quote would take on a life of its own,
becoming a symbol of the era's sexism. Mary King remembers it differently.
"It drew us closer together, because, even in that moment, he was poking fun
at his own attitudes." If Carmichael shared the sexist views of his generation
regarding women's roles in politics, he fought hard against these blinders,
and Mary King remembered him as "one of the most responsive men" to
"Sex and Caste." Howard student, SNCC worker, and Summer Project volunteer Jean Smith Young similarly recalled that Carmichael treated her with
respect, a sentiment echoed by Martha Prescod Norman Noonan. The joke's
lasting reverberations, however, would prove overwhelming. Shorn of context, Carmichael's words damaged his personal reputation, cost him political
credibility in feminist circles, and unfairly minimized SNCC's democratic
culture. Almost fifty years after Waveland, Hayden attempted to correct this
error in an essay, "In the Attics of My Mind," which discussed how she viewed
women in SNCC:

> Nonviolent civil disobedience created a new community of folks will-
> ing to risk everything for their beliefs. Together as this community,
> I thought, we were new people, free of the old stereotypes of gender,
> class, and race. This was the beloved community and the point was to
> organize it everywhere, redeeming the culture, undermining the old
> power structures. Women's culture and black culture, merging for me
> in the southern freedom movement, especially in SNCC, free of the
> constraints and values of the white patriarchy, would lead the way.[11]

In the short run, SNCC's precarious financial health overwhelmed Waveland's historic significance. On November 22, Cleve Sellers, the project director at the Mississippi town of Holly Springs, wrote to Jim Forman about his
local project's dismal economic situation. Mounting costs for auto repairs,
utility bills, legal aid, and office rent far exceeded the $200-per-month sti-
pend from SNCC's Jackson office. Without northern aid, Sellers informed
Forman, all would be lost. Sellers said he had remained relatively silent about
debates over structure at the last staff meeting since it was only "the service
the structure renders" that really counted. Sellers concluded his letter with an
ultimatum disguised as a plea. Unless Forman could provide Holly Springs
with the necessary resources to effectively operate, he would resign in two

weeks. Carmichael, Sellers' good friend and mentor, was the first person copied on the letter.[12]

Sellers was not alone in his frustrations. Ruby Doris Smith Robinson in Atlanta had earlier complained to Forman about feeling overworked and underappreciated. The quick-witted and intelligent Ruby had been among Forman's first recruits in 1961 and among his best decisions. Her no-nonsense demeanor endeared her to some while alienating field staff and Summer Project volunteers, who found her too rigid. A dedicated administrator and occasional field participant, she stretched her considerable talents beyond human capacity. She found herself juggling the needs of local staff, the executive committee, and Forman, whose enduring wish was to build a structure capable of handling competing interests. Ruby dismissed talk from northern whites that she was "bossy" just as she rejected staff complaints of her ill temper. On the brink of resigning, she pulled back out of a principled sense of responsibility. Growing tensions between field staff and headquarters found project staff sniping that headquarters remained disconnected from the routine dangers they faced every day and administrators reporting that SNCC members brandished recklessness like a badge of honor.[13]

The debate over structure versus improvisation was important, and Carmichael sympathized with both sides. He remained in Greenwood through December 1964, running interference for local activists harassed by authorities and plotting a strategic retreat to the relatively virgin territory of Alabama. He based this decision on his experience supporting programs designed by others. Intent on implementing a project based on his personal understanding of American politics, Carmichael relentlessly pursued the creation of independent politics capable of transcending the Democratic Party. He hoped that this new project might transform democracy from the ground up by investing political power in poor blacks in the rural South's Black Belt. The "test case" for Carmichael's theory that independent politics offered black people the best chance for both freedom and self-determination would take place in Lowndes County, the buckle of Alabama's Black Belt.[14]

CARMICHAEL WAS DETERMINED to make 1965 a year devoted to independent black political organizing. But he remained unsure of just how to achieve this ambitious goal. He found the cure for his troubles in a most unlikely example: Martin Luther King's audacious voting rights campaign, which quickly turned Alabama into a center of national civil rights protest.

Carmichael's quiet admiration for King grew steadily after each encounter, and he credited him with teaching other blacks how to face racial terror without fear. King entered the New Year as a Nobel Peace Prize winner, an award he received the previous December in Oslo and that cemented his status as a global human rights leader. SNCC officially judged King's campaign for voting rights in Selma to be a diversion from the real work of long-term organizing. In keeping with organization philosophy, however, individuals remained free to participate. For a variety of reasons, Selma mesmerized SNCC, including members who voiced their disapproval of the entire proceedings only to reverse course and others too afraid to admit to being drawn to King's celebrity. Carmichael belonged to a third contingent determined to build a sustained project in the rurals—the plantation-strewn areas most dangerous yet critical to bringing full citizenship to sharecroppers—and gambling that King's presence in Selma might help facilitate such organizing. Alabama's burgeoning civil rights activity had even attracted Malcolm X, whose February 3 visit to Tuskegee and trip to Selma two days later marked his last appearance in the South before his assassination on February 21. Malcolm's death upset Carmichael and other SNCC workers who were becoming increasingly open to his radical politics. SNCC had carefully observed Malcolm's political evolution during his last frenetic year alive. Malcolm's two tours of Africa in 1964 touched SNCC's internationally minded activists, including John Lewis, who toured Kenya shortly after Malcolm's visit. Malcolm's overtures to the young radicals in SNCC included sharing a stage with Fannie Lou Hamer in New York three months before his assassination. From the grave, Malcolm offered Stokely a portrait of a revolutionary life cut short but jam-packed with Middle East pilgrimages (where Malcolm embraced orthodox Islam and became El Hajj Malik El Shabazz), fearless political debates, and a personal sincerity that Carmichael would spend the rest of his life emulating.

On Sunday, March 7, Alabama state troopers routed civil rights workers attempting to march into Montgomery over Selma's Edmund Pettus Bridge. John Lewis sustained the day's most visible wound, a gaping skull fracture courtesy of a club to the head. That same day, Carmichael arrived in Selma by charter flight from Atlanta (where he had been in town seeking an official transfer to Alabama) with Jim Forman and Faye Bellamy, a new staff member who had arranged Malcolm X's Selma visit. During a 3:00 AM meeting with

King and his trusted second-in-command man, Ralph Abernathy, Carmichael urged SCLC staff to defy an injunction prohibiting marching. Staff who had privately chided Sunday's march as showboating now supported Tuesday's efforts as a defiant stand against fear. Sunday's violence emboldened the resolve of local organizers such as Willie Ricks, a theatrical orator nicknamed "Reverend" for his preaching abilities, who on Tuesday led a portion of the crowd in exhortations from Brown Chapel. Carmichael marched at the head of the line with King on Tuesday. Stokely, in jeans, work boots, and a hooded overcoat, was impassively smoking. It would be the last time that Carmichael participated in a demonstration of this scale in virtual anonymity.[15]

Monday, March 15 was the day Alabama law specified for voter registration. Carmichael was staying at the Ben Moore Hotel in Montgomery. From his fourth-floor window, he saw mounted police officers rout helpless demonstrators. He tried to get to the marchers to help them, but shuttered exit doors at the hotel delayed him. Waves of despair overcame him. Carmichael's emotional response to the police violence against demonstrators pushed him over the edge. SNCC workers found him only intermittently lucid and staggering afterward and hustled him to the Montgomery Airport. Carmichael's delayed response to the day's trauma left him shrieking in grief before a bewildered police officer. He crumpled to the floor as friends and colleagues soothed him.[16]

On the evening of that day, March 15, 1965, President Johnson spoke about civil rights to a joint session of Congress. The televised address upstaged both quotidian struggles being waged in Selma and the plight of democratic warriors such as Carmichael. President Johnson invoked "the dignity of man and the destiny of democracy" in an address that cast events in Selma as part of a historic pantheon that stretched from Revolutionary War battles at Lexington and Concord to the South's surrender at Appomattox, ending the Civil War. "There is no pride in what has happened in Selma," said Johnson. "There is no cause for self-satisfaction in the long denial of equal rights of millions of Americans." The president openly confronted, like Kennedy before him, a national reluctance to publicly admit to historic and contemporary racial oppression against blacks. "But there is cause for hope and for faith in our democracy in what is happening here tonight," he said. At a high point in a speech of many peaks, Johnson concluded with a signal quote from the movement that he now held up as embodying American democracy's very essence: "Because it is not just Negroes, but really it's all of us, who must overcome the crippling legacy of bigotry and injustice. And—we—shall—overcome."[17]

Johnson's speech represented the strongest presidential endorsement of civil rights since John Kennedy's historic televised address on June 11, 1963. Johnson's forty-five-minute speech elicited a wave of conflicting emotions that ranged from joy to disbelief and anger among the elected leaders in attendance. Three dozen separate bursts of applause rewarded the speech's uncanny mix of poetry and politics.

Johnson's speech boosted King's efforts to complete the Selma-to-Montgomery demonstration. In Selma, speaking with his advisers, King correctly identified Jim Forman, who advocated night marches and was prone to rhetorical outbursts in full view of the press, as a disruptive force. King complained that tension with SNCC had produced "an agony of spirit" that sapped his usual optimism. Under pressure from journalists and civil rights leaders such as Roy Wilkins to denounce Forman, King refused but off the record judged SNCC to be naïve. King steered a course of public diplomacy while privately confessing his belief that SNCC was under the spell of radical political ideologies. During a conversation with Harry Belafonte on March 19, King accused Forman of purposeful disruption that pushed the movement to the brink of violence, while Belafonte questioned the mental stability of SNCC's intense executive secretary. Resolved in their judgment of SNCC's recklessness but convinced that peace offered the best course of action, King and Belafonte made plans to broker a settlement as soon as possible.[18]

Carmichael matched Forman's intensity but stayed clear of aggressive outbursts. He preferred to focus on ways to use the planned march to crack open hostile terrain. Stokely recognized Forman as SNCC's strongest administrator: Jim was patient, disciplined, and a master parliamentarian who coupled a "willingness to listen to people" with a "relentless" work ethic. Carmichael patterned his bureaucratic ambitions and ideological steadfastness after Forman, the man he recognized as having taught him "how to be uncompromising in one's principles." But he broke with Forman on the subject of King; Stokely pushed for an organizing approach that avoided "automatic conflict" between SNCC and the SCLC in favor of "getting people together." Carmichael regarded King as his generation's greatest political mobilizer, a protean force who easily brushed off criticism from young activists. Unable to compete with King's star power at the national level or with journalists, SNCC outworked the SCLC and King on the ground, where Carmichael smiled and nodded when local sharecroppers misidentified him as one of "King's men." Attuned to these "political realities," Carmichael proposed to build on the momentum generated by King's appearance in Selma to help organize a new project. "So the march," he would recall eight years later, "helped me in my organizing."[19]

Carmichael used Selma's controversy to organize for black political power. Originating in Selma on Sunday, March 21, and concluding in Montgomery four days later, the Selma-to-Montgomery demonstration traveled directly through Lowndes, the county scouted by Carmichael and SNCC field worker Bob Mants earlier in the month. Almost sixty years earlier, W.E.B. Du Bois had conducted a meticulous sharecropping study there, miraculously sponsored by the Department of Labor and inevitably destroyed after its findings proved too provocative. Carmichael participated in the march but spent most of his time making contacts in Lowndes. He resolved to "create order" from the chaos that would remain after King's departure.[20]

Carmichael entered Lowndes on Saturday, March 27, in the wake of white volunteer Viola Liuzzo's murder in that county two days earlier. He was backed by a contingent of hard-nosed SNCC field workers: Bob Mants, Judy Richardson, Ruth Howard, Scott B. Smith, Courtland Cox, and Willie Vaughan. Three days later, Carmichael led two dozen SNCC workers in a procession that stopped along a church near Highway 80, where Liuzzo had been shot. Wright Chapel AME Zion Church was transformed into a place of witness that day and doubled as a staging ground for organizing.[21]

Carmichael, Mants, Richardson, and Smith distributed leaflets at the Lowndes County Training School in White Hall, the county seat. Confronted by law enforcement while passing out leaflets to students, Carmichael forcefully stood his ground, loudly admonishing officers to arrest him or leave him unmolested. John Jackson, a sixteen-year-old student bus driver and son of a prominent local black family, gleefully accepted one of the flyers and discovered his political vocation as a civil rights activist at the expense of his job. John's parents, Matthew and Emma of White Hall, lent SNCC an unoccupied house that would serve as a permanent headquarters and base of operations for the next year and a half.[22]

SNCC staff replayed the lessons of Selma as they organized a new political base in Lowndes County. Although Dr. King was the guiding spirit at Selma, the late Malcolm X was much in their thoughts. Malcolm's passionate pleas for racial solidarity had hovered over Alabama. Staff members acquired tapes of Malcolm's weekly lectures at the Audubon Ballroom in Harlem and disseminated them to workers. Less than three weeks before his death, Malcolm had visited Alabama, speaking to students and civil rights workers at Tuskegee Institute, a SNCC recruiting ground, and at Brown Chapel AME Church in Selma. Malcolm's brief stop in the state represented a capstone of his complex relationship with SNCC. A few weeks earlier, he had invited Fannie Lou Hamer and SNCC's Freedom Singers to one of his outdoor rallies in Harlem, where he lauded the former sharecropper turned civil rights activist as one of the nation's most important freedom fighters. By the time Malcolm visited Selma, SNCC's relative caution toward his political rhetoric had bloomed into open admiration. From the grave, Malcolm's spirit now gripped SNCC's political imagination, but it would be King's example that provided cover for Carmichael's entrée into Lowndes.[23]

CHAPTER SEVEN

Lowndes County: New Directions

April 1965–May 1966

STOKELY CARMICHAEL'S BELIEF THAT BLACK POLITICAL POWER RESIDED IN the will and political self-determination of local people helped to create the original Black Panther Party. For Carmichael, the Panthers offered the best vehicle for promoting radical democracy in Alabama. Unbeknownst to him, the Panthers would, in many ways, become one of the most enduring elements of his legacy. They would also be among the most misunderstood. Carmichael's activism helped shaped the Black Panther Party in both Lowndes County, Alabama, as well as its more famous counterpart, founded in Oakland, California, in October 1966 by urban street toughs turned activists. Carmichael's involvement with the Panthers showcased two important sides of his character that are sometimes difficult to reconcile: the organizer and the political celebrity. Alabama's version of the Panthers relied on Carmichael's organizing instincts to take advantage of a bureaucratic loophole that turned independent politics in the South from a dream into a reality. Here the group's success hinged on the slow, patient organizing more commonly associated with civil rights than with Black Power. Such distinctions meant little to Carmichael, whose organizing in Lowndes remained fueled by the belief that democracy's most important shareholders were those who had been denied citizenship for so long.

The Black Panther concept would travel from the heart of Dixie to the Bay Area in a dizzying reinvention that refocused the snarling animal from a defensive posture to one of revolutionary foreboding. Oakland's newly formed Black Panther Party for Self-Defense, in one of their first acts, drafted Carmichael as a field marshal, determined to attach themselves to his burgeoning iconography. For a time, Carmichael embraced both of these contrasting visions of the Panther before settling into the leather-jacketed glamour of urban militants whose activism he helped inspire but whose politics he soon grow weary of. Carmichael's activism in Lowndes helped launch the Black Panthers, North and South, into the national imagination and into history.

Carmichael applied political lessons learned in the Delta to Lowndes, a county he would live in for over a year. Two pivotal events marked his time in Alabama. Organizationally, he helped to launch an independent political group, nicknamed the Black Panther Party, whose symbolism would almost instantly transform the black freedom struggle. The rise of the Panthers, first in Lowndes then in Oakland, California, signaled Carmichael's transition from regional organizer to national political leader, a development aided by national profiles in *Look* magazine and *Who Speaks for the Negro?*, an important anthology examining civil rights leaders. The second event was the brutal death of his friend and fellow Lowndes organizer Jonathan Daniels. Carmichael reacted to Daniels' death as if he had lost a brother, but generally refused to discuss these feelings in public. Personal experience fueled Carmichael's political behavior, and this instance proved no different. Daniels' death increased his commitment to a style of independent politics that would turn the Black Panther Party from a local curiosity into a national phenomenon. Oakland proved to be the most creative and volatile outpost on this score, and two young activists and part-time troublemakers, Huey P. Newton and Bobby Seale, would claim the Panther image as their own by the fall of 1966. Carmichael's activism in Lowndes served as an inspiration to urban militants eager to adapt the Panther symbol to local conditions. But the image of Carmichael in sunglasses and leather jacket in 1968 in full Panther regalia obscures the quotidian struggles that gave birth to the group. Before the glamour of Oakland, there was the harsh, dreary, and frightening reality of Lowndes.

IN ALABAMA, LOCAL PEOPLE SEARCHED for strength and purpose through self-rule. Farm subsidies, labor rights, sharecropping, criminal justice, and healthcare were the black community's chief concerns and the basis for county-wide politics. If Mississippi activists dreamed of using the federal government as a battering ram for reform, civil rights workers in Alabama proposed starting a grassroots movement that would produce community-wide change.[1]

Spring turned to summer as Carmichael led SNCC workers in canvassing the entire county. A typical day began early and included approaching rural shacks where residents shared early morning meals of fried chicken and grits but remained noncommittal about the risky prospect of becoming politically active. As always, Carmichael attracted talented people to the cause. Volunteer Gloria Larry chanced upon Carmichael speaking in Selma and followed him to Lowndes as much out of personal interest as political commitment. Jonathan Daniels, a white seminarian student who had bonded with Stokely over a shared passion for philosophy and a practical interest in social justice, traveled to Lowndes as an observer.[2]

On Sunday, August 8, in the little town of Fort Deposit, Carmichael spoke at the town's first mass meeting, of five hundred people, in Bethlehem Christian Church. White vigilantes buzzed around menacingly outside the church, while inside movement leaders conducted a voting rights seminar. At the meeting's conclusion, FBI agents cordoned off access to the church to allow a clear path away from Fort Deposit, but a small group of whites trailed the departing caravan for five miles before receding into the darkness. Fort Deposit's youthful militants vowed to test the 1964 Civil Rights Act's new public accommodations laws in spite of SNCC's warnings that the risk behind such efforts far outweighed potential benefits.[3]

On August 6, Lyndon Johnson signed the Voting Rights Act into law in a public ceremony that featured King, who was given a presidential pen for posterity. The law, which included federal safeguards designed to prevent southern states from denying the black vote, represented the culmination of the Selma demonstrations. But if King's star power helped usher in the right to vote, it would be Carmichael and SNCC's work in Lowndes that pressured the government to ensure local follow-through. Four days after Johnson signed the Voting Rights Act into law, federal registrars arrived in the Black Belt counties of Marengo, Hale, Dallas, and Lowndes. In Lowndes, they set up headquarters at Fort Deposit, which made it, rather than the county seat in Hayneville, the site of the area's civil rights activity. Newspaper reporters alerted by SNCC to the simmering conflict swarmed Fort Deposit on the morning of August 14, the day of a planned protest. FBI agents milled about while Carmichael spoke to young people of the dangers of violent retalia-tion. A crowd of one hundred blacks stood in line outside the post office for voter registration as demonstrators arrived downtown by car and on foot. An ambush cordoned off the first line of picketers as dozens of armed men descended onto the scene. Reporters from *The Southern Courier* (which sym-pathetically covered the civil rights struggle from 1965 to 1968) and *Life* mag-azine covered the story by car. The journalists traveled in a group for their own protection but still found themselves fleeing local vigilantes.[4]

Then there was the one time when Stokely actually almost welcomed being arrested. En route to Lowndes County Jail in Hayneville, Carmichael and driver Chris Wylie along with three local young people were pursued by a truck filled with white troublemakers, who menaced them with a knife and blocked them from proceeding. After a nervous Wylie accidentally hit the truck while trying to get away, they all headed to the local police station. Charged with reckless driving and leaving the scene of an accident, Carmi-chael and Wylie were locked up in Lowndes County Jail. "That was the one time," recalled Carmichael, "that I was not sorry to be arrested."[5]

But then their day took an ominous turn. Local authorities transported Carmichael and the others back to Fort Deposit that evening under mys-terious circumstances. Evening reports, filtered out of Fort Deposit and Hayneville, described roaming white mobs outside the local jail, intimida-tion, and threats of violence. Inquiries from SNCC staff, locals, and the Jus-tice Department probably saved Carmichael's life that night. The next day, Carmichael and Wylie were transported back to Hayneville. Stokely and Wy-lie shared a cell with Jonathan Daniels in the Hayneville county jail. After authorities released five underage prisoners on the first night, eighteen re-mained, including four SNCC workers, Daniels, and a white Catholic priest, Father Richard Morrisroe. Bob Mants posted bond for Carmichael and Wylie on Wednesday, August 18th, but there was not enough bond money, and so Daniels was left in jail. He was released two days later.[6]

Friday, August 20th, Jonathan Daniels became a martyr to the cause. He and seventeen-year-old Ruby Sales, a protester who had also just been re-leased, went in search of Coca-Colas in Hayneville. Suddenly, shots rang out. Daniels threw his body in front of Ruby to protect her. But he was hit, and a second volley killed him. In shock, Sales crawled to safety while noting that Father Morrisroe lay writhing on the ground in agony, a victim of the scat-tered gunfire. He and Ruby would survive.

Carmichael heard the news of his friend's murder while traveling back to Lowndes from Selma to sign bonds for the release of the prisoners. Amid the aftershock of Daniels' murder, Carmichael informed reporters that Hayneville and Selma had turned into tinderboxes. "Sheriff Clark has deputized over 300 whites in the past few hours," he warned. Back in Selma to organize a response to Daniels' killing, he called in reinforcements from projects in Mississippi, Arkansas, and Washington for a two-week "crash drive" that drew experienced organizers and expert drivers. Cleve Sellers lashed out at the Justice Department's John Doar in a telephone conversation over the decision to send FBI agents from Selma to Lowndes. "Obviously," Sellers sarcastically remarked, "you didn't waste the cream of the crop on us." That remark so outraged Doar that SNCC staff suggested a one-day cooling-off period. Meanwhile, SNCC gave a CBS crew permission to enter SNCC's local headquarters in Lowndes, Freedom House, and film interviews. It was a privilege granted to the sole news organization that had offered SNCC unrestricted access to its taped eyewitness reports. CBS's behavior was in direct contrast to the government's. Federal procedure of taping witness statements but offering no protection from local reprisal had rubbed salt on a festering wound at SNCC, whose internal reports criticized the government for advising witnesses to "run and hide the best they can." On August 21, SNCC's Selma office issued a statement that linked events in Lowndes to larger national stirrings for racial justice. "The brutal slaying of the Rev. Jon Daniels and the shooting of Father Morrisroe is but another page in the blood-stained history of Alabama, another page in the history of Lowndes County, and another blot on the blood-soaked image of this nation."[7]

Carmichael spoke of Daniels at a Sunday evening mass meeting attended by John Lewis. Shedding tears for the fallen martyr missed the point, he said, since they could not bring him back from the dead. Instead, those who soldiered on in the wake of disaster could "resurrect" themselves. But Daniels' death shattered Carmichael, who blamed himself for allowing him entrée into Lowndes. "I had a lot of appreciation for him," he remembered over two decades later. Carmichael considered Daniels a rarity: a white volunteer who listened more than he proselytized, capable of grappling with hard questions about race, democracy, and power. Daniels' connection to the Episcopal Church also resonated with Carmichael, who had cordial relations with the church's Washington, DC, diocese, which let NAG use its facilities to conduct meetings.[8]

May Charles accompanied Stokely to Daniels' funeral in Keene, New Hampshire. She would remember the trip as the rare occasion her son directly involved her in movement business. The car radio stayed silent during the trip. And in Keene, Carmichael wept as he grieved with Daniels' parents. "I do think that was the hardest thing my son ever had to do in the movement," she recalled. Over a thousand people viewed Daniels' body at Keene's St. James Episcopal Church. The coffin lay in state for over a day and a half; a funeral and afternoon memorial service included a message of condolence from President Johnson. Carmichael and a group of mourners sang a tearful rendition of "We Shall Overcome" at Daniels' grave. Stokely rarely mentioned Daniels in public, and observers have virtually ignored the death, but it was pivotal in shaping Carmichael's political evolution. His subsequent identification with Black Power offered no room for complicated interracial friendships forged in support of the black vote in rural Alabama. So Daniels' death would be airbrushed out of Carmichael's public persona. But as one journalist suggested, the Carmichael who believed in democracy's powers to heal the South's racial wounds remained permanently scarred by Jonathan Daniels' murder. Jack Nelson, a veteran civil rights reporter, wrote, "Daniels' death and acquittal of his slayer by an all-white jury seemed to be a traumatic experience for Carmichael."[9]

Carmichael responded to Daniels' murder by organizing for radical democracy in Lowndes. Jack Minnis, SNCC's enterprising research director, provided the opening for rural political activism in Alabama's Black Belt that would soon reverberate all the way to California's urban ghettoes. Responding to Carmichael's earlier inquiry, Minnis suggested that state law offered room for independent politics. Beyond minute bureaucratic details lay the novel discovery that blacks in Lowndes could legally form their own political party. Minnis' report dovetailed with Carmichael's parallel efforts to organize a South-wide People's Conference capable of galvanizing "coalitions of people without power." In a September 2nd memo, Carmichael elaborated on his plan to organize "unrepresented people. . . . Many ideas have come through the mail," he wrote, "which for SNCC folk is what we call a miracle." Among the topics suggested for discussion at the planned conference (tentatively scheduled in Greenwood), the most far reaching would be what he benignly described as "political parties."[10]

The creation of the Lowndes County Freedom Organization (LCFO) fulfilled Carmichael's dreams of organizing unrepresented people. LCFO distinguished itself from the Mississippi Freedom Democratic Party by choosing a black panther as its symbol, noting the animal's color and ability to defend itself. The Black Panther Party's southern roots, although destined for obscurity, illustrated Carmichael's continuing dedication to community organizing. Yet the concept soon became something more—a tangible symbol that transcended geographic regions and seemed readily adopted by urban militants across the nation and, over time, around the world. What started out as a local movement for political autonomy came to symbolize far-reaching militancy that would send shockwaves through America.

Going from dream to reality, however, required time, luck, and work. During the second week of December, a reporter interviewed Atlanta SNCC staff as they prepared a ten-page pamphlet on independent politics. The story portrayed SNCC as a group bursting with new ideas but lacking the financial resources to implement them. Northern fatigue over civil rights coupled with SNCC's antiwar stance had precipitated a financial crisis that threatened payroll. Buried in the back pages of *The New York Times*, this early portrait of Lowndes dryly noted that the group would "use a black panther as its party symbol" and perpetuated the myth that the party (which was open to all citizens) would be "all-Negro" by choice. If the mainstream press initially presented the panther as a relatively benign symbol, SNCC immediately recognized it as something more. *The Student Voice*, SNCC's monthly newsletter, featured a snarling black panther on the right side of the masthead framed by the words "Lowndes County Freedom Organization" and "One Man—One Vote" underneath. A caption beneath the panther provocatively asked "WILL THE PANTHER EAT THE ROOSTER?"—a reference to the Alabama Democratic Party's symbol and its controversial accompanying slogan, "White supremacy for the right."[11]

The Black Panther Party grew out of Stokely's experiences in Mississippi, Atlantic City, and Alabama's Black Belt. His vision of American democracy stretched beyond the imagination of the Constitution's framers. "Lowndes County is going to be very interesting," he observed in an interview with *The Student Voice*, "as indicative of what could happen across the country when propertyless people" acquire political power. Carmichael neglected to mention that the Black Panther Party in Lowndes "was an armed party," a pragmatic decision made in the face of racial terror. His organizing experience in the Deep South had taught him that democracy sometimes required guns.[12]

Carmichael began the New Year of 1966 mourning the unexpected death of yet another friend. On January 3, Sammy Younge, age twenty-one, was passing out "One Man—One Vote" bumper stickers at a voter registration drive in Macon County, Alabama. He was shot and killed in Tuskegee following a dispute with a gas station attendant over the use of a restroom. The murder sent SNCC workers into a frenzy and Carmichael into a temporary depression. The news hit Carmichael especially hard since he knew Younge, who had made a name for himself as chair of Tuskegee Institute's campus SNCC affiliate and as a field secretary. Living more or less permanently in Alabama over the past year, Carmichael frequented Tuskegee's campus, where students revered him as a dynamic and charismatic organizer. Less than a week before his death, Sammy had unexpectedly visited Freedom City, the tent city in Lowndes that housed sharecroppers evicted for working with SNCC. Sammy had told Stokely that the movement had become his life; he said he hoped to start a Black Panther chapter on campus. Survivor's guilt gripped Carmichael in times like these. "I just got me three bottles of wine," he confided to Jim Forman, "and drank one for me and one for Sammy and one for Jonathan Daniels." Younge's death spurred short-term controversy and catalyzed SNCC's increasingly public embrace of radical politics. For James Forman, "Sammy's murder marked the final end of any patience with nonviolence—even as a tactic." It also served as inspiration for his book, *Sammy Younge Jr.: The First Black Student to Die in the Black Liberation Movement,* which turned the martyred Younge into a heroic symbol of what radicals now called a movement for black liberation.[13]

Meanwhile, Atlanta staff responded with a statement linking Younge's death to the escalating war in Vietnam. The statement made SNCC the first major civil rights group to publicly oppose the Vietnam War. It was an eloquent argument about the fundamental nature of American democracy. It questioned the nation's ability to advocate for free elections abroad when it seemed unable to defend them at home. Vietnam exposed racial and economic fault lines that battered SNCC's veneer of public cooperation with federal officials. The statement praised "Americans who prefer to use their energy in building democratic forms within this country." It suggested that civil and human rights activism represented a valid although no less dangerous alternative to the draft. "We urge all Americans to seek this alternative," they concluded, "knowing full well that it may cost them lives—as painfully as in Vietnam."[14]

Before Sammy's death, SNCC had been privately deliberating about the war. Writing and presenting the statement broke through the inertia that had gripped the organization. Gloria Larry helped draft the statement, honed after vigorous debate by SNCC's twenty-three-member executive committee and approved without objection. John Lewis, who two days earlier had requested that President Johnson send federal marshals to several Alabama counties, read the statement to Atlanta reporters.[15]

SNCC's words of fire reached the White House on Friday, January 7, prompting the Johnson administration to organize a counter-statement signed by prominent civil rights leaders. But Julian Bond, still basking in the glow of his recent election to the Georgia State House, told a reporter that he supported the statement, setting off a tsunami of negative publicity. Within days, Georgia's House voted to exclude a disbelieving Bond from taking his seat. Mainstream response to SNCC and Bond ranged from Roy Wilkins' artfully worded repudiation to more sustained criticism from *Time* and *The Wall Street Journal*. In private meetings with Vice President Hubert Humphrey, Wilkins and the head of the National Urban League, Whitney Young, urged Humphrey to rethink the administration's relationship with SNCC. Wilkins and Young characterized SNCC as the black sheep of the civil rights family deserving a reduced status. King floated above the fray, offering words of support for SNCC and leading a protest rally in Atlanta to the state capital, where he defended Bond's pacifist views.[16]

An essay by Carmichael in the January 8 *New Republic* was a prelude to the coming firestorm that would link antiwar protests with Black Power radicalism. In "Who Is Qualified?" Carmichael imagined a version of American democracy broad and deep enough to fulfill ancient yearnings of black strivers whose current living conditions echoed the nation's antebellum past. Intellectually provocative, analytically bold, and historically insightful, the essay drew from Carmichael's experiences in the Deep South. "I wouldn't be the first to point out the American capacity for self-delusion," he began gently. Black sharecroppers, he argued, lacked even "the education to get an education," a phenomenon aided and abetted, ironically, by a civil rights movement opening doors primarily to the well trained. "The South is not some odd, unique corner of the nation," he insisted, "it is super-America." Echoing James Baldwin's *The Fire Next Time*, Carmichael proceeded to outline another America where black exclusion remained a long-standing tradition. Blacks lacking the three criteria for inclusion in American society—

money, political connections, and education—belonged to a fraternity of the excluded that included poor whites too mesmerized by racial blinders to realize their membership in a national community of the dispossessed. "For a real end to exclusion in American society, that society would have to be so radically changed that the goal cannot really be defined as inclusion," he observed.[17]

In *The New Republic,* Stokely characterized democratic impulses emerging from Lowndes as a kind of small miracle produced in the aftermath of the Democratic Party's betrayal of "unqualified" black sharecroppers in Atlantic City. Radical democracy for Carmichael meant that poor blacks could not only exercise the vote but rise to political leadership at the local and national level. Rather than embrace a Democratic Party they recognized as "a crew of racist bullies and killers," blacks in Lowndes reached into what Martin Luther King characterized as the nation's "great wells of democracy" to sketch a more hopeful political future. "They wanted to redefine politics, make up new rules, and play the game with some personal integrity," wrote Carmichael in a succinct description of the Black Panther Party. "Out of a negative force, fear, grew the positive drive to think new."[18]

This last line captured the essence of independent organizing taking place in Lowndes. Efforts at organizing the Black Panther Party thrived as winter turned to spring. SNCC staff met twice weekly with local people to go over the nuances. Civics lessons about the power of citizenship and voting rights in Lowndes centered on the pragmatic use of local government that proved revelatory to blacks in Alabama. The use of pamphlets with hand-drawn cartoons illustrated the role of elected officials and the power of the vote. John Hulett, a local civil rights leader and one of only two blacks in the entire county who was registered to vote, facilitated SNCC's organizational inroads. Dark-skinned, intelligent, and wiry, Hulett, a native of Lowndes, had cut his teeth as an activist in Birmingham during the 1950s. A proud member of the NAACP, he had served as a bodyguard for Alabama civil rights leader Fred Shuttlesworth and provided security for Martin Luther King when he came to Birmingham. In 1959, Hulett returned home, with a shotgun, to take his place as both the family patriarch (his father was ill) and an American citizen. The combined efforts of Carmichael, SNCC workers, Hulett, and grassroots activists helped create what the best history of Lowndes called a "more democratic political culture rooted in freedom politics."[19]

Independent politics was formally introduced in Alabama on Saturday, April 2. It was the founding gathering of the Black Panther Party. "This meeting is very different from any other meeting taking place in the state because the candidates are not important," Carmichael observed. "It is the organization that is important."[20]

The decision to organize independently angered black power brokers and civil rights groups connected to the Democratic Party. While independent activists struggled to field a slate of Panther candidates, Carmichael and SNCC courted controversy by calling for blacks to boycott the May 3rd Democratic primary and vote for independent candidates in the fall general election. He claimed to be "unconcerned" about the possibility that the boycott might hurt the election hopes of black and white moderates, and even if it meant re-electing Selma's notoriously racist sheriff, Jim Clark, who, in a sign of moderation, recently stopped wearing a button emblazoned with the words "Never." Carmichael told a reporter that Clark's more moderate opponent would reward Democrats with unearned credibility in the black community. "To ask Negroes to get in the Democratic party is like asking Jews to join the Nazi party," he said. Courtland Cox echoed similar sentiments in more measured tones. "The Negro can't control the Democratic Party on the state or county levels in Alabama," Cox explained, "and he ought to organize something he can control."[21]

The New York Times called SNCC's organizing efforts in Alabama political sabotage. In an editorial the paper claimed that "extremist elements in Alabama's civil rights movement have adopted a rule-or-ruin attitude toward the forthcoming Democratic primary there that can only produce frustration and defeat for the state's Negroes." The rebuke served as a direct reply to Carmichael's defiant assertions that the election of segregationists in Alabama would illuminate the essentially bankrupt nature of the Democratic Party. SNCC's proposed boycott, according to the *Times*, represented "destructive mischief-making" and revolutionary posturing. The paper called for voting rights defined not by Alabama's black residents but by those who urged locals to "fuse their strength with liberal white voters" so as to achieve racial equality. Such criticism reflected the increasingly divergent meanings that terms such as democracy, freedom, and citizenship now had—a far cry from the theoretical abstractions of journalists and intellectuals. The Black Panther Party represented an embrace of a radical democratic vision, one that frightened the state's Democratic political machine and made mainstream civil rights groups uncomfortable.[22]

SNCC's call for independent black politics in Alabama set it on a collision course with the SCLC. Martin Luther King's organization was urging blacks to support liberal candidate Richmond Flowers in May's upcoming gubernatorial Democratic primary. In April, King spent six days traveling to seventeen different towns in Alabama, where he extolled a pragmatic vision of black political participation. For SNCC, King's visit capped off an unfortunate spectacle engineered by aide Hosea Williams in the weeks leading up to the primary. Relishing the role of political boss, Williams engaged in the kind of vulgar horse trading that Carmichael and SNCC deplored, arguing that since blacks knew little about politics and lacked the time to learn, they were required to support white candidates offering the best deal. Although King refused to demonize the concept of grassroots democracy, his tour of the Black Belt in support of the Democratic Party saddened SNCC's leadership and members. But Carmichael's hunch that Lowndes might answer national questions about politics and democracy proved to be the tip of the iceberg. Meanwhile, however, agitation for democracy in one tiny Black Belt county elicited open scorn from *The New York Times*, the SCLC, the NAACP, and the Democratic Party, which all tripped over themselves to repudiate a movement founded in the nation's bedrock political ethos.[23]

Local people in Lowndes acted as if they were too busy to notice criticism by northern white liberals. On May 3, nine hundred blacks in Lowndes County seized control of their political destiny by attending a nominating convention for seven local offices—including sheriff, tax assessor, and seats on the school board—at Haynesville's First Baptist Church, a half mile from the county courthouse. In the run-up to the convention, and as King toured the Black Belt, movement leaders had held nightly mass meetings, and Carmichael warned the Justice Department of imminent race war if the Black Panther convention was not allowed to take place in Hayneville. These efforts succeeded. Carmichael watched with unabashed pride as sharecroppers voted to place a Black Panther on the ballot for the upcoming November election. Surrounded by poll watchers, journalists, and locals, he observed volunteers check the paperwork of citizens attempting to cast their first vote. "We wanted to make it all legal," he told the crowd. The strict rules included ordering voters to keep guns from the polling place. During an inspection of one location, an elderly woman handed Stokely an ancient pistol. "Best you hol' this for me son," she said gently. "I'ma go cast my vote now. I'ma vote for the Panther an' go home."[24]

Memories of Jon Daniels' death almost certainly washed over Stokely that day. At one point, a photographer snapped a picture of Carmichael playfully hugging a little black girl and relaxing with residents outside the nominating convention. He was smiling broadly and casually dressed in a white shirt and jeans, and the photo captured a side of Carmichael that the press would often ignore. Just as in the Delta, local people in the rurals were inspired by Carmichael's courage, impressed by his intelligence, and enjoyed his robust sense of humor. He returned their affection in small and large ways, playing with children, respectfully greeting adults, and adopting traditional folkways as if they were his own. Interviewed by a journalist for *The Militant* newspaper shortly after the nominating convention, Carmichael exuded brash confidence. He found no difference between Alabama Governor George Wallace and Chicago Mayor Richard Daley. He claimed that observation as justification for blacks interested in racial and economic justice to "smash the Democratic Party" in Alabama and elsewhere. Carmichael tied the birth of the Black Panther in Lowndes to the lessons of Freedom Summer, where northern white support introduced political and organizational restraints. Bitter memories from Atlantic City made Carmichael reserve special enmity for the Democratic Party: "I talk about only the Democratic Party because it lied. And a lot of people don't know that yet. Negroes vote as a bloc in the Democratic Party but it lied. It said it was good, it said it was nice, it said it was liberal, it said it was for peace, it said it was for Negroes. And it lied. I know it lied."[25]

Despite this latest organizing success, Carmichael remained restless. The exhilaration produced by organizing victories proved short-lived. As one of the creators of the Black Panther symbol fast inspiring black militants around the country, Carmichael might have ridden to fame on this basis alone if not for a fateful return to Mississippi. Election day in Lowndes marked the end of his life as a local organizer. Within two months, millions of Americans would come to know him as a larger-than-life agitator: the twenty-five-year-old SNCC chairman and black revolutionary whose Black Power call resounded through the nation like a war cry.

CHAPTER EIGHT

The Meredith March

May 8–June 29, 1966

STOKELY CARMICHAEL'S ELECTION AS SNCC CHAIRMAN ON THE HEELS OF the Lowndes County vote made him the organization's national face. The episode carried its own mythology, since John Lewis had initially won re-election before losing after a second vote was called on procedural grounds. Carmichael's victory signaled the strength and political skills of staff connected to Howard University and supportive of the politics associated with the Black Panther Party and independent organizing. The "de-election" marked the beginning of the end of the heartbroken Lewis' relationship with SNCC and fractured his friendship with Carmichael. He would blame the entire fiasco on the departing Jim Forman. Ruby Doris Smith Robinson took over as executive secretary from Forman, and Cleve Sellers retained his position as program secretary. The symbolism attached to Carmichael's victory altered SNCC's public visage. Future historians would cite his chairmanship as the beginning of the group's decline, marking its evolution from a tiny nonviolent priesthood into a fervid and doctrinaire organization that turned its back on the very democratic impulses that its creation had spurred. The narrative cast Carmichael as the charismatic young leader who singlehandedly corrupted the most important grassroots civil rights organization of the era. Carmichael's election helped transition SNCC in the public imagination from the remarkable collection of activists whom Harry Belafonte memorably characterized as "the combat troops of democracy" to a group of militant black nationalists whose experiences in the South burdened them with overwhelming racial trauma.[1]

And now came one of the crucial turning points in Stokely Carmichael's life. James Meredith, who integrated the University of Mississippi in 1962, began a one-man march through the Magnolia State. On the second day of his journey, he was shot and injured. Meredith's solo trek was inspired by his belief that a black man should be able to walk through Mississippi without fear. His subsequent injuries turned into an unexpected rallying point for movement leaders, most notably Carmichael. Meredith's shooting in Mississippi sparked national sympathy demonstrations and an outpouring of support from civil rights leaders, including Stokely, who interrupted his tour of SNCC projects upon hearing the news. The Associated Press's Nashville bureau reported just after 6:30 P.M. that Meredith had been killed, an error traced back to a journalist mistaking a Memphis reporter's statement that Meredith had been shot "in the head" for Meredith "had been shot dead." Despite a correction less than an hour later, much of the first wave of radio and television reports parroted the AP's early coverage. From Chicago, comedian and activist Dick Gregory vowed to march eight hours from the place where Meredith had been shot. Roy Wilkins, fresh off a plane from Washington, expressed shock when reporters told him the news. CORE's new chairman, Floyd McKissick, promised to recruit one thousand volunteers to finish the march while the group's ousted leader, James Farmer, claimed the shooting illustrated the movement's unfinished business. In Atlanta, King called the shooting a "dastardly act" and promised to visit Meredith at Bowld Hospital immediately. James Lawson arrived at the Memphis airport in a station wagon large enough to seat nine and chauffeured both expected (King) and unexpected (Carmichael) civil rights leaders to Bowld. Since meeting Carmichael six years earlier, Lawson took an instant liking to him but remained baffled, even after all of these years, by Stokely's behavior (he had not informed Lawson of his arrival).[2]

The Meredith March in Mississippi from June 7 to 26, 1966, turned Carmichael into an icon. Symbolically, it introduced a new generation of leadership to the national civil rights landscape. Carmichael became an overnight media sensation and the nation's most important black radical since Malcolm X. The march represented the last great demonstration of the civil rights era's heroic period and the first national glimpse of the Black Power Movement that Carmichael would come to personify and lead. Debates over nonviolence versus self-defense grabbed headlines, but the march revealed deeper fault lines. Mississippi exposed tensions between the civil rights old guard and new faces over the trustworthiness of Lyndon Johnson, the sincerity of white liberals, and the movement's overall direction. The phrase "Black Power" effectively harnessed the political movement (previously led by Malcolm X) that had paralleled and intersected, like a fever dream, with civil rights struggles all along. Carmichael, through the act of naming this unacknowledged force in American politics, turned the Meredith March into a watershed historical event. Forevermore, the civil rights movement would be defined by what occurred before and after this march. Carmichael now took his place alongside Martin Luther King as one of America's two most important black political leaders. Carmichael used his one-year tenure as SNCC chairman to thrust himself into the stratosphere of American politics, emerging as the youngest black leader of national repute since a twenty-six-year-old King burst onto the national scene during the Montgomery bus boycott. While his use of the term "Black Power" in Mississippi served as his national launching pad into the rarified world that straddled political controversy and celebrity, his rich experience as an organizer ensured him of a kind of enduring longevity that would outlast most of his contemporaries.

He experienced his first weeks as SNCC chairman through a blur of interviews, press conferences, and speaking appearances. Carmichael sparked immediate controversy by declining an invitation to the White House Civil Rights Conference. On Monday, May 23, Carmichael, clad in sharecropper's overalls and accompanied by Ruby Doris Smith Robinson and Cleve Sellers, read a prepared statement accusing Lyndon Johnson of violating "the human rights of colored people in Vietnam" and, as if further provocation were necessary, questioned the relevancy of racial integration. They refused to meet the president on the grounds that the Vietnam War made him an unsuitable human rights advocate. "Political and economic power," insisted Carmichael, "is what the black people have to have."[3]

The New York Times treated Carmichael's election as a major event. It published a photo of him talking to a sharecropper in Alabama underneath a caption that read: "BLACK PANTHER." The accompanying story balanced fear that SNCC remained vulnerable to foreign ideologies (including communism) with the truth that the group still practiced nonviolence and retained white organizers: "Mr. Carmichael does not advocate violence but neither does he believe in turning the other cheek." Like Malcolm X, he rejected the notion that all black institutions bred inferiority. "White schools are best, all right," explained Carmichael, "but only because they get more money than the Negro schools." Perhaps based on his personal experiences at Bronx Science, he described communism as passé. "We don't have any master plans," he noted. "We just believe in putting power in the hands of the poor and letting them make their own plans." *Time* magazine predicted that Carmichael's election would transform an organization already considered "the most aggressive of the civil rights groups, sometimes appalling older outfits by its sheer bullheadedness." SNCC's recent work in Alabama attested to a tenacity that, *Time* admitted, retained a certain emotional power but ultimately presented a political dead end.[4]

Newsweek characterized SNCC's changing of the guard as a figurative "Growl of the Panther" fueled by a combustible mixture of radical politics and avant-garde posturing. Instructively, in an assessment repeated until it became part of the historical record, *Newsweek* contrasted this new incarnation of SNCC with a nostalgic past of interracial activists who had organized 1964's Freedom Summer. The article's lingering image, besides that of a snarling Panther foisted on the movement by Carmichael, was its description of the new chairman effusively discussing SNCC's embrace of black empowerment in southern politics while John Lewis cleaned out his desk in the background. "Coalition's no good," explained Carmichael to the reporter. "'Cause what happens when a bunch of Negroes joins in with a bunch of whites?" he asked rhetorically. "They get absorbed, that's what. They have to surrender too much to join. . . . Black people got to act as a black community, and the Democratic and Republican Parties are completely irrelevant to them." This was a declaration of war borne from experience in Atlantic City two years earlier and more recent struggles in Lowndes. "I know we're gonna be on the outside now, we're gonna be on our own," he said. "But we've learned, in the past six years of trying to redeem the white man, that we don't have any alternative now but to go this way." Washington columnists Rowland Evans and Robert Novak memorialized the "good" SNCC and its 1960 heyday as "idealistic college students" whose courage stood in stark contrast to the contemporary radicals poised to betray the larger civil rights effort. In a preview of future press coverage of the coming Black Power phenomenon, *The New Republic* sprinkled outright distortion (that Lowndes County blacks disallowed whites in their movement) on top of a posture of bewildered disappointment. In the *New York Post,* Roy Wilkins called SNCC a group of "black racists" whose political line represented a perverse inversion of South Africa's apartheid regime. Unable to acknowledge that the group's project in Alabama could be both pro-black and integrationist in its embrace of democratic principles, Wilkins added to the national condemnation of Carmichael's SNCC.[5]

THE MARCH AFFORDED CARMICHAEL an extended opportunity to spend time with Martin Luther King, one he would make good use of politically and personally. Privately the thirty-seven-year-old King and the twenty-four-year-old Carmichael enjoyed each other's company. They found common ground in a shared love for black culture, books, and philosophy. Both men loved the rural customs and unadorned folkways of southern black culture. Their relationship stretched back to the early 1960s when Carmichael, then a student at Howard, represented SNCC at a seminar in nonviolence that King conducted in Washington. During the Summer Project, Carmichael had hosted King, chauffeured him from the airport, arranged for his meals and accommodation, and provided a bodyguard for his stay in Greenwood. Over time, King and Carmichael's cordial acquaintanceship grew into a deeper friendship. The more established King adopted an almost fatherly mien with the young SNCC leader whom he hosted for intimate dinners in his Atlanta home.[6]

Organizers of the Meredith March hoped to compel the placement of federal voter registrars in Mississippi counties where the black vote remained embattled. Grenada, Tallahatchie, Bolivar, Scott, Holmes, Panola, Hinds, Quitman, Tunica, and Sunflower would never roll off the tongue of most Americans but in a very real sense represented the battleground for democracy in Mississippi. The demonstration aimed to register black voters in parts of America that had last experienced glimpses of genuine democracy in the nineteenth century.[7]

The Meredith March officially began on Tuesday, June 7. Centenary Methodist Church on Mississippi Boulevard in Memphis served as the march headquarters, and SNCC staff issued a stream of telegrams alerting national contacts of their plans. During a bedside visit with Meredith in Memphis, King promised reporters that they were planning a march that would dwarf Selma's. At a press conference Carmichael, in a T-shirt and jeans, appeared restless and sullen sitting next to King, who was wearing a suit and tie, while a bearded and grim-faced Cleve Sellers listened in the background. King suggested that the march's purpose was to drag Mississippi's race relations into the twentieth century and renew pressure on Lyndon Johnson to fulfill the sacred promises on behalf of blacks that he had frequently made. "We want to put President Johnson on the spot," said Carmichael.[8]

The day began modestly with about two dozen marchers walking in ninety-degree heat broken by intermittent rain showers. Dick Gregory and his wife, Lillian, led a small group headed north toward Memphis, symbolically retracing Meredith's steps. He quipped to reporters that it was safer for a man to walk in outer space than for a Negro to travel in Mississippi. "If one shot from the bushes can frighten a whole nation," Gregory mused, "we're in trouble." The main group traveled south on Highway 51 and almost immediately ran into trouble after state troopers ordered them off of the road. With their arms linked together, Carmichael, King, McKissick, and Sellers continued to step forward. King told one officer that they would continue to march on to Jackson, and in an instant the entire group was forced off the road. Sellers fell down to the mud on one knee but retained enough strength to balance a wobbly King, the startled victim of an officer's shove. Preparing to take the blow meant for King, Carmichael lunged forward only to be held back by King, still clutching tightly to his right hand. "Get Stokely," King pleaded to no one in particular, "somebody, lay on him." Sensing the possibility of instant disaster, King led the group into a parley on the side of the road near an ice cream stand as an agitated Carmichael demanded reporters grant them a moment.[9]

The brief conference clarified a course of action to march on the side of the road single file. State troopers periodically photographed the demonstrators, behavior that inspired photojournalists to do the same to the troopers. Cars filled with gawking passengers drove by out of curiosity or anger or both. Black Mississippians living in shacks that occasionally dotted the landscape came out to see the fuss. Women and children dressed in frayed cotton smocks nervously responded to solicitations to look, smile, or even join. King's chants of "Freedom!" competed with SNCC's cries of "Uhuru!," Swahili for "Freedom!" Reporters, overhearing discussions along the march, noticed that King and Carmichael bonded over mutual contempt for white moderates. "We were looking for white moderates in Alabama," Carmichael ruefully observed while marching. "Now we're looking for white moderates in Mississippi." His words set off an impromptu search for "the most ironic definition" of the term, which came by way of King. "He's interested more in order than justice," he explained. Complaints of muddy shoes did little to dampen the day's high spirits. When they neared the town of Coldwater in De Soto County, they concluded for the day.[10]

Back in Memphis, an overflow crowd of one thousand rallied at a mass meeting of local and national leaders. Charles Evers, the ambitious and temperamental brother of the martyred Medgar, drew cheers with a line about playing the role of a black cowboy against white vigilantes. Roy Wilkins and Whitney Young touted the moment as an opportunity to pass new civil rights legislation. Waves of applause greeted Carmichael's flat refusal to plead for rights guaranteed at birth. "I'm not trying to beg the white man for anything I deserve," he said. "I'm going to take it." Floyd McKissick produced the evening's most memorable line in a scathing reference to the Statue of Liberty. "They ought to break that young lady's legs and throw her in the Mississippi," remarked the disgusted CORE leader. King paid tribute to Meredith's courage and offered a cautious optimism that balanced out the doleful nature of the evening's speeches. "We can transfer a dark yesterday into a bright tomorrow," he said.[11]

Competitive debate over strategy continued past midnight at Memphis's Lorraine Motel, where less than two years later King would be assassinated. Wilkins' imperious nature contrasted with King's humble demeanor and strained his relationship with Carmichael. The Urban League's dashing president, Whitney Young, matched Wilkins' austere racial politics. Their business-oriented civil rights approach prized compromise over demonstrations and legal covenants above emotional protests. Wilkins and Young joined King, SCLC aide Bernard Lee, Stanley Wise of SNCC, McKissick, Sellers, and Carmichael for the planning session and immediately made their presence felt by insisting that SNCC (represented by Carmichael and Sellers) would be entitled to only one vote.[12]

In person, Carmichael and Wilkins instantly recognized each other as enemies. Beyond personal enmity, there were several sticking points. The Deacons for Defense and Justice, an armed black self-defense unit operating in parts of Louisiana and Mississippi, would provide march security. The group's advocacy of armed self-defense rubbed Wilkins and Young the wrong way. The dispute over the Deacons was resolved after King agreed to let the Deacons protect civil rights workers as long as the march remained nonviolent. Both Wilkins and Young found the planned march manifesto's critique of the Johnson administration too radical for their taste. King moderated what turned into a withering debate between Wilkins (born 1901),

Young (1921), and Stokely (1941), three generations of civil rights activists. Wilkins outlined a plan designed to leverage the Meredith shooting into legislative progress on the upcoming civil rights bill while maintaining a cordial relationship with the White House, a perspective that Young enthusiastically endorsed. McKissick sided with Carmichael on the crucial points of including local people in the march and the participation of the Deacons. King struck a middle course, finding value in both sides, but agreed to the radical manifesto. At one point a visibly angry and sleep-deprived Carmichael dispatched Wilkins and Young with intellectual and political arguments and started to scream and curse at them. Carmichael responded to their continued defense of the Johnson administration by attacking "that cat the president," a remark that made Wilkins livid. "Don't give me any of 'that cat the president' crap, Stokely," he snapped, before departing.[13]

MARTIN LUTHER KING BEGAN Wednesday's march by reading a contentious manifesto that described Mississippi as a living symbol of "every evil that American Negroes have long endured." Reading words reminiscent of the tone used by black America's martyred prosecuting attorney—Malcolm X—King issued a "public indictment" against moral and political failures rooted in racial discrimination that stretched from Mississippi to the federal government. As they walked down the highway beneath an oppressive sun, verdant crops growing in red earth added grave beauty to the scene. Demonstrators traveling by motorcade to rendezvous at Coldwater joked about the gleaming blue "Welcome to Mississippi" road sign just inside of De Soto County. "We're going to walk straight south," said King, as if bracing military troops for another day of battle.[14]

The text of the official Manifesto of the Meredith Mississippi Freedom March was released on Thursday. Intended as a "massive public indictment and protest of the failure of American society, the government, and the state of Mississippi," the document characterized the Magnolia State as symbolizing historic evils against black citizens. Four demands were addressed to Lyndon Johnson: a request for 600 mobile federal registrars to patrol the Deep South; a presidential directive to "actively enforce existing federal law to protect the rights of all Americans"; an amendment to the proposed 1966 civil rights bill to expand jury provisions to include proportional black representation and extend Title VII of the 1964 Civil Rights Act to allow state and local governments to hire more black law enforcement officials; and a budget to ensure economic opportunity and political self-determination for blacks in the urban North and rural South.[15]

While organizers awaited reaction to their manifesto, the demonstration continued. It was a day marked by unusually cool temperatures in the 60s. Twenty-six whites joined a group of 155 people on Friday. King's absence left Carmichael, Ralph Abernathy, and McKissick as the most visible leaders. In Sardis, where the group ate lunch at St. Matthew Missionary Baptist Church, their ranks swelled to over two hundred. Carmichael spoke to reporters about turning Mississippi into what one journalist correctly described as "a black power base." He promised that SNCC would "break open all of these counties and get people organized for black power." During a lunch break, Carmichael rang an enormous, ancient plantation bell housed on a church ground that, in another era, summoned enslaved Africans from cotton fields. Now, the crowd chanted "Freedom" every time it tolled. Journalists contrasted the belligerent demeanor on display in Mississippi with a more soothing portrait of 1965's Selma-to-Montgomery voting rights demonstration. Traveling through "virgin territory" untouched by civil rights protests, Carmichael exemplified, according to one reporter, a "truculence never shown in the Alabama demonstration."[16]

On Sunday, June 12, King discussed new plans to detour through some of the Delta's nether regions, where the majestic presence of dignified marchers would inspire black voter registration. The new route would extend the march through June 26, requiring an extra week of logistical planning, strategy sessions, and evening rallies. Teams of canvassers set out to rally large swaths of the Delta, which stretched from Vicksburg to Memphis buffeted by the Yazoo and Mississippi Rivers. Throughout the day, organizers bantered with sharecroppers, temporarily halting the cotton hoeing for impromptu civics lessons. A busload of seventy-five new arrivals from Chicago increased the group to over 250 by the afternoon, and the line moved forward about four miles before returning to their campsite in the small town of Enid for the evening.[17]

Stokely missed Monday's march for a SNCC meeting in Atlanta called in part to stem the growing tide of negative media reports. In Atlanta, Carmichael contrasted what he characterized as SNCC's nuanced definition of racial integration with media stereotypes that portrayed him as an advocate of racial separatism. His ten-minute opening address meditated on SNCC's efforts to weave America's racial and economic crises together despite the media's stubborn refusal. The national conversation about race pivoted on examples of blacks attempting to gain access to all-white schools, neighborhoods, and communities instead of addressing why such integration was necessary. In the American imagination, integration remained a one-way street where a handful of qualified blacks invaded mainstream society. "No other groups in the country have to move out of their neighborhood to get a good house in another neighborhood," he said. "And there's no need for black people to have to move out of their neighborhood to find good housing."[18]

Cleve Sellers, Carmichael's best friend and confidant, noticed a closeness develop between Martin Luther King, Stokely, and himself along the march route. King proved open to discussing the need for a positive black racial identity, that is, for what young militants like Sellers and Carmichael were calling "black consciousness." For Sellers, King's behavior proved revelatory. "He turned out to be easygoing, with a delightful sense of humor. We had an opportunity during the discussions to present our ideas and our approach to struggle. His mind was open and we were surprised to find that he was much less conservative than we initially imagined," Sellers would write in his autobiography. For SNCC activists in Mississippi, the Meredith March had the unanticipated effect of redeeming King. The march allowed Sellers, Carmichael, and others to see King through new eyes.[19]

Marchers arrived in tiny Grenada on Tuesday, June 14, Flag Day (which honors the American, not the Confederate, flag). With a population of less than eight thousand, Grenada's reputation as "a white supremacist stronghold" made it a dangerous target. King arrived back from Chicago, and the swelling line doubled to five hundred when they passed through Grenada's black section. They had walked nine miles, and freedom songs and jubilant chants accompanied them as they crossed the Yalobusha River Bridge, beckoning locals to join them. Downtown, protesters placed an American flag atop a monument of Jefferson Davis, the still-beloved Confederate president. CORE's George Raymond and the SCLC's Robert Green publicly mocked the statue. "Give us the flag of freedom," bellowed Green. Raymond climbed on top of Davis' likeness and called him a "joker." Hundreds of seething white bystanders watched the proceedings as demonstrators cheered. Signs for segregated bathrooms had mysteriously disappeared, so town officials put them back up, as black marchers lined up to use the white washrooms anyway.[20]

Five hundred blacks spontaneously gathered at the courthouse that evening in hopes of registering to vote. "If we can't registrate, we're going to demonstrate!" they shouted, playfully creating a new word to rhyme. The march continued, unexpectedly, into the night. It had been a day of heightened energy on the part of protesters and weary resignation from officials whose patience now reached its breaking point. After highway patrolmen led the march from Grenada's poorly lit black section to the courthouse's brick headquarters in the business center, King expressed disappointment over broken promises to keep registration offices open. As bewilderment turned to anger, King met privately with police officials before addressing the tense crowd from the base of the Confederate monument, where he preached a message of determined patience, announced a new agreement with city officials to hire black registrars, and implored marchers to come out in greater numbers the next day. The dramatic breakthrough in Grenada gave the march a temporary narrative of slow but steady progress. In contrast to Selma's epic battle and relatively straightforward cast of heroes and villains, the Meredith Mississippi March had offered a portrait of the movement as a fragmented hodgepodge of competing interests. Victory in Grenada inspired what one reporter characterized as a "new mood" among marchers. With spirits secure in the triumph of dozens of black voters registered by six newly hired black schoolteachers, the march continued its ambitious detour into the Delta.[21]

Carmichael returned to Mississippi on Wednesday, June 15, in time to visit familiar Delta towns. "I woke up this morning to find out that there were riots in Florida and Chicago," he wrote to Lorna Smith, a sixty-eight-year-old white Freedom Summer volunteer who became close to Stokely in Mississippi and remained a loyal friend amid the Black Power controversy. "I do not know what it will take to make the people in this country realize the danger we're in." He maintained that blacks needed to create "institutions through which they can carry on with the democratic processes."[22]

He maintained a faith in radical democracy, but one tied to the ability of blacks to transform political institutions:

> While SNCC will never become a racist organization, there has to
> be an understanding that the black people who need us most in this

country are the disenfranchised black people. And if in fact, people
are to move on they must build black institutions through which they
can carry on with the democratic processes. That means they must
have political and economic institutions that they control. That isn't
to say they are anti-white. We are going to divert our energies to help
build these institutions.

Smith's relationship with Carmichael took shape two years earlier, when
she served as a volunteer in Greenwood working out of SNCC's ad hoc library during Freedom Summer. Smith traced her political love affair to a
chance encounter when Stokely unexpectedly served as a chauffeur to a mass
meeting in Greenwood. Smith sat entranced as Stokely spoke before an audience of six hundred "with such power, carrying the audience." She predicted
on the spot "that if left alive" Carmichael was destined for greatness. In one
of her letters to Stokely, Smith cheerfully recounted how her seventeen-year-
old granddaughter had just received an A after mesmerizing high school
classmates with a civil rights presentation using her grandmother's Stokely
Carmichael scrapbook. Smith's devotion to setting the record straight about
Carmichael's recent election made for the striking, seemingly contradictory
picture of a white female senior citizen passionately defending Stokely to local SNCC supporters and serving as an informal fundraiser, publicist, and
press liaison. To combat media-fueled rumors that SNCC had dispatched its
white leadership, Smith quoted verbatim from a recent telephone conversation with Stokely: "There has been no split in SNCC. No white members have
been thrown out. White members are on the National Board. Concentration
in the future is to be on bloc voting, as the only method Negroes can win an
election in the South." Smith's renegade appreciation for Carmichael's and
SNCC's embrace of black political self-determination made her one of the
few whites whose respect for Stokely increased after his Black Power advocacy. She compared him to her childhood hero, Upton Sinclair, the muckrak-
ing social-democratic writer, and hoped that her dreams for him would be
"accomplished by your wonderful mind" rather than political violence associated with black militancy. Smith defended Carmichael before despairing
white friends based on a nuanced understanding of Stokely's political beliefs.
"I'll have faith in you," she wrote, "until you give me cause not to have." In lieu
of an imagined break that would never come, Smith fired off angry letters
to magazines and newspapers correcting the latest anti-Carmichael screed,

fondly recalled dinner with Stokely at her son's "hillside home in Orinda" during the winter of 1966, and devoted her political energies to counseling fading white liberals about the way in which Black Power enhanced, rather than negated, their collective moral responsibility toward the promotion of racial justice.[23]

Carmichael, who had always found reading Smith's remarkable letters cathartic, now discovered similar relief in writing to her. Their deepening friendship served as a hidden testament against myths about Carmichael's hardening anti-white attitude fast becoming legend. "We are working in this country for true integration," wrote Carmichael, which meant that whites and blacks would have to move into each other's neighborhoods at an equal pace. "Until you have this," he observed, "you do not have true integration." He concluded his letter by disclosing his thinking behind the upcoming foray in the Delta. "I can't think of anything nice to say except that I rerouted the March on Mississippi through Greenwood in memory of you."[24]

Grenada's hospitality and the cooperation of state officials curdled as the march traveled from Holcomb to Greenwood escorted by a diminished police contingent, arbitrarily reduced from twenty to four. Governor Paul B. Johnson Jr. complained at a press conference that he refused to "wetnurse a bunch of showmen" and traced the reversal of his decision to offer demonstrators maximum protection to the march's unexpected metamorphosis into a traveling voter registration campaign. The governor's erratic behavior added to a day filled with shifting moods.[25]

Meanwhile, more than a week of walking through Mississippi took its toll on morale. Black workers in the tent kitchen admonished white volunteers for discarding plastic utensils, luggage was routinely lost or misplaced, cars were late for pickups, and bathrooms were scarce at many rest stops. Some drew strength from the rough conditions while others passed time cracking jokes, singing, and sketching portraits and cartoons of fellow demonstrators. Two veterans from Selma's more celebrated march stubbornly retained their commitment to weather the storm: James Leather was the one-legged supporter who walked a few miles on crutches each day, and Mississippi native Henry Smith proudly sported his rose-colored lapel pin attesting to his having trekked the entire way from Selma to Montgomery.[26]

Charles Evers, one of the march's sternest critics, rejoined, convinced, he claimed, of the potency and sincerity of its voter registration outreach. Recovering from his home in Pleasantville, New York, James Meredith questioned the NAACP's support, remarking that he disapproved of the group's cozy relationship with the Johnson administration. The unexpected momentum forced Whitney Young to reconsider his withdrawal, and the Urban League's involvement now hinged on Meredith's return. By the time the march wound its way through Carroll County in Greenwood, minor insults had escalated into outright humiliation as city officials refused permission to camp on the grounds of a black elementary school.[27]

Carmichael remained composed on Thursday afternoon as he drove past the proposed campsite, Stone Street Negro School, and observed police talking with activists putting up tents. "That ain't no problem," he said. "We'll put them up anyway." He based his decision on having received prior permission from local black leaders. In defiance of police commissioner B.A. Hammond's warning, Carmichael walked over and placed his hand on a tent and was immediately arrested along with SNCC field secretary Robert Smith and CORE activist Bruce Baines.

The picture of Carmichael being handcuffed by two police officers made the front page of the next day's *New York Times*, while the *Los Angeles Times*'s second-page photo captured an indelible image of a nightstick-wielding officer descending upon Stokely, just as he began to raise the tent. For Willie Ricks, whose canvassing missions in the Delta included voter outreach and testing SNCC's new Black Power slogan on unsuspecting sharecroppers, Carmichael's arrest offered an irresistible opportunity. Ricks' infectious belief in social justice, as well as his ability to convey this belief instantly to strangers through speeches that both exhorted and cajoled, made him one of Stokely's most effective political surrogates. For the next several hours, like a rogue pied piper, Ricks primed the crowd for Carmichael's return, which came more than five hours later, after he had posted a $100 bond.[28]

Stokely's appearance at Broad Street Park electrified six hundred supporters. With Ricks by his side urging him to unveil the new slogan, Carmichael gave a brief history of his deep political ties to Greenwood's black community. "This is the twenty-seventh time that I've been arrested. I ain't going to jail no more," he told the large crowd. He repeated the last line for emphasis: "I ain't going to jail no more." Blacks would never achieve justice without the capacity for self-rule, he said. Carmichael spoke in a language that distilled the hopes, fears, and anguish of an emerging generation of black liberation advocates. "All we've been doing is begging the federal government," he insisted. "The only thing we can do is take over."[29]

What the black community must now start proclaiming, he said, was "Black Power!" Like a preacher standing before an outdoor flock of hungry parishioners, Carmichael began a rhythmic call and response. "We want Black Power!" he repeated five times in rapid succession. "Black Power!" came back the reply each time. Carmichael's desire that Magnolia State courthouses "be burned down" in order "to get rid of the dirt" drew howls of approval. "Everybody owns our own neighborhoods except us," he explained. "We outnumber the whites in this county; we want black power." He repeated the phrase again, as both he and Ricks had done since the march's first days. "That's what we want. Black Power!"[30]

CARMICHAEL'S SPEECH ON JUNE 16, 1966, instantly transformed the aesthetics of the black freedom struggle and forever altered the course of the modern civil rights movement. For Stokely, the power of ideas mattered only if they were applicable in the real world. He now defined Black Power, or political, economic, and cultural self-determination, as the vehicle for achieving radical democracy in America. Black Power became a transcendent call for a new generation of political activists even as it echoed centuries-long struggles for political self-determination. "These ideas and feelings had been building up," Carmichael would recall later, "building and percolating upward from the grass roots of our struggle for years, especially during the 1960s." A natural-born communicator whose speech, voice inflections, and stage presence remained influenced by his Trinidadian childhood, Bronx and Harlem adolescence, college years in Washington, and time spent among sharecroppers in Mississippi and Alabama, Carmichael commanded the stage as a new kind of black radical. The speech's critical phrasing and raw emotion lent a measure of urgency to the entire proceedings, as did Carmichael's habit of gesturing, by slashing his hands through the air and pointing, for emphasis. The backdrop of Greenwood's night made Carmichael's eyes glow against the evening darkness. His bronze skin, erect frame, and passionate demeanor evoked images of the Harlem street speakers he had attentively listened to as a teenager. Carmichael's tendency to make fun of black preachers obscured his respect for their mesmerizing oratory; he admired their sense of timing, cadence, and showmanship. His rhetorical flair, previously confined to movement circles, gained a national audience that evening. For the rest of the march, people would be discussing Black Power as a critical turning point in the national civil rights struggle and Stokely as its spokesman. The speech, which appeared spontaneous, represented the culmination of strategic debates within SNCC. Greenwood, SNCC's strongest base in the Delta and a place where both residents and the police chief knew Carmichael, proved to be the perfect launching pad for a slogan that would soon resonate around the world.[31]

King returned to Mississippi on Friday, June 17, with the major controversy over Carmichael's Black Power speech still swirling. During an early morning meeting, King asked Carmichael to stop using the Black Power slogan, a suggestion he rejected while insisting that the term's use reflected an organizational, rather than individual, decision. As a thousand people gathered under a broiling sun at a large rally outside the Leflore County Courthouse in Greenwood, King softened the charged undercurrent swirling around Carmichael's Thursday night speech by defining Black Power as the ability to wrest concessions from white authority on the road to interracial brotherhood. "We are here because we are tired of being beaten, tired of being murdered," said King. From the courthouse steps, he defined Black Power as the "ability to make the power structure say yes even when it wants to say no," a development that the *Los Angeles Times* suggested made Carmichael and King appear to be speaking "with almost one voice."[32]

Carmichael echoed aspects of King's speech in sharper terms. "The only way we can change Mississippi is with the ballot," he urged. "That's black power." Carmichael proposed Black Power as both a political philosophy and a radical framework for expanding democracy through local political power. Blacks needed to shed their embarrassment over being black and elect a sheriff whose broad nose, thick lips, and kinky hair reflected a symbol of power rather than a source of shame. "That doesn't mean we are anti-white," he said. "We are just developing pride."[33]

Sunday, June 19, saw Stokely's debut on a nationally broadcast news interview show. As the march gained momentum in Belzoni, he went to Washington to appear on CBS's *Face the Nation*. In a suit and tie, Carmichael projected an aura of serene confidence (mindful of advice he had received from black journalist William Worthy about his demeanor on national television) as he sparred with reporters about the merits of Black Power. The discussion found Carmichael defending political self-determination as the movement's logical next step as *Face the Nation*'s moderator, Martin Agronsky, and *Boston Globe* reporter James Doyle pressed him on his willingness to use violence. His calm demeanor turned the discussion into an intellectual debate on the merits of American democracy as practiced by black sharecroppers. Carmichael's admission that he viewed nonviolence as "a technique" rather than a philosophy surprised Agronsky and Doyle, and he once again purposefully linked domestic racial struggles with Vietnam. Since America justified "dropping bombs in Vietnam to ensure free elections there," Carmichael observed, the nation could afford "to do no less for freedom in Mississippi." After all, he explained, "there is no reason why black people should be fighting for free elections when they don't have it in their own country." Carmichael spent the rest of his national television debut presenting an alternative civil rights narrative, rooting landmark voting rights legislation in racial uprisings, maintaining the right of local black communities to gain political self-rule by any means necessary, and highlighting racial oppression's almost invisible economic contours.[34]

Stokely's *Face the Nation* appearance was the first of two nationally televised interviews related to the march that Sunday. That evening, the man whose shooting had inspired the march, James Meredith, appeared on NBC's *Meet the Press.* There, he casually recounted how FBI agents stood by and watched him get shot.

Carmichael's national television appearance coincided with the media's reappraisal of the march. "What began as a disorganized contentious assembly of civil rights leaders who couldn't agree on strategy," observed James Doyle, had become a courageous assault against regimes of racial segregation that remained largely out of sight, tucked away in tiny hamlets, "those little Faulknerian towns for which the Mississippi delta is infamous."[35]

Jet magazine, which had published horrific images of Emmett Till for a generation of black activists including Stokely, offered extensive coverage of the march in its latest issue, which featured James Meredith on the cover. *Jet* identified Carmichael as a new breed of radical, and accompanying photos featured him and King leading marchers on a bridge from DeSoto County into Tate County, Mississippi, known as "Terrible Tate." The story recounted Carmichael's scuffle with state troopers at the march's outset as depicting a shifting mood among blacks, a changing of the guard illustrated by Stokely's confession to the magazine that he had been prepared to die at that moment.[36]

As Carmichael recalled bleeding for democracy in the pages of *Jet*, King spoke in Philadelphia, Mississippi, on Tuesday, June 21, at a memorial for

Freedom Summer martyrs Michael Schwerner, James Chaney, and Andrew Goodman. King's stately presence did little to halt violence as local whites assaulted marchers and newsmen during the day and terrorized the black community at night. Main line marchers traveled a distance of forty miles into Sunflower County to canvass for voters, and SNCC field secretary Charles McLaurin led groups of local blacks in Black Power chants in front of sullen whites at the new courthouse downtown. A late-arriving Ralph Abernathy tried to temper "Black Power!" with rival chants of "Freedom!" That evening, King addressed a large rally in Yazoo City, where his calls for interracial cooperation resonated with listeners more than Willie Ricks' passionate Black Power appeals.[37]

Violence on Tuesday in Philadelphia followed the march into Canton on Thursday. In the afternoon, Carmichael and King led two columns to Canton's courthouse, as sheriff's deputies stalked the lawn grounds beneath magnolias. "The time for running has come to an end," proclaimed Carmichael, slicing the air with his finger as he spoke. "You tell them white folks in Mississippi that all the scared niggers is dead! They've shot all the rabbits, now they'll have to deal with the men!" With just over twenty-five miles to Jackson, protesters ran into the mercurial nature of Mississippi's racial politics that evening after being denied permission to camp on the grounds of a local black school. After a rally at the Madison County Courthouse, Carmichael ordered the crowd toward the school to erect tents in spite of opposition. A parade of one thousand singing marchers walked fifteen blocks to McNeal Elementary School's athletic field recruiting more foot soldiers along the way.[38]

Organizers and demonstrators worked by flashlight erecting tents in the dark. At 8:40 P.M., troopers warned the assembled to disperse and within minutes released tear gas canisters into a group of 2,500 demonstrators. A thousand more receded into the night, frightened by the sight of approaching police decked out in helmets and gas masks. Seventy-five Mississippi highway state patrolmen originally dispatched to protect demonstrators reversed course and fired tear gas and indiscriminately pummeled them. Carmichael and McKissick led chants of "Pitch the tents!" and leaders attempted to restore order as crowds scurried away from the school grounds. A gas canister struck Carmichael in the chest, flooding him with painful memories of Cambridge, Maryland, when he was hospitalized after exposure to tear gas. Over thirty years later, he could still vividly see the serene King's calm amid the "sickening thud of blows" directed at helpless women and children. "They were kicking and clubbing people lying on the floor to escape the gas," he remembered.[39]

Troopers assaulted a Roman Catholic priest with a shotgun butt and tackled a freelance photographer, throwing him into a ditch. Odessa Warwick, a veteran demonstrator who last faced down authorities at the historic Pettus Bridge, judged Canton's violence to be "worse than Selma." More than a thousand sought refuge alongside King at Asbury Methodist Church. The Justice Department's John Doar, who had praised state officials in Grenada a week before, now cursed both sides for their refusal to compromise. Even as he tried to reorder the demonstration, King lamented that police protection had turned into an attack force: "Anyone who will use gas bombs on women and children can't and won't protect anybody."[40]

On Friday, King made good on his promise to return to Philadelphia. Three hundred activists faced a boisterous crowd of over 2,000 whites desperate for retribution in spite of a heavy law enforcement presence. Mayor Clayton Lewis allowed marchers to demonstrate on the steps of Neshoba County Courthouse and hold a rally. The crowds in downtown Neshoba were the largest since the previous year's county fair. Huge throngs of whites traveled from as far away as Meridian (forty miles) to witness a bizarre kind of racial theater.

Police ropes forced adults and children to strain for a good view of King while others managed to watch from the courthouse's second floor. Bottles, eggs, and assorted projectiles began raining down just as a local white minister led the assembled in prayer. Carmichael gestured defiantly at the sea of white faces before publicly expressing disappointment and anger over the nation's unrealized democratic potential. "The people that are gathered around us represent America in its truest form," he shouted. "They represent a sick and resisting society that sits in the United Nations and gives lip service to democracy."[41]

———————————

THE CROWDS GREW LARGER UNTIL, on the last day, they became enormous. And celebrities joined in. A Saturday night party at Jackson's black Tougaloo College included Marlon Brando and Burt Lancaster. On Sunday, June 26, an estimated 12,000 to 25,000 people rallied at the state capitol building in Jackson. It was the largest civil rights event in Mississippi's history. Al-most two thousand marched from Tougaloo at 11:00 A.M. under escort from Hinds County sheriff's deputies, and Mississippi highway safety patrolmen and Jackson police joined the large throng as they approached the city lim-its. Carmichael, dressed in blue overalls and sunglasses, and King, casually attired in a white shirt and straw hat, flanked Meredith, who donned the pith helmet he had been wearing when he was shot. Carmichael personally directed an aide to "bring those folks who have been doing most of the walk-ing up front here," well aware that the movie stars Burt Lancaster and Mar-lon Brando now jockeyed for position on the march line. Police treated civil rights workers and demonstrators with contempt that nearly turned violent. "Goddamn you, nigger, move that truck or I'll blow your goddamn head off," ordered one officer to Robert Green, who had received special per-mission from police to drive a truck alongside the march. Green managed to maintain his cool driving the truck away as a chorus of whites yelled, "Shoot! Shoot!"[42]

Tensions between SNCC and the SCLC continued along the hot walk toward the capitol. When an SCLC minister countered a chant of "Black Power!" with "Freedom Now!," Meredith raised his African walking stick and shouted him down. Cleve Sellers doled out Black Power signs and stickers, as did other SNCC staff determined to use the day's platform for long-term political goals.[43]

A CBS News Special Report carried live coverage of speeches intercut with correspondent John Hart's on-camera interviews from the capitol. Pow-erful images of state troopers pushing demonstrators off of the grass at the Leflore County Courthouse contrasted with host Harry Reasoner's dispas-sionate voice-over narration. Much of the footage gave a human face to a march most Americans had only read about in newspapers. An image of King speaking with Leflore's sheriff and Carmichael in sunglasses by King's side offered a portrait of the two leaders as collaborators rather than antago-nists. In Itta Bena, demonstrators snapped pictures of a burning cross, turn-ing a symbol of racist provocation into a souvenir from Mississippi's civil rights front. At a Yazoo City rally, Ernest Thomas of the Deacons gave an im-passioned speech. After Reasoner announced that Meredith remained silent on the question of violence, the report cut to an interview with Carmichael, who claimed to "stand mute" on the subject as well.[44]

White power was out in force. Two hundred members of the Mississippi National Guard's 112th Military Police Battalion surrounded the capitol's southern face. Hundreds of state troopers sporting blue and green helmets and armed with riot gear formed a security perimeter around the white-domed capitol; the Knights of the Green Forest, a Ku Klux Klan splinter group, turned up in full regalia, and local white youth proudly waved Confederate flags. Bystanders heckled passing demonstrators as "monkeys!" and during a live television interview with Hart, one unidentified young man proclaimed a dislike of "niggers" because they "stink." Black people were interviewed, too. A man from Hattiesburg voiced his approval for the day's events, as did an older gentleman from Vicksburg. Pressed by Hart as to how the march would bring about freedom, one young black woman paused and then replied, "I don't know, just freedom," while a student from Jackson State declared that more protests were needed.[45]

Demonstrators reached the capitol just before 4:00 P.M. Andrew Young, one of King's closest lieutenants and the future Atlanta mayor, introduced a local minister to read scripture and asked news helicopters to back away from the stage. Thousands of American flags waved by the predominantly black crowd marked this final rally. The enormous crowd strained to hear speeches that rumbled with intermittent clarity from the main stage. Meredith recalled his graduation from Ole Miss in 1963 and expressed a stubborn faith in his father's belief in the innate decency of white folk despite his shooting. A "system of white supremacy," he said, using a term that would become popular as the decade progressed, shackled blacks and whites to a world ruled by fear. Lawrence Guyot, who had sparred with Carmichael over the use of electoral politics in Mississippi, spoke of self-determination and was the first speaker to mention Black Power. Cheers rose after Guyot proclaimed that neo-colonialism, Black Power, and white supremacy were issues that required national attention. CBS broke away from Guyot's speech to reassure viewers that the police had the situation under control. Dr. Alvin Poussaint, of the Medical Committee for Human Rights and soon to become America's best-known black psychiatrist, drew knowing applause when he claimed that the civil rights movement had "done more for the mental health of Negroes in this country than anything else," and Whitney Young, back in the fold after angrily leaving the march weeks earlier, reminded the crowd of the tangible goals of "jobs and education" that guided the entire proceedings.[46]

Within the crowd, SNCC workers passed out stickers and placards featuring a dangerous-looking black panther whose message was both a warning and a clarion call: "Move on Over or We'll Move on Over YOU." Willie Ricks waded into groups of people snatching American flags distributed by the SCLC before being calmed down by an Episcopal minister. Ricks' unpredictable energy could veer onto the edge of appearing unhinged but just as quickly reveal itself as the peculiar method of a brilliant, if unconventional, organizer. Vinnie Jones, a scowling Brooklyn CORE activist, walked around with a furled-up flag and a sign around his neck that would become Muhammad Ali's calling card the following year: "No Viet Cong ever called me nigger." Lorna Smith, who had joined the march on Saturday just in time to enjoy the entertainment at Tougaloo and listen to Stokely's brief speech, sent a message to the speaker's platform informing Carmichael of her presence. The indefatigable Smith managed to snake through the crowd for a brief reunion. "I won't bother you anymore," she protested after grabbing his arms and kissing him. "You do understand, don't you," replied an apologetic Carmichael, before returning to the stage.[47]

The live broadcast hour did not carry Carmichael's or King's speeches. Carmichael sounded Black Power themes without ever chanting the phrase by declaring that, "if a black man is shot in the state of Mississippi, we will move to disrupt this country." He promised that, the next time white authorities gassed and beat nonviolent marchers, blacks would be prepared: "We need some black power to put black men in their ranks to protect us instead of buildings." King adopted a more diplomatic, but perhaps no less combative, tone. His epic dream of interracial democracy had turned into a nightmare, he said to cheers. According to King, the Meredith March would "go down in history as the greatest demonstration of freedom in Mississippi."[48]

The next day, a feisty Carmichael appeared before a bleary-eyed press corps on the terrace of Tougaloo's student union to unleash a teasing round of banter that earned him the affectionate nickname "Snickly" from journalists. "All right treacherous one, take that cigar out of your mouth!" he said, cajoling a journalist out of a semi-slumber, before pulling a "Black Panther" water pistol from his overalls and spraying the unsuspecting reporter in the face. Carmichael greeted Hosea Williams with the same practical joke, along with a chant of "Black Power!" "My God," replied a dazed Williams moments before heading into an SCLC debriefing session, "and he's a national civil rights leader!" Williams confided to reporters that SNCC's political maneuverings made Carmichael perhaps the first civil rights leader in history to use Martin Luther King to further his own personal ambition. Williams conceded, however, that the tide had turned against the proponents of nonviolence, noting that rumblings of discontent had reached Alabama. "If Negroes in Alabama talk about getting guns and killing white folks," said Williams rubbing his temples, "imagine what it's like in Harlem."[49]

In the days following the march, Carmichael would do more than imagine, embarking on a speaking tour that would include big cities such as Detroit, Los Angeles, New York, and Chicago. Tuesday in Atlanta, a weary King confronted the fallout from a march he now described as a missed opportunity. King weaved a critique of Carmichael's calls for Black Power and a denunciation of SNCC workers' desecration of the American flag during the march finale into a rhetorical tapestry that acknowledged how larger social forces producing "broken promises" and "deferred dreams" now enveloped his optimistic vision of American democracy. For Carmichael, such criticism missed the larger point of Black Power's ability to touch evils that went beyond Mississippi in search of hope that transcended political legislation. The next day, Stokely turned twenty-five.

Chapter Nine

The Magnificent Barbarian

July–September 1966

Mississippi's high drama catapulted Stokely into the political space last occupied by Malcolm X. Cast as Martin Luther King's new foil, he refused to play this role, going out of his way to praise the civil rights leader even as he forged a defiant path toward a political reckoning that frightened supporters and foes alike. The FBI, White House, and national intelligence agencies took Carmichael as seriously as they did King, at times more so, since they feared that he might personally start a national race war. Carmichael's easy humor, good looks, and intelligence made him a telegenic star, an outlaw anti-hero whom crowds mobbed in Harlem as if he were a movie star. Not everyone counted themselves as admirers. In the media, Stokely's multifaceted persona was boiled down to a simple duality: the intelligent, well-spoken, and handsome college graduate and former sit-in activist vs. the fire-breathing and violence-prone militant promising to wage war against white America. Carmichael received both the adulation and antagonism with the practiced humility and easy swagger of a young man groomed for great things while still a teenager. He reveled in aspects of his newfound celebrity, which included the kind of instant recognition everywhere that he previously commanded only in movement circles. Fame also turned friends and colleagues into critics and, more importantly, made Carmichael the target of coordinated surveillance efforts by federal, state, and local authorities that now reported virtually his every move to the White House.

Carmichael's stratospheric ascent placed him at the vanguard of black radicalism. Like Malcolm X, he defined struggles for racial and economic justice as part of a larger human rights agenda. On national television, Stokely offered an intellectually sophisticated and passionately erudite defense of Black Power and showcased the way in which the movement comprised more than the sum of its philosophical and political parts. Although he refused to provide an encapsulated definition of the term, his discussion of Vietnam carried a far-reaching indictment of the fundamental failings of American democratic institutions. Whereas Malcolm X's critique of American democracy rarely made headlines, Carmichael's words attracted national controversy.

The media hailed him as the next Malcolm X. The historian Lerone Bennett's exhilarating *Ebony* profile cast Stokely as the soul of a new movement—a charismatic, brilliant cosmopolitan whom anonymous SNCC compatriots dubbed "the Magnificent Barbarian" in homage to his ability to inspire ordinary people and alienate powerful figures in equal proportion. "No other young man," observed Bennett, "with the possible exception of Martin Luther King, Jr., has risen so far so fast." A picture of Stokely standing next to Lewis Michaux, the owner and operator of Harlem's African National Memorial Bookstore and a mentor to Malcolm X, evoked the historical figure who haunted the Black Power era. "Malcolm X is still living," Michaux told him; "when you walked in, Malcolm smiled." In certain instances, Carmichael's profile traveled beyond Malcolm's. If Malcolm's full historical importance would only be achieved posthumously, Carmichael enjoyed the status of legend during his lifetime.[1]

The Black Power phenomenon roiled national centers of American politics. Lyndon Johnson, whom Carmichael targeted with increasing frequency in public, predicted in private that SNCC's new chairman would be killed within three months. Senator Robert Kennedy, the former attorney general, now New York senator, and the challenger for the heart and soul of the Democratic Party, publicly described the term "Black Power" as "very damaging," since, he thought, it made bystanders out of a white community whose actions were primarily responsible for the nation's racial crisis.[2]

Carmichael's notoriety as a Black Power advocate and King's well-known commitment to nonviolence seemed to place them on a collision course that paralleled King's combative relationship with Malcolm X. Mutual respect and personal friendship between the two prevented this from happening, but King made clear his distaste for the new slogan, if not its substance and meaning. Even as Carmichael argued that the Black Power controversy provided a necessary "forum" for blacks, King characterized the call as a distraction from the raw "evils of Mississippi and the need for the 1966 Civil Rights Act."[3]

Roy Wilkins matched the enthusiasm of *Ebony's* flattering Carmichael profile with unfettered criticism that made national headlines. At the First Methodist Church in Los Angeles on July 5 during the NAACP's annual convention, Wilkins characterized Black Power as racism in reverse that could potentially lead to "black death." The NAACP executive secretary dismissed efforts to explain Black Power's meaning as an intrinsic example of the term's bankruptcy. "It is a reverse Mississippi, a reverse Hitler, a reverse Ku Klux Klan," he proclaimed. Following Wilkins' keynote, a blond neo-Nazi rushed the stage and began yelling racial invectives at the audience of two thousand. He was battered off the stage by an usher in a startling sequence of events that the African-American weekly *Los Angeles Sentinel* characterized as "Black Power in Action."[4]

Lyndon Johnson discussed Black Power in more restrained terms during an afternoon press conference from his Texas ranch. If Black Power's underside represented, as its critics suggested, unrelenting racial violence, then Johnson had been well acquainted with this side at least since the previous summer, when five days after he signed the Voting Rights Act, a riot exploded in Watts, Los Angeles. A traffic stop sparked the violence, which surpassed Harlem's riot the previous summer and engulfed large parts of South Central Los Angeles, including Will Rogers Park, where Stokely would address a large audience of blacks the next year. Poverty, racism, and ritualized police brutality lay at the heart of the riot, which black militants immediately described as an urban rebellion, drawing a line in the sand between how local people and law enforcement interpreted events. The August 11–18 Watts rebellion grew as much from economic misery as from the frayed relations between the Los Angeles Police Department and local blacks that sparked the immediate conflagration. Watts represented a national tipping point in race relations that violence in Harlem in 1964 and Birmingham a year earlier had merely hinted at. Since the start of Johnson's presidency, he had been the witness to three consecutive summers of racial upheaval, and Carmichael's Black Power slogan gave full-throated name to new realities the president was loath to acknowledge. Responding to a question about racial unrest in American cities, Johnson pledged support for increasing employment opportunities and ending discrimination before addressing the growing furor. "We are not interested in black power and we are not interested in white power," Johnson explained in his slow Texas drawl. "But we are interested in American democratic power, with a small 'd.'" Beyond differences of race, generation, and ideology, both Carmichael and Johnson were keen students of power. Carmichael's vision of American democracy contrasted sharply with Johnson's. President Johnson had ruthlessly suffocated democratic stirrings among Mississippi sharecroppers two years earlier in service of party unity, and his view of democracy combined New Deal rhetoric with the brutal pragmatism of machine politics, where political compromise and corruption existed in creative tension. Carmichael's political imagination promoted radical democracy as a simultaneous sword against racial and economic injustice and shield against white supremacy and political exclusion. In Atlantic City's aftermath, Carmichael defined democracy as Promethean fire whose power and potential transcended Jim Crow segregation and the ballot. Democracy's ultimate purpose had less to do with restoring a sense of racial and economic justice that never existed than in creating a new American society whose deeds matched the eloquence of its words.[5]

Carmichael spent much of the summer of 1966 touring the nation in an effort to define Black Power and reimagine American democracy. In Philadelphia, Pennsylvania, on Sunday, July 17, over a thousand people jammed the Church of the Advocate to hear him outline Black Power's contours. From the pulpit, Carmichael gave a complex address that grafted Vietnam, Black Power, and civil rights onto a political and historical tapestry. He chastised white students as playing at being revolutionaries. "You are rebelling to wear a beard and smoke 'pot' and we are fighting for our lives." Carmichael criticized Bobby Kennedy for speaking against Black Power, noting that it was "presumptuous of him to even comment on it." Carmichael disputed the popular misconception that he was anti-white before proceeding to describe the cultural revolution he was now promoting. "Baby we're just trying to get them off our backs. No longer must we say the white man is Alexander the Great, but instead Alexander the Barbaric. I'm getting tired of looking at television and seeing Tarzan beating up black people. I want to see some of those black people beat the hell out of Tarzan and send him home." It left black jazz singer Nina Simone in tears. "What black people in this country need," he told an audience that included white liberals, "is to talk to each other and stop talking to white people." Whereas civil rights operated as a translator between the black masses and white liberals, Black Power spoke in the clarifying language of the oppressed. Following Malcolm X's example of plainspoken eloquence, Black Power "was geared to talk the way that the black community talks and if Johnson doesn't like it that's tough, because we don't like the jive he's putting down either." To the audience, Nina Simone expressed appreciative wonder over Carmichael's ability to publicly express thoughts she had carried since childhood. "I have been thinking of some of the things I have heard tonight since I was three years old," she said. Simone was universally admired by black radicals for her powerful song of protest, "Mississippi Goddamn!" written in the aftermath of 1963's Sixteenth Street Baptist Church bombing that killed four black girls in Birmingham, and her involvement in the black freedom struggle only grew as the decade progressed. Simone's tearful confession momentarily silenced the crowd, turning the boisterous rally into a sacred political space that provided a glimpse of Black Power's political and emotional resonance among local communities.[6]

On July 28, Carmichael joined Representative Adam Clayton Powell Jr. in Washington, where they announced plans for a Labor Day Black Power conference. Both men wore business suits and represented two generations of black activism. Powell's long-time racial justice advocacy made him a natural supporter even as his self-aggrandizing showmanship and personal scandal added to the movement's reputation as a refuge for political scoundrels. Carmichael's bright political future marked him as a potential heir to both Malcolm X's polarizing legacy and Powell's legendary rhetorical brio. He praised Powell's long civil rights record and ignored his boastful, if accurate, reminder that he had actually originated talk of black power before Stokely.

Carmichael told reporters that the conference would extend invitations to a cross-section of civil rights leaders, including King, whom Carmichael held up as the movement's most powerful figure. He took pains to define Black Power as "power coming from black people" and informed reporters that respect, rather than fear, was the movement's main objective. "We're going to bring black people together," he said.[7]

Carmichael visited Chicago the next day. The stop was part of a speaking tour designed to capitalize on his growing fame and the public's huge appetite for his voice. His appearance in the riot-torn city competed with Martin Luther King's keynote address at a mass meeting that same evening. Stokely spoke at two rallies on the South Side of Chicago (largely avoiding the violence-plagued West Side of Chicago), made local radio and television appearances, attended press conferences, and sat for a television interview with Irv Kupcinet, who had counted Malcolm X as a frequent guest.

Carmichael met with King in Chicago and extended a personal invitation to the planned Labor Day conference on Black Power with Representative Powell in Washington. Carmichael left the meeting convinced that his invitation had been accepted, although the SCLC leader told reporters that he required board approval. Although they were cordial and friendly in private and respectful and deferential in public, the relationship between Carmichael and King remained complicated. In front of reporters in Lowndes shortly after Chicago's West Side erupted in racial violence, Carmichael mocked King's efforts at forging a peace accord. Tilting his head back and puffing out his chest, he launched into an expert impression of King. "I must have some concessions," he said. "You must give some concessions." Carmichael most comfortably expressed his opposition to King through humor, although each man's political themes and style rubbed off on the other. In Chicago, where Black Power served as a war chant for some rioters, Carmichael's influence could be seen in King's speeches touting self-affirmation and race pride. Similarly, Carmichael's public efforts to create coalitions among ideologically diverse black leaders and organizations reflected a political maturity that exposure to King accelerated. Mutual affection and enduring respect prevented the public break reporters craved, but privately King and Carmichael each fretted over the wisdom of the other's political strategy.[8]

Chicago media compared Carmichael's and King's separate political itineraries. The next day's coverage in the *Chicago Daily News* contrasted Carmichael's rhetorical fire with King's more soothing tone. The paper noted that young people flocked to hear Stokely while adults were mesmerized by King. Whereas Carmichael evoked the image of impenetrable walls of discrimination that barred blacks from the promises of American citizenship and democracy, King urged their removal. But the generation gap noted by news coverage missed some important nuances. Carmichael could find no quarrel with King's cogent description of "a triple ghetto" shaped by "race, poverty, and human misery" but remained skeptical of the nation's capacity for radical social transformation. While "they differed on several points, including non-violence," King and Carmichael remained bound by "a demand for immediate equal opportunity for the Negro." Carmichael's emergence as King's most visible public adversary contrasted Malcolm X's role in the growing perception among the press and parts of the public that acknowledged common themes, if not strategies and tactics, in the rhetoric of both men.[9]

Meanwhile, Carmichael was, surprisingly, being defended by the nation's chief law enforcement officer. As Stokely toured Chicago, Attorney General Nicholas Katzenbach found himself in the awkward position of defending Carmichael on a Sunday morning political interview show against accusations by Ohio Senator Frank Lausche that a Black Power conspiracy ignited recent national civil disturbances. Calling such talk a "tragic mistake," Katzenbach traced the roots of urban rioting to a painful legacy of discrimination and a shameful lack of resources. In private, FBI director J. Edgar Hoover offered an alternative riot theory, insisting that the Communist Party's vast tentacles gripped a wide range of civil rights organizations. Hoover's warning, culled from a leaked Senate subcommittee document, amplified a growing mythology that identified Black Power as the bombshell secret behind growing racial unrest.[10]

Amid civil disturbances in Cleveland, Omaha, and Chicago, Carmichael faced accusations of instigating a near-riot in Atlanta on Tuesday, August 2. Police there had stopped a car carrying three SNCC workers. Before long, a crowd of passersby gathered at the scene. What started as a routine charge of making an illegal turn and blocking an intersection turned into a tense racial standoff after the driver of the car refused to accept the citations and several police cars arrived on the scene. When one officer threatened to arrest the driver, the crowd began to chant "No!" and warned the police that they would have to arrest everyone. A black officer defused the situation through a compromise that included the acceptance of the traffic citations by SNCC but no arrests. At one point, Carmichael mounted a car and told the crowd, now swelled to several hundred, that Black Power had prevented any arrests. "This is what black people can do if they stick together," he said. Two black physicians active in local civil rights politics who happened on the scene provided a miniature portrait of the black middle class' complicated relationship to Black Power. Otis Smith and Roy Bell expressed empathy for the frightened white police officers, pride in the black sergeant who helped defuse the situation, and worry over the movement's disruptive potential. Police officials amplified these concerns, telling reporters that, "When Carmichael showed up, they really broke loose." Newspaper accounts that Carmichael led an angry crowd in Black Power chants portrayed SNCC and its leader as daredevil agitators capable of harnessing the pent-up rage swirling in the black ghetto.[11]

An August 5th *New York Times* profile, under the headline "Black Power Prophet," burnished Carmichael's reputation as the movement's leading architect and most charismatic spokesman. The story described him as a young man who possessed a "fine-cut" and "friendly" face, whose graceful and relaxed demeanor hid a passionate temperament rooted in his Caribbean upbringing. Stokely archly described his interracial social life at Bronx Science High School. "Liberalism is an extension of paternalism," he noted. He now believed that the same whiff of condescension he spotted in the parents of white playmates when he was growing up existed among white activists in the movement. Alongside new revelations about Carmichael's personal life, the *Times* published SNCC's Black Power position paper, written the previous spring by militants from the group's Atlanta chapter, put forth as evidence that the group's new trajectory had been long planned. The ensuing chronology, which suggested that Carmichael was influential in formulating the paper, made good copy but poor history. The actual authors were hardline militants and dissidents in Atlanta's Vine City project, publishers of the radical newspaper *Nitty Gritty*. The ensuing controversy found Carmichael defending whites from criticism that he regarded as narrowly ideological and led to the eventual ouster, accompanied by mutual recriminations, of several Atlanta staffers. In the aftermath of the Meredith March, Carmichael's public statements seemed to support the sentiment that Atlanta staffers had expressed, but there were significant differences, including Carmichael's advocacy of pragmatic, if limited, interracial coalitions. The collectively written paper, although authored by apostates eventually driven out of the organization, became a lasting artifact of transformation, forever linked to Black Power's dramatic arrival on the national stage.[12]

The same day as the *Times* profile appeared, Lyndon Johnson mentioned Carmichael twice from the White House during a telephone conversation with AFL-CIO vice president Joseph Beirne. They were discussing national labor unrest, including a crippling month-long airline strike. Johnson told Beirne that he had talked to AFL-CIO President George Meany twice earlier in the day about "what makes Stokely Carmichaels," equating SNCC's leader with a growing climate of social crisis and political dissent. Johnson invoked "Stokely Carmichael" as a metaphor for the kind of political turmoil the White House sought to avoid in ongoing labor disputes. The second time he mentioned the SNCC chairman, the president fumbled over his name, managing a complete pronunciation of "Stokely," and getting halfway through "Carmichael," before giving up and announcing that, "we don't want a hellraiser." Johnson's circumspect public proclamations concerning Black Power masked a growing preoccupation with Carmichael's political activities. A brilliant politician, masterful legislator, and shrewd political operator, Johnson now regarded Carmichael as a genuine threat.[13]

The next day, August 6, Luci, one of the president's daughters, was getting married. Outside the church, protesters carried signs that read "Build homes in Washington, don't burn villages in Vietnam" and "Hey, Hey, LBJ. How many kids did you kill today?" A second, larger demonstration marched to the White House, site of the wedding reception. Rallies in New York, where SNCC member Ivanhoe Donaldson spoke, and San Francisco reflected the breadth of antiwar activism as well as SNCC's leading role in defining such protests as part of a larger global movement against American imperialism. The Washington rally's scheduled keynote, Stokely Carmichael, sent a message of "greetings and solidarity" from Cleveland, where he was continuing his speaking tour. There he raised the call for Black Power to new rhetorical heights by igniting a fresh burst of controversy: "When you talk of black power, you talk of building a movement that will smash everything Western civilization has created." Carmichael's discussion of ending Western civilization, combined with an earlier comment about "bringing this country to its knees," sent media and political figures into a state of shock.[14]

If mainstream media attacked Carmichael as a villain, the Nation of Islam's newspaper lionized him. *Muhammad Speaks* called him a breath of fresh air in the stale arena of black leadership, highlighting excerpts from his speeches that expressed admiration for Elijah Muhammad and the Black Muslims. The courtship between Carmichael and the Messenger of Allah, as his followers called Elijah Muhammad, was a sensitive affair, however. Accompanied by Cleve Sellers, Carmichael visited Muhammad at his sprawling Chicago mansion, where the Messenger spoke in an asthmatic whisper about his life and about divine intervention. Carmichael spent most of the August 7th meeting silently gazing at the frail, elderly Muhammad and mentally comparing him to his hero, Malcolm X. Born Elijah Poole in 1897, the Georgia native had overcome a sharecropper's limited education to become leader of one of the most important black religious and political groups of the twentieth century. Muhammad's most important decision was to mentor and cultivate Malcolm's X's intellectual and organizing prowess on behalf of the Nation of Islam. For a while, Muhammad and Malcolm worked in tandem, an aging king and dashing prince determined to build a sprawling political kingdom. But by the early 1960s Elijah Muhammad feared that Malcolm was growing too powerful and steering the group into unchartered political, rather than purely religious territory. Their inevitable break unleashed the vengeful side in Muhammad, who advised true believers that apostates, even Malcolm, were worthy of death. Stokely ignored this backstory and chatted with Muhammad like an eager young apprentice. If Muhammad's understated charisma paled in comparison to Malcolm's, his sly sense of humor endeared him to Stokely. "It looks to me that this here movement must be starving these fine young men," Muhammad said, as Carmichael and Sellers feasted on a lavishly prepared meal. But his visit yielded a more austere political harvest as Muhammad refused to extend the full organizational backing of the Black Muslims without Stokely's religious conversion. If neither man convinced the other to embrace new political and philosophical orientations, the generally pleasant atmosphere cultivated more than a superficial alliance. By private instruction, the Messenger placed Stokely under the protection of the Fruit of Islam, an order that recognized him as a political jewel worthy of being defended by the paramilitary unit of the NOI. Carmichael would find deeper political chemistry with Louis Farrakhan, one of Malcolm X's most promising former protégés turned mortal enemy.

Muhammad Ali, the NOI's most important draw in the aftermath of Malcolm's departure, joined the group for dinner. He was all restless energy, athletic swagger, and playful banter. Stokely instantly bonded with the twenty-four-year-old Ali. He recognized in Ali a fellow changeling: a natural performer whose unassuming intelligence and lack of formal education made others quick to underestimate him. Carmichael's meeting with Ali symbolically connected two seemingly distant vocations, sports and community organizing. Over the course of the next several years, they frequently encountered one another and in a way changed places, with Carmichael becoming a global celebrity and Ali slipping into the role of antiwar activist. If Ali offered Carmichael personal inspiration, then Stokely provided the heavyweight boxing champ with political affirmation. The next year, Ali's draft refusal and increasingly confident political opposition to the war could be traced, at least in part, back to Carmichael. Stripped of his title and disallowed from boxing over the next four years, Ali would emerge as a global symbol of antiwar defiance whose principled draft resistance made him a hero to black Americans.[15]

Faced with a vast array of negative media attacks, Carmichael attempted to positively shape his national profile. On NBC's morning show, *Today,* he cited yellow journalism, in both print and news media, as the scourge behind a growing white backlash. "The projection of black power has been given by the white press," insisted Stokely. "They're the ones who maliciously distorted it." Certainly the mainstream media continued to debate it, casting negative judgments in editorials, cartoons, and opinion columns that at times matched the polemical tone they accused militants of adopting. Anecdotal evidence supported Carmichael's claims of media bias. John S. Knight, publisher of the *Detroit Free Press* and the *Miami Herald,* publicly warned that "the white man's role is not being made easier" by militants, while an editorial run in the Hearst chain of newspapers, which included at least eight major dailies, repudiated Black Power as "a step toward separatism, or apartheid, theories wholly inconsistent with the American way." The *Chicago Tribune* dismissed the movement as chatter from "hotheads," while *The Wall Street Journal* smugly observed that, "the Negro needs the white man far more than the other way around." The liberal *New York Times* and its West Coast counterpart, the *Los Angeles Times*, approvingly quoted King's critique of the term, while influential columnists James Reston and Joseph Alsop thought the phrase portended a turn toward violence. Although *The Christian Science Monitor*, *The Boston Globe*, and the *Boston Herald* provided more nuanced views, they lacked the prestige, influence, and circulation of the newspapers and magazines offering fervid condemnation.[16]

On August 10, in a speech in Detroit, Stokely urged blacks to refuse military induction. South Carolina Congressman Mendel Rivers wrote to Attorney General Katzenbach asking if Carmichael's words violated the Selective Service Act, which penalized individuals who aided in the avoidance of military service. Marvin Watson, special assistant to the president, telephoned the FBI the same day to relay special instructions from Johnson. Watson informed FBI assistant director Cartha "Deke" DeLoach that Johnson "was very concerned about the activities of Stokely Carmichael" and about reports suggesting ties between SNCC and the Communist Party. Johnson personally requested information about the bureau's surveillance of Carmichael and a detailed memorandum of his activities "at least several times a week." DeLoach reassured Watson that the FBI had excellent "coverage on Carmichael" and ordered the Domestic Intelligence Division to send twice-weekly memos to the president "in connection with this matter." Johnson must have surely

been disturbed to find out that Stokely was pursuing a new alliance with the
Nation of Islam.[17]

On Thursday, August 18, Carmichael called for unity in a series of meetings that energized New England militants and drew him closer to Louis
Farrakhan. Born Louis Eugene Walcott, the Bronx native was raised in Boston's Roxbury neighborhood by a mother (like Malcolm's) who hailed from
the Caribbean. Farrakhan abandoned a promising career as a calypso singer
after converting to Islam. Malcolm X, who was eight years older, embraced
Farrakhan as a younger brother and protégé. In the aftermath of Malcolm's
departure from the Nation, however, Farrakhan led the calls for violent retribution against Malcolm. Within the NOI, Farrakhan now occupied the space
left by Malcolm. He would eventually be rewarded for his loyalty with a plum
post as head of Temple No. 7, Malcolm's old mosque in Harlem. Farrakhan's
presence as head of the Nation's Temple No. 11 in Boston helped make the
city a headquarters of Black Power activism. At a private reception at the
Roxbury restaurant Estelle's, Carmichael and Farrakhan began an enduring
political friendship bound in a mutual belief that racial solidarity trumped
ideological differences.

Almost as if to publicize this point, "Louis X," as the press still referred
to him, attended an event later that evening at Harvard. Carmichael began
his speech, with his trademark humor: "Good evening, it's a pleasure to be in
the intellectual ghetto of the north." A packed crowd of eight hundred predominantly white Harvard students listened intently as Carmichael lectured
on Western civilization's unspoken allegiance to violence. He cited Vietnam
as the latest example of a fundamental contradiction plaguing American democracy and admitted that he was going "stark raving mad" over the nation's
bombing assault against the North Vietnamese. "If I had to admit I was part
of that," he confessed, "I think I'd commit suicide." While his antiwar activism
made him popular among blacks, it proved a source of controversy nationally.
Carmichael mentioned a recent Harris Poll claiming that only nineteen percent of blacks supported him; he challenged King, James Meredith, and Ralph
Bunche to go on a speaking tour of the ghetto to more practically gauge his
appeal. He acknowledged Farrakhan with the traditional Muslim greeting—"A
Salaam Alaikum"—and introduced him to the audience as a special guest.[18]

Stokely and Farrakhan continued their public friendship. They held
a press conference two days later outside the Blue Hill Avenue offices of
NEGRO (New England Grassroots Organization) in Roxbury. At one point,

Carmichael disputed widespread quotes attributed to him that he never met any whites he could trust, noting that his exact words were that he "had never known a white politician who could be trusted." Carmichael and Farrakhan's appearance offered novel approaches to black unity as both men insisted that liberation would only be achieved through the combined powers of political self-determination and love.[19]

Farrakhan's reference to Carmichael as "one of us," in his introduction, sent FBI agents scrambling to decipher whether the SNCC chairman had joined the Black Muslims. Agents pursued other wild goose chases as well, including erroneous reports that Stokely had attended the National Convention of the Communist Party of the United States of America. The next issue of *Muhammad Speaks* splashed photos of Stokely and Farrakhan walking side by side in Roxbury in an accompanying story that credited Elijah Muhammad's groundbreaking teachings for Carmichael's success. Boston's black newspaper, *The Bay State Banner*, published front-page coverage of Carmichael's visit, which put the city on the map as a center for Black Power organizing.[20]

Fresh from his meeting with Farrakhan, Carmichael appeared on the August 21st edition of *Meet the Press*. There he characterized America's involvement in Vietnam as immoral, and in doing so tied Black Power to antiwar activism for the first time on a nationally televised forum. His calm demeanor, easy eloquence, and thoughtful manner rattled journalists expecting raw polemics. His business suit and slight drawl (a combination of Trinidad, the Bronx, and Mississippi perhaps never before heard on national television) gave him the disarming air of a young professor. He joined Roy Wilkins, Whitney Young, Floyd McKissick, and James Meredith in NBC's Washington studio for a special ninety-minute broadcast, while Martin Luther King appeared via satellite from Chicago. In a widely publicized appearance Carmichael debated civil rights leaders and parried with the show's moderator and reporters while defending Black Power and offering incisive criticism against the war. Carmichael also laid down an unequivocal gauntlet regarding his own military service: "No, I would not fight in Vietnam, absolutely not, and I would urge every black man in this country not to fight in Vietnam."[21]

Four days later, he spoke in Newark, whose population was predominantly black but whose mayors were always white. In front of the Stella Wright Homes, a housing project in the city's Central Ward, Carmichael leapt on top of a station wagon and decried the status of blacks "pent up in these projects and these rundown homes." For twenty minutes he discussed white racism, community control, and challenged the four hundred assembled to assert themselves in new and provocative ways, plaintively noting that authorities did not fear the potential of racial violence in Newark. That evening, Carmichael spoke for over an hour to an enthusiastic and vocal crowd at the second-floor headquarters of Operation We Care, the Central Ward's local anti-poverty board. "You should have already taken Newark, NJ, over because it belongs to you," he told them. Taking off his jacket and tie and perspiring heavily, Carmichael called blacks in the armed forces mercenaries and vowed to continue his antiwar stance. "The only way to stop me," said Carmichael, "is to kill me or put me in jail and when they do, I'm going to organize the brothers there." Both the grittier afternoon crowd of the Stella Wright Homes and the attentive evening audience of local black militants, poverty board members, and city officials interrupted Carmichael's speeches with frequent applause and laughter. Reporters marveled at Carmichael's interactions in bars, private homes, and community centers as he effortlessly crisscrossed through Newark. In classic Stokely fashion that left journalists scratching their heads, he ended his visit at an interracial fundraiser at the home of some Jewish supporters.[22]

Carmichael's meteoric rise to national fame proved to be a double-edged sword. The controversy over Black Power made him a bona fide star on the national speaking circuit, an eagerly sought-after lecturer whose fees provided SNCC with a rare source of steady income. It also projected Carmichael as the unquestioned leader of an organization that eschewed hierarchy. Staff openly rebelled against his growing ego, and some, like Ruby Doris Smith Robinson, now derisively called him "Stokely Starmichael." Robinson, newly elected executive secretary and bureaucratic combatant, voiced sharp objections to the cult of personality surrounding Stokely. Robinson agreed with Black Power in principle. In fact, on the last day of the Meredith March, she and Jim Forman had been shouting "Black Power!" chants along with Willie Ricks. Robinson grew concerned that growing fame enabled Carmichael to casually bypass the checks and balances of SNCC's executive structure, where past chairmanships played visible, though largely symbolic, policy roles.[23]

Stokely's rhetoric now ran past Robinson's comfort level. In an internal memo, SNCC struggled with the reverberations from "Stokely's projection since his election to the chairmanship"—a phenomenon that altered the group's internal democracy. Ironically, Black Power facilitated Stokely's "growing capture by the country" at the expense of SNCC's organizational health and long-term political goals. Overwhelmed communications staff proved no match against major newspapers and magazines in efforts to define Black Power. And so they proposed a drastic solution: "The best move we could make is for Stokely to step out of the chairmanship by expressing fear over being isolated as a national leader." The memo couched the proposal as more of a suggestion than a conclusion, noting that Carmichael's "role is with SNCC and the SNCC staff."[24]

SNCC's organizational strength seemed to decline in proportion to Carmichael's growing fame. Once-robust projects withered and the loss of John Lewis and Julian Bond (who had left to pursue a political career) hurt the group's public image. Efforts to organize northern projects under their new philosophy came under intense pressure from local and federal authorities. FBI informants alleged that tensions within SNCC reached a crescendo that August, resulting in Carmichael handing in his resignation letter to the central committee, effective October 21, a letter it declined to accept.[25]

THE DAY AFTER LABOR DAY, Carmichael attended a contentious meeting with Atlanta Mayor Ivan Allen that was a prelude to a life-altering confrontation. Ostensibly there to broker an agreement regarding the treatment of twelve SNCC members arrested the previous month outside a military induction center, the encounter foreshadowed disaster. The meeting at City Hall began awkwardly with Carmichael refusing to shake the mayor's outstretched hand and spiraled downward from there. Allen declined Carmichael's entreaties to release the SNCC defendants as a federal charge beyond his jurisdiction. Unable to convince the mayor to accord the prisoners better treatment, the group briefly prevented Allen from leaving before it departed peacefully.

The shooting of a black man suspected of car theft in Atlanta's Summerhill neighborhood later in the day brought SNCC to the scene. Carmichael arrived shortly after the early afternoon incident and primed local residents for a demonstration. "We're going to be back at four o'clock and tear this place up," he said, voicing words whose meaning would be the subject of legal proceedings in the coming months. A lower-middle-class neighborhood located a few blocks from city hall and the state capitol, Summerhill's racial demographics had changed virtually overnight due to white flight, but its proximity to government power and Atlanta's new $18 million sports stadium gave it a high level of services and support. Carmichael announced that SNCC would return within two hours, spreading the word via a reporter from a local black radio station who accompanied him to the shooting. During a radio interview that aired locally shortly before violence flared, he promised to organize a protest rally that would "tear this city upside down." Asked by the reporter what he meant by these remarks, Carmichael hedged. "Well, I think the black people of this country are afraid to protest, and legitimately so, that's my own feeling. And that they must be urged and coerced to come out of that fear, to wake up, to tear up that fear."[26]

Back at SNCC's Atlanta office, Carmichael directed William Ware to the intersection of Capitol and Ormond, where he immediately set up a bullhorn connected to a sound truck emblazoned with the figure of a black panther. By late afternoon, reports coming in to Carmichael at SNCC headquarters made the risk of his appearance in the neighborhood a necessary burden of leadership that would be interpreted as an act of provocation. He got to the scene and remained for ten minutes, just long enough to survey the escalating revolt and provide visible evidence that connected him to a riot.

Cleve Sellers, Ruby Doris Smith Robinson, and Ivanhoe Donaldson were on hand as news of the shooting flashed through Summerhill. Police placed Ware in custody for operating a sound truck without a permit as hundreds of locals arrived on the scene. Mayor Allen came with police reinforcements as local youth surged forward with angry shouts of "kill the white bastards, kill the cop," and hurled whatever objects were handy. Allen waded into a crowd of onlookers, some of whom shouted "Black Power!" with fists raised in the air as the mayor stood impassively, protected by his personal chauffer, police captain George Royal. The mayor pleaded with onlookers to return to their homes while SNCC workers counseled residents to stand their ground in defiant witness.

Clad in a gray suit, white shirt, and dark tie, Allen hopped on top of a police car and addressed the crowd. Among the sea of black faces watching the mayor was Carmichael, who could relate to Allen's impulsiveness if not his judgment. An intuitive reader of large crowds with an anthropologist's feel for the emotional temperature of impassive gatherings, Carmichael quickly retreated from the scene. For a few moments, the city appeared on the brink of a reprieve as the mayor established a tenuous rapport with angry residents. Then, just as quickly, order vanished as the surging mass toppled Allen from the car. Shaken but uninjured, the mayor bounded back on top of the vehicle and once again pleaded for calm. A young man police later identified as an unnamed SNCC worker vaulted atop the car with a competing message: he urged the crowd to cleanse the city's racism with a scourge of violence comparable to Watts. Allen's patience disappeared, and he ordered police to "get the shotguns" and fire tear gas in an effort to disperse a crowd now ballooned to one thousand.

A political liberal who had endorsed the March on Washington and supported the 1964 Civil Rights Act, Atlanta's mayor now turned intransigent in the face of racial unrest. Reporters, police officials, and innocent bystanders scrambled for cover in a chaotic, tear gas–stained scene. Capitol Avenue, the riot's epicenter, formed a bucolic backdrop, with its simple two- and three-story homes neatly poised on tree-lined streets. Police arrested over sixty people, and at least fifteen suffered injuries, including five children overwhelmed by tear gas. Martin Luther King Sr. and other civil rights leaders raced to the scene under police escort after the violence was quelled. "Can't some of us call Stokely and tell him we would like to talk to him?" King asked Allen. "He goes before the trouble starts," replied the mayor. "I saw him leaving when I came up." One hundred state troopers supplemented a force of city police seven times larger by nine at night, when the mayor informed Governor Carl Sanders that the riot had at last ebbed.[27]

Wednesday's front-page headlines traced the worst incident of violence in Atlanta's modern history directly to Carmichael. Ralph McGill, the publisher of *The Atlanta Constitution,* described Allen as "impeccable, bareheaded, distinguished looking"—and brave enough to face down a mob of angry blacks. News stories portrayed Allen as a courageous liberal politician who virtually single-handedly faced down the militant agitator. Allen embraced this narrative, acting like a movie sheriff intent on protecting his town: "If Mr. Carmichael is looking for a battleground, he has created one, and he will be met there at any place and time he chooses," he warned. At a press conference reviewing the previous day's event, the mayor admitted that the riot's roots lay in over a century of racial segregation, but just as quickly focused his attention back on Carmichael. "If he has any wares to peddle, he had better find a more fertile field," Allen declared. "But if he wants to come back where he was yesterday, he will find me there to meet him."[28]

Like two political candidates making last-minute election-day appeals, both Carmichael and Allen toured Summerhill's riot-torn area on Thursday.

Carmichael arrived first, shadowed by ten policemen, pleading his case to local residents and denying Allen's public accusations against SNCC. "The racist mayor and white racist papers said we started a riot and ran," said Carmichael. "We did not start it and we will not run away." Neither would Atlanta police. They searched for any pretext to detain him. The flimsy one they came up with was the suggestion that Carmichael had attached an unauthorized Black Power sticker to a local woman's door even as SNCC staff were blanketing the area with leaflets detailing their version of events.[29]

Atlanta officials, meanwhile, debated whether to charge Carmichael with insurrection, a crime that carried the death penalty in Georgia. Ohio Representative Wayne Hays blasted him on the floor of Congress as the mastermind behind recent riots in Atlanta and Cleveland. Mayor Allen toured Summerhill on the heels of Carmichael's exit, offering improved social services, support for the pending 1966 civil rights bill, and praise for local civil rights leaders who repudiated Tuesday's violence. Allen presented his personal biography (as a former segregationist turned racial liberal) as proof of his sincerity.

Police arrested Carmichael at SNCC headquarters near the Atlanta University Center's strip of historically black colleges, around 11:00 P.M. on Thursday, September 8. The charges were inciting a riot and disturbing the peace. Accompanied by attorney Howard Moore and SNCC staff, including photographers who snapped photos, and covered by journalists, Carmichael entered the Fulton County jail with $6 and an armload of books. Carmichael's arrest hurled SNCC into crisis mode. He waved a preliminary hearing during an early Friday morning appearance at Atlanta Municipal Court. He refused to answer questions and was transported from city to county jail. Atlanta's authorities now regarded Carmichael as a walking contagion spreading the virus of urban militancy, so they placed him in an isolation cell. The next day, Moore filed a lawsuit in federal court charging city officials with scapegoating both Carmichael and SNCC. *Carmichael v. Allen* successfully placed Atlanta's mayor and criminal justice system on the defensive while innovating a legal strategy destined to make Moore the darling of civil libertarians everywhere.[30]

Ralph McGill's widely read front-page stories in *The Atlanta Constitution* depicted SNCC as a once-proud civil rights organization now ruled by a band of anarchists who cultivated anti-white sentiment and nursed apocalyptic grudges against society. Offering more scandal than proof, McGill alleged that one of SNCC's main leaders suffered from a psychological disorder and that the entire group had become nothing more than an elaborate communist front. National print media followed suit. *Time* magazine, in a story headlined "Stokely's Spark," called the riot "a peculiar and perverse triumph" for Carmichael and included a photo of Stokely being fingerprinted by police. SNCC's remaining contingent of white supporters fought back, headed by Boston University professor Howard Zinn. Zinn, a former Spelman College professor, had taken an instant liking to Stokely since their first meeting outside of a church in Albany, Georgia, during the early 1960s. Occasional reunions in Greenwood and personal interviews conducted by Zinn for academic writings on SNCC deepened their bond. From Boston, Zinn defended Carmichael as both a political symbol and a friend.[31]

Carmichael's arrest reverberated through national politics. Liberal and conservative politicians scapegoated him for outbursts of urban rioting. "A vote against me is a vote for Stokely Carmichael," declared Massachusetts attorney general and Republican senatorial candidate Edward Brooke. Poised to be the first black man elected to the Senate since Reconstruction, Brooke positioned his moderation as a bulwark against the politics of racial grievance that Carmichael typified in the white imagination. *The Boston Globe* lauded Brooke as "the only major political figure on the scene to arouse the distaste of members of SNCC and the [far-right-wing] John Birch Society." Brooke's campaign placed race in the background in hopes of promoting the handsome candidate's universal appeal backed by solid intellectual and political credentials. Carmichael's regular media appearances forced Brooke's hand. By October, Brooke responded to questions of a white backlash by touting his candidacy as the antidote to Carmichael's increasingly harsh criticism of American society.[32]

In fact, most politicians, especially those running for office, including Republicans and Democrats, were running from Carmichael. In Massachusetts's Democratic Senate primary, during a live television debate, Boston Mayor John Collins condemned him. A Mississippi congressman asked Defense Secretary Robert S. McNamara to draft Carmichael. North Carolina's governor and chief justice denounced him and worried that Atlanta's violence might spread further south. A Georgia official called SNCC the "Non-student Violent Coordinating Committee," a not unclever turn of phrase that critics had been using for some time. Moderate black leaders like Whitney Young and conservative ones such as Dr. John Jackson of the National Baptist Convention joined in repudiating Atlanta's violence. Dr. O.W. Davis, who had witnessed Carmichael's minor confrontation with the Atlanta police a month earlier, called him "an albatross around our necks, a parasite on the community." The newly formed Good Neighbor Club distributed seven hundred "I am a good neighbor" stickers in Summerhill to serve as a friendly warning against canvassing SNCC staff. Black moderates who quelled violence in Atlanta's rough Vine City neighborhood the day after the riots publicly repudiated Black Power, and persons unknown vandalized SNCC's newsstand near its Atlanta Project, the site of SNCC's militant group that had authored the Black Power position paper. *The Washington Post*'s front-page coverage three days after the riot crystallized the popular conception of the entire affair in a report that claimed virtually the entire city of "Atlanta put the finger on Stokely Carmichael and his wild SNCC crew who were on the scene as big as life."[33]

Martin Luther King struggled with political damage stemming from media coverage of Carmichael's arrest. King discussed potential fallout over the arrest with an adviser, Stanley Levison, on Friday evening. He predicted that Carmichael would most likely serve jail time and would soon reach out to him for assistance. King planned to shift focus of the incident from Carmichael to the economic conditions that caused it. Carmichael's arrest placed new pressures on King's stalled Chicago campaign to promote slum clearance and anti-poverty legislation and the broader movement's goals of highlighting racial injustice in northern cities. Privately, King told SCLC staff that he agreed with Carmichael's emphasis on black political, social, and economic power yet remained baffled by his tactics. Atlanta's volatile racial politics and unpredictable civil rights terrain made King wary of encroaching on SNCC's political territory, but he instructed Hosea Williams to send staff into Summerhill and Vine City to test the local political temperature. The FBI matched King's trepidations with bureaucratic intensity. Agents monitoring SNCC's New York office reported that the chapter featured just one white member even as they accessed the group's local bank account to glean sensitive financial information. Meanwhile, Immigration and Naturalization Service officials probed Carmichael's citizenship status in hopes of finding precedents to deport him back to Trinidad.[34]

Some whites were willing if not exactly eager to push for civil rights and integration. But national fatigue over racial militancy was setting in. *The*

Saturday Evening Post, published in Philadelphia, Pennsylvania, not Philadelphia, Mississippi, typified the half-heartedness, hypocrisy, and bad faith of white America:

> We are all, let us face it, Mississippians. We all fervently wish that the Negro problem did not exist, or that, if it must exist, it could be ignored. Confronted with the howling need for decent schools, jobs, housing, and all the other minimum rights of the American system, we will do our best, in a half-hearted way, to correct old wrongs. The hand may be extended grudgingly and patronizingly, but anyone who rejects that hand rejects his own best interests. For minimum rights are the only one we are willing to guarantee, and above these minimum rights there is and will continue to be a vast area of discrimination and inequity and unfairness, the area in which we claim the most basic right of all—the right to be stupid and prejudiced, the right to make mistakes, the right to be less and worse than we pretend, the right to be ourselves. When the majority right is threatened, the majority will react accordingly—with results that could be disastrous to all of us.[35]

The editorial defended white supremacy as part of the nation's birthright and warned of coming racial violence against social justice movements advocating the transformation of a racially intolerant democracy into a multiracial one.

Almost as if in response to the *Saturday Evening Post's* editorial, Carmichael wrote a letter from jail. It was published in the October 2nd edition of *The Sunday Ramparts,* a San Francisco–based radical paper. In it, he defined the uproar over SNCC's Black Power call as a naked expression of white supremacy. Carmichael argued that SNCC's increasing radicalism had alienated it from past supporters. As long as SNCC confined its activism to southern bastions of racial segregation, the group enjoyed moral and financial support from scores of northern white liberals. Yet after discovering "that racism was not an isolated phenomenon peculiar to the South," SNCC quickly found itself abandoned by liberal allies. If SNCC regrouped by embracing Black Power, white northerners and southerners revealed their common interest in keeping blacks powerless. Carmichael's letter openly questioned whether SNCC's liberal supporters ever truly supported the group's insurgent vision of

American democracy. In contrast to King's celebrated letter from a Birmingham jail cell, written on April 16, 1963 (which memorably characterized civil rights protesters as bringing the entire nation back to "those great wells of democracy dug deep by the founding fathers"), Carmichael's jail missive remained destined for obscurity. It connected SNCC's activism during the first half of the 1960s to urban rebellions in Harlem and Watts, judging institutional racism to be less an exception to the rule and more "the national policy of the United States, an integral part of what is known as 'the system.'"[36]

After posting bond on Thursday, September 16, a defiant Carmichael discussed his future plans on a local radio program. "As long as there are injustices, there will be demonstrations and Atlanta might as well get used to it," he said. "If they want to stop demonstrations, they should stop messing with black people." Carmichael's week in jail represented his first extended stay in one place since becoming SNCC chairman. His indictment on a reduced charge of misdemeanor riot offered a victory of sorts along with a smaller bond amount. He rationalized his decision to leave jail as a political one, since "there is a need for people to be outside, having proved that the arrests were illegal."[37]

In Washington, meanwhile, the new civil rights bill that the Meredith Marchers had vowed to strengthen, now suffered defeat. The Republican minority leader, Senator Everett Dirksen, refused entreaties to end a filibuster of it. Joseph Rauh, a civil rights lawyer who, with Eleanor Roosevelt and Hubert Humphrey, had founded the Americans for Democratic Action (ADA) in 1947, called Dirksen the "biggest asset" to Carmichael's incendiary brand of politics. The black newspaper, the *New Pittsburgh Courier,* delved into American history to counter myths of white backlash as simply a continuation of the nation's long-standing Negrophobia: "It is more like a whiplash to the Negro, and as the blows continue to rain down upon his bared back the pain is going to become more severe." *The New Journal and Guide*, a black weekly published in Norfolk, Virginia, placed blame for the defeated civil rights bill squarely on Carmichael's shoulders, warning readers that the "sooner the Negro community rejects the alien philosophy and tactics of the many STOKELY CARMICHAELS fomenting unrest and disorder around the nation," the better off blacks would be. Anonymous White House officials echoed this sentiment by suggesting that Carmichael's anti-white posture derailed the new civil rights bill. At a cabinet meeting in late September, Lyndon Johnson blamed Carmichael for the defeat of the bill and said he was a "young man" who didn't know "his rear end from his elbow." *The Boston Globe* defended Stokely and traced his loss of faith in traditional civil rights measures to a climate of racial fear and hostility as old as the republic itself. An editorial in the black newspaper, *The Chicago Defender* titled "How to Silence Stokely," was particularly lucid: "By this date, it is reasonably plain the entire white community despises the insides of one Stokely Carmichael." The paper offered the "childishly simple" solution of ending institutional racism, rather than "shooting Carmichael dead," as a cure for his "wild and turbulent cries."[38]

CHAPTER TEN

"A New Society Must Be Born"

September–December 1966

STOKELY'S ANTIWAR SPEECHES AND DRAFT STATUS COMBINED TO MAKE HIM a powerful symbol of defiance, for both radicals and conservatives, of the increasingly controversial Vietnam War. Throughout the second half of 1966, politicians and bureaucrats urged military officials to draft Carmichael and send him to Vietnam even as he vowed to go to jail rather than fight. His bold antiwar posture garnered renewed controversy but also further praise, especially from college students who sympathized with words of fire directed against Lyndon Johnson. Carmichael defined the Vietnam War as a microcosm of the many ills plaguing American democracy. At first, he called for an end to the war. Later, he would call for America's military defeat. Carmichael's reputation transcended American borders, stretching into the political consciousness of black soldiers in Vietnam. The *Baltimore Afro-American*'s report of discrimination facing "tan servicemen" in Saigon featured black GIs who embraced Carmichael's militancy. "We have manifested a 100-per-cent pride in being black," explained one soldier. "We want to be black . . . even in Vietnam. Damn the civil rights bill. We want our constitution."[1]

Carmichael's brilliant essay "What We Want" in the September 22nd issue of *The New York Review of Books* defined Black Power as a political philosophy born of deeply personal experience. He blamed SNCC for serving as an unwitting buffer between white society and the black masses, as racial interpreters who helped to maintain the illusion that American democracy required little more than reform. SNCC and other civil rights groups underestimated the depth of institutional racism, the jagged edges of democracy, and the deep-seated hostility of whites against even the appearance of black advancement:

> For too many years, black Americans marched and had their heads broken and got shot. They were saying to the country, "Look, you guys are supposed to be nice guys and we are only going to do what we are supposed to do—why do you beat us up, why don't you give us what we ask, why don't you straighten yourselves out?" After years of this, we are at almost the same point—because we demonstrated from a position of weakness. We cannot be expected any longer to march and have our heads broken in order to say to whites: come on, you're nice guys. For you are not nice guys. We have found you out.

According to Carmichael, blacks, disabused of blind faith in whites, could now embark on a political mission to transform the nation on their own terms. Black Power's significance lay in its uncompromising assertion that blacks could independently define social, political, and cultural phenomena. This meant wrestling with the way in which race and class shaped hope, opportunity, and identity. SNCC's time in the Mississippi Delta and Alabama's Black Belt convinced its young organizers that power could alter the wretched socioeconomic conditions faced by black sharecroppers. Yet even this change, Carmichael admitted, would provide only incremental relief: "Ultimately, the economic foundations of this country must be shaken if black people are to control their lives."

"What We Want" intellectually disarmed some of Carmichael's fiercest critics and in the process announced SNCC's chairman as a formidable thinker. For readers of *The New York Review of Books,* the essay was a revelation that easily transcended clichés surrounding black radicalism. "We won't fight to save the present society, in Vietnam or anywhere else," Carmichael concluded. "We are just going to work, in the way that *we* see fit, and on goals *we* define, not for civil rights but for all our human rights."[2]

Shortly after Carmichael's essay appeared, CBS News broadcast on September 27 a special report, "Black Power, White Backlash." Carmichael, wearing the African robe given to him by Guinean President Sékou Touré (via Jim Forman), spoke to correspondent Mike Wallace from SNCC's Atlanta headquarters. Carmichael once again defined Black Power as an act of political self-determination and countered Wallace's attempts to link the slogan to violence. "Now, I'm not concerned about the question of violence," said Carmichael. "It seems to me that will depend on how white people respond. If white people, in fact, are willing not to bother black people because they are black, then there's going to be no question of violence." Carmichael described urban riots as "rebellions," offering an alternative to Wallace's "white backlash" thesis. From this perspective, waves of civil unrest in black communities reflected the depths of a social order created and maintained by white society. The cure for violence, he said, lay in black consciousness. Political self-awareness would lead to community control over housing and resources and turn ghettoes into thriving neighborhoods. "And the means you will use to achieve all of this?" asked Wallace. "Any means necessary," replied Carmichael.[3]

Offered the chance to speak directly to white America, Carmichael issued a stark indictment:

> I would say, "Understand yourself, white man." That the white man's burden should not have been preached in Africa, but it should have been preached among you. That you need now to civilize yourself. You have moved to destroy and disrupt. You have taken people away, you have broken down their systems, and you have called all this civilization, and we, who have suffered at this, are now saying to you, you are the killers of the dreams, you are the savages. . . . Civilize yourself.[4]

Two days after the CBS broadcast, Carmichael was the subject of a wiretapped conversation between Martin Luther King and Stanley Levison. National unrest disappointed King, who recounted his recent conversation with Whitney Young when both men contemplated resigning from their respective organizations, a thought Levison dismissed as insufficiently symbolic. The gubernatorial nomination on Georgia's Democratic ticket of the openly segregationist Lester Maddox depressed King. He and Levison discussed Carmichael's role in shaping contemporary political currents and jointly agreed "Stokely must be politically isolated." They discussed how moderate civil rights leaders found Carmichael's behavior appalling, suggesting that he be treated as a "black Trotskyite," and blamed Maddox's nomination on Carmichael. FBI informants reported that King had received assurances from Carmichael that same evening that he would temporarily halt Black Power demonstrations until after the mid-term elections. The accord formed part of a back-channel request from President Johnson to ease the pace of escalating racial tensions connected to civil rights demonstrations.[5]

Carmichael spoke to a packed audience of Black Power militants in Detroit on Tuesday, October 4. At least fifty whites joined thirteen hundred blacks at Black Power theologian Reverend Albert Cleage's Central Congregation Church. Cleage, along with attorney Milton Henry, who also spoke, represented the vanguard of the Motor City's black militants—activists whose extensive political portfolios included establishing intimate alliances with Malcolm X that stretched back to the 1950s. Henry was a former air force lieutenant, and his political association with Malcolm X thrust him into the upper echelons of black political radicalism by the early 1960s, buoyed by keen business instincts that found him marketing black political radicalism through his own media company. Henry's introduction paid tribute to Malcolm and Stokely while noting the historic vulnerability of radical black political leaders. "We need to erect monuments to our Stokely Carmichaels everywhere while we still have them" since "we didn't do it to Malcolm," said Henry with a tinge of personal regret overwhelmed by a cascade of applause that continued as Carmichael walked to the podium.

Before speaking, Carmichael paid his own tribute to Rosa Parks, whom he called his "hero" and who was now serving on Michigan congressman John Conyers' staff. "Individualism is a luxury you can no longer afford," Carmichael said in a speech that balanced his anti-Vietnam message with an indictment of the black middle class as racial poseurs who abandoned their less successful brothers and sisters in urban ghettos. Over repeated interruptions of applause, Carmichael touted the creation of cooperative stores, credit unions, and insurance companies as more humane an alternative to modern-day capitalism, applauded Muhammad Ali and Adam Clayton Powell as symbols of Black Power, and vowed to make black people recognize their own beauty, which they remained frightened of. "I'm six foot one, 180 pounds, all black and I love me," said Stokely. "We're not anti-white, it's just that as we learn to love black there just isn't any more time for white."[6]

Carmichael's electrifying appearance at Central Congregation brought together two generations of civil rights and Black Power activists, offering a new genealogy of both movements. The presence of Parks, lauded as the spark of the Montgomery Bus Boycott and symbolic progenitor of the Civil Rights Movement's heroic period, elegantly reflected the era's ideological and organizational diversity. Cleage and Henry illustrated the often-times hidden passions and spectacular ambitions of a northern black freedom struggle that, in certain instances such as Detroit's Walk for Freedom, converged with more-conventional civil rights demonstrations. Carmichael (whose business suit hinted at the civil rights movement's lasting influence on him) represented the most unique political activist of his generation, having served on the front lines of southern civil rights demonstrations and northern Black Power insurgency. Stokely now served as a living bridge between civil rights and Black Power activists.

But moderate civil rights leaders were publicly opposing Black Power. In a manifesto statement issued on October 13, Bayard Rustin, A. Philip Randolph, Wilkins, Young, and National Council of Negro Women president Dorothy Height, but not King, signed a statement titled "Crisis and Commitment" denouncing Black Power. King's signature was noticeably absent. Only in private would he discuss the issues raised in the statement. Meanwhile, in a New York television studio on *The David Susskind Show*, Carmichael dismissed those who blamed him for tipping primary election results in Georgia and catapulting Ronald Reagan to front-runner status in California's gubernatorial race. "If I'm responsible for all of these elections," he quipped, "SNCC wants me to run for president." In Atlanta, reporters pestered King, conspicuously absent from the anti Black Power screed, for comment on the entire matter before wrestling tepid words of support for Stokely that Friday's headlines twisted into a whole-hearted endorsement.[7]

In California, Reagan deftly exploited racial fears in the weeks leading up to the November election. Reagan's outspoken criticism of Carmichael served as a prelude to his blood feud with the Black Panthers and enmity toward radical activism in general. On Tuesday, October 18, Reagan sent Carmichael an open telegram asking him to cancel an appearance at the University of California, Berkeley, that "could possibly do damage to both parties." California's embattled incumbent, Edmund G. "Pat" Brown, rejected Reagan's overtures to join him in his request and accused his challenger of pandering to conservative voters and black militants. "Carmichael and his black power friends are doing everything they can to defeat me and elect Reagan," Brown lamented. "They don't want peaceful progress, they want panic in the streets and publicity. And Reagan serves their purposes by helping to give them both."[8]

If politicians were scapegoating Stokely, in private he was getting it from all sides at SNCC. His lecture and speaking fees were now SNCC's main source of income and an invaluable organizational resource if properly harnessed. Though Carmichael rationalized his schedule as an example of political commitment to the movement, the constant attention and adulation he received in black communities fed his ego.

Things came to a head at a central committee meeting in Knoxville, during the weekend of October 22–23. On Sunday, Carmichael, in an Oral Report of the Chairman cloaked as a *mea culpa*, passionately defended his tenure. "Rhetorically, there have been a lot of mistakes made," he admitted. Since the last central committee meeting, Carmichael had spent the bulk of his time up north, visiting experimental SNCC offices in New York, Boston, and Chicago. Carmichael suggested correctly that his rhetorical excesses jeopardized SNCC's embryonic northern inroads and placed the group in an even more precarious political and financial state. But North and South were very different. "One of the problems we have in the North," he lamented, "is that we do not understand political machinery." Carmichael offered the rare but telling admission that, despite his considerable gifts, national leadership required new levels of political sophistication. Carmichael reported that across the nation, projects were in a state of disarray: Los Angeles and San Francisco offices moribund; Atlanta's in flux; Harlem's promising efforts at community control offset by opposition from Bayard Rustin and Whitney Young; Alabama in danger of having only one organizer, H. Rap Brown; and Mississippi sorely missing the leadership and presence of Cleve Sellers, who had as program secretary frequently traveled with Stokely and was no longer able to concentrate on local organizing. In a move that would have surely have made Jim Forman smile, Carmichael tasked the central committee with instilling unprecedented levels of organizational discipline, instead of merely assuming people were "working on our programs."[9]

Verbally chastised by Ruby Doris Smith Robinson, Faye Bellamy, future program secretary Ralph Featherstone, and others, Carmichael preached consensus by suggesting the central committee establish clear "guidelines" for his public speeches. Beyond petty jealousies and private grievances over Stokely's celebrity, staff chafed against public perception that their new chair controlled them and grimaced each time his personal opinions ran ahead of, or contradicted, organizational policy. Chastened, he expressed regret for political transgressions and promised to halt his speaking tour after December 10 to focus on staff development and SNCC's "internal structure."[10]

Efforts to contain Carmichael's rhetorical escapades paralleled SNCC's organizational crisis. Two-thirds of the group's 135 members now operated in Atlanta or northern cities. The South's remaining staff suffered from creeping disorientation over SNCC's Black Power thrust, a feeling exacerbated by a lack of resources, apathy, and burnout. Efforts in Harlem, Philadelphia, and Chicago offered promising opportunities to transplant SNCC's organizing prowess to cities but just as often invited new waves of official repression. The remainder of Sunday's meeting broke along twin fault lines of ambition and dysfunction, resulting in plans to send a delegation to Africa in the New Year, assign a fundraiser to southern projects, and pay the rent for Atlanta staff by cutting salaries in half. Some of the proposals, most notably for establishing SNCC's International Affairs Committee, would flourish amid organizational decline over the next two years but most would remain stillborn. Jim Forman urged the group to develop long-term political education programs, recommending a period of study to prevent growing apathy and political lethargy. Five and a half months into his chairmanship, Carmichael complained that it was "impossible" to serve the dual roles as "administrator and fundraiser," already guessing that he would spend the rest of his tenure fundraising.[11]

Carmichael struggled to fulfill his role as SNCC chairman even as acting attorney general Ramsey Clark and FBI official Deke DeLoach debated prosecuting him on federal charges. The FBI pressed Clark for wiretap surveillance of Carmichael, sensing an opportunity to corner the inexperienced AG. Clark refused the bureau's request for telephonic surveillance, fearing a public relations disaster if news of the wiretap leaked, noting Carmichael's reputation as a civil rights leader, and not wishing to risk future legal prosecution. Sensing DeLoach's disappointment, Clark asked him if the bureau "would elaborate" on its reasoning for the Carmichael wiretap. DeLoach replied that director Hoover's request came at the insistence of the president, who "wanted to make absolutely certain the FBI had good coverage on Carmichael." Absent microphone surveillance, the bureau's investigation remained hamstrung, and since Carmichael's "activities and statements bordered on anarchy," the FBI felt comfortable with the request. While the bureau had Carmichael's Selective Service records, they had failed to procure his college files and required fresh intelligence regarding "where Carmichael was getting his money, whom he was taking orders from, whom he associated with, and his plans for the future." Fearful of communist subversion in the black movement, the FBI imagined that Carmichael received direction from foreign outposts; it routinely investigated wild rumors and false sightings that connected the SNCC chairman to the Communist Party and related organizations.[12]

The Carmichael wiretap request exposed a rift between Hoover and Ramsey Clark that would grow over the next two years. DeLoach's efforts to box in Clark by leveraging the White House's interest failed. Even as Clark took pains to relay a message to Hoover that he was not "deliberately delaying action on the Carmichael request," he steadfastly refused wiretap approval. Clark's political independence and reverence for civil liberties and the rule of law made him a political enemy of the FBI, whose forces he nominally led. Hoover considered Clark's philosophy of "combating crime through an attack on poverty" both politically naïve and dangerous. As attorney general, Clark refused calls to arrest Carmichael on sedition charges and developed a thoughtful, deliberative political style that made him the rare White House official who balanced growing hysteria around Black Power, race riots, and social unrest with political restraint.[13]

Justice Department officials debated Stokely's fate on the same Thursday that he reported to a pre-induction facility in New York City. Carmichael's fitness to serve in Vietnam would hinge on the results of his latest medical evaluation. Draftees, mostly from the working and welfare classes, fought the Vietnam War, on the American side, and the draft exemptions of celebrities were given particular scrutiny in the media. Stokely's draft status ranked behind actor George Hamilton (who was dating a daughter of President Johnson) and Muhammad Ali as the public's third-most popular Selective Service inquiry. After a preliminary interview with a psychiatrist, Carmichael arrived at St. Albans Naval Hospital in Queens for physical and mental tests. Carmichael's vociferous antiwar speeches placed his 1-Y exemption (available for service in emergency, but exempt because of health or other reasons) under official scrutiny, but he refused to back down. On Friday, Carmichael returned for a final medical evaluation. After completing his exam, Carmichael departed the induction center's rear entrance in a vain effort to avoid journalists. "I'd rather go to Leavenworth," he told reporters, insisting that he would refuse to serve "on the grounds of my own conscience." From the induction center on his way to a brief reunion with Mummy Olga in Harlem, Carmichael teased reporters that he wore tinted granny glasses "because they make me look non-violent," joked with the cabdriver that all this media attention meant that "somebody must have stolen something," and, once he arrived at his destination, wolfed down a plate of rice and beans and chatted with relatives. Determined to hail down a black cabbie on Harlem's 125th Street to take him to the airport, Carmichael paused as a Puerto Rican taxi pulled up. "Close enough," he said and hopped in. At Kennedy Airport, before boarding a flight to California, Carmichael repeated his promise to go to prison rather than Vietnam.[14]

The interest of the FBI and White House in Stokely's draft status surpassed that of journalists, politicians, and the general public. Naked political calculations fueled the White House's secret request to the FBI in September concerning Carmichael's Selective Service status. The FBI responded three days later, furnishing sensitive information deliberately withheld from Ramsey Clark. The confidential records revealed that Carmichael's first pre-induction exam on January 21, 1965, resulted in his draft status reclassification from 1-A to 4-F, which rendered him medically ineligible for service. The evaluating psychiatrist misidentified his civil rights activities as taking place in CORE rather than SNCC but concluded that his arrests revealed no inherent pattern of antisocial behavior. Disqualified for medical reasons, Carmichael took a second physical examination a year later, on February 14, 1966. "Has had two additional episodes of decompensation," the examination noted, "in the past following the shooting of two of his friends." The "decompensation," or paralytic nervous breakdown, followed the killings of Jonathan Daniels and Sammy Younge. Both incidents burdened the usually self-assured Carmichael with bouts of inconsolable grief and a sense of helplessness, which he overcame through organizing. The chief medical officer of the induction center gave Carmichael a "Y" symbol following this second examination, making him eligible for military service in times of war. They suggested his status be re-evaluated and updated after one year.[15]

At the University of California, Berkeley, on Saturday, October 29 with his pre-induction physical weighing heavily on his mind, Carmichael delivered his most important antiwar speech. This galvanic address, carried by newspapers across the nation, made him America's leading critic of the Vietnam War. He arrived at Berkeley with better antiwar credentials than Martin Luther King. The speech marked a crucial turning point in antiwar activism among white radicals in the New Left who organized the conference. It also showcased Carmichael's complicated relationship with white activists. Three months earlier, Carmichael had brokered the release of a joint antiwar statement with SDS president Carl Oglesby. Now, his effective linking of Black Power insurgency to the war in Vietnam offered white activists a new entrée into the black movement if they dared. Carmichael's presence in Berkeley explicitly invited whites to participate in a larger anti-imperialist movement that SNCC had sketched at the beginning of the year in its controversial antiwar statement. But, as usual, Stokely did so on his own terms. He admonished student activists for their reticence in opposing the draft with the imposing authority of an icon who had defiantly proclaimed his draft resistance before Muhammad Ali, but he offered no specific organization vehicle or interracial alliances to facilitate this objective. Following Carmichael's speech, SDS would take matters into their own hands, organizing a vast array of campus antiwar activism. Over the next two years, the Black Panthers would offer SDS and the wider New Left access to participate in the broader revolutionary struggle that Carmichael and SNCC first outlined. Despite his reluctance to actively work with white radicals, Carmichael's bold antiwar rhetoric provided the intellectual and political contours for whites to engage in a global assault against American imperialism. Stokely's increasingly hard public line against the possibility of interracial alliances obscured his continued personal and professional relationships with whites. Away from the media gaze, he followed his Berkeley speech by attending a party in San Francisco's Haight-Ashbury neighborhood, where he openly consorted with white friends and intimates in a manner that contrasted with his public stance. Carmichael enjoyed the sexual freedom, casual use of marijuana, and social pleasures that both the times and his celebrity status offered. Before fame, Stokely possessed the charm and charisma to attract the attention of a variety of women. After, his opportunities and appetites increased.[16]

At Berkeley, Carmichael's discussion of Black Power's relationship to larger failures of American democracy soared into the high ground of rhetorical eloquence as it plumbed the racial and historical depths of black life. Standing at the podium of the Greek Theatre, scanning the overwhelmingly white crowd, Stokely might have rationalized his presence at Berkeley as a kind of missionary work, since, as he remarked at an earlier press conference, "it is white institutions which perpetuate racism within the community." In California, Stokely entered the ranks of black America's iconic leaders, joining a pantheon that stretched from Frederick Douglass' abolitionism to Ida B. Wells' turn-of-the-century anti-lynching campaigns, through the controversy between Booker T. Washington (accommodation) and W.E.B. Du Bois (activism), the Marcus Garvey movement, and Malcolm's and King's parallel and morally charged political and religious crusades.[17]

Dressed in a suit and tie, he resembled a campaigning politician. Carmichael's conservative attire contrasted with the radical themes he preached in a clipped accented voice. Like an itinerant evangelist, Carmichael turned the Greek Theatre into a mass political meeting that took on the energy of an outdoor religious revival. He diagnosed America's rulers as sick with the disease of racism. Before the biggest audience so far in his speaking career, Carmichael defined racism's uncanny influence on every aspect of American life, one that he challenged Berkeley students to dismantle. "A new society must be born," he thundered. "Racism must die. Economic exploitation of non-whites must end," said Carmichael. "Martin Luther King may be full of love, but when I see Johnson on television, I say: 'Martin, baby, you have got a long way to go to accomplish anything.'"[18]

The great contradiction of the civil rights movement was that although whites were "the majority" and thus accountable for "making democracy work," blacks inevitably bore the burden of this responsibility. Blacks faced death on the racial front lines of the South even as most whites recoiled from such sacrifice. "The question," according to Carmichael, was, "how can white society move to see black people as human beings?" In hundreds of talks over the next year he would hone this theme into a dazzling stump speech that imagined novel connections between race and war and found intimate kinship between Black Power and American democracy.[19]

Carmichael sounded like a university professor: "The philosophers Camus and Sartre raise the question of whether or not a man can condemn himself. The black existentialist philosopher who is pragmatic, Frantz Fanon, answered the question. He said that man could not." Born in Martinique in 1925, Fanon settled in France as a young man and became a psychiatrist. During the French-Algerian War, he supported the Algerian Front de Libération Nationale (FLN). His book, *The Wretched of the Earth,* an exegesis on revolutionary violence's powers of renewal, partially obscured a radically humanist philosophy that implored oppressed people the world over to search for new forms of humanity free of racial and economic exploitation. Translations of Fanon's French-language books afforded him a global following that ran past his premature death from cancer in 1961 at age thirty-six. Media depictions of Carmichael invariably portrayed his temperament as running hot, ignoring the cool side that enjoyed precise intellectual and philosophical discourse.[20]

Carmichael implored those in attendance to use their individual will to form a collective barrier against escalating war. Echoing Sartre, Carmichael criticized national political leaders who made war instead of peace. "There is a higher law than the law of a racist named [Secretary of Defense Robert] McNamara," said Carmichael, "a higher law than the law of a tool named [Secretary of State Dean] Rusk, a higher law than the law of a buffoon named Johnson—it is the higher law of each of us." Waves of applause overtook his defiant roll call of White House officials escalating the Vietnam conflict. "We can't move morally against Lyndon Baines Johnson," he contended, "because he is an immoral man who doesn't know what it is all about. We must act politically." He challenged his student audience to question the basic assumptions about American democracy and join SNCC in exposing "all the myths of the country to be nothing but lies." Carmichael reveled in highlighting America's moral and political failures even as he indicted white liberals as feckless and white students as unsophisticated. "It is white people across this country who are incapable of allowing me to live where I want to live—you need a civil rights bill, not me," he said. "I know I can live where I want to live." This last line drew a burst of applause and helped to introduce a larger discussion of white privilege that became the core of the speech:

> The question then is how can white people move to start making the major institutions that they have in this country function the way it is supposed to function. That is the real question. Can white people move inside the old community and start tearing down racism where in fact it does exist—where it exists. It is you who live in Cicero and stop us from living there. It is white people who stop us from living there. It is the white people who make sure we live in ghettos of this country. It is white institutions that do that. They must change. In order for America to really live on a basic principle of human relationships, a new society must be born. Racism must die. The economic exploitation of this country on non-white peoples around the world must also die—must also die.[21]

Hysteria greeted Carmichael's Berkeley speech. Governor Pat Brown and his Republican challenger, Ronald Reagan, both decried Carmichael's appearance although each knew that it boded well for Reagan, already riding a wave of popularity buoyed by "white backlash" against black militancy. In Washington, Ramsey Clark received a fresh batch of requests from congressmen to prosecute Carmichael for promoting draft evasion. The Mississippi senator and arch-segregationist James Eastland telegrammed Clark that Carmichael's "reckless and inflammatory speeches" promoted "acts bordering on treason." But Stokely found at least one high-profile supporter, who intensely watched his every move despite an outward pose of studied disinterest. At a press conference in Norfolk, Virginia, following a sermon that warned against racially separate paths to power, Martin Luther King defended Carmichael's antiwar posture, telling reporters he would be the first to support an individual whose political actions were motivated by a call to conscience.[22]

———————

FROM GALVANIZING ANTIWAR PROTEST in Berkeley, Carmichael shifted his attention back to Lowndes, where two years of activism were culminating in a watershed election. Shortly before that election, which was to be held on Tuesday, November 1, he wrote, "I'm always thinking of Lowndes County." Two days before Lowndes County's historic election, Carmichael's efforts to organize an ad hoc protest in Selma, Alabama, about one hundred yards east of the infamous Pettus Bridge, triggered his latest stay in jail. Selma's mayor, Joe Smitherman, explained the arrests of Carmichael and two other SNCC activists as a prudent move to prevent violence, noting that the entire scene was eerily reminiscent of Atlanta's recent riot. After a weekend in jail, Carmichael posted bail just in time to join almost seven hundred people at Monday night's meeting at Mt. Moriah Baptist Church in Hayneville. Carmichael's appearance would be bittersweet, as it marked the symbolic end of his active involvement in Lowndes County politics. His appearance closed the circle begun nineteen months earlier in the wake of the Selma–Montgomery march, when he first entered Alabama with little more than the determination to organize against the grain of conventional civil rights politics.[23]

At Mt. Moriah, Carmichael delivered a passionate valediction that boiled nineteen months of organizing, marches, arrests, demonstrations, and killings down to an unwavering belief in radical democracy. Seven months earlier, Carmichael had given a bold speech at Mt. Moriah celebrating the first anniversary of the Lowndes County Freedom Organization:

> They always call it the Black Panther party because it sounds fright-
> ening, and because it encourages and reflects the physical and sexual
> fear whites have of Negroes. The symbol of the Alabama Democratic
> Party is the rooster, but you don't hear anyone calling it the White
> Cock Party. . . . Don't be afraid, 'cause you're black and nappy-headed
> and got a broad nose, that you can't handle power. Don't you let 'em
> shame you. Don't you ever talk about anything all black is bad, 'cause
> you're hating yourself. We're gonna find the blackest, most nappy-
> headed nigger and make him sheriff just to spite the white folk.[24]

In classic Stokely fashion, he challenged residents to overcome their fears
and support one of their own for high office. Now, Carmichael imagined the
next day's vote as a reckoning that would prove that blacks could "rock this
whole country from California to New York City!" He played to the religious sensibilities around him, reminding them that, "When Moses crossed
the Red Sea he left some people behind. We are going to leave some Uncle
Toms behind." Blacks in Lowndes would, at long last, be able to "say goodbye
to shacks, dirt roads, poor schools" and dream of living in the "fine brick
homes" historically reserved for whites. It was a powerful moment, one that
defied accounts that portrayed Black Power as brash, angry, and lacking clear
political objectives. As Stokely would later remark, "All the uninformed editorial writers throughout the country, all the panic-stricken whites in insu-
lated suburbs across this land should have been there that night." Through a
flash of humor on that election eve, Carmichael instantly relayed the way in
which future chroniclers would interpret tensions between civil rights and
Black Power as an insurmountable chasm: "When you mention Selma, people say—There's some mean white folks down there. But when you mention
Lowndes County, they say—There's some mean niggers down there!" Black
Power's origins, at least in Lowndes, mimicked the slow, patient community
organizing commonly associated with SNCC's heyday. This story would
prove, in the short run, too unruly, as symbols of snarling black panthers
overwhelmed the image of Carmichael locking arms with those at Mt. Moriah singing "We Shall Overcome" before hugging and kissing streams of
supporters leaving the church. Carmichael's empathy for poor black sharecroppers remained the unspoken heart of his personal and political saga.[25]

November 8, a bright and clear Tuesday, witnessed hundreds of Lowndes
County residents quietly, and unapologetically, vote for the black panther.

Drivers traveling west on Highway 80 were greeted in Lowndes by a large sign emblazoned with a picture of the fierce panther crouching just between the words "Montgomery" and "Selma," "PULL THE LEVER FOR THE BLACK PANTHER AND GO ON HOME!" Caravans of drivers shuttled voters to the polls. Reports of election irregularities spread instantly, and SNCC staff raced to combat a wide range of violations. Black voters received pre-marked ballots in certain precincts, were accompanied by whites in others, and faced widespread harassment and intimidation. At least one supporter was savagely beaten, and Fort Deposit vigilantes fired gunshots as Carmichael left a filling station. In an election plagued by voter fraud committed by plantation owners, all seven Black Panther candidates lost, but important precedents were established. White supremacy in Lowndes was doomed, and the drive for self-determination through the ballot was unleashed nationally. SNCC's monthly *Movement* newsletter defiantly characterized the election results as the dawn of a new political era: "LOWNDES COUNTY: Candidates Lose, but Black Panther Strong."[26]

Democratic breakthroughs in Lowndes worked in reverse at the national level as Republicans made historic congressional gains and added six governorships, including Ronald Reagan's landslide victory in California. "Stokely Carmichael and the New Left helped elect a number of 'white backlash' governors, Congressmen, and sheriffs," read a typical post-election analysis. At least one prominent black politician successfully leveraged Carmichael's notoriety to national prominence. Edward Brooke's triumph over former Democratic Governor Endicott Peabody, despite campaign visits by Bobby Kennedy and Hubert Humphrey, made him the first black man elected to the United States Senate in the twentieth century. Brooke's late-stage campaign mantra that "a vote for me is a vote against Stokely Carmichael" proved to be inspired. One columnist credited Carmichael as "the greatest vote getter of the day," a consequence of politicians' ability to scare up votes in a manner that defied party affiliation and common sense. Race altered long-standing political alignments, ushering in a redrawn electoral map that threatened the Democratic Party's majority in both houses of Congress and the presidency. Lyndon Johnson had anticipated as much, remarking, after signing the Voting Rights Act, that the Democrats had given up their southern electoral majority for a generation. Johnson's prediction proved overly optimistic in the long term (it would be lost for two generations at least) and painfully accurate in the short term. Racial divisions stoked negative political impulses based on fear, anger, and resentment. Elections pivoted on neither history nor truth but on the raw power of emotion and gut feelings. On this score, Carmichael's incisive analysis of backlash as an ancient problem dressed in new clothing did little to blunt its effectiveness in the national political arena. Both Republican and Democratic politicians publicly recoiled against Black Power as unabashed racial mischief even as they embraced rhetorical attacks against Carmichael as a conduit to angry white voters.[27]

The FBI continued to mark Stokely as a threat to democracy, despite his heroic efforts on behalf of the disenfranchised. On Thursday, November 17, Walter Yeagley, the assistant attorney general, sent a Justice Department memo to J. Edgar Hoover informing the FBI director that Carmichael's public antiwar statements failed to merit sedition charges. At the FBI's request, the Justice Department had pored over Carmichael's *Meet the Press* transcript, statements following his October pre-induction exam, and the well-publicized Berkeley speech. But all three instances failed to meet the legal threshold for prosecution. "In light of the foregoing," Yeagley wrote, "we have concluded that the facts do not warrant any further investigations for a violation of sedition statutes." Carmichael flew to San Francisco that same day for a week-long Bay Area visit that included public speeches, high-profile television and radio interviews, and private fundraising receptions. This crucial West Coast swing of his speaking tour reflected SNCC's efforts to coordinate the region's thriving but diffuse Black Power landscape.[28]

While the FBI searched for new avenues of prosecution, on November 15, Stokely addressed the subjects of the Vietnam War, democracy, and civil rights before 1,200 students at Yale University: "We are faced with a situation where powerless conscience meets conscienceless power. . . . Martin Luther King has the compassion of no one else in the world. I see him getting hit over the head and afterwards talking about building up love through nonviolence. But when I see Lyndon Johnson on TV, I say 'Martin baby, you've got a long way to go.'" He described Black Power as a reclamation project, one that resisted white guilt over racial oppression and black self-loathing based on the nation's racist culture. "When you're able to negotiate from a position of strength, only then will there be meaningful dialogue." Carmichael called for a national racial dialogue that moved beyond integration, which he characterized as a concept "formulated by a tiny group of Negroes who had middle-class aspirations." As he now did in all of his talks, Carmichael took the time to discuss the Vietnam War. "I think it is absolutely hypocritical for the government to talk to me about non-violence when the United States is bombing the hell out of Vietnam," said Carmichael. "I can't understand this in my own mind."[29]

Following his appearance at Yale, Carmichael toured the Bay Area speaking to college students, welfare rights organizers, and local activists. Huey P. Newton and Bobby Seale were two of the Bay Area militants most eager to meet him. The previous month, the close friends, part-time political activists, and some-time troublemakers, had founded the Black Panther Party for Self-Defense in Oakland. The sons of transplanted black southern migrants, Newton and Seale came of political age in an era that viewed young black men more as budding criminals than as law-abiding citizens. Named after Louisiana's tragically heroic Governor Huey P. Long, Huey Percy Newton divided his energies, with equal intensity, in pursuit of social justice (leading to community college and law school) and criminal activity that included jail stints. Six years older than Huey, Seale had an idiosyncratic mix of patriotism and rebellion that earned him a dishonorable discharge from the air force but made him wary of pro-Castro Cuban revolutionaries as an affront to his love of country. During the early 1960s, they dabbled in radical politics as a venue for self-improvement but judged their more experienced peers as lacking Malcolm X's rare combination of street credibility and political sincerity. Alabama's experiment in Black Power politics reverberated all the way to Oakland through a hard-nosed volunteer named Mark Comfort, an acquaintance of Newton and Seale who helped spread the panther symbol to the Bay Area. Comfort had been one of a group of secretly armed election-day sentries in Lowndes.[30]

By the time of Carmichael's visit, Newton and Seale formed a fragment of California's sprawling archipelago of political radicalism. Soon, they would emerge as leaders of the most controversial organization of the era. For now, they requested Carmichael's assistance to affirm their importance amid a cascading wave of competing groups even as their political ambition far surpassed their humble origins. Huey's grave affability impressed Carmichael even as he reserved judgment on the more loquacious Seale. Newton's quick smile balanced his naturally brooding intensity, a combination that Carmichael found refreshingly appealing. Carmichael judged the twenty-four-year-old Newton's talent for attentive listening remarkable and marked him as the rare activist more interested in studied observation than polemics. In private, Carmichael mediated tensions between various local factions, including Newton and

Seale's Oakland group, created only the month before, over which organizations could properly identify as Black Panthers. He declined to confer special
privileges on any group, correctly recognizing that such an action would only
escalate a volatile political situation. Carmichael sought a diplomatic solution
to political tensions compounded by personal grievances over turf, prestige,
and ideology that stretched back years. In his final meeting with local militants, Carmichael preached themes of racial solidarity that Newton and Seale
respectfully listened to even as they made plans to consolidate a fledgling
group of revolutionaries into a political vanguard.[31]

From the Bay Area, Stokely traveled to Los Angeles to speak before a
crowd of 6,500 at Will Rogers Park, in Watts, site of the previous year's massive civil disorder. Local television and radio crews covered the event while
FBI agents and undercover police and sheriff's department officers provided
more clandestine witness. Claims that local militants planned to burn nearby
oil fields and damage Los Angeles's Civic Center placed law enforcement
and military agencies on high alert with secret orders to arrest Carmichael
if he used incendiary words that could incite a civil disturbance. On the day
of Carmichael's speech, the FBI disseminated an intelligence report documenting ongoing surveillance and planned contingencies to the president,
secretary of state, army, air force, secret service, and defense intelligence
agency. Dressed in a suit and tie, Carmichael stood casually perched on top
of a pickup truck bed and spoke through a makeshift loudspeaker, seemingly oblivious to the organized chaos around him. It had been a year, three
months, two weeks, and a day after the start of the Watts rebellion, and Carmichael was speaking before the largest assembly of black people he had ever
addressed. Shouts of "Tell them how it is!" and "That's right!" greeted his
examination of Vietnam and American race relations. He implored blacks
in the audience to be proud of their unique beauty and condemned Western
culture as bankrupt. "Whites have made us hate ourselves," he told them. "We
should never blame ourselves for our plight."[32]

Black men carrying two-way radios ordered white reporters and cam-
eramen to the back of the crowd. Demonstrators carried signs reading "I
heard you in Berkeley" and "Give 'em Hell, Stokely" as jazz filtered through
the park. "There is a new breed of black people in the country today," said
Stokely. "My mother scrubbed floors so I could have black power." Blacks
"lauded Massa Johnson" after he appropriated the phrase "We shall overcome" on behalf of civil rights legislation, Carmichael argued, "but you will

not hear him yell 'black power.'" For forty minutes he galvanized the assemblage with talk of renewal born of bitter despair. "If what they said was true, if you could make it on hard work, black people would own this country lock, stock, and barrel. . . . I know black power is good because so many white folks came out against it." Carmichael's two raised fists thrust high in the air marked the end of the speech as waves of cheers and applause filled the park's open spaces.[33]

Alongside the political exhilaration of such moments as those at Will Rogers Park, organizational difficulties continued at SNCC. On December 1, about a hundred SNCC staff met at the Peg Leg Bates Country Club in Kerhonkson, New York, owned by the one-legged black tap dancer Clayton "Peg Leg" Bates, to consolidate, review, and critique the group's programs. Staffers hoped that the resort-like setting might encourage open discussion about the Black Power controversy, the role of whites in SNCC, and the group's future direction. Carmichael's opening remarks suggested interracial organizing still had a place within SNCC. He urged the seven remaining white staffers to continue to organize in white communities and serve as fundraisers. Carmichael's pragmatic view of SNCC's racial makeup failed to satisfy Atlanta Project members, including George Ware, who made the question of white participation a litmus test of the organization's willingness to practice political self-determination. Over the next three days, stunned veterans and largely silent white staffers witnessed the group's intense and tortured deliberation regarding an issue that most considered relatively minor.

Jim Forman watched the contentious proceedings in horror. For him the deliberations reflected SNCC's "rock bottom" in terms of leadership, political vision, and personal behavior. At a session to discuss a police raid on Chicago's SNCC office for marijuana possession, Forman almost snapped when he realized that "some of the leadership were so high from smoking pot that they could not participate in any meaningful discussion." Carmichael almost certainly belonged to the cohort of SNCC leaders whose recreational marijuana use Forman perceived as having "encouraged the corruption" of SNCC. During one meeting, the denigration of Fannie Lou Hamer as an unsophisticated rube by militants convinced of their own political wisdom represented SNCC's symbolic nadir. Overwhelmed but resolute, Forman proposed a doomed motion to disband SNCC and send any remaining funds to Guinea's revolutionary government in Africa. Forman's affinity for Marxist visions of class struggle made him skeptical of a purely race-based Black

Power formulation. Similarly, his enduring respect for process made him view the Atlanta nationalists' sometimes deliberately provocative statements as an ominous sign of SNCC's deteriorating internal culture.[34]

A resolution dismissing white members passed during a 2:00 A.M. vote by 19–18, with dozens of members absent or abstaining, underscored Forman's anxiety and provided the final epitaph to the group's public image. Now, anguished private confrontations were played out in public as a Carmichael-led witch hunt: a Black Power–inspired purge designed to erase SNCC's interracial past even at the cost of ending the group's last slender ties to white moral and financial support.

Dedicated staff found time to conduct organizational business amid the sniping. Beyond one faction's obsession with white participation, the Peg Leg Bates retreat became a site of important new business. A general agreement established nationwide freedom organizations modeled after Lowndes and symbolized by the black panther. Plans called for grassroots entities that would serve both as political parties and as social action groups organized around housing, welfare, education, and economic priorities, complete with a youth division. Looming over this ambitious agenda was the question of whether the skeleton staff possessed the expertise, unity, and will to execute the ambitious policy goals. Carmichael found the entire ordeal, as well as the false aura of myth it perpetuated, depressing. In his autobiography he largely glossed over the event, seemingly content to let his long record of interracial political and personal relationships speak for itself. For Carmichael ally Judy Richardson, the retreat represented the beginning of the end of her involvement in SNCC. The sight of Atlanta Project members "kicking in doors" frightened the level headed Richardson. Trust established through living and working together on the front lines of grassroots political organizing now bumped into corrosive levels of personal hostility "that seemed to override any connecting bonds" within SNCC.[35]

———————

FROM THE POLITICAL DRAMA of the Peg Leg Bates retreat, Stokely returned to more personal matters in New York City. On December 10, he attended his sister Lynette's wedding and stood in for Adolphus by giving the bride away during a Saturday afternoon ceremony at the family's long-standing house of worship, Westchester Methodist Church in the Bronx. An integrated crowd of about one hundred, including the wife of the Ugandan ambassador, attended the interracial couple's nuptials. Followed by African-American photographer Gordon Parks for an upcoming *Life* magazine profile, Carmichael found brief respite at the wedding reception, which doubled as a rare visit home, where he answered questions about his life in between rounds of banter with May Charles. Carmichael scored a historic legal victory three days later when Atlanta's federal court struck down Georgia's insurrection laws as unconstitutional, paving the way for his eventual clearance on rioting charges that dated back to September.[36]

He barely had the chance to absorb the good news before participating in a debate with his former mentor turned nemesis Bayard Rustin. In many ways, the debate, at Hunter College in New York, represented the dénouement of their complicated political relationship. Rustin's energetic denunciation of Black Power and Carmichael in recent months had drawn stark political lines between the two, who remained friendly, if wary, political adversaries. Privately, Rustin still regarded Carmichael as "essentially a humanist, terribly bright, and always willing to put his body on the line." The month before their debate, Rustin had stumbled across "some old pictures" and "was struck by the resemblance between me and Stokely." Troubled by a political rift that seemed to grow wider each day, Rustin found solace in their still "personally friendly" relationship and comfort in the knowledge that "if I were in deep trouble he would come to my aid, as I would help him if he needed it."[37]

Five years after Rustin's legendary verbal duel with Malcolm X at Howard University, Carmichael now assumed the role of radical provocateur. When he was a teenager and college student, Carmichael's admiration for Bayard's social democratic ideals, nuanced pacifism, and oratorical brilliance made him gloss over Rustin's pragmatic allegiance to the Democratic Party and organized labor. Rustin's loyalty to the Johnson administration, despite the Vietnam War, disappointed Carmichael politically and pained him on a more personal level.[38]

At Hunter, Carmichael and Rustin debated the future of the civil rights movement, finding common ground in the fact that without dramatic political action escalating racial violence would continue. "Lyndon Baines Johnson had better wake up or all our cities will be in a constant state of insurrection," proclaimed Carmichael. He distinguished individual prejudice from institutional racism, reasserting a novel approach to race relations that would remain an enduring, yet unacknowledged, part of his intellectual legacy.[39]

Rustin had recently compared Black Power's efforts to solve racial injustice to trying to cure cancer by using a topical antiseptic. Now he trumpeted the Freedom Budget (inspired by A. Philip Randolph) as a practical solution to pressing economic and social problems facing poor blacks. He acknowledged that Johnson's focus on Vietnam increased the probability of civil disorders, but remained steadfast in his belief that blacks needed interracial allies. Rustin explained his support for the president as "the lesser of two evils." Carmichael pounced on this answer, arguing that blacks needed creative alternatives based on their intimate knowledge that "this is a racist country from the top to the bottom, from left to right."[40]

A Louis Harris poll released on Monday, December 19 seemed to support Rustin's position. Carmichael's approval rating stood at just 2 percent among whites and 18 percent in the black community in contrast to Martin Luther King's 64 percent rating, although whites' three-to-two disapproval of King reflected the depth of the nation's racial crisis. Critics interpreted Carmichael's poll numbers as if he were a politician "felt by both whites and Negroes to be a harmful influence on civil rights progress" instead of a radical activist whose growing fame and genuine appeal in the black community transcended statistical surveys.[41]

Despite Carmichael's low poll numbers, his image provided brisk business for newspapers and magazines. Throughout December, *Esquire* magazine placed splashy ads in newspapers, headlined "The Black Power of Stokely Carmichael" and touting an in-depth profile that promised an unvarnished portrait of black rebellion as personified by "one man's defiant, angry protest against racial injustice." Another *Esquire* ad, "A Report on Stokely Carmichael and his POWER: Color it black," packaged black radicalism as the SNCC chairman's personal brand, a dangerous but thrilling commodity.[42]

If Carmichael remained an outlier among mainstream Americans, the counterculture embraced him. At a December 22nd SNCC benefit at the Village Theater in New York's East Village, Carmichael joined saxophonists Archie Shepp, Marion Brown, and Jackie McLean and poet A.B. Spellman for an insouciant evening of music, poetry, and politics. Posters splashed all over the East Village trumpeted his keynote, as did the theater marquee. A sizable audience rewarded this advanced publicity and reflected Carmichael's celebrity. Possessed of the uncommon ability to project an aura of charismatic friendship to friends and foes alike, Carmichael immediately put the audience at ease with a splash of humor.

The technical backup to the show was a bit haphazard. The room was almost totally dark when Stokely came onstage. Wires from the speakers for the musicians provided an obstacle course for even the agile Stokely. "I'm talking to an amorphous mass of blackness," Carmichael remarked to hysterical laughter. Like a seasoned performer he continued an improvised routine even after the lights came on. "I'm going to find which one belongs to the CIA," he quipped while untangling microphones from the earlier jazz performance. Carmichael shifted from jokes to politics, unleashing an expert imitation of Lyndon Johnson—"We shall overcome, mah fellow Americans"—criticizing the Vietnam War, and, in the next breath, announcing Jesus Christ as the world's most foremost revolutionary. He briefly addressed his own mortality: "They got Malcolm pretty easy but they'll have to take a harder shot to get me." Carmichael finished his fifteen-minute speech with a brief segue way back to Archie Shepp. "I really dig this music," said Carmichael. "It's my kind of Christmas music," he said, before singing a few lines of "Jingle Bells" and walking off stage.[43]

CHAPTER ELEVEN

"Hell No, We Won't Go!"

January–July 10, 1967

CARMICHAEL'S REMARKABLE YEAR HAD ELEVATED HIM ALONGSIDE MARTIN Luther King as one of the most influential and reviled figures in American politics. He experienced a disorienting transition from a full-time political organizer into a national icon whose personal celebrity at times overshadowed his political exploits. Carmichael's notoriety obscured SNCC's diminishing organizational base and fundraising capacity. A dizzying speaking schedule compounded these difficulties, offering scant time for the organizing necessary to restore SNCC's faltering political capabilities. For the first time since college, he found himself looking for new political opportunities. Trips to Puerto Rico and Canada whetted his appetite for the kind of international travels that had been Malcolm X's trademark. Carmichael's deepening involvement in antiwar protests popularized the chant of "Hell No, We Won't Go!" into a national slogan and pushed Martin Luther King toward his own, more celebrated, critique against the war. Carmichael increasingly focused his political energies and intellectual interests in pursuit of political terrain that transcended domestic politics. He longed to participate in the undiscovered world of anti-colonial upheavals, political rebellions, and international revolutions. The unquestioned symbol of black radicals in America, Carmichael set his sights on the risky proposition of transitioning into an international revolutionary.[1]

Carmichael's most remarkable transition pivoted on his ability to project himself as a thoughtfully outspoken antiwar activist whose influence extended beyond Black Power militants into the world of peace activists and human rights advocates, most notably Martin Luther King. He was just twenty-five, but the pace of history burdened Carmichael with the responsibility of displaying a wisdom and maturity that belied his youth. It wasn't easy and didn't always end well. Carmichael spent the first half of the year torn between claiming the mantle of Black Power radical and pursuing the more difficult role of political statesman.

Stokely spent the New Year defending embattled congressman Adam Clayton Powell Jr. in Washington. Powell faced corruption charges even as his loyal constituents defended him as a powerful black politician under unseemly attacks from a racist system. On January 10, inside the House of Representatives, as Powell's colleagues voted against reinstating him, outside Stokely spoke to a thousand demonstrators protesting the House action. News that Powell's illustrious and at times infamous career teetered on the brink of extinction attracted a broad section of activists who viewed the development as racially motivated. Carmichael emerged as Powell's most visible supporter, instructing the large crowd to focus their organizing energies on the White House. "The main cat you focus on is Lyndon Baines Johnson," said Carmichael, who described the president as an old-school political boss who controlled blacks through the Democratic Party machine. The cure, he insisted, was "not to bloc vote but to black vote."[2]

Edward Brooke's dramatic political ascension paralleled Powell's fall. Brooke, escorted by Massachusetts senior senator Ted Kennedy, entered the Senate Chamber to a standing ovation from his new colleagues. Brooke and Powell both utilized controversy over Carmichael's Black Power cry to advance their political ambitions. Whereas Brooke parlayed this advance largely through deft rhetorical maneuvers that repudiated Carmichael's brand of militancy, Powell alternately praised and teased the young SNCC chairman (as he had often done with Malcolm X) in an effort to assert himself as the pragmatic godfather of the entire Black Power enterprise. Powell boasted to his friends in Congress of having recruited the "entire spectrum of Negro leadership behind me—all the way from Roy Weak Knees (Wilkins) to Whitey (Whitney) Young to Martin Loser (Luther) King to that kook Stokely Carmichael."[3]

Powell's afternoon speech represented a valediction of sorts. In contrast to his demeanor inside the chamber, where he spoke in hushed whispers about personal and ethical lapses, outside the Harlem legend told demonstrators to withhold federal taxes, spread the word about his dismissal around the country, and mark the day as the beginning of a national decline in American political life. "This building," said Powell as he pointed toward the Capitol with his cigar, "houses the biggest bunch of elected hypocrites in the world." His ten-minute speech hinted at forming a third party and grand plans to stoke political revolutions that he had neither the energy nor enthusiasm to embark on.[4]

As THE SUN SET ON AN ERA of racial militancy in national politics, Carmichael made his most important professional decision since running for chair of SNCC. He pressed on with a grueling speaking schedule, but on Irv Kupcinet's Chicago television show, broadcast on Thursday, January 12, he announced he would not seek re-election as SNCC chairman. Publicly, he characterized his decision as a procedural matter, assuring Kupcinet that he had no intentions of retiring from the movement. Privately, an exhausted Carmichael made plans to return to Washington as a full-time organizer. Away from the spotlight, Carmichael met with local Chicago militants and defended his appearance at predominantly white schools as a matter of financial survival, noting that most black groups could not match his speaking fees. Carmichael's trip to Chicago followed an established routine organized by Cleve Sellers, who often traveled with him. Brief moments of relaxation marked late nights that often drifted into early-morning after-parties. Carmichael's travel schedule, celebrity, and wandering eye made a steady romantic relationship difficult. Indeed, since Mary Lovelace's surprise wedding, Carmichael's personal life seemed adrift in a series of sexual conquests that marked him as an energetic but discreet womanizer.[5]

SNCC's organizational woes also continued. Marion Barry, SNCC's first chairman, resigned from the Washington office in January to begin a journey that would culminate in his election as D.C. mayor in a little over a decade. "I do not think we ought to open a D.C. office," Stokely observed in an archly written memo, "unless we have some new people who are willing to go there and do some work." In addition to Washington, he suggested that SNCC either close the Los Angeles office or find a new staff capable of fundraising and reaching out to the black community in Watts. In a flurry of memos, Carmichael tried to make sense of organizational decline while cataloguing deficiencies that extended to San Francisco's once sparkling fundraising apparatus. The central committee responded with action, suspending the Los Angeles office and dismissing its full-time staff member, closing the Chicago office, and accepting Barry's resignation. They also wielded more control over Stokely's speaking schedule. They vetoed an appearance on *Firing Line,* the conservative William F. Buckley's public-affairs TV show but agreed to his participation in a Bay Area political conference. Their directive that "Stokely is always to be accompanied by a SNCC staff person at his engagements" was one that Carmichael almost certainly chafed at.[6]

Carmichael was defining Black Power in an expanded historical context. At a January 16th appearance at Morgan State University in Baltimore, he invoked Frederick Douglass' message about "power conceding nothing without demand," as a nineteenth-century version of Black Power. His debt to Douglass transcended their shared interest in political self-determination, dazzling oratory, and knack for earning national publicity. The premier self-made man of his generation (alongside Abraham Lincoln), Douglass innovated a tradition of black political activism that inspired the likes of Marcus Garvey and Malcolm X. If Douglass remained the embodiment of nineteenth-century black political self-determination, Carmichael now claimed his place within this tradition. "This country has been able to make us ashamed of being black," he observed. "We must stop imitating white society and begin to create for ourselves and our own and begin to embody our cultural patterns so that we will be holding to things that we have created, and holding them dear." This act of self-definition would lead to a critique of America's failure to live up to its lofty ideals of freedom and liberty. "You must begin to understand the nature of this country called America, which exploits all other, non-white countries," he said, offering a clear definition of what many radicals now called imperialism. Stokely had once had an unwavering belief in radical democracy, but he now confronted a growing realization that America, far from being a global beacon of freedom, was in fact an empire. He closed his speech with a generational plea: "When we began to crawl, they sent six million people to an oven and we blinked our eyes. When we walked they sent our uncles to Korea. And we grew up in a cold war. We, this generation, must save the world."[7]

Eldridge Cleaver, an ex-convict turned journalist, accompanied Stokely to Morgan that day as part of a writing assignment for *Ramparts* magazine. Cleaver lingered over Carmichael's words, laughed at his jokes, and marveled at his ability to establish instant rapport with his audience. A convicted felon and self-confessed rapist, Cleaver had transformed himself into a radical writer. In prison, he had begun a love affair with his lawyer, Beverly Axelrod, who introduced him to leading Bay Area intellectuals, including the editors of *Ramparts*, a formerly liberal Catholic magazine undergoing an evolution into one the era's most influential New Left publications. Cleaver's physical appeal paralleled his budding literary pursuits. Dangerously handsome with the imposing six-foot-two bearing of a former athlete, the thirty-one-year-old Cleaver found a political mentor in the twenty-five-year-old Carmichael. Cleaver's instant admiration for Carmichael began a professional relationship that would mature into a personal friendship doomed by petty jealousies, organizational rivalries, and mistrust. A member of the Nation of Islam in prison, Cleaver had followed Malcolm's exit into apostasy. In addition to chairing the Bay Area's Malcolm X Afro-American Society and turning his rented Fillmore-area brownstone into an intellectual and cultural salon for Black Power activists, Cleaver entered Carmichael's politically intoxicating orbit.

In late January, Stokely (without Cleaver) visited Puerto Rico. Ella Baker, who had worked with Puerto Rican nationalists in New York in the 1950s, helped arrange the itinerary. Her international vision of the movement had influenced Stokely, and the trip was a realization of this vision. The trip appealed to Cleaver and other Black Power activists eager to discover a shared international history of racial and colonial oppression. On January 24 Carmichael arrived in San Juan to throngs of cheering supporters. Local activists and students representing the Movimiento de la Independencia Puertorriqueña (MPIPR) and the Federación de Universitarios Pro-Independencia (FUPI) organized his tour. Carmichael gave a brief speech at the airport in halting, broken Spanish, before being whisked away to La Perla, a ghetto bordering the ocean. From there he traveled to a local cemetery to visit the gravesite of Pedro Albizu Campos, a legendary hero of Puerto Rican independence, who had died in 1965. Stokely's entourage reconvened later in Old San Juan, where he read a statement to reporters expressing SNCC's support for Puerto Rican independence. "Our people are a colony inside the United States," he said; "you are a colony outside of the United States." He vowed to resist American military efforts to recruit blacks and Puerto Ricans into the armed forces. "We have experienced with our own bodies and our own blood what this so-called U.S. democracy means," Stokely declared.[8]

Carmichael's visit to Puerto Rico sent FBI and Foreign Service Bureau agents scurrying to keep pace with his travel schedule. Carmichael's arrival in advance of an island-wide July vote to choose between independence and statehood fanned partisan flames on both sides of the political divide. Wearing sandals, blue jeans, and a wide-brimmed hat that made him look like a brown-skinned *campesino,* Carmichael led an antiwar student demonstration the next day on the streets of San Juan. Carmichael and over two hundred demonstrators marched from the University of Puerto Rico in Río Piedras to a military induction center in Fort Brook escorted by fifty helmeted riot squad officers. In the barrio of Santurce, dozens of local police offered protection against rock- and egg-throwing anti-Communist hecklers as Carmichael completed a seven-mile trek. Supporters carried a large sign reading "*Apoyamos el poder Negro en los estados unidos,*" and raucous chants of "Puerto Ricans, Yes—Yankees, No!," competed against cries of "Puerto Ricans, Yes—Russians, No!" a development Carmichael blamed on anti-Castro Cubans. He gave a brief address at the Fort Brook rendezvous point, assuring the crowd that blacks would "not fight the dirty war in Vietnam," before rain ended the rally. Carmichael spent the last day of his visit in Mayaguez, where he merged themes of Puerto Rican independence and Black Power. He departed San Juan on an evening flight but not before holding a press conference with independence advocates to announce the signing of a joint alliance forged in a "common struggle against U.S. imperialism" between SNCC, MPIPR, and FUPI, which continued a pattern of establishing coalitions with political outliers.[9]

Three days after leaving San Juan, Carmichael headlined the final day of a Black Power conference in San Francisco. Participants included Maulana Karenga, whose ubiquitous presence demonstrated Stokely's ability to consolidate black radicals on the West Coast into a coherent political force. Karenga, the bald and loquacious leader of the Organization Us (which stood for "Us blacks"), was doing important work, forging local bonds with militants who shaped the movement's grassroots character. Karenga's offbeat brilliance made his love of African culture and ritualized expression of racial solidarity sometimes rub urban militants the wrong way. His obvious intelligence, puckish sense of humor, and sartorial flair seemed ready made for mass consumption, yet enduring fame would elude him although not his ideas. Overshadowed by the leather-jacketed allure of the Black Panthers, the Organization Us would endure, like jazz, through invented cultural flourishes (primarily through Kwanzaa) that would be adopted by generations of black Americans.[10]

Another soon-to-be-major West Coast figure, Huey Newton, also attended the conference. He had first met Stokely the previous November. He was brimming with ambitions for his Black Panther Party for Self-Defense that far exceeded the group's modest resources. Still embroiled in competition with rivals over naming rights, he dreamed of fashioning the type of national political party of which Carmichael himself often spoke.

Carmichael was fresh from Puerto Rico, and his speech explored the conference's theme of "black survival" through a discussion of the urgent need for national politics attuned to world affairs. Black militants interpreted Governor Ronald Reagan's political ascendancy as the first step in a nationwide counter-revolution. Carmichael's speech reminded them that only a lack of political imagination prevented black political control of the Bay Area. "We must begin to think international politics and alliances [and] align ourselves with people of color around the world who are also oppressed." If Carmichael's early activism had made him an eloquent proponent of radical democracy, he now railed against conventional notions of American exceptionalism. "We are determined to tear up the pie," he said, "because to get a piece of that pie one has to be antiblack. SNCC says and is determined to be successful and black." At the conclusion of his speech, the audience of seven hundred at the Russian Center of San Francisco gave him a standing ovation.[11]

In between standing ovations in various venues, Stokely struggled to catch up with his voluminous correspondence. He sent personal letters to James Baldwin promising to "get us some Black Power" and expressed more intimate sentiments to female companions from Albany, Georgia, to Paris, France. Carmichael's good looks, charm, and celebrity afforded him the opportunity for frequent post-lecture romantic encounters with politically engaged female admirers. "All I could say is that I would like to see you again," he wrote to Gloria Madden, "but that is just impossible because I'll be in and out of the country from now until the summer (my schedule is already preplanned) and nothing looking near to or by Cleveland."[12]

At twenty-five, Stokely regarded his romantic relationships with women as secondary to his primary role as a political activist and organizer. Nonetheless, he devoted considerable energy to maintaining a complex array of romantic entanglements. He regretted his punishing traveling schedule, joked about his fear of commitment, and made plans for future assignations. "I just find myself grasping," Carmichael confessed to Madden in early February, a description that accurately reflected the emotional and physical toll that life as a national political leader exacted. As emotionally distant with women as he was sexually passionate, Carmichael left a string of paramours in a perpetual state of romantic limbo.[13]

Carmichael's burgeoning celebrity attracted a coterie of high-profile personal and professional admirers. Eldridge Cleaver observed Carmichael's travails through a lens of personal envy and political ambition. Cleaver's position as a staff writer at *Ramparts* and other connections allowed him to maintain a relatively secure lifestyle while providing eager white radicals an entrée into black militancy. The tiny Black Panther Party for Self-Defense, for different reasons, attracted both *Ramparts* and Cleaver. A Malcolm X memorial in February featured a contingent of armed Panthers escorting Malcolm's widow, Betty Shabazz, to the *Ramparts* offices. In the confusion that followed, there was a near shootout between police and Panthers. The drama earned Cleaver's newfound respect for a group of militants eager to recruit him.[14]

If the Black Panthers appealed to Cleaver's sense of danger, Carmichael inspired more intellectual ambitions. In the weeks following the Black Panthers' confrontation with police, Cleaver continued to travel with Stokely on assignment for *Ramparts*. His *Ramparts* essay "My Father and Stokely Carmichael," portrayed Stokely as the leader of a new era freed from the humiliating accommodations of the past. In Cleaver's opening description of SNCC's decrepit Chicago offices, the blaring sounds of John Coltrane playing in the background became a soundtrack to hip movement activists. The fleeting presence of Cleaver's father, who briefly accompanied him to SNCC's offices in search of Carmichael, served as the article's opening salvo. Traveling in the middle of a freezing Chicago winter, Cleaver observed and wrote, with a barely concealed mixture of pride and admiration, about Carmichael conducting television interviews, meeting with local militants, and speaking before a predominantly white audience at the University of Chicago. Cleaver had personal reasons for feeling indebted to Stokely, who introduced him to SNCC worker Kathleen Neal. She would, following a whirlwind romance, become his wife. A brilliant speaker, eloquent writer, and accomplished activist in her own right, Kathleen catapulted her way into the front ranks of the Bay Area's burgeoning political radicalism. As Kathleen Cleaver, she would become the Black Panthers' communications secretary and one of the best-known female Black Power activists of the era.

"Stokely Carmichael," wrote Cleaver, "is the first of his stature to finish a college degree." Cleaver positioned Carmichael as the latest in a black nationalist pantheon that included Malcolm X, Elijah Muhammad, and Marcus Garvey. He praised Stokely's six years of service in the South as a courageous tour of duty that prepared him to lead a larger revolutionary movement. For Cleaver, the combination of Carmichael's intellectual agility and mass appeal offered historic opportunities. He held up Carmichael's plans to tour Africa as part of a necessary cosmopolitanism that soared above the cosmology of the Nation of Islam and the racial separatism adopted by some black militants. Cleaver would take Carmichael's dictum of establishing "specific alliances on specific issues" as potent collateral against whispers that questioned his close interracial personal and professional contacts. Carmichael's youthful vitality and unparalleled ability to evoke fear and admiration in intimate and large-scale encounters made a lasting impression on Cleaver. Barely three months out of prison and with a full three years left on his parole, Cleaver requested permission to accompany his hero on a tour of Africa. The request pivoted on Cleaver's status as a journalist and, if granted, would take him to exotic locales, including Egypt, Liberia, Guinea, Ethiopia, and Ghana. But because of his "short time on parole" and past parole violations, permission was denied.[15]

Carmichael's ability to mesmerize white audiences rivaled his hold over Cleaver and black militants. Seven thousand Berkeley students listened in rapt attention to Carmichael's February 17th account of his years as a local civil rights organizer. After five years of nonviolent direct action, Carmichael said, white authorities could no longer brutalize him without fear of retaliation. "If he touches me, I'm going to try and kill him." Carmichael challenged Berkeley's students and the larger New Left to become radical missionaries in an effort to cleanse America's racist soul. "Fight to take over," he admonished, "and fight to find white leaders who are civilized." Political transformation required a new generation to "change the whole society," which included "taking over the corporate structure and running it." The next morning, he fielded questions from over a hundred participants who attended an invitation-only Black Power conference held at the Masonic Temple in Los Angeles. Then he flew to New York to attend a Malcolm X memorial.[16]

Following the Malcolm X commemoration, Carmichael left the country for a brief speaking tour of leading Canadian universities. At Montreal's McGill University, on February 23, he spoke before an audience that found his combination of physical appeal and intellectual provocation irresistible. The next day, the Trinidadian born, one-time Trotskyite, and life-long Marxist historian C.L.R. James joined dozens of blacks, among a sea of white students, at Carmichael's February 24 lecture at Sir George Williams University, also in Montreal. James' eclectic writings on Haiti, class struggle, and cricket made him an intellectual hero for radicals drawn to his imaginative blend of intellectual theory and revolutionary politics. James had been deported from the United States to England in 1953 because of his radical politics, but his influence extended to black militants in Detroit, Caribbean revolutionaries turned statesmen, and newly elected African rulers. Carmichael's speech, demeanor, and charisma impressed James, who wrote to him shortly after. Old enough at sixty-six to be Stokely's grandfather, James identified Black Power as the culmination of mass political energies harnessed by world historic figures including Marcus Garvey, George Padmore, and Frantz Fanon. Thus began an occasional correspondence and cordial political relationship that found the elderly Trinidadian offering the wisdom of a lifetime spent studying historical materialism to Carmichael. The standing ovation that ended Carmichael's presentation rivaled the wild cheers and large crowds that greeted his appearance, the same day, at the Université de Montréal.[17]

From prestigious Canadian universities, his punishing schedule continued into March, with a swing through western Pennsylvania. There he spoke at two universities and a church in Pittsburgh (where he invoked a popular chant—"Beep, Beep, Bang, Bang, Ungowwa Black Power"—that young people would continue to repeat years after his lecture), followed by a lecture at Saint Vincent College in Latrobe. His March 2nd itinerary in Pittsburgh offered an instructive view of his typical speaking schedule in major cities. Appearances at the University of Pittsburgh and Point Park Junior College were supplemented by a press conference during the day and capped off by an evening, standing-room-only lecture at Ebenezer Church in front of a predominantly black crowd of several thousand.[18]

As Carmichael spoke in Pittsburgh, Lyndon Johnson returned to the scene of one of his finest hours as president. Johnson's unannounced visit to Howard University reaffirmed his commitment to racial justice in a symbolic effort to recapture the urgent momentum that galvanized his historic commencement address almost two years earlier. "I don't want to turn back," he promised a surprised crowd of students, faculty, and staff on hand to celebrate Howard's centennial anniversary. Symbolically, Johnson's appearance suggested that the president's faith in the struggle for civil rights remained steadfast. "I have come back to Howard today to renew my commitment to that task," he pledged, "and to tell you that so long as I live, in public or private life, I shall never retreat or amend that commitment." The widely covered speech received warm applause from Howard's audience and showcased the political sophistication of a generation of black college students intelligent enough to support the starkly divergent visions of American democracy of both Johnson and Carmichael.[19]

Carmichael returned to Atlanta for a few days. There, he lent support to members of NOI Temple No. 15, who had recently engaged in a violent altercation with the police. Then he presided over a grueling SNCC central committee meeting, where long-festering wounds over the increasingly erratic behavior of Atlanta Project members reached a boiling point. On Saturday, March 4, the central committee convened to discuss the recent firing of two Atlanta Project staffers, a maneuver sanctioned by Carmichael and Cleve Sellers to end disputes over the proper use of SNCC-owned vehicles. Because of SNCC's personal intrigues there, staff referred to Atlanta as "Peyton Place," after the TV soap opera. Jim Forman clung to a desperate hope, "that despite our fumblings and our fucked-up internal situations," SNCC remained the radical black movement's political face, albeit one undergoing a painful re-evaluation.[20]

For Carmichael, SNCC's transformations meant that he had to dramatically curtail speaking to white audiences. He said, "Personally I have three more engagements before white audiences" before he would retire from the college lecture circuit. Having reached "the conclusion that SNCC will not move into the black community and begin fund-raising until we go broke," he scheduled twenty-two speeches at black colleges over the next two months in advance of a May staff meeting. Carmichael characterized his visit to Pittsburgh, where he stayed an extra day organizing an Afro-American club, as a model for his future speaking engagements. He had concluded that SNCC had "to direct our attention to black people only." He also announced plans to roam Alabama, Mississippi, and southwest Georgia in hopes of lending his experience to ailing projects. "I'm tired," he lamented, "of being a showpiece." These last remarks were partially fueled by Carmichael having observed vendors hawking one-dollar buttons of his likeness that grinned when shook, an image that sent staff into convulsive laughter.[21]

And then on March 14, at Lafayette College in Easton, Pennsylvania, the personal and political collided. Stokely delivered what would have been a standard stump speech decrying American involvement in Vietnam, except that his appearance came the day after his local draft board had changed his classification from 1-Y to 4-F, exempting him from military service.[22]

With his own military service resolved, Carmichael continued to link Black Power and Vietnam as part of a radical critique of American racism that defined the nation as an empire whose imperial ambitions threatened humanity's future. Martin Luther King was perhaps the individual most affected by Carmichael's high-profile antiwar message. That spring King definitively amplified Carmichael's seasoned antiwar rhetoric in a measured, resolute speech that sent shockwaves across the nation and around the world. King's April 4th address at New York's Riverside Church lent international stature and moral clarity to antiwar speeches that Stokely had defiantly delivered as SNCC chairman. At Riverside, King balanced his personal disappointment in American democracy with weary hope. "The world now demands," he pleaded, "a maturity of America that we may not be able to achieve." King's words now resound with an authority that would in later years swell. But, shortly after the Riverside speech, he found himself in the uncomfortable position of having to disabuse some observers that he was simply echoing Carmichael's antiwar stance. He needn't have worried. King's peace advocacy impressed future historians as a daring rejection of the status quo, just as association with Black Power would muffle Carmichael's stridently eloquent antiwar advocacy. King's bold antiwar talk made efforts to negatively link him to Carmichael—whispered since the Meredith March—easier for critics who correctly identified both men as political revolutionaries. "If Negroes hope to continue to make progress, they had better get responsible leadership and repudiate the Kings and Carmichaels," warned the *Chicago Tribune* on April 6.[23]

At Tennessee State University on Friday, April 7, Carmichael urged four thousand students to wake up from their political stupor and fight for black rights. He detailed the difference between institutional racism and individual prejudice; the real enemy was not prejudiced individuals but racist institutions: "You're going to fight institutionalized racism; the reason it is able to perpetuate itself is because of power. Not love. Not morality. Not nonviolence, but power. And if you're going to check it, you need power to counteract the power that is used to perpetrate . . . institutionalized racism in this country. That's Black Power."[24]

His appearance at the historically black school represented a triumph of self-determination, after three thousand students had signed petitions urging administrators to uphold freedom of speech over fears of subversion and let him speak. "We must become masters of our own terms," he said. Only black people could define themselves. "We are not savages," he told the room full of black students. "We are not culturally deprived. We are not apathetic. We are not lazy [but] beautiful, black, intelligent, aggressive people," he proclaimed to applause.[25]

He chided students for ignoring a political revolution gripping the entire globe "and you don't even know how democracy works in your own little Nashville." The more he ridiculed them, the more they cheered. "You ought to organize and take over this city, but you don't do it because you don't want power." The day before, Carmichael briefly conferred with Martin Luther King, in town to address Vanderbilt University's "Impact Symposium." The sight of Carmichael and King together offered a jarring image of the potential for black social and political transformation. Carmichael introduced King to his new friend Eldridge Cleaver, who had accompanied Stokely to Vanderbilt. Cleaver would remember the moment as a time when Carmichael's mere presence "threw the entire state into an uproar."[26]

On Saturday, Carmichael addressed a capacity crowd at Vanderbilt, where he delivered a radical critique of American democracy. It was based on a *Massachusetts Review* essay on black power he had written with former NAG member and *Hilltop* editor Michael Thelwell. His easy humor remained intact, however, as he only half-jokingly ordered "the honkies of *The Banner*," the conservative Nashville daily, to "leave because you will not begin to understand the lecture that I am about to give." That evening, unrelated bedlam broke around Nashville's black Fisk University, where Carmichael had spoken the previous day. The violence left three students wounded by gunfire, dozens injured, and almost one hundred in jail. Cries of "Black Power!" pierced through a confrontation between Fisk students and riot police, which had begun as a Saturday evening demonstration over the arrest of a black student at a nearby restaurant and escalated into a small riot.[27]

By Sunday, violent flashes spread to Tennessee State's campus, leaving Nashville in a confused state of spreading panic linked together by Carmichael's presence. Rioting in the wake of his brief visit fulfilled the warnings of the *Nashville Banner*, which vilified Carmichael as an "interloper" and "firebrand" in advance of his appearance. *The Nashville Tennessean* defended Carmichael as a test of First Amendment freedoms, noting that he represented merely the most powerful voice of a movement the region ignored at its own peril. Shades of Atlanta hovered over the Fisk disturbance after one local black leader practically accused Carmichael of igniting the flames of Nashville's riot through militant proxies. Carmichael's volatile image contrasted with his recent appearance on WPLN's *Nashville Forum,* where he chatted amiably about independent politics, quoted the Book of Job to explain black people's right to self-defense, and deliberated on Frantz Fanon. One panelist on the show lamented that his militancy frightened white liberals eager to confront America's racial sins. "Well then, if you want to make up for the sins, you go to the sinners," replied Carmichael. *The New York Times* responded to the Nashville disturbance by writing SNCC's epitaph, describing the group as financially insolvent and Carmichael as a "romantic young man who busies himself speaking mainly to white audiences who are intrigued by his inflammatory rhetoric."[28]

If Nashville showcased Stokely's romantic side, a speech in New York soon hinted at a newfound revolutionary pragmatism. On Saturday, April 15, King, Carmichael, and hundreds of thousands of others marched from Central Park to the United Nations, as part of the Spring Mobilization to End the War in Vietnam. The two men's appearance together marked them as friendly political adversaries whose seemingly disparate constituencies united in opposing the Vietnam War. The two shared top billing with Harry Belafonte, Dr. Benjamin Spock, and the event's organizer, James Bevel, as speakers in front of the UN. If Carmichael's imaginative blend of civil rights, Black Power, and Vietnam elicited anger, King's efforts inspired reactions that ran the gamut from betrayal to rage to condescension. Without mentioning him, the NAACP repudiated the notion of linking civil rights and peace movements as a "serious tactical mistake," while King's fellow Nobel laureate Ralph Bunche publicly urged him to resign from the movement or maintain a decorous silence on Vietnam.[29]

In New York, Carmichael linked arms with King, Spock, Belafonte, and Bevel in the march's front ranks, which led swelling numbers of demonstrators that city officials put at one hundred thousand and rally organizers claimed as four times larger. It was the largest peace demonstration in American history. Three thousand local police officers were joined by the less visible presence of FBI agents and surveillance teams who observed marchers gather at

Central Park's Sheep Meadow destined for the United Nations Plaza. Two more Central Park staging areas bustled with activity in advance of the noon start time as demonstrators listened to folk singers, rock and roll bands, and poetry. Dozens of Cornell University students burned their draft cards in an act that marked a symbolic shift in the public rejection of war and inspired a hundred more young men to join them in creating an improvisational fire they kept contained to a coffee can.[30]

At noon, a cavalcade of demonstrators began a four-hour procession toward the United Nations. Black nationalists from Harlem, white housewives from Westchester, poets from Greenwich Village and the East Village, and college students from all over joined the march route. Counter-demonstrators hurled eggs and paint at protesters but were kept largely in check by police. Carmichael and King walked along the front line of the march protected by peace marshals deployed by Ivanhoe Donaldson, in a reprise of security measures that dated back to Selma.

From the platform erected at the United Nations Plaza, Carmichael repeated his antiwar proclamations amid chants of "Black Power!" He was serving, for the first time since the Meredith March, as a powerful warm-up act for Dr. King. "I am here today," he began, "not just as the chairman of the Student Nonviolent Coordinating Committee, not just as an advocate of black power, but as a black man [and] human being who joins you in voicing opposition to the war on the Vietnamese people." Invoking Malcolm X, he questioned the values of a nation willing to wage war in the name of liberty and deploy American military strength against the Third World under the guise of freedom. "We black people have struggled against white supremacy here at home," observed Carmichael. "We therefore understand the struggle against white supremacy abroad." Carmichael declared public support for "Dr. Martin Luther King's stand" and reminded listeners that his Nobel Prize showed "that at least in Sweden, the connection between ending war and ending racism is clear." He challenged his critics to consider a Biblical quote: "What would it profit a man to gain the world and lose his soul?" Carmichael juxtaposed the moral clarity of the Nuremberg Trials in the aftermath of the Second World War with contemporary silence regarding Vietnam. "Where is the voice of conscience today?" he wondered. "We have not only a right to speak out. We have an obligation."[31]

As he often did in such large public settings, Carmichael assumed the role of professor. Here he was delivering a seminar on American imperialism, a system that enabled the nation to casually smother anti-colonial impulses even as it professed its commitment to spreading democratic freedoms around the world:

> We maintain that America's cry of "preserve freedom in the world" is a hypocritical mask behind which it squashes liberation movements which are not bound, and refuse to be bound, by the United States' cold war policies. We see no reason for black men, who are daily murdered physically and mentally in this country, to go and kill yellow people abroad, who have done nothing to us and are, in fact, victims of the same oppression. We will not support LBJ's racist war in Vietnam.[32]

Carmichael chastised Ralph Bunche "up on the 38th floor of this building" who "once marched against police brutality in Selma, Alabama" but "today condemns those of us who speak out against the war." Bunche's hypocrisy mirrored the president's, since LBJ continued to talk of peace "while Napalming Vietnamese children." The massive size of the gathering offered an alternative to this political misery: "In your great numbers lies a small hope."[33]

His speech delivered words of fire but extended a political olive branch to those brave enough to recognize the sacred political ground shared by peace activists and Black Power radicals. Carmichael judged the Mobilization an enormous success. He was impressed by the massive turnout, which convinced him that young people held the key to transforming American society. Perhaps the sea of faces evoked a tinge of nostalgia in Stokely, who effusively praised the gathering in private to the point of discussing the possibilities of interracial democracy. He found the entire event moving enough to write to Lorna Smith that young people, both black and white, offered American society its last best hope. With trusted white friends and colleagues, Carmichael still held out hope for a revolutionary future that featured interracial coalitions.[34]

Carmichael and King met later that night at Harry Belafonte's sprawling New York City apartment. Their still-warm personal relationship smoothed over rough patches of conversation that found Stokely interpreting King's Riverside address and UN appearance as being influenced by his own antiwar posture. Carmichael reveled in the fact that his contrarian advocacy of Black Power and an end to the Vietnam War could jolt King into action and found it too irresistible, at least in private, not to mention it personally. Carmichael's performance softened some of his most ardent critics inside the movement. Stanley Levison, whose enmity had raged since Atlanta's riot, conceded that Carmichael's efforts at rapprochement affected the demonstration positively.[35]

The African-American photographer Gordon Parks visited Carmichael in the Bronx shortly after his United Nations speech as part of a *Life* magazine profile. Carmichael touted King's Vietnam stance as an example of their shared recognition of common foes. "The people who support the war in Vietnam are the same ones who keep their foot on the black man's neck in this country. Bigotry and death over here is no different from bigotry and death over there." Carmichael described his antiwar stance as the logical outgrowth of a Black Power philosophy that transcended purely racial appeals to political change. "I suppose it's pride, more than color, that binds me to my race," he told Parks. "And I'm learning that the concern for blackness is necessary, but that concern has to go further than *that* to reach anyone who needs it." He echoed Courtland Cox's line about blackness being necessary but not sufficient. Recognition of his own mortality hovered over his conversations with Parks. "Mississippi taught me that one's life isn't too much to give to help rid a nation of fascists," an experience that allowed him to view the prospect of death as the necessary corollary to a lifetime of revolutionary struggle.[36]

Carmichael's insouciance struck a chord in Parks. Parks (an equally adept writer, memoirist, and raconteur) and Carmichael bonded over shared reputations as mavericks. "Stokely gives the impression," Parks observed, that he could "stroll through Dixie in broad daylight using the Confederate flag for a handkerchief." Carmichael's unshakable antiwar position evoked conflicting feelings in Parks, whose son served as a tank gunner in Southeast Asia. Parks wondered which of the two young men's fight was more just. Finding "no immediate answer," he concluded that, "in the face of death, which was so possible for the both of them, I think Stokely would surely be more certain of why he was about to die." Stokely Carmichael had become, for Parks and millions of other black Americans, a surrogate son.[37]

NEAR MIDNIGHT ON THE LAST SATURDAY IN APRIL, Martin Luther King telephoned Stokely at his Atlanta office. A night owl who operated on a few hours of rest, Carmichael waged a losing battle with sleep and keeping up with his administrative duties. In private Carmichael and King shared a teasing rep-artee that took the edge off of their mutually stressful lives. After exchanging pleasantries, King invited Carmichael to attend Ebenezer Church services the next day. Performing his expected role in their usual banter, Carmichael initially balked before King's relentless pleading wore him down. "Something special happening, Reverend?" asked Carmichael. "Well . . . I'll be preaching," replied King. Carmichael teased that he enjoyed King's ability to "make me tap mah feets," but this joke fell on deaf ears. "I really do want you to be there tomorrow," said King, "because . . . tomorrow . . . before my congregation . . . I'll be making my statement on the war." A pause of over thirty seconds fol-lowed before Carmichael finally spoke in a tone barely above a whisper. "I'll be there, Dr. King. I'ma be in the front row of that church." After hanging up, Carmichael immediately contacted Cleve Sellers to inform him of their new plans.[38]

Unusual circumstances beyond Carmichael and Sellers' appearance on Ebenezer's front pew marked the Reverend King's Sunday morning sermon. Reading from a prepared text, King mocked America's narrow application of nonviolence. "There is something strangely inconsistent about a nation and a press that will praise you when you say be nonviolent toward Jim Clark," said King, referring to Selma's brutally racist sheriff, "but will curse you when you say be nonviolent toward little brown Vietnamese children!" He praised Muhammad Ali as a courageous dissenter who chose personal conscience over material splendor even at the risk of imprisonment. King's elevation of Ali as a youthful champion of peace implicitly acknowledged Carmichael's trailblazing anti-war activism. Ironically, both Ali and King would achieve a kind of romantic identification as antiwar icons in a manner that would elude Carmichael. King's passionate speech injected an air of mournful outrage into the national debate over Vietnam and drew stark lines between com-peting visions of American democracy that his political activism had helped creatively blur over the past decade. Carmichael led the entire congregation in a standing ovation.[39]

The next day, Stokely's best friend was undergoing a rite of passage for young men their age. Cleve Sellers was to be inducted into the army, and Stokely accompanied him. Friends and confidants, the volatile Carmichael and the even-tempered Sellers drew strength from their contrasting person-alities. Just as Stokely masked an imposing intellect behind a cool pose, the deceptively fierce Sellers hid a quiet rage behind a placid, at times stoic, exterior. At the induction center, Sellers remained standing when told to step forward and made national news by refusing to serve in the army. Carmichael found the fact that sixteen SNCC workers had been called up by local Selective Service suspicious and told reporters that none of them, including Sellers, would serve. "They are drafting Negroes to commit genocide against their race," Stokely said.[40]

Four days later, Carmichael released an internal exit report from his year as SNCC chairman. "We have been able in the last year to change the milieu of the country in terms of how it views Civil Rights," he wrote. "Our job now IS TO ORGANIZE." The report advocated independent politics, community control, and grassroots organizing in urban ghettoes and rural hamlets as part of an expansive freedom agenda.[41]

Carmichael's bold talk reverberated to the upper echelons of American politics. On the Friday after Cleve Sellers refused military induction, members of the House Armed Services Committee pelted Assistant Attorney General Fred Vinson with questions about why Carmichael had yet to be prosecuted for sedition. Vinson's defensive admission that Carmichael's "outrageous" antiwar speeches did not cross legal bounds was met with skepticism. Louisiana representative F. Edward Hébert suggested forgetting the First Amendment to "show the American people that the Justice Department and Congress were trying to clean up this rat-infested area." After pointing out the Constitution's inherent protections of dissident speech, Vinson was asked by another member for his personal opinion of Carmichael's now famous "Hell no, we won't go set!" catchphrase. He replied, "I think it is an outrageous statement that is under the protection of the First Amendment in the circumstances he made it." Vinson's citing of precedent dating back many decades to Supreme Court Justice Oliver Wendell Holmes did little to placate impatient politicians. In an ominous sign that elected officials now regarded them as partners, committee members singled out Carmichael and King by name throughout the hearing. "How can the Carmichaels and Kings stand before the American people and incite violation of the law while the Justice Department stands idly by?" demanded Hébert. With a rhetorical sleight of hand, King's critics attempted to discredit him through association with Carmichael.[42]

Carmichael's new public association as King's unlikely political partner on the subject of Vietnam coincided with the end of his tenure as SNCC chairman. SNCC's annual elections during the second week of May clarified Carmichael's organizational status, with H. Rap Brown as the new chairman along with two new executive committee members. Outside Paschal's Motel in Atlanta, Carmichael addressed reporters about the administrative change, introducing Rap Brown, program director Ralph Featherstone, and executive secretary Stanley Wise, who replaced the gravely ill Ruby Doris Smith Robinson. Carmichael sat next to a dour-looking Brown, whose sober demeanor masked nervous energy over assuming national leadership at the tender age of twenty-three. Sporting a denim jacket, sunglasses, a medium-sized afro, and a mustache that drooped over the sides of his mouth, Brown looked the part of a Black Power revolutionary. His distinctive Louisiana drawl lent his urbane expressions of racial solidarity with far-flung African independence movements a measure of folksy authenticity. It also hid political shortcomings. Sensing that reporters mistook Brown's anxiety for meekness, Carmichael preemptively set the record straight. "People will be happy to have me back when they meet him," he cracked.[43]

The slightly awkward press conference mirrored Brown's transition to the chairmanship. Carmichael's enormous star power overshadowed Brown's initial efforts to establish a public identity as well as SNCC's plans to expand its civil rights portfolio to include human rights and increase its political reach to the international arena. Brown, perhaps too eager to prove himself, would soon indulge in over-the-top rhetoric that seemed designed to out-Stokely Stokely.[44]

While Rap Brown became SNCC's new chairman, the FBI's focus remained on Carmichael. On Tuesday, May 16, FBI Director J. Edgar Hoover released portions of the director's congressional testimony, made three months earlier, to the news media. Hoover accused Carmichael of being under the direct control of communists and anti-American subversives. New allegations charged Carmichael with maintaining contact with communist front groups. FBI phone lines buzzed with reporters clamoring for more information, only to be told that Hoover's testimony stood "on its own two feet and we can add nothing." Reporters confronted Carmichael in Grand Rapids, Michigan, about Hoover's charges. Instead of the expected fireworks, Carmichael calmly requested that Hoover prove the charges, adding that the FBI director, who was seventy-two years old, should retire.[45]

Hoover's testimony overshadowed shocking reports of a police raid at two homes in suburban Grand Rapids, where investigators found weapons

Selma, March halted at the bridge, March 9, 1965 (Stokely Carmichael, far left; MLK, Jr. fifth from left). The Jack Rabin Collection on Alabama Civil Rights and Southern Activists, Box 4, Items 050. Courtesy of Historical Collections and Labor Archives, Special Collections Library, The Pennsylvania State University.

Civil rights leaders Dr. Martin Luther King Jr. (left) and Stokely Carmichael (right) participating in a voter registration march after originator James H. Meredith was shot on June 6, 1966. Photo by Lynn Pelham/Time Life Pictures/Getty Images

Stokely Carmichael speaking at a meeting at a small church building.
Jim Peppler/ Southern Courier/ Alabama Department of Archives and History,
Montgomery, AL.

Stokely Carmichael carrying a young woman down the road during the Meredith March in
Mississippi. Jim Peppler/ Southern Courier/ Alabama Department of Archives and History, Montgomery, AL.

Stokely Carmichael addressing a crowd in front of the Neshoba County Library in
Philadelphia, Mississippi, during the "March Against Fear" begun by James Meredith in June
1966. Jim Peppler/ Southern Courier/ Alabama Department of Archives and History, Montgomery, AL.

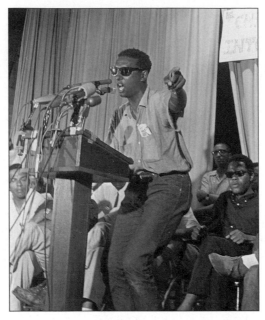

Stokely Carmichael speaking to an audience during the "March Against Fear." Jim Peppler/ Southern Courier/ Alabama Department of Archives and History, Montgomery, AL.

Humor enlivens wedding preparations as the family gets together. Enjoying Carmichael's jokes are (from left) his mother, his sister, Judy, and Sinclair Greenidge, Stokely's cousin (1968). Courtesy Johnson Publishing Company, LLC. All Rights Reserved via AP Images.

Stokely Carmichael speaks in London in July 1967. Photo by Bentley Archive/Popperfoto/Getty Images

Stokely pals with Gloria Richardson at his wedding, while Guinean Ambassador Achkar Marof maintains the light mood (1968). Courtesy Johnson Publishing Company, LLC. All Rights Reserved via AP Images.

Stokely Carmichael walking down Auburn Avenue during Martin Luther King, Jr.'s funeral procession on April 9, 1968. Jim Peppler/ Southern Courier/ Alabama Department of Archives and History, Montgomery, AL.

Stokely Carmichael with his wife Miriam Makeba and others walking in Martin Luther King, Jr.'s funeral procession on April 9, 1968. Jim Peppler/ Southern Courier/ Alabama Department of Archives and History, Montgomery, AL.

Stokely Carmichael is shown with his wife Miriam Makeba and attorney Howard Moore after testifying for the Senate subcommittee in 1970. Photo by Afro American Newspapers/Gado/ Getty Images

Carmichael speaks during an engagement at his former school, Bronx Science High School, in New York in December 1985. Photo by David Fenton/Getty Images

linked to a plot by white supremacists to assassinate Stokely. FBI investigators picked up chatter about harming Carmichael from a group stockpiling grenades, artillery shells, fourteen sticks of dynamite, and two submachine guns. The bureau claimed no jurisdiction over the matter publicly but privately found enough plausible evidence to suggest those arrested posed a threat to Carmichael's safety. A police escort transported Carmichael from the airport to his hotel, and reinforcements were on hand for his appearance at Fountain Street Church in downtown Grand Rapids, where an audience of almost two thousand listened to a speech bursting with references to Frederick Douglass, Malcolm X, and Jesus. Carmichael capped off his evening by visiting Grand Rapids' black community, where he spoke at the Trinity Church to a small group of teenagers, still buzzing over reports of thwarted assassination plots, suburban arsenals, and FBI vendettas.[46]

On Thursday, amid the fallout from Hoover's charges, Carmichael made a brief stop in Jackson, Mississippi, to attend the funeral of Ben Brown, a student activist killed the previous week during rioting at Jackson State. Stokely was en route to an afternoon visit to Southern University in Baton Rouge. Investigators from Mississippi's secret Sovereignty Commission snapped photos of Carmichael, Sellers, Willie Ricks, and local Tougaloo activist Howard Spencer at Jackson's airport. Carmichael knew Ben Brown, a highly regarded civil rights worker, from SNCC's Summer Project. The funeral reunited Stokely with Mississippi activists Owen Brooks and Lawrence Guyot, who joined over seven hundred mourners at the Masonic Temple on Lynch Street, where they gathered in stifling heat to eulogize a fallen hero. Carmichael arrived just in time to hear Brooks preach a sermon that called for a political reckoning to cleanse the Magnolia State. Carmichael remained composed throughout the service, but the funeral undoubtedly evoked painful memories of Jonathan Daniels and Sammy Younge and perhaps increased a growing preoccupation with his own mortality.[47]

————————————

IF STOKELY'S STATUS AS A NATIONAL LEADER complicated his hopes to resume grassroots organizing, events in California would soon make it impossible. Huey Newton's brash decision to send an armed convoy of Black Panthers to the State Capitol in Sacramento on May 2 triggered bursts of panic and near hysteria that simultaneously burnished the young organization's celebrity and jeopardized its already slim chances of longevity. Newton's gamble poised the Black Panthers on a tightrope between daring improvisation and reckless bravado that mixed threats of violence with the exhilarating spectacle of street-corner toughs as political revolutionaries. The Black Panthers imagined a world not yet in existence, but one that they thought they could will into being. Newton's subsequent drafting of Carmichael into the BPP continued a pattern that marked the Panthers as visionaries daring enough to confer the rank of field marshal on Carmichael, with a public commission to "establish revolutionary law, order and justice" over the United States.[48]

A *New York Times* article in the late summer resuscitated the waning buzz from the group's Sacramento adventure. "The Call of the Black Panthers," by *Ramparts'* assistant managing editor Sol Stern, featured a soon-to-be-iconic photo of Newton. Wearing an open white dress shirt and a black leather jacket, Newton sat pensively holding a rifle in one hand and a spear in the other, with African shields carefully strewn across the floor. The image evoked poetic juxtapositions between the past and present, the modern and the ancient, that suggested black revolutionaries needed a potent knowledge of history and politics. For Stern, the Panthers' limited impact on the Bay Area's civil rights scene made them less of a political phenomenon than a sociological one. Against the backdrop of national urban civil disorder, the Panthers—with their melodramatic statements, bombastic posture, and dead serious swagger—demanded attention. The article lingered over Newton's photogenic looks and smoldering intensity, showcased co-founder Bobby Seale's charisma, and documented the Oakland Police Department's enmity. With characteristic brio, the Panthers inflated membership numbers, spoke of mounting a global revolution against American imperialism, and convened sparsely attended rallies.[49]

The Black Panthers drafted Carmichael into their organization that summer, identifying him as the most important radical of his generation. *Muhammad Speaks*, perhaps wistful for the days when Malcolm X struck fear into the white mainstream, cheerfully observed that America was "quivering under the searing lashes" of Carmichael's words.[50]

June 11 found Stokely in rural Autauga County, next to Lowndes and forty miles outside of Montgomery. At an outdoor meeting, his typical exhortations advocating self-defense proved too much for the police, who arrested him. The arrest coincided with the premiere that evening of an NBC news documentary, "After Civil Rights—Black Power." Footage of Stokely opened the program, and he was brilliant. Addressing a multiracial audience, he said, "The first man in this country to die in the war for independence was a black man named Crispus Attucks! A black man!" The audience applauded. Stokely paused, then stunned the audience: "He was a *fool!* A fool. He got out there and got shot for white folks while his brothers were enslaved all over this country. He should have gotten his brothers together to take care of natural business." In light of the upcoming fourth anniversary of the March on Washington, the documentary broadcast vivid scenes that evoked the recent past's expansive hopefulness. Black Power, according to narrator Sander Vanocur, provided evidence that dreams imagined four short years ago had been displaced by the anger of urban militants.[51]

Stokely was incarcerated in Autauga County Jail in the small city of Prattville. By the next day, the presence of over one hundred national guardsmen from Montgomery and Alabama state troopers left Prattville in a virtual state of martial law. In Chicago, hearing of Carmichael's arrest, activists threatened new types of "racial upheaval" if he was injured. Rumors spread that authorities had snatched Stokely from jail to be lynched. While Stokely was in jail, white vigilantes fired into a home where black militants, including SNCC activists, had converged to plot a response to Carmichael's arrest. Police cordoned off a twenty-block area of Prattville's black community searching for people who had allegedly fired on officers that same night. State troopers and national guardsmen searched every home in the area rounding up dozens of frightened residents, but found only one double-barreled shotgun, one 22-caliber rifle, and one spent shotgun shell. Ten locals were taken into custody in the early morning of June 12. Carmichael posted bond on Tuesday, June 13, and departed Autauga County Jail, surrounded by National Guard troops. The same day President Johnson nominated Thurgood Marshall to become the nation's first black Supreme Court Justice.[52]

Racial violence in Alabama spread to Tampa, Florida, sparked by the police killing of a black teenager. On Wednesday, as Carmichael and Rap Brown drove to SNCC's Atlanta headquarters, newspapers reported outbreaks of violence in at least half a dozen cities, ranging from sporadic flares in Youngstown, Ohio; Newark, New Jersey; and Watts, to more significant upheavals in Tampa and Cincinnati. Rioting in Cincinnati amplified national anxiety over deteriorating race relations, a situation that Rap Brown's Thursday night appearance there only exacerbated. Brown's prediction that Cincinnati would burn until the departure of national guardsmen he described as "honky cops" increased his own political notoriety at a high cost. Brown's inflammatory polemics cast him alongside Carmichael as one of an infamous duo spreading national racial disorder. Brown's remarkable ability to offer memorable provocations to newspaper reporters and in speeches would outpace his long-term political effectiveness.[53]

On Saturday, June 17, Stokely visited Boston's Roxbury neighborhood. His star-crossed relationship with the nation's Cradle of Liberty, which helped galvanize support for Edward Brooke, would soon touch the city's local politics. Boston was in the midst of a mayoral election with no less than twenty-six candidates. They included Boston Schools Committee member Louise Day Hicks, an outspoken advocate of maintaining segregated schools. Boston Schools Committee chairman and mayoral candidate John McDonough warned that Hicks' potential victory offered "an open invitation to the Stokely Carmichaels" to plot racial strife in a city brimming with ethnic and class conflicts. The mayoral election, which pitted Hicks against the eventual winner of the primary and the general election, thirty-nine-year-old racial moderate Kevin White, offered a prelude to angry controversies over school busing that would grip the nation in the early 1970s.[54]

Despite Carmichael's bold words regarding Black Power, it was his antiwar stance that most troubled LBJ. During a July 10th meeting with FBI investigations chief Deke DeLoach, Johnson characterized Carmichael as one of three black political activists who required tight surveillance (the other two were King and CORE's Floyd McKissick). The meeting followed Johnson's request to the bureau the previous month to find Carmichael's sources of funding. He remained unsatisfied with the FBI's answer that Carmichael's prodigious speaking schedule supplemented his annual $4,500 income as SNCC chair. DeLoach restated long-standing and uncorroborated charges that King's personal adviser, Stanley Levison, was a high-level communist. He called obscene Carmichael's recent demand for an almost $2,000 speaking fee at the University of Wisconsin (he settled for $1,300). Johnson floated the idea that the bureau leak information about Carmichael to friendly journalists. Then the president shifted to a second line of attack in the form of House Un-American Activities Committee hearings for Carmichael and McKissick, an idea waved off by DeLoach as futile, given the committee's low standing among the public. Johnson concluded the meeting with a hope that Carmichael's "anti-Vietnam activities" would remain under tight surveillance.[55]

CHAPTER TWELVE

The World Stage:
London, Cuba, and Vietnam

July 13–September 5, 1967

STOKELY CARMICHAEL'S INTERNATIONAL TRAVELS REPRESENTED THE CULMINATION of his personal desire and political need to forge relationships with global revolutionaries. Carmichael's five-month world tour in 1967 helped make Black Power a global export while turning him into an international icon. Hailed by revolutionaries in Cuba, Algeria, and Vietnam, Carmichael's trip placed Black Power at the center of global liberation narratives. His time abroad further radicalized Stokely, convincing him that revolutionary violence served as a necessary corollary to social and political transformation. His overseas travels helped to shape his evolving political outlook. The radical tone and pugnacious tenor of Carmichael's overseas speeches enraged American officials, politicians, and other citizens in general. Overseas, Carmichael popularized the notion that America was a declining empire and embraced the rhetoric of anti-imperialism with a fervor that made SNCC activists nervous and American officials angry. The discovery of kindred spirits around the world came, in many instances, at the cost of further alienation back home. If Cuba, Vietnam, and Europe offered intoxicating political adventures, Africa provided the most enduringly profound experience, one that would lead him to embrace revolutionary Pan-Africanism. International travel showcased Carmichael's genius for political improvisation as well as his affinity for intellectual provocation. Carmichael left the United States as a radical political activist, but returned a revolutionary. His international travels served as more than an apprenticeship in the particulars of global insurgency. Abroad, Carmichael felt free to experiment with his politics and adapt to his surroundings. Local conditions shaped the content of his speeches. The opportunity to meet with famous revolutionaries galvanized Stokely, whose confidence grew the more he traveled. For the first time since coming to America as a boy, he could imagine another life for himself on distant shores. Exposure to countries brimming with revolutionary possibilities made him skeptical of America's ability to change. Hailed as a bold oracle of the black revolution, Carmichael found a measure of peace in the political battlefields of the Third World.

Stokely's entry on the world stage began in London. Accompanied by SNCC activist George Ware, he arrived there on July 15 to attend a two-week-long Dialectics of Liberation conference, which opened that day. The conference attracted a formidable line-up of prominent radical intellectuals: the German philosopher Herbert Marcuse; the Scottish psychiatrist and best-selling author of *The Divided Self*, R.D. Laing; the revered Marxist historian and activist C.L.R. James; journalist John Gerassi; the sociologist Paul Goodman; Julian Beck, the founder of the Living Theatre; and poet Allen Ginsberg. Stokely would speak on July 18. Angela Davis, a twenty-three-year-old African-American Marxist and perhaps Marcuse's most precocious student, attended the conference and found a rapport with the group of activists who accompanied Stokely around London. "As I listened to Stokely's words, cutting like a switchblade, accusing the enemy as I had never heard him accused before, I admit I felt the cathartic power of his speech," Davis vividly recalled decades later. Her own Marxist beliefs placed her at odds with black nationalists who openly dismissed socialism as unsuitable for African Americans, but she spent enough time with Stokely in London to ask him for political contacts for her planned return to California. Meanwhile, British newspapers described Stokely as a "phenomenon" whose "slogan is Black Power" and whose skin color constituted "his country."[1]

Quoting Sartre and Camus, Carmichael captivated journalists with stories that mixed the personal and the political in mysterious and revelatory ways. In the racially mixed and already volatile working-class neighborhoods of Brixton, Hackney, and Notting Hill, Carmichael recounted how an early infatuation with Western civilization (in Trinidad and the Bronx) waned upon his discovery of the black world's hidden treasures and the white world's horrific transgressions. Dubbing Malcolm X his patron saint, he said that riots in the United States were actually rebellions and predicted that escalating violence was inevitable in a nation born in blood. When he commented that he might be shot by the end of the year, reporters asked him why. He replied, "We are challenging the United States of America who have unchallenged rule of the world, that's why."[2]

Carmichael met with students at Africa House, a headquarters for progressives of all colors. Michael X (born Michael de Freitas), England's celebrated Black Power activist, fellow Trinidadian, and Malcolm X disciple, regaled Stokely with his dark humor. The two became fast friends, and Carmichael and Ware wound up living at de Freitas' place for part of their stay, much to the disappointment of conference organizers. In London, he reunited with C.L.R. James, who confided in him that Michael X's glamorous façade hid unpleasant and dangerous secrets, a warning that Carmichael dismissed, having already accepted de Freitas as a colorfully disreputable ally. (James was right: in 1975 Michael X was tried for murder in Trinidad and hanged.) Stokely reunited with Biafran poet Obi Egbuna, the founder of the Universal Coloured Peoples' Association, whom he had first met in the States a year earlier. Armed with savvy local guides, Carmichael attended political meetings in Islington, where civil rights groups vied for political control over Britain's volatile racial landscape.[3]

Carmichael experienced London through the eyes of a visiting dignitary, and the trip showcased his international popularity. The British public and media treated him like a rock star. Documentary filmmakers shadowed him to conference sessions and through the city; he filmed a BBC interview. Carmichael's international celebrity made local police nervous, as his very presence turned outdoor speaking venues into mob scenes. At these rallies, Carmichael found the raised fists of Asians in the crowd, notably Pakistani youth, a surprising aspect of a colonial system that relegated its nonwhite immigrant population to the nation's political fringes. The boisterous reaction of multiracial crowds to Black Power speeches tailored to Britain's complex history of colonialism, combined with Carmichael's heated polemics, gave government officials pause. Special Branch agents amassed evidence for prosecution under Britain's Race Relations Act, which banned hate speech designed to incite racial violence. For over a week, Carmichael roamed parts of North London in sunglasses and a dashiki regaling Caribbean militants with stories about black history, the power of self-determination, and the strength derived from racial consciousness, while Special Branch took copious notes.[4]

On July 18, Carmichael delivered a major speech at the Dialectics of Liberation Conference. The conference was held at the Roundhouse, an enormous former steam engine repair shop, in Camden Town's Chalk Farm. A ramshackle domed architectural wonder, the Roundhouse's past life included stints as a warehouse for London Metropolitan Transit vehicles, which lent the decrepit building the slightly nostalgic flavor of the British industrial working class.

At the Dialectics Congress, Carmichael identified American imperialism as the main threat to human rights, social justice, and racial equality. "What we're talking about around the United States today, and I believe around the Third World, is the system of international white supremacy coupled with international capitalism," he said. "We're out to smash that system. People who see themselves as part of that system are going to be smashed with it—or we're going to be smashed."[5]

In his speech, with typical erudition, Stokely outlined a global revolutionary struggle between the world's colored population and the West: "The people of the Third World are going to have to stop accepting the definitions imposed upon them by the West. Frederick Douglass, the great black leader of the 1800s, said that a slave seeks his liberation when, and only when, he stops obeying a master." Carmichael described Western civilization as morally and politically bankrupt. "One of the biggest lies that Western society could have done was to name itself Western civilization," he declared. "At best, it's a misnomer; at worst, and more correctly, it's a damn lie."[6]

He defined Vietnam as an imperial war connected to American capitalism but rejected conventional Marxist solutions, in which only an interracial class struggle could trigger a successful political revolution. Carmichael remained skeptical of white capacity to recognize black humanity and forge political solidarity with the Third World. "United States capitalists never cut down on their domestic profits to share with workers—instead, they expanded internationally, and threw the crumbs from their profits to the American working class, who lapped it up," observed Carmichael. "The American working class enjoys the fruits of the labors of the Third World Workers. . . . The proletariat has become the Third World, and the bourgeoisie is white Western society." It was an audacious speech, bold enough to criticize sacred principles of historical materialism in a room filled with some of the world's foremost Marxist theorists.[7]

During lunch break, Stokely held court outside the Roundhouse, enjoying a rare sight of the British sun as students pelted him with questions. C.L.R. James' afternoon speech rebuffed Carmichael's talk of Third World solidarity in a gentle enough manner that Carmichael and Michael X felt compelled to stand up and cheer at its conclusion. Toward the end of his visit, he returned to the Roundhouse as part of a panel that included Allen Ginsberg. Carmichael began his ten-minute talk by refusing to discuss violence, one of the conference's main themes, preferring instead to focus on "relevant things" that people could actually control. "Why not?" shouted a voice from the audience. "I don't know, because maybe you're powerless," replied Carmichael to a murmur of applause. Calling blacks "African Americans"—two decades before the term would be embraced—Carmichael gave a brief address on the failures of liberals to confront white supremacy. Ginsberg defended hippies as cultural explorers playing an important role in toppling Western society's historic biases against indigenous traditions and folkways. As he put it, whites were "beginning to explore for the first time the universe of consciousness of other cultures besides their own." Carmichael rejected this point, comparing hippies to privileged runaways who would "return to their culture within a year or two," but Ginsberg replied that "there's no culture to return to."[8]

On July 24, Stokely announced that he was leaving the country sooner than scheduled. He would have to cancel a series of scheduled political meetings. Clandestine efforts to remove him from Britain's domestic racial politics had increased as he drew crowds in Notting Hill and Brixton. The press, though critical of his fiery polemics, seemed drawn to him and pleasantly surprised by his sense of humor. While the conservative *Daily Sketch* accused him of inciting violence in ethnic immigrant enclaves and urged deportation, *The Sunday Telegraph* expressed grudging admiration for Stokely's intellectual erudition, noting that his public talks, although "laced with sarcasm," drew "heavily on such well-known philosophers as Sartre, Camus, Machiavelli, and Lewis Carroll." The leftist *Tribune* was impressed by Carmichael's "blunt yet engaging manner" but taken aback by some of the things he said. In a lengthy profile, Colin McGlashan in *The Observer Review,* which was Labour-oriented, noted Carmichael's ability to "talk like a ghetto hustler, a black sharecropper, or a university intellectual." Stokely spoke of his celebrity persona as a phenomenon separate and distinct from his real self: "The name Stokely Carmichael was the invention of the white press. I'll not live up to the rules they make for me." Instead he aimed to "take all the admiration and love other black people give me and try and spread it amongst us." McGlashan presented Carmichael as political royalty, a reluctant prince on the cusp of "inheriting Malcolm X's throne" as "the world's chief symbol of black militancy." His international tour drew him closer to the political seasoning and cosmopolitan network that such a role both assumed and required. But McGlashan warned, "Carmichael's tragedy and his people's may be that the world will give him neither the time nor the understanding he needs."[9]

British authorities offered neither time nor understanding. Rumors swirled that the Home Office had asked Carmichael to leave, and Scotland Yard offered a terse "no comment" when asked about his sudden departure. Home Secretary Roy Jenkins ordered a full report on Carmichael's activities from Special Branch even as officials denied having anything to do with his exit. Roy Sawh, a local anti-racist activist who conferred with Carmichael during his time in London, claimed that Special Branch had contacted Stokely at his North London residence and asked him to leave.

Stokely had a place to go. After his Dialectics speech, Cuban officials invited him to attend the upcoming Organization for Latin American Solidarity (OLAS) Conference in Havana. Meanwhile, it is likely that Stokely's visit to England had a positive effect: two days after his departure for Cuba, Home Secretary Jenkins unveiled plans to introduce tough new anti-discrimination legislation in Parliament as a pre-emptive strike against the kind of urban unrest gripping America.[10]

DETROIT WAS BURNING as Carmichael and Ware arrived in Havana on July 25. Violence in the Motor City had begun after police raided an illegal after-hours spot on Twelfth Street. Local residents responded to this routine bit of intimidation with an unprecedented burst of fury that unleashed citywide destruction. Sniper fire, billowing clouds of smoke, and looting plagued large swaths of the city and seemed to fulfill the prophecy of Carmichael and others that the United States was on the precipice of a race war. Michigan Governor George Romney, a Republican presidential hopeful, toured the city's devastation by helicopter and said it looked like it had been bombed. President Johnson and Romney cracked down, sending in the army and national guard. The initial violence and law enforcement response left forty-three dead, thirty-three blacks and ten whites. America's largest eruption of urban violence since Watts less than two years before, Detroit became a powerful symbol of national anxiety over race relations, urban decline, and violence.[11]

In Havana, Stokely descended from the Cubana Airlines plane in a black jacket and open collar white shirt and was met by high-ranking officials. He was whisked away by a limousine to Santiago on the island's eastern edge. If British authorities regarded him as a pariah, the Cuban government welcomed him as black America's unofficial prime minister. The day he arrived, Havana's domestic news service published a translation of one of his London interviews in which he expressed political solidarity with Latin American revolutionaries, traced his first encounter with the Cuban Revolution back to the visit Fidel Castro made to Harlem in 1960, and hailed Che Guevara as a hero. He called violence in US cities a civil insurrection whose participants resembled Latin American freedom fighters.[12]

Carmichael's words in Cuba spread around the world. Cuba's *El Mundo* and *Granma*, Paris's *Le Monde*, and the Algerian Press Service all published his statements, as did newspapers in Rome, Poland, Yugoslavia, Hanoi, Rio de Janeiro, Santiago, and Dakar. Left-wing scribes from *The Militant*, the *National Guardian*, *Ramparts*, and *The Worker* featured sympathetic reporting that stood in stark contrast to that of the mainstream contingent. In interviews and press conferences, Carmichael proved himself to be an affable raconteur: quick-witted, spontaneous, and eloquent. He parried with Latin American and European journalists who reveled in the back-and-forth banter. *Le Monde*'s special correspondent described Carmichael, in a sports shirt and dark sunglasses, as possessing the bearing of "an athlete at rest," and Vienna's *Arbeiter-Zeitung* called him the "strangest Latin American" at the Cuban conference. In truth, his speeches and interviews in Cuba gave pause to all sides of the Cold War, including the Chinese, who sanguinely quoted his praise for Chairman Mao Tse-tung without reporting a word about the conference; the Soviets, upset over OLAS's rejection of Moscow's line of peaceful coexistence with imperialism; and European leftists, uncomfortable with Carmichael's talk of revolutionary violence and racial solidarity.[13]

Cuban media portrayed him as the iconic figure of America's black revolt. George Ware thought that the Cubans treated Carmichael as some "mythological creature" temporarily roaming their island. Gregarious, perpetually smiling, with an easy demeanor, Carmichael impressed and charmed supporters and critics alike. He also made for good press, providing an endless stream of commentary broadcast around the world. In one breath, he discussed four centuries of white supremacy and indicted Abraham Lincoln as a racist, and in another he declared that Cuba had "the most marvelous army in the world, and also the most beautiful women." He enjoyed the accommodations almost as much as the sight of local women. The Cuban government lodged Carmichael and Ware in the Havana Libre Hotel, formerly the Hilton, and supplied their guests with the finest rums and cigars. Elizabeth "Betita" Martínez and Julius Lester, SNCC colleagues, joined them there, having just arrived in Cuba to attend an arts festival in Havana. Martínez served as Carmichael's translator for much of his visit, while Lester, a gifted photographer, provided a pictorial record of the trip.[14]

On Wednesday, July 26, before an audience of one million people, President Fidel Castro introduced Stokely as one of America's "most distinguished" civil rights leaders. They were in the expansive José Martí Plaza in Santiago de Cuba, a picturesque city with breathtaking views of the Caribbean. It had been at Santiago that Castro declared victory on January 2, 1959, over the dictatorial regime of Fulgencio Batista. With Stokely looking on, Castro then launched into one of his trademark long speeches, this one lasting two hours and twenty-five minutes. Every time Castro mentioned Stokely Carmichael, there were waves of applause and cheers.[15]

The ceremony commemorated the fourteenth anniversary of Castro's ill-fated attack on the Moncada Barracks that began his journey from obscure rebel to revolutionary hero. Domestic concerns dominated Castro's address, but themes of American race relations surfaced. "The U.S. colored population, victim of discrimination and exploitation," proclaimed Castro, "is rising up more and more with astonishing valor and heroism to demand its rights and resist force with force."[16]

Carmichael and Castro became friends. They spent three days conversing through interpreters. Stokely told one reporter that the conversations were the "most educational, most interesting, and most enlightening of my public life." Castro chauffeured him around Cuba's eastern shores of Santiago by jeep to the Sierra Maestra, where he grabbed Carmichael by the shoulders to point out famous battles and forgotten skirmishes. Castro's love of precise details of military and political strategy appealed to Stokely's bookish side and made these conversations less tales of heroic derring-do than a lively political seminar. They bonded as fellow revolutionaries who cultivated equal interests in political and intellectual pursuits. Their time also stirred memories of his days as a "little nationalist in Harlem" inspired enough by the Cuban Revolution during his junior year at Bronx Science to join the Fair Play for Cuba Committee.[17]

Carmichael's time in Cuba scandalized America. Rowland Evans and Robert Novak, Washington-based political reporters whose column made for required Beltway reading, alleged that SNCC represented nothing less than "Fidel Castro's arm in the United States." Conservative William F. Buckley characterized Carmichael as "giving the Communists a postgraduate course on the art of revolution." The Justice Department announced plans to confiscate his passport on his second day in Cuba, triggering an international game of cat and mouse that would continue, with near misses, in several countries until December.[18]

Carmichael's spectacular international adventures placed new pressures on the State Department. Alabama's lieutenant governor and Florida's secretary of state sent to the State Department recent resolutions, passed by their respective state legislatures, requesting that Stokely be denied re-entry to the United States. Private citizens and business and civic leaders sent detailed inquiries demanding punishment for his unauthorized Cuban trip. State Department officials diplomatically confessed that there were limited legal options for banning Carmichael from returning home and cited a recent Supreme Court decision (*United States v. Laub*) curtailing criminal prosecution against citizens violating travel restrictions. "There is no provision of law which authorizes any agency of the federal government to deny a citizen's re-entry to this country," Winthrop G. Brown, assistant to the secretary of state, apologetically informed Alabama Governor Lurleen Wallace, but he promised to "to take such appropriate action as is authorized by law with respect to Mr. Carmichael's conduct abroad."[19]

As Carmichael's travel schedule gripped the American imagination, Lyndon Johnson designated the last Sunday in July a National Day of Prayer for Reconciliation. National soul searching for the roots behind racial unrest found religious and civic leaders pleading for constructive solutions beyond partisan politics. More often, however, riot politics ushered in a mean season of ideological posturing, with calls for laws against rioting and rioters. California Governor Ronald Reagan called looters "mad dogs," while others identified communist conspiracies as the causes of riots, though Detroit's police chief denied that communists had anything to do with the riots in his city. Black newspaper editors railed against the passage of any "Stokely Carmichael anti-riot legislation" as a diversion from the larger forces behind urban violence. House Judiciary Committee chairman Emmanuel Celler, a noted critic of Black Power and no friend of the former SNCC chairman, offered a remarkable critique of anti-riot legislation: "I loathe Stokely Carmichael and his ilk; if I were a hangman or a gravedigger there's no one I would rather serve . . . but despicable characters should not goad us into passing a bill of this type." But each passing day offered more incendiary Carmichael quotes. On the national day of prayer, he said, "The United States is going to fall. I only hope I live to see the day." Meanwhile, eighty-five-year-old Illinois Democratic representative Barratt O'Hara argued against the legislation, noting that it would make it illegal for boys from Indiana and Illinois to squabble over watermelons. But, by early August, Attorney General Ramsey Clark had seen enough and contacted the FBI to obtain speeches and radio and television tapes of Carmichael's visit to Cuba.[20]

Carmichael would fondly remember his time in Havana as "eye-opening, inspiring, and mind-blowing." Cuba introduced Stokely to the human frailties of revolutionaries, the humble dignity of Cuban peasants, and the gregariousness of Fidel Castro. As he later wrote, "For me, the international struggle became tangible, a human reality, names, faces, stories, no longer an abstraction. And our struggle in Mississippi or Harlem was part and parcel of this great international and historical motion. It was both humbling and inspiring. I felt recommitted, energized."[21]

For the duration of the nine-day OLAS conference, which began on July 31, the day after the US national day of prayer, Carmichael dominated the event. The conference was held at the Havana Libre Hotel. On opening day, Stokely sat on the rostrum with Raúl Castro, Fidel's younger brother. A huge poster of Simón Bolívar, the hero of Latin American solidarity, was emblazoned with a caption that succinctly captured the spirit of the coming days: "The duty of all revolutionaries is to make revolution." These words had guided the gathering of the Tri-Continental Congress held the year before in Havana and placed Cuba at odds with its Soviet benefactors' diplomatic policies. Tensions between Cuban and Soviet officials remained strained enough for *Pravda* to publish a stinging anti-Castro rebuke written by Chilean communist leader Luis Corvalán.[22]

On August 1, as the inaugural plenary session convened, Carmichael, along with George Ware and Julius Lester, conducted a press conference in the Havana Libre attended by over one hundred reporters. The event quickly turned into an international relations seminar with the assembled reporters and foreign correspondents playing the role of fascinated, if at times combative, students. Several times Ware supplied the fast-talking Carmichael with key historical details while Lester railed against assumptions that portrayed SNCC as Stokely's personal fiefdom.

Carmichael brashly presented himself as the unquestioned spokesperson for black political radicalism in the United States. He identified the Watts rebellion as the starting point of a revolutionary consciousness among African Americans and pledged enduring solidarity with guerrilla fighters from North America to Vietnam. He dismissed the theme of nonviolence incorporated into SNCC's name as an outgrowth of a moribund historical moment. At its conclusion, the gathered press corps gave him a standing ovation.[23]

Carmichael's rhetorical firebombs took him from being a bit player in *New York Times* bureau chief James Reston's dispatches from Havana to center stage. A Cold War liberal with easy access to the Johnson White House, Reston took personally Carmichael's statements to the press attacking America. In Santiago, he introduced himself to Carmichael, who flatly informed an astonished Reston that if America went to war with Cuba, "the white boys are going to fight it out alone." In the fall, Reston would recount this conversation in detail to FBI agents but for the moment remained dumbfounded by the sheer audacity of the "very surly" Carmichael's brazen remarks. Reston devoted an entire dispatch to exposing "Stokely Carmichael's Game" in Havana. He described Carmichael as an arrogant peacock "strutting around" Havana with impunity from both American law and accepted standards of Negro protest. "Carmichael is too intelligent and cynical not to know what he is doing," lamented Reston.[24]

The majority of American press coverage proved equally critical. "Carmichael Lauds Cuban Communism" screamed *The Washington Post* on the August 2nd front page. The *Chicago Tribune* pounced on Carmichael's vague threats of reprisals against American leaders who killed black militants to surmise that "Stokely Hints Assassinations" in a story sourced by Reuters. Carmichael's reported hit list included Lyndon Johnson, Secretary of State Dean Rusk, Defense Secretary Robert McNamara, and British Prime Minister

Harold Wilson. His talk of guerrilla warfare sent American intelligence figures scrambling, including the exasperated CIA Director Richard Helms, who
fired off a secret memo to Johnson that promised to shed light on emerging
connections between Latin American insurgencies masterminded by Castro
and those imagined by Carmichael.[25]

Carmichael found better rapport with the foreign press. In the Uru-
guayan leftist daily *Marcha,* Carlos María Gutiérrez wrote a profile that
highlighted the personal chemistry between Carmichael and Ware. Gutiérrez
portrayed SNCC as a tightly disciplined group of organizers who followed a
strict chain of command, and wrote that Ware compared SNCC to guerrilla
fighters. The State Department collected other such reportage. One writer
in Prague's *Literární Noviny* seemed to sum up the contention of some in
the United States that Carmichael was a pawn of the Communist East: "The
words of Stokely Carmichael come to us from the West, but they are being
brought by the East Wind."[26]

Carmichael addressed the OLAS conference on Wednesday. His sudden
appearance at noon, three hours ahead of schedule, caught Western journalists off guard but not international reporters who were tipped off to the
change and joined a standing-room-only audience of fifteen hundred to
hear Carmichael deliver a twenty-minute speech that would help make him
a global icon.[27]

"We share with you a common struggle," he began. He identified "white
Western imperialist society" as the main threat to humanity. "Our struggle
is to overthrow this system that feeds itself and expands itself through the
economic and cultural exploitation of non-white, non-Western peoples—of
the Third World." He emphasized a transcendent solidarity capable of establishing more "humanistic societies." He eulogized the civil rights movement
as a well-meaning but ill-fated reform effort hopelessly overmatched by the
predatory nature of American imperialism. The Stokely Carmichael who
had previously advocated radical democracy now moved toward embracing a
philosophy of anti-imperialism that included a radical critique of capitalism.
In a way, his OLAS remarks combined the Marxist intellectual and political
works of his youth with the writings of Third World revolutionaries:

> We are moving to control our African-American communities as you
> are moving to wrest control of your countries, of the entire Latin con-
> tinent, from the hands of foreign imperialist powers. There is only

one course open to us: we must change North America so that the economy and politics of the country will be in the hands of the people, and our particular concern is our people, African-Americans. . . . For the total transformation to take place, whites must see the struggle that we're engaged in as being their own struggle. At the present time, they do not. Even though the white worker is exploited, he sees his own best interest lying with the power structure. Because of the racist nature of this country, we cannot work in white communities, but we have asked those whites who work with us to go into their own communities to begin propagandizing and organizing. When the white workers realize their true condition, then alliances will be possible between ourselves and them.[28]

If the Third World offered hope for political solidarity capable of toppling America's postwar empire, Black Power remained the language of action. "Black Power is more than a slogan," he argued, "it is a way of looking at our problems and the beginning of a solution to them. It attacks racism and exploitation, the horn of the bull that seeks to gore us."[29]

Carmichael's description of capitalism as a metaphorical bull must have pleased the delegates in Havana, since many considered Fidel Castro to be Latin America's revolutionary matador. In Havana, Stokely eulogized the civil rights movement:

The "civil rights movement" did not actively involve the masses, because it did not speak to the needs of the masses. . . . Eventually, the United States Congress passed a Civil Rights Bill and a Voting Rights Bill, assuring us of those rights for which we had been agitating. By this time, however, more and more of us were realizing that our problems would not be solved by the enacting of these laws. In fact, these laws did not speak to our problems. Our problems were an inherent part of the capitalist system and therefore could not be alleviated within that system.[30]

Carmichael's presence in Cuba practically overshadowed Castro, whose four-hour-long keynote speech came at the end of the conference. The Cuban president paid particular attention to "Comrade Stokely Carmichael," who was seated next to him. Castro promised that assaults on Carmichael would reverberate from Latin America all the way to the States, where Stokely would be returning "under my protection." A Saturday evening reception for OLAS delegates at the Revolutionary Palace featured the spectacle of Soviet diplomats eating caviar and sipping champagne and of the newfound political intimacy between Fidel and Stokely, who spent the evening huddled with the Vietnamese delegation.[31]

Shortly after the conference ended, Carmichael boarded a flight for Vietnam by way of Madrid. Less than an hour later, the plane returned to Havana. Cuban agents had learned that American officials planned to confiscate Carmichael's passport in Madrid. Cuban intelligence proved correct, and US consular officials were left waiting in vain for Carmichael's arrival. A revised itinerary placed him with the returning Soviet delegation on a seventeen-hour flight from Havana to Minsk and then on to Moscow, where he spent two days before departing for Beijing. On August 9, George Ware, who had proved an indispensable traveling companion in Cuba, attempted to slip back into London via Switzerland only to discover that the anti-Carmichael ban made British officials place him on an America-bound airliner due to "his close association with Stokely Carmichael." Two days later, British authorities arrested Michael X, Carmichael's favorite host in London, for violating the Race Relations Act.[32]

Carmichael arrived in a China awash in a Cultural Revolution reflected in the striking visual iconography of the Red Guard. W.E.B. Du Bois' widow, Shirley Graham Du Bois, headed the tiny community of black expatriates, which included Robert F. Williams, a relatively recent arrival who had found Cuba to be ideologically suffocating. Carmichael and Du Bois met for dinner almost immediately and forged an instant friendship. Small, determined, and intelligent, Du Bois reminded Stokely of his mother. She returned this sentiment, adopting him as a political son. The second wife and widow of W.E.B. Du Bois, Shirley Graham was a personal confidante to the first president of Ghana, Kwame Nkrumah, as she had been to Malcolm X. Over dinner, Carmichael told her he was toying with the idea of giving up his passport, a suggestion she rejected as folly, before promising to introduce him to the recently deposed Nkrumah.[33]

From China, Carmichael headed to North Vietnam, the country that had been central to his antiwar speeches over the past year. He arrived in Hanoi under the cover of early morning darkness. He immediately marveled at the technological ingenuity of the North Vietnamese, who had created a system of mobile bridges and underground tunnels that withstood tenacious US bombing. He was impressed by the Vietnamese people's ability to prevent war from defining "their attitude toward life." Carmichael addressed a public meeting in Hanoi where local and national political leaders greeted him as a visiting diplomat. He spoke about America's racial travails, highlighted the black movement as the leading edge of antiwar resistance, and unleashed his "Hell no, we won't go!" slogan before an approving crowd.[34]

Private lunches with President Ho Chi Minh and Prime Minister Pham Van Dong were balanced by public receptions with delegations from the Viet Cong (the National Front for the Liberation of South Vietnam) and the Vietnam Afro-American Solidarity Committee. President Ho, the author of the anti-colonial treatise *The Verdict of Colonialism*, regaled Stokely with stories of listening to Marcus Garvey in Harlem, and Carmichael surprised him by expressing knowledge of Ho's relatively obscure writings on lynching. Ho, perhaps remembering Garvey's missionary zeal to establish a black fatherland, asked Carmichael why black Americans had yet to return home to Africa. Carmichael's promise that such a return "remains the ultimate goal" expressed more of a personal desire than a collective sentiment.

Privately, Carmichael and Vietnamese officials exchanged frank opinions about class struggle and nationalism, with communist leaders expressing dismay over Stokely's stubborn refusal to discard black nationalism as a core part of his political beliefs. "During our discussions I had one slight, recurrent problem with the cadres," Stokely remembered. "The leadership was clinging to Marxism-Leninism as the only path to socialism." Despite a philosophical disagreement over the merits of black nationalism, Carmichael and his Vietnamese hosts managed to build a warm political relationship. But if Carmichael's Vietnam sojourn lacked the racial controversy of his London trip or the incendiary spectacle of his Cuban visit, it offered something equally important: the chance to be an eyewitness to a people engaged in a revolutionary struggle. Time spent with North Vietnamese intellectuals, workers, peasants, and children placed a human face on an unfolding political tragedy he had publicly railed against over the past eighteen months.[35]

There were rumors that Stokely was collaborating with Vietnamese officials who were planning show trials of captured American soldiers. In this uneasy atmosphere, he departed Vietnam to begin a new momentous journey to his spiritual homeland.[36]

CHAPTER THIRTEEN

The World Stage: Africa

September 6–December 11, 1967

STOKELY CARMICHAEL BEGAN HIS FIRST VISIT TO AFRICA ON WEDNESDAY, September 6. The first stop was Algeria. The French-Algerian War of 1954–1962, marked by Algerian guerrilla warfare, had ended in President Charles de Gaulle's grudging acceptance of independence. The war became a legend among radical activists around the world as a triumph against Western imperial powers. Mustapha Bouarfa, head of the Algerian delegation to OLAS, had arranged Stokely's trip under the auspices of the National Liberation Front (FLN). FLN officials carefully orchestrated Carmichael's visit, providing access to virtually all government offices and generous press coverage. The *Moujahid* had announced his impending arrival in September. The newspaper characterized him as the symbol of black protest hounded by American officials who wished to "decapitate" Carmichael in hopes of ending domestic racial insurrection. Upon his arrival at the Algiers airport, Carmichael embraced the country as his "homeland" and "one of the most revolutionary countries in Africa." Carmichael spoke to reporters about his recent Vietnam tour, pointing out that political leaders and peasants expressed outrage over racial oppression. "Here is a people on whom bombs fall daily, but who worry about the hell that awaits me personally in the U.S.," he marveled. Carmichael toured agricultural and industrial fields over the course of ten hectic days and met with high-ranking officials, who welcomed him as a fellow revolutionary.[1]

By 1967, Algeria was synonymous with a brutal romanticism captured in the 1966 docudrama film by Gillo Pontecorvo, *The Battle of Algiers*, which became an instant classic. Carmichael's presence in Algiers unfolded like a cinema verité about a black American revolutionary who had waged non-violent war in the Deep South traveling all the way to Africa to be tutored by guerrillas wise enough to liberate and rule a nation. September 7 marked his first full day in Algiers, and the start of a series of meetings with top FLN officials, local political leaders, and media. Dressed in army boots and fatigues, Carmichael greeted Cherif Belkacem, the FLN's secretary general, and commandant Si Larbi as comrades in arms. He openly embraced Algeria's nationalization of American oil companies. "We have been pillaged too," he told Larbi, "and we are beginning to take it back."[2]

The next day, Carmichael speculated about opening a SNCC or Black Power office in Algiers to maintain contact with Algerian and other African liberation movements represented there. The FLN's support added to rumors that Carmichael had secured financial backing from Algeria to set up an international revolutionary base. A late-night visit to the Kasbah included a tour of homemade bomb and grenade factories used during the war of independence and memorialized in *The Battle of Algiers*.[3]

On Saturday, Carmichael visited the head of the government-owned energy company, Sonatrach. He attended a lunch hosted by North Vietnamese Ambassador Nguyen Van Phat, where he resumed a conversation about Afro-Vietnamese solidarity begun in Hanoi. In the evening he went to the Algiers International Fair, where the Syrian ambassador gave him an official reception. The next day, Carmichael traveled to Oran, where he addressed a conference of government representatives. On Monday he toured collective farms and a glass factory, chatting with workers alongside FLN representatives. Then he delivered a speech at Oran's National Theater, where light-skinned Algerians squirmed in their seats at his racially combative language. American officials called the incident the "only humorous" moment of Carmichael's visit.[4]

In a three-page interview published in the Monday, September 11th edition of the official FLN publication, *Révolution Africaine*, Carmichael discussed guerrilla warfare as the key to a domestic revolution in America. His comments identifying the United States as "the most disgusting country in the world" echoed the government's anti-Western sentiments even as his race-oriented politics concerned the more class-conscious elements. Ubiquitous American embassy officials observed that Carmichael "appears to be blooming in the heady atmosphere of anti–United States anti-imperialist Algeria." Carmichael's interview with the Middle East News Agency expressing unqualified support for Arab independence made the front page of the next day's *Egyptian Gazette* under a caption "Carmichael: Negroes 'on Side of Arabs,'" which might have been more accurate if the term "Negroes" had been replaced with "SNCC." He characterized Israel as a proxy for American imperialism in the Middle East and hinted at his coming embrace of Pan-Africanism, adding that "maybe a return to Africa is not too preposterous." Wednesday's *Gazette* lauded Stokely's bold words in a supportive editorial, "Carmichael, U.S. Rebel," whose title succinctly captured his image among international revolutionaries.[5]

At political conferences in Algiers and Oran, Carmichael described Black Power as part of an international struggle against imperialism. He expressed partisan support for conflicts raging in the Middle East in the wake of the Arab-Israeli Six-Day War fought in June of that year. Carmichael's speeches often drew energy from his audience, and in Algeria he discovered a particularly well-suited match. His extensive advocacy for Palestinian liberation contrasted with Martin Luther King's vocal support of Israel's right to statehood and political self-determination. Similar remarks expressed in Havana had remained obscured by the audacity of his Cuban trip, but now his foray into Middle East politics made American foreign policy experts nervous. Vietnam remained a consistent theme of his press conferences, including a September 13th affair, where he discussed ratcheting up black antiwar activism. He expressed support for his friend Muhammad Ali, who, early in the year, having refused induction into the army, had been stripped of his heavyweight boxing title. Ali himself had made a similar defense of Carmichael's personal character at an outdoor rally in Philadelphia four days earlier. "I don't condemn Stokely," said the beleaguered former heavyweight champion. "I believe there is sincerity in his heart."[6]

US embassy officials characterized Carmichael's political sentiments less charitably than Ali had. Carmichael's international tour elicited reports that expressed rage, hostility, and awe. Damage control remained paramount for officials trying to protect and burnish America's image in countries already skeptical of democracy. Consular bureaucrats in Algiers summed up Carmichael's presence with a resigned admission of the trip's impact. "It would be extremely difficult to measure how much harm he generated for the United States; it is abundantly clear that he did no good."[7]

Mustapha Semhi, a *Révolution Africaine* correspondent with deep ties to the FLN, counted himself among a minority in Algeria immune to Stokely's charms. "I talked to Stokely Carmichael for eight hours—with Cherif Belka-cem and alone," he reported to an Algerian embassy officer, "and really you know, he wasn't very serious." The FLN's former Paris bureau chief thought Carmichael intelligent enough but blanched at his talk of revolutionary violence. If Semhi found Stokely's rhetoric too facile, he considered the Algerian government's indulgence of Carmichael appalling. Carmichael's ten days of unlimited access to virtually every government branch combined with generous coverage in *Révolution Africaine* and *El Djeich* (the Algerian army weekly) rubbed the politically doctrinaire Semhi the wrong way and, in the process, soothed the wounded egos of American officials, who reported the critique under the subject heading "Stokely Wasn't All That Great."[8]

SNCC's Jewish allies must have agreed that "Stokely wasn't all that great." Fresh on the heels of a pro-Palestinian article published in the *SNCC Newsletter* that alienated liberal Jewish supporters, Carmichael poured further fuel on the controversy by equating Zionism with racism, as the United Nations would do in 1975, by a vote of 72 to 35. What SNCC regarded as anti-imperialism others defined as naked anti-Jewish sentiment, a perspective echoed by a *Boston Globe* editorial branding the group the "KKK of the New Left." For Carmichael, Zionism disguised imperial ambitions in the cloak of indigenous nationalism. Algiers' domestic news service quoted him suggesting that the "solution to the Palestine question lies in taking up arms." Such bold talk endeared him to his Algerian hosts and impressed radicals sympathetic to the Arab cause even as it ensured that charges of anti-Semitism would follow him from North Africa to the grave.[9]

Algerian officials fêted Carmichael, producing indelible memories. "In Algeria I was treated royally," he happily remembered, "almost like a *rais* [head chief]." Ten days into his stay, on September 15, Carmichael flew to Cairo as the guest of a local Afro-Asian solidarity group. "I am a primarily a man of peace," he said, "but through violence I shall destroy those who deny peace to us." In Cairo, Carmichael contemplated what basis there could be for black liberation in the United States. Speaking with David, the son of Shirley Graham Du Bois (and stepson of W.E.B.), he said, "Once we begin to fight and the third world also begins to fight, the economic security of the white worker will be reduced, because the economic security of the white worker comes from the fact that he exploits the sweat of African-Americans and the people of the third world. Once his economic security is reduced and he becomes economically unstable, then he too will begin to fight. And then you will have the grounds for establishing a real people's democracy in the US."[10]

If American democracy's image remained permanently tarnished in Carmichael's eyes, Africa—with its indigenous liberation movements, revolutionary governments, and enormous potential—now captured his imagination.

Carmichael's tour of Africa and the Middle East continued in Damascus three days later, where he addressed the Syrian Committee for Afro-Asian Solidarity. He met with Prime Minister Yusuf Zuayyin before returning to Algiers on September 23. There he discussed "the problems of youth and international solidarity" with FLN officials. Off the record, his Algerian hosts pledged full support for Carmichael's political efforts in the United States, including a promise of official recognition and formal diplomatic ties and military training for him and SNCC, an offer he turned down (the Black Panthers, later offered similar support, would accept it). Algeria's revolutionary history appealed to Carmichael's cosmopolitan side, and he recognized his time in Frantz Fanon's adopted homeland as being a part of "a uniquely favored historical generation." His stay in Algiers concluded as it began, with a meeting with Cherif Belkacem, whose hospitality had afforded him free rein. Carmichael resumed his first extended trip as an adult outside the United States in Conakry, Guinea, on Tuesday evening, September 26, disembarking from a Soviet Aeroflot flight from Algeria. He arrived as an honored guest of the Eighth Congress of the Democratic Party of Guinea. Amid rumors that the government wished to avoid controversy, however, he did not address the congress.[11]

Guinea's tropical climate reminded Stokely of Trinidad, and the sweet and pungent tastes of fruits and vegetables evoked long-dormant childhood memories. The environment struck him as both comfortingly familiar and refreshingly new, a place where nights under the stars inspired poetry: "Suddenly the moon became a presence in my consciousness once more." Conakry's scenic coastal backdrop complete with coconut palms and mango trees reminded him of the picturesque splendor of Port of Spain. Single-story wood buildings and their concrete two-story counterparts formed Conakry's modest skyline nestled on a bay and bracketed by green mountains.[12]

Carmichael's stay in Conakry, just like his tours of parts of the Middle East, followed on the heels of Malcolm X's several trips to Africa. In November 1964, Malcolm had arrived in Guinea and was introduced to President Sékou Touré, who had praised him for advancing "the struggle for dignity."

Malcolm X, in both symbolism and substance, helped to pave the way for Carmichael's reception in Guinea.[13]

Shirley Graham Du Bois paid him an unexpected visit on his first day and immediately introduced him to Kwame Nkrumah, who had been ousted in a coup the previous year. Touré had named Nkrumah Guinea's co-president and one of his advisers, but Nkrumah plotted his return to power in Ghana and in Carmichael found an important ally. Nkrumah's coastal villa on the Kolaya shore hid the harsh reality of political exile. The *Osagyefo* (or redeemer of his native land) and Carmichael took an instant liking to each other. Resplendent in a white collarless Nyerere suit, the diminutive Nkrumah gazed at the tall, rather haggard-looking Carmichael, who, despite donning a fresh shirt, was still tired from his trip. It turned out to be a largely one-sided conversation as Nkrumah lectured on the metaphysical ties between blacks and Africa. Carmichael sized up Nkrumah as the rare combination of statesman and intellectual that he aspired to be. Nkrumah had degrees from Lincoln University and the University of Pennsylvania, and his fluency in English allowed Carmichael to bond with him in a manner he never would with the Francophone Touré.

More good news followed after Shirley Graham Du Bois casually mentioned an upcoming concert featuring Miriam Makeba. Carmichael's growing celebrity made his second meeting with Makeba in seven years markedly different from the first, and the South African singer waved off Du Bois' efforts at formal introduction for the kind of casual intimacy afforded by mutual fame.

At thirty-five, Miriam Makeba was an established international star. She spent holidays at the home of Sidney Poitier, counted Elizabeth Taylor as a fan, and received after-show visits from entertainment legends like Bing Crosby. Her singing, which included protest songs about racial apartheid in her homeland, made her one of the most recognizable figures of the era. In 1962, Makeba and Harry Belafonte had sung at President Kennedy's 45th birthday celebration in Madison Square Garden. Although her appearance was overshadowed by Marilyn Monroe's sultry performance of "Happy Birthday, Mister President," Kennedy requested a meeting with Makeba, which Belafonte arranged. "I just wanted you to know, Miss Makeba, how very glad and how proud I am to have an African artist participate in my birthday celebration," the president told her.[14]

Miriam recognized Stokely as a familiar face from television, while he had never forgotten her. "We've met before," he reminded Makeba, "at Belafonte's." They began an intensely passionate affair that would bloom into marriage against the backdrop of global political events. This time, Stokely's timing proved fortuitous, especially as it came on the heels of a recent falling out between Makeba and her "Big Brother," Harry Belafonte, over whether to continue to sing the Hebrew song "Erev Shel Shoshanim" in the aftermath of the Arab-Israeli Six-Day War. In her autobiography, Miriam would claim that she had not suggested that Belafonte and she stop singing the song, but merely told him about the opposition of some her African diplomatic contacts. Belafonte, however, remembered their private conversation very differently. Belafonte and Makeba each accused the other of attempted censorship, and the dispute severed a once-close professional and personal relationship.[15]

Mutual physical attraction and a shared affection for Africa made for a particularly intoxicating romance that ignored a nine-year age difference between them. He found Miriam's international stature and artistic excellence as attractive as her beauty and quiet strength, while Makeba succumbed, as many women did, to Carmichael's combination of humor and intelligence. They snatched intimate moments together as guests of the Guinean state. Her extensive international networks matched her physical beauty and artistic talents. African leaders and dignitaries adored Makeba, whose passionate stage performances made her a beguiling and at times seductive figure. Kwame Nkrumah had invited her to Ghana in 1965. President Julius Nyerere personally issued Makeba a Tanzanian passport after South Africa revoked hers. Makeba's celebrity unlocked the doors to African and Third World embassies, where she and soon Stokely were treated like royalty. Her close personal relationship with diplomats and knowledge of the United Nations were unique for a performing artist. Makeba possessed enough charm to bring presidents to their knees, and she and Sékou Touré in fact developed a special relationship that found Stokely and Guinea's president competing for her attention.[16]

Stokely Carmichael and Kwame Nkrumah recognized each other as political soul mates. They found common ground, as would be their habit, in one of Nkrumah's ideas. Carmichael's overnight reading of the manuscript of Nkrumah's soon-to-be-published book *Handbook of Revolutionary Warfare* convinced him to serve as the American organizer for the *Osagyefo's*

proposed All African People's Revolutionary Party. The conviction that a robust Pan-African movement held the key to both of their political fortunes
overcame Nkrumah's initial skepticism about exporting an idea conceived
primarily for the African continent. For Carmichael, their relatively brief discussion of building a Pan-African political party in the United States would
become his life's work.

Nkrumah invited Stokely to meet Sékou Touré just before the co-presidents
entered a session of the party congress, and Carmichael marched in lock-
step between the two men to thunderous "spontaneous, intense, powerful"
applause. Despite Touré's dramatic gesture, a kind of innate formality would
mark their relationship, which, until their later years together, lacked the
personal warmth, political chemistry, and familial affection forged between
Carmichael and Nkrumah. Mutual respect and admiration characterized
Carmichael and Touré's relationship, but each remained subconsciously wary
of the other, a distance perhaps exacerbated by a language barrier between
the French-speaking president and the English-speaking revolutionary.[17]

On Stokely's fourth day in Conakry, a US Embassy consular officer spotted
Carmichael at the G'bessia Hotel as he ate breakfast with Shirley Graham Du
Bois, and immediately requested his passport. The maneuver represented a
middle ground between compelling foreign governments to expel Carmichael and ignoring him. Deciding that coercion, even through back channels, would only "serve Castro-Carmichael propaganda," State Department
officials crafted a letter threatening legal action if he continued to use an in-
valid passport. The scenario required that Carmichael accept the letter from
a consular official.[18]

"No, Stokely, no! Don't do it. That's exactly what they did to Du Bois,"
screamed Shirley Graham. The tense scene turned unintentionally comic as
Carmichael responded on cue. "I don't want anything to do with it! I don't
want anything to do with it!" he replied, repeating the phrase as a rehearsed
defense against efforts to inform him that his passport had been officially
revoked. Saved by the intervention of Du Bois and a Guinean bodyguard
assigned for his protection, Carmichael retained his passport.[19]

On the first Monday in October, Carmichael and Makeba paid a surprise
visit to the People's Militia of Guinea. Orders to halt exercises were almost
drowned out by the cheers of the militia's men and women waving rifles in
the air. The young soldiers of the Fifth Battalion of Guinea's local militia included women practicing grenade throwing and target practice with rifles, an

exercise that Carmichael eagerly participated in. After years of shedding his own blood in search of higher democratic values in the United States, Carmichael now upheld revolutionary violence as the cure to a world ensconced in suffering. Makeba's international stature surpassed Carmichael's, and under a steady rain she gave a brief speech about the hopes for liberation of South Africa.

That same day, Carmichael and Makeba attended a luncheon at the Cuban Embassy, where they mingled with dignitaries and guests, who were quite in awe of Makeba's mesmerizing ability to convey the depths of colonial oppression in her powerful songs. Carmichael's three-week stay in Guinea represented nothing short of a political introduction to the high-stakes world of African politics, where he played the role of eager student to the demanding Kwame Nkrumah. He departed Conakry for the Club des Pins, Algiers, with immediate plans to visit Tanzania and a promise to return to Guinea permanently to work and study under Nkrumah.[20]

On October 7, while Carmichael was in Guinea, Ruby Doris Smith Robinson died of lymphosarcoma in Atlanta. She was only twenty-five. One week later, scores of her friends and colleagues in SNCC joined Robinson's family for a funeral service. Clifford Robinson, Ruby Doris' husband, and her two-year-old-son Kenneth Touré were in the packed church as friends, including John Lewis and Julian Bond, reminisced about a death they blamed on racism as much as they did on cancer. Sékou Touré sent a telegram from Guinea expressing condolences. New associates of SNCC, most notably Eldridge Cleaver, the Black Panthers' brooding minister of information, joined faces that Ruby would have found familiar such as Cleve Sellers and Jim Forman. One of Stokely's friends and allies, Maulana Karenga of the Organization Us, had to wait outside, unable to get inside the overcrowded venue. Robinson's death was a major blow for Stokely, who could not attend the funeral. As one of SNCC's most important leaders and original architects, Robinson would openly challenge Stokely even after he had become politically famous. Carmichael, who could be sensitive to criticism, embraced her as a little sister, and her loss contributed to the group's inexorable decline over the next year.[21]

Carmichael returned to Algeria on Wednesday, October 18. The next day he recounted the details of his passport confrontation in a wide-ranging interview with Algérie Presse, the state news agency. Desperate attempts to invalidate his passport reflected a larger effort to stall political alliances whose reverberations threatened the Cold War's grip on the world's political imagination. "What the State Department really wants, in attempting to restrict my movements, is to prevent the inevitable link-up between Afro-Americans and the countries of the third world," observed Carmichael. News of the October 9th killing of Che Guevara in Bolivia intensified Carmichael's preoccupation with mortality. He exclaimed, "When death comes to me, it will come as it did to Che."[22]

The United Arab Republic (UAR), the name Egypt adopted under the presidency of Gamal Abdel Nasser, welcomed Stokely as a revolutionary leader who represented black radicals in the United States. In Cairo on October 20, Carmichael met with UAR officials and local Afro-Asian solidarity groups. During that meeting, he publicly embraced Palestinian self-determination. On October 27, he caught a plane to Dar es Salaam. In Tanzania, Stokely was determined to forge concrete alliances with African revolutionaries, having already corresponded with various liberation groups in hopes of serving with them. Obstacles to such a course included Carmichael's promise to return to Guinea within two months to serve as Nkrumah's personal aide. His budding romance with Miriam Makeba further clouded this picture, but in Africa he imagined a world of endless possibilities.[23]

While his time in Guinea produced romantic and political epiphanies, Carmichael's month in Dar es Salaam sparked international controversy. United States Information Agency (USIA) officials chronicled the fallout from Carmichael's visit as if documenting the aftermath of a political hurricane. In December of that year, they observed, after he had left, "He was certainly the most vivid personality to hit this comparative backwater in a long time and his heart would beat faster if he knew how frequently he is still talked of, at smart Oyster Bay cocktails, in student beerhalls, and perhaps even in village 'pombe' [beer] shops." Dar es Salaam was one of the world's most dangerous and exotic cities. There, operatives from Europe, the United States, and other parts of the world trafficked in real and imagined intrigues. A familiar political force steadied Stokely in Dar's treacherous political waters. Cuban Embassy staff drove him around the city, a task that turned into a full-time job as he struggled to answer numerous speaking requests. Housed at the Palm Beach Hotel, Carmichael could often be seen chatting with Tanzania's Minister of Lands, Settlement, and Water Supply, Mohammad Babu, an ally of Malcolm X's. President Julius Nyerere met with Carmichael for over two hours, and the ruling party, TANU, arranged logistics. Nyerere was a hero to Pan-Africanists in America. His definition of socialism as *Ujamaa,* or cooperative economics, impressed black nationalists searching for a viable alternative to American capitalism. Stokely's most instructive meetings, however, took place with guerrilla fighters. A private conference with Eduardo Mondlane, the Mozambican leader and head of FRELIMO, one of Africa's most respected liberation groups, reassured him of the political integrity of revolutionaries he had too casually dismissed upon his initial arrival in Africa.[24]

British reporter David Martin interviewed Carmichael for the *Standard,* a local paper, on his second day in Tanzania. In a wide-ranging, front-page story, Carmichael argued that only armed struggle would bring about African liberation and disputed enemy casualty figures reported by guerrilla leaders. Although he praised Mohammad Babu, rumors that Carmichael described African leaders as "worthless" and Julius Nyerere as "a clown" would haunt his stay. His most provocative, and ill-advised, comments centered on a general denunciation of certain African revolutionaries with a fondness for skirt chasing and white women.[25]

On November 2, Stokely addressed a capacity audience at University College's Theatre Hall. He was interrupted by frequent shouts of "Black Power!" Then Miriam Makeba capped off the event with songs about Africa's unfolding revolution.

The couple's reunion in Tanzania inspired a short romantic holiday. Miriam was going to the United States, and Stokely entrusted her with a letter and some money for his mother. In the Bronx, May Charles received Miriam into the Carmichael family with only some residual feelings of competition for her son's affections. His sister Janeth would accompany Makeba on a tour of Guinea that December, fulfilling a lifelong dream to visit Africa.[26]

Stokely's intemperate statements regarding African revolutionaries drew criticism from some important potential allies. Representatives from South Africa's African National Congress (ANC) published an editorial entitled, "Brother Carmichael . . . We Disagree," accusing him of being politically ignorant, rhetorically offensive, and personally naïve. The ANC detailed the evolution of its long human rights campaign in South Africa, recounted its contemporary military efforts in Rhodesia, and dared "Mr. Carmichael to venture into these areas and take stock of enemy casualties." One of Africa's most respected liberation groups labeled him an amateur whose eagerness to meddle in global political affairs betrayed the worst kind of political arrogance. "Raving and ranting in no way enhances the cause of Africa nor does it help our Afro-American brothers who are suffering the indignities" of white supremacy. American newspapers trumpeted the editorial's harsher quotes with cheerful headlines ("Free African Group Blasts Stokely View," "Carmichael Decried by Africans," and "African Group Accuses Carmichael of Hatred") that broke an American press blackout in effect since Cuba. The reality of African politics blurred distinctions between guerrillas and revolutionaries, statesmen and dictators, and made Carmichael's blunt analysis ring false to indigenous leaders who had spent a lifetime combating colonialism. The heady mixture of adulation and unprecedented access to Third World revolutionary leaders fueled Carmichael's already formidable ego. He had arrived in Dar, despite protestations to the contrary, determined to teach as well as to learn, only to discover a more complicated political terrain in Tanzania than he had anticipated.[27]

Carmichael proved enormously popular with local Tanzanians despite such missteps. At Kivukoni College, on the other side of the bay from Dar, Carmichael addressed an audience filled with students, American and British teachers, Cuban diplomats, and, of course, two USIA officers studiously taking notes. Students smiled at his jokes, nodded in knowing agreement when he discussed "the traditional inferiority complexes" of blacks in Africa and America, and let out delighted shrieks as he advocated purging Tanzania's white advisers and teachers. In a nod to the ANC's advice about re-evaluating the African Revolution, Carmichael admitted the need to study the history of Dar's assorted liberation groups before issuing stinging indictments. But he proceeded to do just that, although he extolled the virtues of armed conflict against the Portuguese, who were engaged in fierce struggles, most notably in Cape Verde, Guinea-Bissau, Angola, and Mozambique, to maintain their colonial power in Africa. Carmichael boarded a ferry back to the city under the bright stars of the African night on his way to another speaking engagement at the University of Dar es Salaam. There he offered a moving eulogy for Che Guevara before being besieged by autograph-seeking students.[28]

At the end of his time in Tanzania, Carmichael was reminded of the country and the struggle he had left behind. Huey Newton was in prison on charges of murdering an Oakland police officer in late October. Stokely spoke at a rally in support of him. Carmichael left Tanzania with painful lessons about African politics, where independence rested on fluid alliances, ancient histories, and indigenous cultures that remained incomprehensible to even sympathetic outsiders. Before returning "back to hell," he offered a "special message to the people of this country, particularly the youth, and that is that the revolution must continue."[29]

He traveled back to America's burning political infernos through Europe, where the Left embraced his uncompromising antiwar stance. If Carmichael's tour through Africa struck outsiders as a quixotic search for long-buried racial and cultural roots, his radical statements about Vietnam in Europe sounded alarm bells. Carmichael arrived in Uppsala, Sweden, a university community thirty-five miles outside of Stockholm, on the last Monday in November to deliver a series of lectures and meetings with local antiwar activists. Over the course of two days in Sweden, which included an appearance on television, he remained defiant about the prospects of criminal prosecution back home. "I am prepared for any punishment from prison to death," he said.[30]

On Wednesday morning in Copenhagen, Jean-Paul Sartre welcomed him to the headquarters of the tribunal that Sartre and the British philosopher Bertrand Russell were conducting on US war crimes in Vietnam. Carmichael was one of the original members of the tribunal's eighteen-person jury, and the visit offered him the chance to participate in the tribunal. Pham Thach, North Vietnam's Health Minister and the tribunal's first witness, paid tribute to Carmichael "for his fight against racial discrimination in the United States" and efforts to foster Third World solidarity. The tribunal drew an impressive array of writers, artists, and activists from over a dozen countries in a largely successful effort to forge an intellectual base for resistance to the Vietnam War and the draft.[31]

Stokely stayed for just the morning session before departing for Oslo that afternoon. That night he addressed a capacity crowd of two thousand at the Oslo Student Union at Blindern in measured but effective tones about the Vietnam War. Carmichael's detailed foreign policy criticisms, which called for Norway's withdrawal from NATO, impressed participants and journalists. Asked during the question-and-answer session if he planned to return home in light of Arizona Senator Barry Goldwater's calls for him to be tried for high treason, Carmichael remained resolute. "Absolutely," he answered before adding that in two weeks Goldwater would have his chance. An editorial in *Arbeiderbladet*, Norway's daily Labor Party newspaper, captured the duality that lay at the core of Carmichael's impassioned speech against a country: "he hates so bitterly and . . . also loves so highly."[32]

Carmichael capped off his Scandinavian tour with an evening talk at a large concert hall in downtown Stockholm before heading to Paris accompanied

by a photographer and two Swedish journalists with plans to cover his political activities in France and the United States. Despite warnings from the
Swedish police that French officials regarded him as an "undesirable," he was
determined to address a large antiwar demonstration in Paris before returning home.[33]

The French police detained Carmichael at the customs gate at Orly Airport on Tuesday, December 5, setting the stage for a short but memorable
stay in Paris. The Interior Ministry called him an "undesirable person," and
French officials offered him a seat on a plane the next morning "to a destination of his choice." He was held incommunicado at Orly for seventeen hours,
and his predicament reminded him and others of the time when France
barred Malcolm X's entrance less than two weeks before his death. Meanwhile, Stokely's allies secured a prominent attorney, Madeleine Lafue-Veron,
to help craft their formal protest to the Foreign Ministry. A group of expatriates, activists, and intellectuals who dubbed themselves the "Friends
of Stokely Carmichael," issued a statement expressing disappointment "that
France, the most liberal of countries," denied Stokely entrance "especially in
view of Gen. de Gaulle's position on the Vietnam war."[34]

Amid speculation that President de Gaulle had personally intervened on
Stokely's behalf, the French government lifted the quarantine and granted
him a three-month visa. His detention and release dominated the front page of
the American-owned, Paris-based *International Herald Tribune* over the next
two days. Lafue-Veron traced the government's turnabout to old-fashioned
lobbying: "Many ministers were contacted during the morning. There was a
general feeling that the expulsion was contrary to French policy."[35]

Pleasantly surprised, Carmichael praised de Gaulle as a peaceful statesman, in contrast to the war-mongering Lyndon Johnson. Carmichael's
statement reflected both common ground with de Gaulle on the subject of
Vietnam and a more nuanced understanding of contemporary realpolitik.
"The man likes me, my ideas and my work," he told a reporter without ever
mentioning de Gaulle. Behind the scenes, his scheduled appearance at a
government-sanctioned antiwar rally forced high-level officials to weigh the
political consequences of barring Carmichael against the short-term controversy of allowing him to speak.[36]

That evening, four thousand attended an antiwar rally at the Palais de la
Mutualité in Paris' Left Bank. The crowd cheered as Carmichael, dressed in
an open collar shirt and sports coat, strode to the stage, his two fists raised,

before settling beneath a giant poster of Che Guevara. In the background were Viet Cong flags and a Christmas tree. For a delicious instant, the predominantly French-speaking crowd stood transfixed at the symbolism of a living revolutionary speaking beneath a portrait of a recently martyred one. "We have not come to France as an act of defiance but . . . to help the Vietnamese people," he said. "Our aim is to disrupt the United States of America, and we think our blood is not too high a price to pay. We don't want peace in Vietnam! We want the Vietnamese to defeat the United States of America!" Waves of applause and cheers reverberated throughout the Mutualité.[37]

Excerpts of Carmichael's comments in Paris made the CBS Evening News Thursday telecast, with correspondent Harry Reasoner summing up his speeches as "a violently anti-American" jeremiad "to audiences from Havana to Hanoi." The broadcast interspersed an excerpt from Carmichael's Paris speech with a provocative snippet from a sit-down interview:

REPORTER: Mr. Carmichael, you said you would shed your blood for the Vietnam cause. Now how and where do you intend to do this?

CARMICHAEL: In the United States of America. The war in Vietnam must be brought to the United States of America. If Ho Chi Minh cannot sleep, Lyndon Johnson shall not sleep. The babies in Vietnam are in threat of their lives, and people in the United States must be in threat of their lives. If fire is raging in Vietnam, then fire must rage in the United States. And as long as the United States oppresses black people inside the United States and oppresses Vietnamese in Vietnam, we have a common bond against a common enemy. And we will fight.

Aware that no amount of editorializing could follow such an audacious statement, Reasoner ended the segment on a note of dry resignation: "Stokely Carmichael speaking in Paris last night."[38]

After the rally, French police surveillance trailed Carmichael to two different safe houses and a secret rendezvous with his female interpreter. His purportedly romantic assignation happened a little before the appearance of the front-page headline in the *International Herald Tribune*—"Carmichael at Paris Rally As French Reverse Stand." Stokely emerged as a brown-skinned political magician, capable of swaying Foreign Ministry officials and French intellectuals in a display of political theater that had charmed even the most jaded political observers.[39]

He spent the next day in clandestine political meetings. An early afternoon visit with Russell Tribunal member Laurent Schwartz was followed by
a three-and-a-half-hour off-the-record political conference with Third World
foreign nationals, black expatriates, and antiwar organizers at the home of
an Indian national. Early Friday meetings with members of Paris's vibrant
community of black American exiles gave way to a late lunch with Swedish
journalists at the Eiffel Tower. His nights in Paris invariably stretched into the
early morning hours. "He returned to his Paris domicile at 4 o'clock A.M. after
having spent two hours in a cabaret," reported his weary surveillance team.[40]

Stokely attended a screening of the antiwar film *Far from Vietnam* (*Loin
Du Vietnam*) at the Cinémathèque française. Then he met with Richard
Perrin, a nineteen-year-old white army private turned peace activist and
deserter. Carmichael and Perrin conducted a joint midnight interview with
CBS News, Dutch television, and *The New York Times* at a Paris apartment.

The news conference had been Perrin's idea, and he expressed open admiration for Stokely, who, along with Muhammad Ali, appealed to his rebellious side. Glimpses of Carmichael's private life emerged the next evening
as he met with Perrin in a smoke-filled Paris bar in between spending time
with his local paramour and then with French antiwar activists, black intellectuals, and political admirers. News of the press conference created a minor
sensation, with journalists wondering how a nice middle-class boy from Ver-
mont like Perrin could wind up sharing the politics of the dangerous Stokely
Carmichael.

Alerted to Stokely's impending arrival in the United States, Nicholas Katzenbach, now undersecretary of state, requested congressional approval to
make unauthorized international travel illegal. Although the move smacked
of naked politics, it underscored a mood in Congress for a political reckoning, and Katzenbach admitted that such legislation "obviously was related to
travel by Stokely Carmichael and others to places such as North Vietnam."
The proposed bill would impose a sentence of up to one year in jail and a fine
of $1,000 for those convicted. Support for such legislation fell along ideolog-
ical lines, with the conservative *Chicago Tribune* daring the Justice Department to "Call Carmichael's Bluff" and the liberal *Washington Post* balking at
the sweeping nature of the proposed law as a move toward totalitarianism.
The black-owned *Chicago Daily Defender*, marveling at Carmichael's ability
to return home without facing immediate arrest, viewed the unfolding scenario as nothing less than "a test of American democracy."[41]

On December 11, Carmichael returned to the United States, landing in New York. The first passenger to get off the Air France Boeing 707 (ahead of three Swedish journalists and filmmakers who accompanied him), Stokely was nattily dressed in a pair of brown corduroy pants, turquoise turtleneck sweater, and checkered sports coat. A United States marshal representing New York's Eastern District and armed with a federal search warrant immediately confiscated his passport, while on the tarmac a hundred supporters chanted "Black Power!" Agents from the State Department, Immigration, and the attorney general's office were also present. The spectacle of federal authority proved more comical than frightening, and Carmichael suppressed an urge to laugh behind exchanged pleasantries. Braced for the possibility of arrest he instead surrendered his passport while registering a strong verbal protest that barely masked his appreciative relief at remaining free. Carmichael's passport photo gave him the look of a brooding matinee idol while visa stamps from London, Cairo, and Tanzania revealed the globetrotting curiosity that lay behind his brown eyes. The wide eyes seemed to promise mischief but could frighten imperial powers and post-colonial outposts such as Jamaica, where the Ministry of Home Affairs had banned Carmichael from entering the country.[42]

Pro-Carmichael militants and media jockeyed for position at Kennedy Airport, a situation that produced an angry exchange between activists and police. Carmichael exited customs to a surging crowd of supporters that included groups of women hugging and kissing him. Professional and amateur photographers snapped pictures, lending the proceedings the hectic feel of a movie premiere. Carmichael sprinted from customs to an awaiting vehicle that departed Kennedy Airport under police escort. Some white taxi cab drivers flipped on their "Off Duty" signs to protest Carmichael's overseas activities, to the chagrin of female supporters who had planned to follow his car back to Harlem. The next day's *Chicago Daily Defender* succinctly captured the entire scene: "STOKELY'S BACK." From the airport, Carmichael and James Forman went to the YMCA on 135th Street and Lenox Avenue in Harlem to meet with Rap Brown. Shortly before 9:00 P.M., Carmichael headed home to the Bronx for a reunion with his mother. But their timing proved off as May Charles was on the cruise ship *Argentine*, where she worked, and it was ready to depart. "Stokely, I want to see you when I return," she told him by telephone. On December 14, *The Barbados Advocate* profiled May Charles' private anguish over a son living in the shadow of constant death, in an article titled "Carmichael's Mother Lives in Fear." "It's a living hell," she said, adding that she died "a thousand deaths" after his every arrest. "Stokely's way is the only way for us now," she said. The writer of the article noted the irony of black nationalist Carmichael's education and upbringing in the Bronx in predominantly white neighborhoods and schools.[43]

The warm feelings that greeted him upon his return would not last. Carmichael's international political ascent paralleled SNCC's declining political fortunes. It also fueled competitive jealousy in Jim Forman, whose evolving politics drew him closer to a more class-based analysis of revolution. The greatest blow had come in October with the death of Ruby Doris Smith Robinson. Stokely was in Conakry when she died, and his return offered an opportunity to reminisce and grieve over her, whose tough criticism of him often strained their relations when he was chairman. Privately, attorney William Kunstler advised him to curtail public speeches in case federal authorities decided to prosecute him on charges related to his travels.[44]

Fallout from his global travails continued as Carmichael emerged as a living Rorschach test for divergent political and cultural sensibilities. His international travails made him a touchstone that transcended politics into the far-reaching stratosphere of American culture. Yaphet Kotto, a talented black stage actor and founder of the Watts Actors Workshop, chafed against people who "ask what I think about Stokely Carmichael," insisting that "he is not my spokesman, and I'm not his." Dr. Benjamin Spock claimed common ground with Carmichael on broad peace initiatives, and writer and feminist activist Gloria Steinem identified him as one of the few living Americans she yearned to interview "because he has the fervor of a convert."[45]

CHAPTER FOURTEEN

Black Panther

December 11, 1967–April 3, 1968

IN A STROKE OF INGENIOUS HISTORICAL TIMING, IN FEBRUARY 1968, THE Black Panther Party named Stokely Carmichael the party's honorary prime minister. The title aptly described his new identity: he imagined himself, like Malcolm X, able to unite disparate strands of the black community into a cohesive political force. Five months of international trial by fire tested his principles, resolve, and will. Despite mistakes, Carmichael's political sincerity remained unquestioned and formed the basis of his singular position as the most important black radical activist of his generation. Yet he remained in organizational limbo, for the first time in almost a decade, without a steady political base. Carmichael returned to America just in time to experience one of history's most momentous years. Bursting with ideas, plans, and emotions that friends and colleagues could barely comprehend, he observed the year's upheavals, riots, and protests with a perspective of a man whose political fate lay in the international politics of Africa and the wider Third World. Travels overseas made him long for the kind of rich, full life that seemed increasingly impossible in the States. Stokely's relationship with the Black Panther Party grew serious, offering a chance to regroup and channel political energies in a manner that resembled his early days in SNCC.

The notoriety of the BPP, if not its actual size, had increased markedly during Stokely's travels. The Panthers had taken a precarious journey from the outer fringes of black politics to its center, a situation made all the more ironic since the group's newfound credibility stemmed from a shootout between Huey Newton and the Oakland Police. While out driving in the early hours of the morning of October 28, 1967, after attending a party celebrating the end of his parole, Newton was stopped by a police officer. The officer and Newton were familiar with one another from earlier confrontations, and a mêlée ensued that left the Panther with a bullet lodged in his stomach and Officer John Frey dead. Carmichael viewed the Panthers as highly motivated political amateurs whom he might be able to shape toward his own political ends. Bracingly confident, the Panthers identified Carmichael as a prized asset capable of tipping the scales in their quest to free Huey Newton from jail. Carmichael found the group, in many ways, just as attractive as they found him. But he hedged his bets, organizing a local Black United Front in Washington to maintain his political independence. Yet the lure of the leather-jacketed rebels whom his activism helped inspire proved for a time irresistible, forever linking Carmichael and the Black Panthers in the historical imagination. Carmichael's efforts on behalf of the group helped shape their public image, identified future areas of strength, and exposed organizational weaknesses and ideological fault lines that would erupt long after his association with the BPP ended.[1]

On December 14, Carmichael returned to Howard University, where he autographed copies of his first book, *Black Power: The Politics of Liberation in America*, co-written with political scientist Dr. Charles Hamilton. The collaboration proved historic, with the Roosevelt University political scientist incorporating Carmichael's missives into a manuscript that illustrated the movement's intellectual sophistication, political ambition, and scholarly insight. Published by Random House six weeks earlier, *Black Power* represented the rare best seller that introduced a new academic and literary genre. Along with two other books published in 1967—Martin Luther King's incisive *Where Do We Go from Here: Chaos or Community?* and Harold Cruse's groundbreaking *The Crisis of the Negro Intellectual: A Historical Analysis of the Failure of Black Leadership*—*Black Power* established black political thought as a mainstream topic of historical and intellectual interest. All three books would become required reading in the Black Studies programs and departments that willed themselves into existence through gritty demonstrations and strategic political negotiations.

With Carmichael overseas at the time of its publication in November, Dr. Hamilton deflected rumors that he had written the book himself. "Stokely has too much of an ego to permit me to ghost write a book for him," he explained to one reporter.[2]

Black Power offers a still-powerful diagnosis of America's tortured racial history. The book contrasts personal prejudice with "institutional racism" and in the process introduced a term whose meaning would resonate well into the twenty-first century. The authors argued that racism manifested itself in all aspects of American democracy, marking it as a systemic phenomenon that encapsulated the entire country. In doing so, Carmichael and Hamilton challenged the intellectual arguments underpinning magisterial works, from Alexis de Tocqueville's *Democracy in America* to Gunnar Myrdal's *An American Dilemma*, that viewed racism as the aberration of an otherwise healthy democracy.

In *Black Power: The Politics of Liberation in America,* Carmichael and Hamilton offered an alternative reading of American history. They replaced optimistic narratives of democratic ascent with the reality of racial oppression, white violence, and a national failure on racial matters. Hope, through self-definition and a reimagining of Western society, sprang from this history of failure. The book was the product of an organizer who saw himself as an intellectual and a scholar who admired political activism, and its tone alternated between searing eloquence and restrained, if incisive, historical and political analysis. Thus, *Black Power* was less a polemic than an intellectually rigorous and theoretically subtle political treatise whose unexpected breadth and depth surprised critics.

In *The New York Review of Books*, Christopher Lasch faulted *Black Power* for its failure to forge "concrete proposals" despite the authors' insistence that they had avoided outlining a political blueprint to prevent the book from becoming immediately dated. In *The New York Times,* Fred Powledge (author of a book that came out at the same time, *Black Power/White Resistance*) expressed similar disappointment but lauded the book's "excellent description" of institutional racism and stimulating discussion of the viability of interracial political coalitions. Albert Murray, an iconoclastic black writer and critic whose sensibilities matched those of his close friend the novelist Ralph Ellison, accused Carmichael and Hamilton of unwittingly adopting the tone of "white do-gooders speaking through black masks." Like Ellison, author of the iconic novel *Invisible Man,* Murray chafed at the faintest whiff of literary, historical, or political orthodoxy, insisting that black culture retained a resilience and vitality that the nation ignored at its own peril and whose trajectory remained hidden from all but the most indefatigable researchers. Chicago activist Al Raby countered Murray's skepticism with full-throated approval of "this cool and reasoned book." For Raby, who knew Carmichael, *Black Power*'s "vigorous attack" on racism and vivid description of "white supremacy in the form of domestic colonialism" was a major contribution to a burgeoning movement literature.[3]

While critics weighed *Black Power*'s intellectual and literary merits, Undersecretary of State Nicholas Katzenbach delivered a confidential memo five days before Christmas to President Johnson on plans to prosecute Carmichael: "You asked that I examine possible avenues for the criminal prosecution of Stokely Carmichael." Katzenbach's sharp legal mind and keen sense of history uncovered a statute dating back to 1799, the Logan Act (which made it a crime to consort with foreign officials for the purpose of "defeating the measures of the United States"), under which Carmichael might be prosecuted. Carmichael's actions in Havana and Hanoi made him ripe for criminal prosecution on these grounds. Public relations and legal obstacles lurked behind this potential opportunity, since the Logan Act had not been the basis of prosecution for the past 168 years. The Supreme Court might reverse such a conviction since, wrote Katzenbach, "hundreds of American citizens probably violate the broad language of the Logan Act every year" without prosecution. Charges of sedition and passport violation were moot since Carmichael's passport bore "no visas or entry stamps" from banned countries. And so, Katzenbach recommended against prosecution.

Instead, Katzenbach proposed charging Stokely with obstructing the draft: "Carmichael's whole series of speeches in April and May 1967 on college campuses and elsewhere would be viewed as a single attempt to obstruct the draft." The approach rested on arguing that in his speeches Carmichael urged citizens "to disregard or return induction notices," a legal stretch that Katzenbach hoped "might stand up in court." Carmichael's speeches in Cuba would be used as an "incriminating admission" for State Department prosecution. Johnson reviewed possible scenarios for Carmichael's arrest and prosecution as Justice officials sought legal advice from the State Department in search of potential witnesses in Tanzania, Sweden, and Denmark who could testify in a federal trial.[4]

Carmichael returned to the Bronx on December 29 just as a report studying black youth in Atlanta identified him as a generational touchstone. The Southern Regional Council issued the first major study of black teenagers' opinions in twenty-seven years. In "Black Youth in a Southern Metropolis," the SRC found that almost half opposed the Vietnam War, and just a bare majority—fifty-one percent—supported nonviolence. Forty-five percent judged whites to be untrustworthy, and the Atlanta area teenagers culled for the study included Stokely Carmichael alongside Martin Luther King as the city's most important black leader. The report predicted that black youth would be "far more aggressive and militant" in the future than "the current advocates of black power." While academics, journalists, and race relations experts grappled with the conclusions drawn from "Black Youth in a Southern Metropolis," Carmichael concluded the year with visits to friends and family in Harlem under the watchful eye of FBI agents temporarily thwarted in their round-the-clock surveillance by traffic jams and bad weather.[5]

In the New Year, Carmichael made building national political solidarity among black activists his primary mission. On Tuesday, January 9, almost one hundred of Washington's key black political leaders met at Carmichael's request at the New School for Afro-American Thought in the city's northwest section to organize the Black United Front (BUF). Outside, reporters waited in frigid temperatures while metropolitan police squad cars patrolled the area. Inside, Carmichael trumpeted the power of racial solidarity over political and strategic differences to a largely approving crowd of community organizers, civic and religious leaders, and civil rights activists. His optimistic demeanor masked private disappointment over the press's ability to publicize a meeting called in secret. Upset over unauthorized leaks, he found comfort in orchestrating successful negotiations with the *Washington Post* for exclusive photos—but not interviews—that featured him outside holding court and inside making points on a chalkboard. He counted many in the audience as close political friends. The presence of racial moderates such as the SCLC's Walter Fauntroy and journalist Chuck Stone lent the entire project broad appeal. Surprise registered among critics and supporters expecting fire-breathing polemics only to find Carmichael playing the role of statesman convincingly enough to be named temporary chairman of a united front featuring some of the city's most respected civil rights leaders.[6]

The BUF reconvened five days later, absent two FBI informants unable to attend due to prior commitments. Local agents consoled themselves with secret knowledge that another well-placed informant hosted a SNCC fundraiser that same evening and "pointed out that Carmichael is suspicious of everyone in SNCC," since he correctly suspected "that there must be an informant in their midst." Whitney Young issued the first public dissent, telling reporters that he planned to resist any hint of a Carmichael takeover of BUF leadership. The NAACP's H. Carl Moultrie echoed Young's reticence, abandoning the united front under orders from the NAACP's national headquarters. Washington's local Urban League "voted to defer association" pending a review of the new group's organizational structure and political goals. Carmichael responded like a seasoned politician, attending morning services at Metropolitan Baptist Church, where he chatted amiably with parishioners and, by the close of services, received a warm greeting from Reverend Dr. E.C. Smith, chairman of a group of ministers that, the day before, had blasted the BUF.[7]

Carmichael's public moderation convinced some black newspapers like the *Chicago Daily Defender* that racial moderates and militants had reversed roles. Conservatives, it seemed, were "doing the finger pointing" and radicals were turning the other cheek. Sunday's front-page *Washington Post* story, "Carmichael Enigma: What Are His Aims?," contrasted the "two Stokely Carmichaels" that had appeared since his global tour. The new Carmichael preached "conciliation and tolerance" to the point of attending church services dressed like a head deacon. The "old" Stokely, "the fire-eating revolutionary," continued to advocate a gospel taken straight from the Old Testament.[8]

Eldridge Cleaver and Bobby Seale witnessed both sides of Carmichael in Washington during the end of January. Cleaver's political activities now outstripped his literary ambitions. The Black Panther Party's minister of information imagined himself, like Carmichael, the leader of a burgeoning revolution. Both had changed since their last meeting, with Carmichael achieving iconic status among black militants and Cleaver's more regional profile expanding as the Black Panthers' notoriety grew. Seale arrived in Washington less than two months out of jail on charges stemming from the Panthers' memorably audacious "invasion" of California's State Capitol the previous spring. The Panthers' daring bravado had put a temporary stranglehold on the entire state of California when they walked into the statehouse armed with guns to protest impending legislation designed to curtail their armed patrols of the police. Virtually penniless and despite mounting personal and family obligations, Seale decided to thrust himself into full-time organizing on behalf of Huey Newton, who was awaiting trial and possibly facing the gas chamber if convicted of murder.

Aided first by coffee and then wine, Stokely, Cleaver, and Seale bypassed competitive urges and nervous tension to negotiate an appearance by Carmichael in Oakland. Cleaver and Seale were impressed, if wary, as Carmichael, driving a rental car, evaded FBI agents, whose job was to stay no less than thirty feet behind him in their car. "He drives like he's crazy," said Seale. Simmering controversy hovered over discussions at SNCC's Washington office, with Carmichael and others objecting to the presence of whites at a proposed Free Huey rally in Oakland and the Panthers reminding him they were simply adopting his past advocacy of strategic interracial alliances. Like a pair of leather-jacketed defense attorneys, they presented their case to a roomful of skeptical black nationalists, who asked them, "Why do you trust white people?" Against the backdrop of Washington's developing Black United Front, their message of interracial unity seemed especially ill-timed; Carmichael's consent to speak in Oakland cut off debate but revealed divergent political and organizing philosophies papered over by the Panthers' political desperation. Cleaver and Seale left with a deep sense of relief mixed with bafflement and anger over Carmichael's refusal to accept their racial politics or acknowledge what they now considered an unnatural fear of whites based on past experiences.[9]

Stokely transitioned from delicate negotiations with the Panthers to a new round of diplomacy with Martin Luther King. Twice during the first week in February, Carmichael and King met to hash over differences and discuss areas of mutual agreement.

During a meeting of two hundred activists at Washington's Church of the Redeemer, King disclosed detailed plans of the SCLC's upcoming Poor People's Campaign, where some three thousand people would camp between the Washington Monument and Lincoln Memorial to draw the nation's attention to the poor. The encampment would be called Resurrection City. Carmichael expressed support for the campaign's goals while maintaining SNCC's and the BUF's organizational autonomy.[10]

Carmichael and King met privately in Washington like fellow apostates. Like old friends engaged in a long-running, if frequently interrupted, conversation, they immediately picked up where they had left off. Carmichael's recent efforts made him suspect in the eyes of more doctrinaire militants, just as King's new adherence to what he called militant nonviolence gave a radical edge to his increasingly bold quest for economic justice. Their potential rapprochement, announced as a bombshell race relations breakthrough in the previous week's *Chicago Defender*, buzzed through Washington intelligence circles. Press coverage of the meeting alternately described it as part of King's

effort to neutralize the violent threat posed by Carmichael and a consolida-
tion of the duo's political alliance.[11]

In person, Carmichael assured King that SNCC's intentions were positive. "Stokely, you don't need to tell me that," replied King. "I know you."
Carmichael questioned King's judgment but never his sincerity and by
Wednesday returned with SNCC's compromise decision to neither endorse
nor denounce the Poor People's Campaign. Their two-hour summit took
place at Pitt's Motor Hotel and would be the last time Stokely would ever see
King alive. As Carmichael left, King suddenly grabbed his hand almost as
if he sensed impending danger. "Stokely, please be extra careful, now," King
pleaded. "Avoid any unnecessary risks. Promise me." Carmichael's natural
tendency to deflect anxiety with humor glossed over the warning, but King's
"unusually somber" last words would remain etched in his memory. A photographer from the *Afro-American* captured for posterity a picture of Stokely,
King, and Jesse Jackson, the young Chicago activist and SCLC aide, above
a caption that described their earlier Tuesday meeting as a "secret parley."
Although lacking a national profile, Jackson was already well-known among
Chicago civil rights activists. A former college football player, Jackson possessed the bearing and confidence of an athlete and spoke in the cadences
of a Harlem street speaker, all of which made him a rising star. His efforts
and drive to make a name for himself at times caused tension between him
and King, who recognized his talent but frowned upon personal agendas. Yet
Jackson remained destined to be considered, more than Ralph Abernathy,
Andrew Young, or Stokely, King's natural political heir. About Stokely, King
privately expressed reservations, confiding to his adviser Stanley Levison that
although Carmichael was now "sweet as pie," he tried to "pull a power play
on us in Washington," in an effort to redirect the purpose of the Poor People's
Campaign. The coup was thwarted only by a lack of support.[12]

Meanwhile, new horrors in the South involved Stokely's best friend.
Cleve Sellers was in South Carolina living with his parents while under indictment as a draft evader. Stokely had been scheduled to speak at the campuses of South Carolina State and Claflin College, but could not make it and
Sellers was a last-minute substitute. A small group of students were picketing
Orangeburg's bowling alley, and a larger one had gathered around a bonfire as a show of symbolic strength for the picketers. On February 8, state
troopers attacked the defenseless students at the bonfire. The Orangeburg
Massacre, as it came to be called, left three students dead and twenty-seven

injured, including Sellers, who was shot in the left shoulder. Sellers' celebrity status as a top Carmichael lieutenant helped to obscure the troopers' ruthless suppression of nonviolent demonstrators. Instead, the media spun crude tales of racial conspiracy inspired by Black Power militants. The next month, Sellers would be sentenced to five years in jail for refusing army induction and receive an extra year on trumped-up charges related to his activities in Orangeburg.[13]

STOKELY'S ALLIANCE with the Panthers would help the group claim the mantle of leadership over the most-radical segments of the black freedom movement. If Carmichael's plans to foster coalitions in Washington and other cities reflected a more pragmatic side, his efforts on behalf of the Black Panthers resurrected the rebel. Carmichael and SNCC aide Carver "Chico" Neblett arrived at San Francisco International Airport on the evening of February 15, and from there a group of Panthers took them to Eldridge Cleaver's residence. Organizers trumpeted Carmichael's upcoming keynote speech at a planned February 17 rally as a virtual guarantee of publicity. He arrived in Oakland at the height of his fame. Reporters were crediting him with the surge of interest in Negro History Week, which had been started in 1926 by historian Carter Woodson and became a precursor to Black History Month. Carmichael's presence offered new revenue streams, providing much-needed funds for Newton's defense, and Stokely's star power paid immediate dividends, turning a jailhouse visit on the rally's eve into a media event. At Berkeley's Sproul Plaza, Stokely, accompanied by Panthers and SNCC staff, bumped into Reies Tijerina, the outspoken leader of the Alianza Federal de Mercedes (Federal Land Grant Alliance), Chicano activists demanding New Mexico's return to indigenous people. The two men embraced amid expressions of mutual admiration and solidarity, emboldened by the awareness that their singular political struggles formed an important part of a larger global tapestry.[14]

Reporters, photojournalists, and news crews jammed the cramped lobby of Alameda Superior Court in anticipation of Carmichael's visit. He arrived at two P.M. in a tan coat but departed wearing a more Panther-appropriate black leather jacket accompanied by a group that included Chico Neblett. One of Carmichael's closest allies in SNCC, Neblett had a reputation as a courageous and tough organizer. His experiences in Mississippi and Albany,

Georgia, made him a veteran of some of the group's earliest days. Chico's older brother, Chuck Neblett, was one of the original SNCC Freedom Singers. Chico and Stokely's friendship went beyond a single organization, and Neblett (who would later change his name to Seku Nkrumah, in homage to Sékou Touré and Kwame Nkrumah) would come to embrace Pan-Africanism as a lifelong political commitment. A man more of deeds than of words, Neblett cut a striking figure: tall, lean but powerfully built, with an afro that made him seem like a militant straight from central casting.

Stokely's personal secretary, Ethel Minor, who would edit much of his correspondence and a book of his speeches, also traveled to California. Intelligent, resourceful, and pretty, Minor, whose past included a stint living in Colombia (where she learned to speak fluent Spanish), had worked as the office manager at Malcolm X's Organization for Afro-American Unity before meeting Stokely in Chicago in 1966 and becoming one of his most devoted political associates. Three years older than Carmichael, Minor found herself working in SNCC's communications department under the supervision of Charlie Cobb. Her political maturity and personal sophistication allowed her to politely resist Stokely's initial romantic advances in favor of a close political relationship that would last for three decades.

Carmichael told reporters that, "Brother Huey P. Newton is going to be freed—or else." He stopped to talk with Armelia Newton, Huey's mother, on his way out of the courthouse. "You gave birth to a beautiful warrior," he told her. Stokely emerged all smiles from his meeting with Huey Newton, but his buoyant demeanor masked political differences between the two. Newton's faith in the ability of protest to leverage his freedom clashed with Carmichael's vigorous insistence that nothing short of a political revolution would alter his fate.[15]

The subject of interracial organizing offered another point of contention, with the self-assured Newton dismissing Carmichael's advice to exclude white radicals from the Black Panthers' political affairs. Newton misread Carmichael's objections to white involvement as an emotional response to SNCC's past history of interracial organizing rather than as advice based on deep political experience. Carmichael's personal admiration for Newton's brash self-confidence did not blind him to the young Panther's political inexperience. It was a trait that hampered their discussion at the prison and in fact infected the entire BPP, perhaps none more so than Cleaver, who concealed a skimpy organizing portfolio behind charismatic bravado. "Our visit," recalled Newton, "lasted just long enough for us to disagree." Carmichael's brief appearance excited the courthouse and energized journalists, who speculated that his presence, along with talk of a Panther-SNCC alliance, might turn a local story into a national one.[16]

Over the weekend, Carmichael delivered major speeches that would propel the Free Huey Movement into the national consciousness and provide the BPP a level of credibility undreamed of just a few months earlier. The Panthers' courtship of Carmichael drew the BPP and SNCC closer just as tensions between Carmichael, Forman, and Rap Brown over control of SNCC's resources, organization, and vision reached a breaking point. Public displays of unity in Oakland, where Rap Brown was named minister of justice and Forman minister of foreign affairs, masked roiling conflicts within SNCC.[17]

Clashes over fame, power, and ideology amplified growing strains between Carmichael and Forman. A widening political chasm undercut a personal friendship that dated back to 1961 when a letter of support from Forman had buoyed Carmichael and fellow Freedom Riders in Parchman Penitentiary. Like a proud older brother, Forman had watched Carmichael's professional and intellectual growth inside of SNCC and encouraged him to assume a larger role in the organization's leadership. Carmichael's initial reticence at providing vocal administrative leadership eventually gave way to his election to chairman, a candidacy that Forman initially supported. But Carmichael's Black Power fame soon overwhelmed SNCC, including Forman, Stokely's handpicked director of international affairs, who quietly fumed at the outgoing chair's improvisational world tour. Carmichael's celebrity and international travels struck Forman as irresponsible, a kind of freelance political activism designed for self-promotion rather than a global revolution. Worse, Carmichael's unauthorized trip to Cuba and widely broadcast statements that seemed to promote racial revolt at the expense of class solidarity rankled both Forman's well-known authoritarian streak and burgeoning Marxism. Forman responded tactically, embarking on speaking tours, promoting the links between Jim Crow and economic exploitation as an implicit rebuke to the far-more-popular Carmichael and cultivating internal support in SNCC through a close alliance with Rap Brown. With his internal base secure, Forman rejected as self-destructive private calls to dismiss

Carmichael from SNCC even as he blamed the former chairman for "creating more confusion and distrust in the movement." Efforts at a personal rapprochement also failed. Carmichael countered Forman's pleas to stop calling whites "honky" or at least connect the phrase to economic exploitation with his own personal admonition that "the blood on the street will kill you if you talk about class."[18]

On February 17, Cleaver officially introduced Carmichael, who was wearing not a leather jacket but a dashiki, as the Black Panthers' honorary prime minister. Race matters ruled the day in a talk that played down class issues that Carmichael had eloquently broached in London and Cuba. Instead, he rebuked socialism and communism as ill suited to combat racial oppression. Carmichael's time as a community organizer in the Deep South made him skeptical of convincing blacks to adopt a political philosophy that seemed to reject their religious and cultural groundings in favor of a purely economic understanding of social injustice. The Pan-African impulses sprinkled throughout Carmichael's address could be traced to his time in Conakry and Dar es Salaam. Pan-Africanism's creative imagining of a diasporic narrative of rupture and reclamation capable of transcending geographic borders appealed to Carmichael as both a philosopher and an activist. Carmichael preached a message of racial solidarity beyond ideological and class divisions.[19]

On a stage filled with ardent proponents of socialism and Marxism, Carmichael dismissed these theories as incapable of confronting the frightening depths of black suffering:

> The ideologies of communism and socialism speak to class structure, to people who oppress people from the top down to the bottom. We are not just facing exploitation. We are facing something much more important, because we are victims of racism. In their present form neither communism nor socialism speak to the problem of racism. And to black people in this country, racism comes first, far more important than exploitation. No matter how much money you make in the black community, when you go into the white world you are still a nigger. The question of racism must be uppermost in our minds. How do we destroy those institutions that seek to keep us dehumanized? That is all we're talking about.[20]

The rest of the speech traversed the international contours of the black freedom movement, marshaling raging conflicts in the Middle East, Vietnam, and Africa as proof that they were living "in a world that's clearly heading for a color clash." Blacks, he argued, must prepare themselves for an epic fight by "organizing our people, and orienting them toward an African ideology which speaks to our blackness." Carmichael promoted "an African ideology" as the necessary unifying thread "to build a concept of peoplehood" for blacks still "wandering in the United States." It was a brave, audacious, at times exasperating, speech, preemptively combating what he considered the Panthers' awkward efforts at spreading class struggle in the black community. He effectively outlined the case for the relevancy of black nationalism even while acknowledging its limits. Convinced from personal experience that black people found Marxist dialectics too cold and impersonal to embrace, Carmichael forged ahead with a vigorous endorsement of Pan-Africanism at a rally sponsored by black militants who called themselves socialists. The Panthers, meanwhile, chafed at the content of Carmichael's speech even as they benefited from its star power.[21]

Carmichael introduced the Black Panthers to the national and international audience the party coveted. Confident in his own organizing abilities, Carmichael stayed above the fray of the palace-level intrigues that marked negotiations between SNCC's Forman and Black Panther operatives led by Cleaver and Seale. Absent the aura of legend attached to Newton, Cleaver remained the most well-known Panther not in jail. His book of autobiographical essays, *Soul on Ice*, published in early 1968, would sell over a million copies in its first two years and establish him as a sought-after speaker, a polemicist waging war on established American institutions.[22]

The next day's rally in Los Angeles featured more participants than the Oakland benefit. Los Angeles Panther Alprentice "Bunchy" Carter, an ex-convict, gang leader, and Cleaver confidant, joined Carmichael, Rap Brown, Forman, and others on stage. The rally foreshadowed violent schisms in California's Black Power Movement. If the Bay Area belonged to the Black Panthers, Maulana Karenga and Us dominated Los Angeles. Karenga channeled this influence through the Black Congress, a consortium of Los Angeles militants who would play a key role in organizing California's Black Power experiment.[23]

At the rally, Jim Forman made note of a kind of historic watershed—so many factions united on one stage: Carmichael, Brown, Seale, and Karenga.

He meticulously described acts of retribution that would take place if any of the leaders on stage were assassinated, before praising the Panthers for having successfully recruited America's "field niggers," ex-cons and former addicts. The concept, inspired by Malcolm X's memorable distillation of class conflict within the black community as being rooted in the divergent worldviews of "House Negroes" and "Field Negroes," identified America's black underclass as the harbinger of a global political revolution. The brief antiwar speech by the Reverend Thomas Kilgore of the Second Baptist Church stressed Black Power's ability to touch secular and religious audiences. "I said to our congregation this morning, men like Stokely Carmichael have a message to tell this country in a time like this."[24]

Carmichael took the podium at just before 7:00 P.M. to preside over California's last unified Black Power rally. "How is this beautiful race of people, black people, gonna survive Babylon?" he asked. Carmichael's address drew from the evening's earlier speeches, and his discussion of Third World solidarity offered a professorial spin on the message of Reies Tijerina advocating cross-racial alliances. His contention that even Uncle Toms deserved a second chance echoed Karenga's and Forman's support for unity even as it amplified points made by Bobby Seale and Rap Brown. The speech represented a summation and capstone, with Carmichael repeating his belief that neither communism nor socialism offered the solution to black oppression in America. Instead, he offered a sweeping definition of Black Power as nothing less than the promotion of a human rights revolution: "We have been so dehumanized we cannot recognize our own humanity and that's what this fight is all about." Cold statistics detailing unemployment, wretched housing, and bad jobs missed the point. "It is a question of our humanity," Carmichael insisted. He repeated the line again, almost as if aware that many of his listeners scarcely made the connection between Black Power and human rights. He told the Los Angeles audience that only blacks could lead the revolution he imagined:

> We do not have that many class structures in the society among us. Communism and socialism speaks to classes. We are talking about races of people. There is a difference. That means to say that we read Mao Tse-tung. . . . Because he has a lot of good things to say. Mao Tse-tung is a great Chinese leader. The greatest Chinese leader there

is. But we need African leaders. That's who we must follow. African
leaders. We are Africans. We are Africans. We are not Chinese. The
Chinese don't go around and bow down to an African. They bow
down to someone in their own image. We have to find people in our
own image who we will bow down to. African leaders. African ideology. Straight down the middle. We're comin straight from a black
thing. No right, left,—none of that junk, straight up black. That's
where we're comin' from.[25]

This portion of his speech offered glimpses of his new identity as a
Pan-African revolutionary. The "We are Africans" line would, by the time
he took the name Kwame Ture, become a signature line of Stokely as a
professional revolutionary and political ideologue. There were still many
changes in store. His public rejection of socialism and communism for a
"black" ideology would, very shortly, develop into vociferous support for an
African-centered vision of socialism.

That night, representatives from the Panthers, the Organization Us, and
SNCC rendezvoused at a cocktail party still buzzing from the day's excite-
ment. The unity marked by the Free Huey rallies that weekend would not
last. Simmering tensions between the Panthers and Us members lurked beneath spectacular displays of unity. Us' cultural flourishes at times obscured
the group's paramilitary side: its *Simba Wachanga* (Young Lions) were an
intimidating security force whose expertise in martial arts and combat
matched the ferocity, if not the actual numbers, of the Panthers. Both groups
recruited ex-gang members, and soon a turf war over whose politics actually
constituted the revolutionary vanguard would erupt. The war was aided by
FBI counterintelligence and youthful egos and would leave a trail of violence amid tattered alliances. Divergent organizational styles and political
philosophies regarding the correct emphasis on culture and politics became
the rhetorical ground for the Panther-Us conflict. But despite stylistic differences, both groups' worst tendencies—strong-arming, intimidation, threats
of violence—mirrored those of the other, setting the stage for a bloody future confrontation.[26]

Stokely's public embrace of Pan-Africanism imperiled his political standing with the Panthers as well as his personal safety. In California, Ethel Minor was shocked to overhear Panthers complaining about how Carmichael's

political line damaged their interracial alliances. Some even whispered threats of violence against the stubborn honorary prime minister. "And it wasn't but a few days before I began hearing Eldridge was pissed off with Stokely's what they called 'cultural nationalism'," recalled Minor. "And his undying love for our people, they didn't relate to that at all. The Panthers didn't relate to that. And within a few days it got so bad that I actually heard some of them talking about bumping Stokely off, that's how bad it was."[27]

Carmichael departed California for Atlanta on February 26 after eleven days of private meetings, speeches, fundraisers, and parties. In Atlanta, he addressed a capacity crowd at Morehouse College, Martin Luther King's alma mater. The audience of two thousand who packed Morehouse's gymnasium attested to his celebrity in Atlanta, where university students admired him even as they maintained their determination to claim a piece of the American Dream that Carmichael disparaged. After discussing Black Power, pride, beauty, and a proposed boycott of the Mexico City Olympics by black athletes, Carmichael read a letter from Rap Brown, written from Orleans Parish Prison in New Orleans. Mixing bombast and militant indignation, Brown described himself as a political prisoner ready to die on behalf of black people. One of Brown's closing lines ("Aggression rules the day") appropriately characterized the tactics of not only Black Power militants but also law enforcement and the federal government. Unbeknownst to Carmichael, his Morehouse appearance signaled the resumption of the blur of speaking engagements largely halted since his return to the States.[28]

In a moving essay, "From Dreams of Love to Dreams of Terror," published that February, James Baldwin chronicled Carmichael's transformation from non-violent kid to outspoken revolutionary. Aptly characterized by Malcolm X as the poet of the black revolution, Baldwin observed echoes of Malcolm's spirit in Carmichael. Born and brought up in Harlem, Baldwin had risen from the depths of grinding poverty to literary heights that had made him, by the early 1960s, the nation's foremost oracle of racial wisdom. In *The Fire Next Time*, his slim volume of two essays on race, democracy, and civil rights published in 1963, Baldwin became one of America's premier literary geniuses, a prophet gifted with the ability to see where others could not, and feel what was most ignored. "I first met Stokely Carmichael in the Deep South when he was just another non-violent kid, marching and talking and getting his head whipped," wrote Baldwin. The memory of the young Stokely served as a prelude to Baldwin's distillation of Black Power:

I have never known a Negro in my life who was not obsessed with Black Power. Those representatives of white power who are not too hopelessly brainwashed or eviscerated will understand that the only way for a black man in America not to be obsessed with the problem of how to control his destiny and protect his house, his women and his children is for that black man to become in his own mind the something less than a man which this republic, alas, has always considered him to be.

The movement's ascent paralleled Baldwin's own burgeoning radicalism. Where others from his generation shrank from the volatile rhetoric of militants, Baldwin embraced Carmichael as a bold warrior whose words reflected the transformation of an entire generation. "Stokely Carmichael, a black man under 30, is saying to me, a black man over 40, that he will not live the life that I've lived or be corralled into some of the awful choices that I've been forced to make, and he is perfectly right," Baldwin wrote. America's relentless pursuit of Carmichael reflected the vindictive behavior of a guilty nation. "If only, I gather, we had the foresight to declare ourselves at war, we would now be able to shoot Carmichael for treason," Baldwin wrote. "On the other hand, even if the Government's honorable hands are tied, the mob has got the message."[29]

If James Baldwin rightfully claimed the title of movement poet bestowed on him by Malcolm X, Carmichael continued in the role of political warrior once played by Malcolm. FBI officials alerted local authorities in Alabama to Carmichael's presence on Sunday, March 10. Alabama public safety officers trailed after Carmichael from his morning arrival in Montgomery to his late afternoon appearance at Mt. Moriah Church in Lowndes, the site of his moving speech promoting radical democracy on the eve of 1966's historic election. Carmichael used his long-standing invitation to address mass meetings in Lowndes to promote a political vision that compared black liberation in America to the controversies that surrounded Jesus and his disciples. Observed by Alabama state troopers, FBI agents, and local informants, Carmichael was also being watched by the state attorney general's office to see if a speech he gave the next evening at Tuskegee Institute provided grounds for his arrest.

At Tuskegee, Stokely challenged students to take America over by force if necessary, while quoting Rap Brown's prison letter from New Orleans: "We are all slaves. No slave should die a natural death." Two thousand people attended the event, which included a Black Power–inspired play, "Back to Black," which advocated a return to African cultural traditions. When Carmichael's typically combative assaults on white supremacy and Vietnam failed to meet the standards of Alabama's beefed-up anti-rioting statute, agents followed him to Tuscaloosa for a speaking engagement at Stillman College, arranged by the new dean of students, John W. Rice Jr. The dean ignored pressure from authorities who viewed Carmichael's appearance as a harbinger of doom and in the process struck up an improbable friendship that introduced Stokely to his precocious daughter and future secretary of state, Condoleezza. Backstage, Stokely expressed gratitude toward Dean Rice for being courageous enough to let him speak. Thirteen-year-old Condoleezza marveled at Carmichael's "calm and courteous" demeanor, which contrasted with the revolutionary she had just witnessed. Over the next two decades, Carmichael's relationship with Dean Rice would go grow into a warm friendship. He regularly spoke at Rice's courses and became a part of the extended family. Stokely loved to debate the merits of socialism with Condoleezza, whom he nicknamed his "petite soeur."[30]

The next day, March 15, Stokely's private life temporarily overshadowed his political activities as news of his engagement to Miriam Makeba became public. The story broke just as SNCC's communications staff circulated an internal memo outlining steps to control Carmichael's speaking itinerary. Backlash against Carmichael's radical politics would mar the couple's happy news and hamper Makeba's singing career and business ventures. Miriam received the first signs of what the future portended while in Nassau, when the Bahamian prime minister canceled her business permits to operate a clothing boutique (Makeba's Hut) and banned her from the island. Makeba's business associates responded with little enthusiasm for an engagement that took them by surprise and signaled the end of lucrative television and concert appearances that had placed her on the cusp of international mainstream superstardom. Her press agent pleaded to the public not to hold the couple's whirlwind romance against Makeba, a musician who just happened to fall in love with the world's foremost black revolutionary. Gossip columnists from Miami to New York speculated about the couple, openly questioning Carmichael's financial motives, and characterizing Makeba as a woman who sang of love only to marry an apostle of hate. Just thirty-six and in the prime of her career, Miriam pressed on even at the cost of irreparable damage to her musical aspirations, a realization that humbled Carmichael. "Unfortunately, Miriam was made to suffer a great deal because of our love," he remembered. The black press fêted the union as a transatlantic political coup that symbolically tied black America to Africa. The bride-to-be addressed the gossipy controversy surrounding them with a poise that disarmed reporters. "I love him and we will get married," she told the *Chicago Daily Defender*. But Makeba's dreams of keeping her "private life separate from my professional life" would prove difficult. The FBI's surveillance of Carmichael now extended to Miriam. "It can be Stokely's mother's house in the Bronx, or it can be the airport. They are there," Makeba remembered. "These faceless white or black men in their suits sitting in their cars and looking at me." Makeba and Carmichael tried to find humor in government harassment by calling the FBI agents their personal "babysitters."[31]

Carmichael introduced Miriam Makeba as his future wife that Sunday before an interracial congregation at Washington's Presbyterian Church of the Redeemer. The appearance served personal and political purposes, continuing Carmichael's vow to address church audiences whenever possible, publicizing his relationship with Makeba, and quelling any rumors that his impending marriage might soften his revolutionary fervor.[32]

Carmichael traveled to Baltimore the next day, where he listened to the poet and playwright LeRoi Jones speak at a local church. Born in Newark, New Jersey in 1934, Jones attended Rutgers, Howard, and Columbia Universities without obtaining a degree. In the 1960s he emerged as one of the few notable black poets of the Beat era. By 1965 Jones had become a radical, after taking trips to Cuba where he met Fidel Castro and leaving behind a white wife and two daughters in Greenwich Village to pursue a new career as the literary avatar of the black nationalist–inspired Black Arts Movement. Jones' most important collection of essays, *Home*, published in 1966, redefined "blackness" from a color the world despised into a revolutionary identity that manifested itself in culture, art, politics, and geography:

> The black man has been separated and made to live in his own country and color. If you are black the only roads into the mainland of American life are through subservience, cowardice, and loss of manhood. Those are the white man's roads. It is time we built our own. America is as much a black country as a white one. The lives and destinies of the white Americans are bound up inextricably with those of the black American, even though the latter has been forced for

hundreds of years to inhabit the lonely country of black. It is time we impressed the white man with the nature of his ills, as well as the nature of our own. The Negro's struggle in America is only a microcosm of the struggle of the new countries all over the world.

Stokely regarded Jones as a practical example of Black Power's cultural and intellectual ferment.[33]

Two days later, Carmichael returned to his alma mater. He addressed one thousand Howard students occupying the university's administration in the kind of daring protest maneuver that NAG, now defunct, had once championed. That evening he appeared on *Controversy 14,* a local Washington current affairs program, where he discussed his father, a topic he rarely addressed in public. "I'd rather die at 26 with a gun in my hand than live to die like my father did," he said at one point, "because he gave all his sweat and all his blood to white folk and I ain't got nothing to show for it." In response to a follow-up question of how his father died, Carmichael offered a bitter elegy. Adolphus Carmichael succumbed to "a heart attack at a young age, working hard, working, bowing, scraping, saying yas suh, yas suh," he explained. "But he was an Uncle Tom, not for me to be an Uncle Tom, he was an Uncle Tom for me to be a man and I'm going to be a man one way or another." Expressions of disappointment mixed with respect continued to accompany his public memory of Adolphus.[34]

In Chicago, Stokely spent Saturday evening listening to Miriam sing at a local nightclub. On Sunday he participated in grueling truce negotiations between the Blackstone Rangers and another local gang, which made him an hour late to address parishioners at St. Margaret's Episcopal Church. Then, at the Masonic Temple in Maywood, Illinois, he delivered an unscheduled, impromptu speech. He was introduced by Fred Hampton, the talented and effortlessly charismatic nineteen-year-old head of the West Suburban NAACP Youth Council and the future leader of Chicago's Black Panther Party. Carmichael and Hampton bonded over their respective oratorical gifts. His Sunday itinerary continued in Gary, Indiana, where he spoke until midnight to a group of sixty local militants before returning to Chicago.[35]

Carmichael spent Tuesday, April 2 in Washington playing peacemaker. A confrontation between locals and store employees at the Peoples Drug Store, a racially integrated establishment on U Street, had drawn police and mutual recriminations. Tension over the manager's decision the previous month to hire security guards to prevent shoplifting had continued into April. The sight of a large crowd gathered around Peoples interrupted Carmichael's efforts to move SNCC's remaining office equipment from their old U Street headquarters to a new storefront a few doors away. He arrived just in time to prevent a crowd of over three hundred people from turning their sporadic brick and bottle throwing into a genuine riot. He stayed long enough to tell the store manager that he was "fed up" with his treatment of black customers. Next, he turned his focus to cooling the inflamed passions of angry neighborhood youth and restless bystanders gathered outside, leveraging political charisma in a successful effort to disperse the crowd.[36]

CHAPTER FIFTEEN

The Prime Minister
of Afro-America

April 4–December 28, 1968

STOKELY WAS IN WASHINGTON WHEN HE HEARD THAT MARTIN LUTHER KING had been shot in Memphis. It was Thursday, April 4. For the next few hours he alternated frantically between SNCC's U Street offices and those of the SCLC, across the street, anxiously awaiting word. King had spent the previous night passionately extolling his radical vision of American democracy in support of striking black sanitation workers. King's support for "garbage men" dovetailed into what had become a final crusade to promote economic justice as a corollary to racial equality.

His last night on earth, King seemed to anticipate his own demise but pressed on with a defiant address that assumed the form of an Old Testament prophet judging a godforsaken land. Four years, seven months, and five days after he had captured the world's imagination at the Lincoln Memorial with a speech that remained defiantly hopeful, King exited the national stage with a final address that was at once visionary and a requiem. "And I've seen the Promised Land. I may not get there with you. But I want you to know tonight, that we, as a people, will get to the Promised Land." The next day, King's prophecy came true while he stood on the balcony of the Lorraine Motel. He was thirty-nine.[1]

At twenty-six, Carmichael was the last survivor of the iconic triumvirate that had included Malcolm X and King. The King assassination gave Carmichael galvanic purpose, convincing him that America's final hope at peaceful redemption had died with the man he admired and had come to love. The tragedy also exposed contradictions, both politically and personally, within Carmichael. He alternated between serene calm and passionate anger. His deteriorating relations with SNCC reached their breaking point shortly after King's death, and he gambled that his alliance with the Panthers might offer the organizational security he still craved. He veered, sometimes uncomfortably, between the high drama of rhetorical bombs and the more contemplative posture of the "Prime Minister of Afro-America," a new title bestowed on him by the Black Panthers. Surrounded by turmoil, Carmichael soldiered on, touring the country delivering radical speeches and narrowly evading federal prosecution. Carmichael's increasingly bitter tone about the possibility of racial equality in America reflected the national despair brought on by war, political assassinations, and urban riots. He found himself surrounded on all sides. Intelligence agencies ratcheted up surveillance, and former friends turned into bitter combatants even as new allies posed unpredictable dangers. It was the last full year Stokely would ever spend in America.

KING'S DEATH TURNED CARMICHAEL, for at least one night, into the rare guerrilla general—one who instructed his retinue to politely ask businesses to shutter their doors. Although not everyone felt obliged to follow orders, for a time things proceeded smoothly. Carmichael led demonstrators through a corridor of drugstores, supermarkets, and theaters, including the Peoples Drug Store, the scene where he had averted a mêlée two days earlier. Carmichael continued to march along U Street closing down Carter's Liquors, the Safeway supermarket, and the Pig N' Pit. Fighting through tears, he led the crowd north on 14th Street, at times deploying aides to spread the word and in other instances simply relaying a terse message to store managers: "King is dead."[2]

Discipline faltered at the Republic Theater, when a teenager smashed through the front window oblivious to peaceful negotiations occurring at the nearby Lincoln Theater. Against the backdrop of broken glass and growing chaos, Stokely snatched a gun from the boy. He ordered the restless crowd to go home, waving a gun in the air to symbolize his own preparation for the coming racial war, while a growing army of mourners gathered for an impromptu public vigil that teetered on the edge of violence. Carmichael warned the restive crowd that race war required disciplined resolve. A hostile crowd of one thousand menaced two black security guards who were saved by the intervention of Carmichael and SNCC. Some businesses, including Carmichael's favorite haunt, Ben's Chili Bowl, remained untouched for the duration of the disturbance, and Ben's would turn into a de facto post-riot headquarters for activists, firefighters, and police.[3]

It was a heroic performance, but ultimately a futile one. Stokely's calm proved a temporary relief. Looting along 14th Street attracted reporters, television cameras, and journalists whose narratives inevitably blamed him for the evening's violence. *The New York Times* report that Carmichael urged people to "go home and get guns" overwhelmed the more accurate *Washington Post*'s firsthand accounts, from "trained Negro reporters," which portrayed him as roving diplomat. An eyewitness statement made to FBI agents a few days later supported this view. As the crowd shouted "Hey, Hey, Black Power!" one observer remembered Carmichael telling people, "Brother King is dead, keep a cool head."[4]

At 10:30 that night, Cleve Sellers practically dragged him from the unfolding riot scene. Stokely had an apartment in Washington since his days as an undergraduate, and now they retreated there with a group of friends. They spent the night and early hours of the morning listening to Carmichael ruminate on his friendship with King. Rain arrived a half hour before midnight, cutting short a period of looting. Thousands of Washington residents unleashed their anger, breaking store windows, smashing car windshields, and looting the same neighborhood that housed SNCC's offices. Youngsters carrying stolen television sets scurried past officers under orders to disperse, rather than arrest, rioters. Observers interpreted late evening showers as a hopeful sign that the city might not burn. Large crowds gathered around King's anti-poverty headquarters on 14th and U Streets even as roving mobs smashed half of the storefronts along a ten-block stretch. The city's tactical squad, armed with helmets, tear gas, and gas masks, dispersed crowds while National Guard units remained on stand-by. Violence in New York, Hartford, Boston, and Jackson, Mississippi, heralded widespread national civil disorders in the wake of King's assassination.[5]

Bobby Kennedy heard news of King's assassination while campaigning for president in Indiana. John Lewis, who had recently joined the Kennedy crusade for president, had accompanied him to the Hoosier state. Kennedy's March 16th announcement of his plans to pursue the White House had been met with relief by Democrats tired of Johnson's prevarications about

Vietnam and scorn by the thousands of young antiwar demonstrators who, in a show of support for Minnesota senator Eugene McCarthy, shaved their beards and cut their long hair in order to get "clean for Gene." Skeptics questioned whether Bobby represented a mere extension of his slain brother or if he could fulfill the goal of racial healing and economic justice that his most ambitious speeches promised. Stokely Carmichael openly rebuked Kennedy as a pretender who, as attorney general, had failed to protect civil rights demonstrators. Indeed, it was Bobby who had approved the FBI's wiretapping surveillance of King. Kennedy's first assessment of King was shaped through Hoover's eyes, but this jaundiced view evolved over time. By 1968, Kennedy and King followed parallel tracks, with both men arguing that America's racial and ethnic diversity constituted potential strength rather than division.[6]

Kennedy announced the news of King's death to a gathering of three thousand people who had come to hear him deliver a campaign speech. Instead, the stunned crowd heard Kennedy offer a moving eulogy for King. In many respects, it was the best speech he ever made:

> Martin Luther King dedicated his life to love and to justice for his fellow human beings, and he died because of that effort.
>
> In this difficult day, in this difficult time for the United States, it is perhaps well to ask what kind of a nation we are and what direction we want to move in. For those of you who are black—considering the evidence there evidently is that there were white people who were responsible— you can be filled with bitterness, with hatred, and a desire for revenge. We can move in that direction as a country, in great polarization—black people amongst black, white people amongst white, filled with hatred toward one another.
>
> Or we can make an effort, as Martin Luther King did, to understand and to comprehend, and to replace that violence, that stain of bloodshed that has spread across our land, with an effort to understand with compassion and love.
>
> For those of you who are black and are tempted to be filled with hatred and distrust at the injustice of such an act, against all white people, I can only say that I feel in my own heart the same kind of feeling. I had a member of my family killed, but he was killed by a white man. But we have to make an effort in the United States, we have to make an effort to understand, to go beyond these rather difficult times. . . .

What we need in the United States is not division; what we need in the United States is not hatred; what we need in the United States is not violence or lawlessness; but love and wisdom, and compassion toward one another, and a feeling of justice toward those who still suffer within our country, whether they be white or they be black.

So I shall ask you tonight to return home, to say a prayer for the family of Martin Luther King, that's true, but more importantly to say a prayer for our own country, which all of us love—a prayer for understanding and that compassion of which I spoke.[7]

Washington canceled its annual Cherry Blossom Festival on Friday. A mournful air hovered over an otherwise warm and sunny spring day, and Carmichael held a mid-morning press conference at the New School for Afro-American Thought. Lester McKinnie introduced Stokely, who insisted that reporters call him "Mr. Carmichael." King's death had triggered raw anger in Carmichael. SNCC staff frisked entering reporters, and Carmichael, wearing sunglasses, spoke in front of enormous posters of Malcolm X and Rap Brown. He eulogized the "one man" imparting lessons of "love, compassion, and mercy" and blamed Lyndon Johnson and Robert Kennedy for King's murder, pointing to the president's threats against the Poor People's Campaign and Kennedy's record as attorney general as proof that former enemies would only embrace King in death. "Bobby Kennedy pulled that trigger just as anybody else," he said. "Because when Dr. King was down south, Bobby Kennedy was Attorney General," and "every time a black person got killed, Kennedy would not move because he wanted votes so he is just as guilty." Carmichael would never reconcile Kennedy's political reticence during the early 1960s with his contemporary embrace of human rights. If Bobby's political sincerity convinced portions of the New Left and even certain Black Power militants that the government could be an ally, Stokely remained equally certain of Kennedy's hypocrisy. Carmichael's searing comments surprised journalists and reporters, including CBS, which decided against broadcasting his press conference in favor of Walter Cronkite's brief mention of the event on the nightly news. A spokesman proudly noted that CBS, during the height of Washington's riots, had shown just a single image of Carmichael on camera.[8]

Stokely's press conference the day after King's assassination placed him at the center of simmering national racial tensions. It had originally been scheduled to discuss Rap Brown's legal troubles stemming from various rioting charges. But of course the assassination was on everyone's mind. Carmichael managed to list some states—Maryland, Louisiana, Florida, Virginia, and Ohio—where SNCC planned to organize. He sidestepped rumors of a general strike by blacks in response to King's assassination. Now, Stokely asserted that white America was responsible for King's death:

> I think white America made its biggest mistake when she killed Dr. King last night because when she killed Dr. King last night, she killed all reasonable hope. When she killed Dr. King last night, she killed the one man of our race that this country's older generations, the militants and the revolutionaries and the masses of black people would still listen to. Even though sometimes he did not agree with them, they would still listen to him.[9]

Carmichael's words, angry, desperate, and remorseful, illustrated King's powerful hold on him personally and politically. Stokely, the world's foremost Black Power advocate, still considered King a transcendent moral leader and older brother. For Carmichael, King's death signaled a loss of hope for the black freedom struggle in America. Reporters, however, focused on Carmichael's more incendiary statements, including his comments after a reporter had asked him, "Are you declaring war on white America?"

> White America has declared war on black people. She did so when she stole the first black man from Africa. The black man has been … patient, has been resisting—and today, the final showdown is coming. That is clear. That is crystal clear. And black people are going to have to find ways to survive. The only way to survive is to get some guns. Because that's the only way white America keeps us in check, because she's got guns.[10]

At a special White House meeting with civil rights leaders that same morning, Lyndon Johnson singled out Stokely as the source behind unfolding national unrest. LBJ repeated erroneous news reports that his own FBI would privately refute. Johnson turned the occasion into an impassioned plea for peace, designating Roy Wilkins, Bayard Rustin, and Whitney Young as unofficial emissaries charged with countering Carmichael's recklessness. The image of the first African-American Supreme Court Justice, Thurgood

Marshall, whom Johnson had appointed, sitting on the president's right side, symbolized for reporters, civil rights activists, and photographers the accurate measure of LBJ's commitment to racial equality. Images of racial bonhomie at the White House contrasted with a feeling of general panic across the city. Thousands of whites fled Washington for Maryland and Virginia in a mass exodus even as young blacks in Franklin Square watched looters roam the streets against a backdrop of cherry blossoms.[11]

Later that day, Carmichael addressed a group of three hundred Howard University students from the steps of Douglass Hall. "Stay off the streets tonight, if you don't have a gun, because there's going to be shooting," he warned, loudly repeating the words over and over as if invoking a political incantation and pulling out a gun that, coupled with his green army jacket and sunglasses, gave him the appearance of a modern urban guerrilla. That evening, Stokely conducted a brief telephone interview with Radio Havana, translated in Spanish and broadcast on Cuban radio. King's untimely death made it "necessary to fully enter into a revolution," he observed. For a brief moment, Carmichael turned into a revolutionary foreign correspondent, detailing how dozens of post-assassination riots constituted a prophetic fulfillment of his Havana speeches.[12]

In the afternoon, Lyndon Johnson ordered four thousand army and national guard troops to Washington. By midnight, authorities counted the dead while chaos gripped the city. One company of troops remained inside the White House while another positioned itself outside the southeast gate. The image of helmeted sentries armed with bayonets and light machine guns in Washington on Friday night seemed to fulfill Carmichael's long-standing prediction of race war. "Both the outbreak of trouble last night and today's renewal of arson and looting followed angry public outbursts on Dr. King's death by Stokely Carmichael," reported *The New York Times*. An official with the Community Relations Service, the White House's troubleshooting anti-riot unit, disputed such one-dimensional characterizations during an interview with FBI agents. Carmichael's behavior in the aftermath of King's assassination positioned him as a belligerent peacemaker even as the press remained determined to portray him as Washington's chief agitator. "White people who so often condemned Martin Luther King as an extremist," wrote syndicated columnists Rowland Evans and Robert Novak, "now will have the pleasure of dealing with Stokely Carmichael." Media hysteria regarding Carmichael reached its peak three days later in a *Washington Post* editorial that asked if he should "have been locked up right away" despite having been charged with no crime.[13]

Carmichael's provocative behavior in Washington, which one newspaper judged to be a "psychotic reaction," paled in comparison to that of the Black Panthers. Two days after King's death, Eldridge Cleaver led a Panther convoy into a wild shootout with police that left seventeen-year-old Bobby Hutton, the group's treasurer and first recruit two years earlier, dead. Bobby's death and the wounding and subsequent incarceration of Cleaver marked the official start of a full-scale war between the Panthers and law enforcement that would escalate over the next two years.[14]

On the Saturday of Hutton's shooting, Lyndon Johnson anchored the nation's grief in a bracing display of political resolve, delivering his second television appeal for calm since King's death. "The dream of Martin Luther King Jr. did not die with him," Johnson promised. Johnson declared Sunday a national day of mourning, ordering American flags to be flown at half-mast over all government buildings, ships, and military and diplomatic facilities until King's burial.[15]

The assassination touched off spasms of urban violence in cities and soul-searching among civil rights activists. Roy Wilkins announced a new campaign for jobs and racial justice while denouncing Carmichael's "gun talk." He touted the NAACP's "Adopt a Cop" program designed to promote better understanding between black residents and law enforcement. Whitney Young publicly attacked both Carmichael and the media: Stokely as a peculiar kind of literary invention, an activist who lacked the political support and organizational backing of everyone except the media, which specialized in a voyeuristic fascination with his overheated polemics. Vice President Hubert Humphrey echoed Young's concerns about the media, telling *Look* magazine that it was time for television and radio to "accept their responsibility in these riot situations."[16]

Of course, King's ideas and works did not die with him. *The Washington Post* posthumously published an op-ed by him ("U.S. Plays 'Roulette With Riots'") on the consequences of federal inaction against urban uprisings just as fresh bursts of violence engulfed the nation. King's discussion of the promise of Resurrection City contrasted with the waves of bitter grief and unapologetic rage that greeted his death. Reports that almost 12,000 soldiers were patrolling Washington to quell upheaval overshadowed King's message from the grave. In Saigon, reaction among American troops split along racial fault lines, with black soldiers expressing palpable grief in stark contrast to their white counterparts. "For many white soldiers, the murder of Dr. King appeared to arouse uneasiness," observed reporter Bernard Weinraub, "accompanied by a surprising lack of sympathy" that included fears that blacks would now follow Carmichael's radical example. *The New York Times'* characterization of Carmichael as "probably the one black leader who rivaled Dr. King in sheer charisma and ability to sway a crowd" amplified this point.[17]

———————————

APRIL 7 WAS PALM SUNDAY. Cool and clear spring weather accompanied a citywide calm reflected in the gorgeous sight of camellias bursting with color along the Mall's reflecting pool, tulips blooming in parks, and crab apple trees sporting delicate shades of pink and white. Bright sunshine made rubble along 14th and 7th Streets resemble parts of postwar Europe, complete with the burning embers from dying fires. Residents and hundreds of sightseers in town for the canceled Cherry Blossom Festival jammed city sidewalks, with tourists surveying the ruins as if on an archaeological expedition and locals leaving church holding the palm fronds that symbolized Jesus's entrance into Jerusalem five days before his crucifixion.

Many came to New Bethel Baptist Church, located on 9th and U Street and poised in between two major riot areas, where Walter Fauntroy preached a morning sermon of reconciliation and forgiveness to an audience that included Bobby Kennedy and Stokely Carmichael. Kennedy, who made brief remarks at Fauntroy's request, toured the area in an appearance that made him a hero to locals. But Stokely regarded RFK as a perverse example of liberal condescension. Carmichael appeared at an afternoon press conference against his better judgment, privately dismissing much of the post-assassination mood as a parallel universe where "too many niggers were calling for peace" during a time of war.[18]

Meanwhile, federal officials ratcheted up their investigation into whether Carmichael's comments after King's murder "may have violated any one of a number of statutes." Spurred by a national outcry that blamed Carmichael for Washington's violence, Ramsey Clark launched a probe of Stokely's post-riot actions. Clark's plans received the approval of Republican House minority leader Gerald Ford, who blamed Washington's riots on "some very inflammatory" statements by Carmichael. Roy Wilkins joined in this condemnation, telling reporters that Carmichael's calm and reasonable demeanor immediately after the assassination changed overnight "as if somebody had come to see him and talked to him" about starting trouble. To tamp down trouble, the NAACP planned to distribute thousands of anti-violence stickers around the country. "Hot Head, Hot Lead, Cold Dead," warned one.[19]

ALL DAY TUESDAY, the nation watched the televised funeral of Martin Luther King from Atlanta. There were two memorial services—one at Ebenezer Baptist Church, where King and his father pastored, followed by a second at King's alma mater, Morehouse College. The conspicuous attendance of politicians at the proceedings upset Carmichael, who felt that their presence dishonored King. Vice President Hubert Humphrey, Senator Edward Kennedy, Senator Eugene McCarthy, and Richard Nixon appeared alongside Sammy Davis Jr., Eartha Kitt, Marlon Brando, and Harry Belafonte. The presence of three announced candidates for president—Robert Kennedy, McCarthy, and Nixon, along with Humphrey, who was expected to announce soon—lent the services the feel of a political event. Jacqueline Kennedy's presence embodied King's posthumous entry into the ranks of American political royalty whose lives were cut short by assassination but whose legacies remained embodied in the stoic grace of their widows.

Carmichael and Miriam Makeba arrived with an escort of raised-fisted bodyguards and associates chanting "Black Power." Shouts of "Stokely, baby!" greeted him as he sat in the same row as New York Governor Nelson Rockefeller and New York City Mayor John Lindsay. Courtland Cox and Ralph Featherstone joined Carmichael as did Maulana Karenga. Fifty congressmen, thirty senators, and mayors from riot-torn cities packed a service bursting with labor leaders, clergy, and notable cultural figures. Ralph Abernathy's sermon that morning suggested that King's death would be remembered as "one of the darkest hours of mankind." King had recently requested that at his funeral service, instead of the listing of his honorifics and prizes, a recording of his speech, "The Drum Major Instinct," be played. And so it was. The speech, delivered on February 4, 1968, at Ebenezer, found King contemplating his death in public, something he did often. "I'd like somebody to mention that day, that Martin Luther King Jr., tried to give his life serving others. . . . Yes, if you want to say that I was a drum major, say that I was a drum major for justice; say that I was a drum major for peace; I was a drum major for righteousness." Following the service, Stokely walked over and embraced Martin's widow, Coretta Scott King, each whispering words of condolence in a moment of intimacy bound by shared grief.[20]

It was three and a half miles from Ebenezer Baptist to Morehouse, where the second service would be held. Fifty thousand people—including Bobby Kennedy in rolled-up shirtsleeves, Governor Rockefeller, and Stokely Carmichael—walked through downtown Atlanta in eighty-degree heat to Morehouse. Over seven hundred policemen and one hundred firefighters were on hand to respond to rumored violence, which never materialized.

At Morehouse, one of King's role models eulogized the fallen leader. Benjamin Mays, the retired president of the college, said that King was a prophet who taught the nation lessons "about war and peace; about social justice and racial discrimination; about its obligation to the poor; and about nonviolence as a way of perfecting social change in a world of brutality and war." The service reached an emotional climax when gospel legend Mahalia Jackson sang "Precious Lord, Take My Hand."[21]

King's final resting place would be at South-View Cemetery, four miles from Morehouse in the family plot beside his maternal grandparents. The fallen hero's hearse was humble: two mules led a simple farm wagon carrying King's cherry-wood coffin. One hundred thousand people, packed in lines six and seven deep, watched the four-mile procession from Morehouse to South-View Cemetery, where dogwoods and green boughs flourished in their springtime bloom. Carmichael, flanked by Cleve Sellers and close friends, periodically flashed a closed-fisted salute to those watching.[22]

STOKELY CARMICHAEL WENT from being a spectator in Atlanta to the center of race controversy in absentia in Baltimore on Thursday. There the state's governor, the little-known Spiro Agnew, blasted a roomful of local civil rights leaders as irresponsible fomenters of racial violence and strife. Agnew turned blaming Stokely for riots into brazen political theater. In a jaw-dropping display that would culminate in his improbable selection as Richard Nixon's vice-presidential running mate, Agnew accused local leaders of abdicating their duty in the wake of the city's recent violence. He charged Carmichael with planning the national wave of riots from Baltimore, based on an undercover police officer's report that he had appeared in the city plotting insurrection the day before King's assassination. It was no coincidence that Carmichael appeared in the city three days before it exploded, claimed Agnew, spinning a conspiracy theory so wildly offensive that it compelled dozens of black leaders to walk out in disgust and immediately issue a statement condemning the governor. Secret FBI reports correctly traced Carmichael's presence in Baltimore the day before King's assassination to his impending wedding, but Agnew's impact rested on bravado more than truth. Like Lester Maddox and Edward Brooke, Agnew gained unimagined levels of national fame and political celebrity from vilifying Carmichael. But whereas Maddox remained marginal on the national political scene and Brooke a political novelty, Agnew would ride a wave of racial backlash to the White House as Richard Nixon's vice president.[23]

As politicians exploited his image for personal political gain, Carmichael stayed largely out of the public eye. On April 24, Carmichael briefly reunited with one of his personal heroes and mentors, Ella Baker, for a tribute in her honor at the Roosevelt Hotel on Madison Avenue. The event drew old friends such as Bob Zellner and Howard Zinn and movement icon Rosa Parks. Carmichael's presence at the interracial gathering attested to his profound respect and love for Baker. In his later years, as he lay dying of cancer, Carmichael cited Ella Baker's leadership as definitive proof that he was not the cardboard misogynist his legendary joke about women in SNCC had made him out to be. "I would not have been taken seriously as a leader of an organization like SNCC if I had not taken seriously the leadership of women," he said. "A woman like Ella Baker would not have tolerated it."[24]

Two days later, Carmichael and Rap Brown visited the turbulent campus of Columbia University. That spring, students went on strike in protest against a range of causes that spanned from racial injustice to the Vietnam War. Students organizing for Black Studies and black liberation had taken over campus buildings in a demonstration that turned the university into a headquarters for radical student activism. Black students, outraged by plans to construct a gymnasium that would deprive Harlem residents of much-needed recreational space, accused the university of being racist and took over Hamilton Hall. Stokely—resplendent in sunglasses, turtleneck, and a Nehru jacket—and Rap Brown entered Hamilton Hall to meet with black student leaders. "Hamilton Hall is a black fortress," declared Brown. The brief visit to Columbia made front-page headlines. Their appearance lent glamour to a dispute that placed the Ivy League school at the center of overlapping controversies about race, community control, student autonomy, and power that were also roiling the nation.

From privileged Columbia, Stokely went to multiracial, explosive Newark. There he spoke at a Central High School rally sponsored by the United Brothers, a local group of Black Power militants and racial moderates that merged community organizing with electoral ambitions. It was led by the radical writer LeRoi Jones, whose beating and arrest at the hands of the police during the previous summer's riot had turned him into a full-time activist. He adopted the name Ameer Barakat, and then, under the mentorship of Maulana Karenga (who himself had gone from Ronald McKinley Everett to Ron Karenga to Maulana Karenga), Amiri Baraka. Jones' increasingly political vision of Black Power combined the cultural flourishes of the Organization Us with urban machine politics and would contribute to the election of Newark's first black mayor, Kenneth Gibson, in 1970. Stokely began his speech by reminding his listeners that Jesus himself extolled the redemptive powers of "the sword not the shield" as he paraphrased one of his favorite passages from the Gospel according to Matthew. For nearly two hours, he regaled nine hundred listeners with stories that connected his experiences in Cuba, China, and around the world with his belief that blacks were engaged in a struggle for their very survival. "We need to help our brothers find their way back home," he said. Waves of applause greeted a speech that, by pre-arrangement with organizers, steered clear of fueling any national race controversy.[25]

On April 29, Carmichael took time away from his political schedule to wed Miriam Makeba. They were married in a small civil ceremony in Washington at Calloway Methodist Church in Arlington. The church's pastor, the Reverend Douglas E. Moore, a former Boston University classmate of Martin Luther King's, officiated. Carmichael and Makeba dazzled: he in a blue Nehru jacket and she in a brown and yellow African dress. The newlyweds rented a house on 16th Street in the part of the city referred to as the Gold Coast for its grand homes. But marriage offered only a temporary respite from their hectic schedules. Both planned to continue their careers, confident that their love could withstand the inevitable long stretches of time apart. The newly married Carmichael gave one of his first interviews to the *Baltimore Afro-American*, where he described "Mrs. Carmichael" as a freedom fighter whose civil rights philanthropy stretched from the Bahamas to South Africa.

Despite "extra worries on my side," Carmichael vowed to maintain his commitment to political revolution. He thought that his admirers would be happy about his wedding, "because I have found someone that I love and who loves me."[26]

The intimate ceremony anticipated a more raucous celebration on Friday, May 16. The couple exchanged vows a second time as part of a lavish African-themed reception, co-hosted by Tanzanian ambassador Akili B.C. Danieli and Achkar Marof, the Guinean ambassador, at the latter's embassy in Mount Vernon, New York. The event offered Stokely time out from BUF meetings, nocturnal visits to the newly erected Resurrection City, and political activism on behalf of the Black Panthers. The couple sauntered into their reception like movie stars. Miriam was in a beige African Bubu hand-crafted for the occasion by May Charles, while Stokely donned a masculine version of the same robe in white, a gift from Sékou Touré. *The New York Times* made note of the reception and an *Ebony Magazine* photographer trailed the newlyweds to the embassy, where they received five hundred guests in a scene that affirmed their status as political royalty.[27]

Achkar Marof proclaimed the marriage to be "the beginning of stronger ties between black people on both sides of the Atlantic." Reverend Moore invoked ancestral spirits in offering a prayer for a successful marriage. He placed Carmichael's call for revolution along a continuum of provocative exhortations that went back to Old Testament prophets. The ceremony drew from Stokely's cultural and theological imagination; his childhood training had included, at the urging of May Charles, at least three close readings of the Bible. The couple declined to exchange traditional Christian wedding vows, instead engaging in a call and response with Moore that announced their union as a collective endeavor whose success depended on a wide circle of familial and kinship networks. Stokely said, "I have found a love and she wears my ring," and Miriam replied, "I have found a love and he wears my ring."[28]

At the celebration, Stokely basked in the presence of his family. May Charles and his sisters Lynette, Judy, and Janeth were now joined by Miriam's grown daughter, Bongi. Familiar faces such as Gloria Richardson and LeRoi Jones appeared as the guests feasted on a buffet of West Indian and African food. The highpoint of the four-hour ceremony occurred when Miriam led a four-song chorus that evoked thunderous applause among the event's overwhelmingly black and brown guests, a uniformity broken up only by some of, as *Ebony* magazine put it, "the world's few decent white people." Then, the five hundred friends, family, dignitaries, and well-wishers joined Stokely and Miriam as they danced to the rhythms of African drums late into the night.[29]

But imaginative new forms of FBI harassment soon dampened the celebratory mood. Newspaper stories about the couple's alleged efforts to purchase a $70,000 home in Northwest Washington's "Gold Coast" would haunt Carmichael throughout the year. The wedding's lavish pageantry also served to reinforce FBI plans to mount a whispering campaign that identified Carmichael as a government agent spying on "racial militants and future racial radicals." According to the FBI memo "Stokely Carmichael–Counterintelligence Program," of July 9, 1968, "The 'whispering campaign' should include overtones that Carmichael is being rewarded greatly by the government for his efforts, which permits him to buy a mansion type house, live lavishly, avoid military service, avoid prosecution for his activities and enjoy a regal life with women, important officials and diplomats." Although Carmichael, like King with the SCLC, eschewed personal wealth by donating all of his speaking fees to SNCC, he enjoyed the trappings of fame and celebrity, which opened the door to the gossip.[30]

While Stokely and Miriam vacationed in Los Angeles, SNCC staff met in Atlanta for restructuring. They elected Carmichael's old Howard classmate Phil Hutchins as program coordinator, under a newly redesigned leadership structure. Hutchins' election signaled the reeling group's shift away from the verbal polemics of the recently convicted Rap Brown back to the grassroots organizing that had been Stokely's forte in the Deep South. If the election of the Newark-based Hutchins sent a message, so did Carmichael's absence. His marriage and rumors of his efforts to purchase the mansion elicited skepticism in mainstream and black newspapers, who questioned his political commitment. "Where's the Old Stokely?" asked *The Chicago Tribune* in an editorial that accused him of losing interest in "stirring up revolution" and destroying capitalism. Television news producers, meanwhile, vied over "who has had Stokely on the least minutes," in a veritable news blackout that continued for over two months after King's death.[31]

During a June 18th party at the Guyanese Embassy in Washington, the couple briefly addressed stories that they planned to buy a Blagden Avenue mansion. Miriam, smiling and unassuming in a manner that beguiled and charmed all, shot down well-wishers who congratulated them on the purchase of their fictitious new home. "That's all rumor," she said. "We live on 16th Street," she added, referring to their rented home. That same day the FBI circulated false leaks that a real estate agency had returned Makeba's $3,500 deposit on the Blagden Avenue mansion for lack of suitable financing.[32]

Support for Stokely came from the intelligentsia, black and white. In an electrifying speech on race, democracy, and human rights at the Fourth Assembly of the World Council of Churches, James Baldwin said that Stokely "may be a racist in reverse, but he is not nearly so dangerous as the people who rule South Africa, or some of the people who govern in my country. . . . He is insisting on saving his soul, and in that he is closer to the Christian conscience than the governor of Alabama." Dr. Benjamin Spock informed an incredulous William F. Buckley that Carmichael was "a very sincere and American-loving person even though he says some things that distress some people from time to time." Jean-Paul Sartre praised him as the rare kind of black speaker who ignored whites in a heroic effort to raise the consciousness of his own people. Howard Zinn sensed that "at his core, Stokely Carmichael is still an integrationist."[33]

For a time, national dreams of racial integration thought to have died with Martin Luther King seemed to carry over in the charismatic and passionate presidential candidacy of Bobby Kennedy. But Kennedy's assassination on June 5 had shattered civil rights activists who viewed him as the last mainstream politician capable of promoting racial equality and healing. Carmichael, however, remained forever embittered at Kennedy's role in harassing civil rights activists, including King.

Meanwhile, the Panther-SNCC alliance buckled as each side feared a hostile takeover. A July 12th announcement that SNCC planned to form a nationwide political party organized under the black panther symbol, suggested the relationship's formal consummation. Behind the scenes, the planned merger stalled, thwarted by clashing egos and divergent political experiences. As Huey Newton's murder trial began, gun-wielding Panthers menaced James Forman in New York. In a prison interview, Newton criticized SNCC for being captives of white liberals, and Eldridge Cleaver referred to the group as "hippies" radicalized by the Panthers.[34]

ON JULY 25, THE STATE DEPARTMENT returned Carmichael's passport as part of a deal that included a signed affidavit that he would stay clear of banned countries. The decision had political and personal implications, as Stokely could now resume his plan to return to Conakry with Miriam. Almost in celebration of his passport victory, Carmichael appeared the next day at a church in Mobile, Alabama, where he spoke words of fire. Accompanied by Panther field marshal Donald "D.C." Cox, he preached a message of guerrilla war that compared the black revolt to the first stage of a prolonged social and political revolution. "It's your town, if you want to burn it, burn it! . . . Don't pray for power, don't beg for power!" he thundered. Then he called for an armed revolution capable of imposing "maximum damage with a minimum of losses of black people." Away from the spotlight, privately, he counseled Mobile's black leaders to adopt a pragmatic version of united front politics that would reduce infighting. That night, a firebomb was hurled into a white-owned pawnshop, the first in a series of unexplained fires that spread through the city during the summer and that authorities traced to Carmichael's visit.[35]

That Sunday, July 28, in New York, Miriam sang at the Harlem Cultural Festival in Mount Morris Park. Stokely was there, enjoying his wife's performance. He thought of Miriam as his personal and political muse. His observation that "politics proceeds out of culture, then turns around and defines culture" seems an apt description of their marriage.[36]

Carmichael spent the early part of August 1968 adjusting to his new marriage, attending BUF meetings, and maintaining communication with the Panthers. The glow from reclaiming his passport faded that month when his native Trinidad banned him from a scheduled September visit. Angry and embarrassed, Carmichael rationalized the decision as proof that Prime Minister Eric Williams was a US puppet. Carmichael's tough talk masked genuinely hurt feelings and cast him as an exile from his Caribbean birthplace. Politics lay behind his exclusion, with sitting governments in Trinidad and Tobago and other West Indian countries fearful that Carmichael's Black Power rhetoric could tip political scales toward opposition parties.[37]

Huey Newton's ongoing murder trial that summer drew Carmichael back to California. Stokely found himself becoming more deeply involved with the Black Panthers. On August 22, at the Alameda County Courthouse, Carmichael, Eldridge Cleaver, and Bobby Seale were in the courtroom as Newton testified to a skeptical jury how a search for enduring peace had resulted in the shooting death of Oakland police officer John Frey. Newton delivered a dazzling performance, elevating the Panthers into a revolutionary pantheon that included the nation's founding fathers. "We would go with

Thomas Jefferson," Newton observed at one point, "where he says that when institutions no longer serve the needs of the people, they must be changed by conventional means or by revolution."[38]

At a break in the trial, Carmichael responded to a torrent of questions about the recent announcement that he had been fired from SNCC. "I still regard SNCC highly and have never publicly attacked it," he explained diplomatically, adding that he found his tenure with the group "enjoyable, pleasant, healthy and educational." Three of Carmichael's key allies in SNCC transitioned to the Panthers with him. Carver "Chico" Neblett became field marshal, directed to organize Panther chapters in the western half of the country. "D.C." Cox would organize the eastern half and Bob Brown a Panther chapter in Chicago. Carmichael's honorific prime minister title obscured a more hands-on organizing approach that helped shape the party's early direction and contributed to both its success and its inner tensions.[39]

Behind the scenes, Carmichael's departure from SNCC turned ugly. His expulsion represented the culmination of a test of wills between Carmichael and James Forman, uneasy colleagues turned political combatants. Carmichael and Forman supporters had squared off in a secret July 22nd meeting in New York, in which Stokely stood accused of orchestrating a power grab via Panther proxies that "almost resulted in the physical harm to SNCC personnel and threatened the existence of the organization." In a separate meeting five days later, the central committee voted to expel Carmichael, a decision only made public in late August to Stokely's surprise and disappointment.[40]

The Newton trial continued. A packed courtroom listened to the twenty-six-year-old defendant recount his personal odyssey from ghetto hoodlum to urban revolutionary in a narrative that mesmerized partisans and critics alike. Outside the Alameda County Courthouse, dozens of demonstrators carried "Huey Lives" signs in a peaceful protest. Afterward, Carmichael headlined a rally in Marin City that featured some of the Panthers' white allies in the Peace and Freedom Party (PFP).[41]

At the rally, Carmichael resurrected themes of capitalism and imperialism missing from his February speeches in Oakland and Los Angeles. In Marin City, he cordially acknowledged the presence of white PFP activists and announced that the era of "entertainment"—where black militants spoke in cresting polemics that made whites cringe—was over. He lectured the audience on capitalism's uncanny ability to breed global economic misery, racism's unforgiving subjugation of blacks, and how color and class

were embedded in a tragic history that explained the roots of Newton's incarceration. Confident enough in his own intellect to impart this education
to a crowd of eager students, Carmichael proceeded to offer socialism and
communism as potential alternatives that piqued his interest but ultimately
did not quite satisfy his own search for a new social vision. Premature talk
of revolution, he warned, lulled activists into celebrating imagined victories.
Armed struggle, exemplified by Castro's Cuba, preceded successful revolutions. Carmichael's talk concluded by criticizing white liberals for their inability to connect eloquent words with practical deeds. "Political equality"
was meaningless without economic equality, but the latter was something
that white liberals were unwilling to fight and die for. Carmichael's talk was
the by-product of both practical discussions with the Black Panthers and his
own efforts to build a united front among Black Power activists. Attuned to
how his earlier dismissal of socialism and communism had alienated key
Panthers, the Marin City speech represented a kind of public rapprochement
between Carmichael and the BPP.[42]

Despite his public show of support, Carmichael's relationship with the
Panthers remained complicated. He hoped to use the group as a base for
national and international political struggles guided by the revolutionary vision of Pan-Africanism he had encountered during his global travels. And
Carmichael and the Panthers' New York chapter had much in common, intellectually and philosophically, despite the national party's Marxist orientation.
The Panthers enjoyed the prestige that Carmichael's international reputation bestowed but stubbornly refused to seriously consider his ideological leanings. Carmichael's August appearances at Free Huey rallies offered
white radicals an olive branch of sorts: he dared them to organize their own
communities as part of a national revolutionary struggle. But adopting the
Panthers' increasingly hard political line would prove difficult. Carmichael
and former SNCC activists, such as Chico Neblett, attempted to influence
emerging Panther chapters via a radical Pan-Africanism at odds with Cleaver's increasingly heterodox Marxist-Leninism. Carmichael and Cleaver's
battle for control of the Panthers proved to be little more than a skirmish.
Cleaver's willingness to use intimidation tactics learned in prison and on the
streets would leave Carmichael looking for a new organization. For much of
the year, Carmichael served as roving Panther ambassador, crisscrossing the
country holding fundraisers, interviews, and rallies with local militants. He
would in later years characterize his relationship with the group as ill-fated

and superficial, but Carmichael was one of the BPP's practical architects and perhaps most important early supporter.[43]

Stokely took a break from supporting the Panthers to travel with Miriam to Dakar, Senegal, on September 5. Senegal's president was Léopold Sédar Senghor, a poet and the legendary founder of Négritude, a Pan-Africanist philosophy to which Black Power owed much. Over the next several weeks, the couple made preparations to relocate to Conakry, Guinea. Kwame Nkrumah was living in exile in Guinea. In conversations with Nkrumah there, Carmichael presented the Black Panthers as a group of revolutionaries committed to the *Osagyefo's* triumphant return to Ghana. With the entitlement of a former president, Nkrumah preached patience, reminding Carmichael that "without a base we can do nothing."[44]

Huey Newton's manslaughter conviction in September and Richard Nixon's narrow presidential win in November accelerated Carmichael's plans for a new political headquarters. Nixon's "law and order" philosophy would make Johnson's Department of Justice appear restrained in its approach to Black Power radicals, a change of fortune that Carmichael understood. Stokely's marriage to Miriam and hopes for the future collided with a palpable concern for his safety. Always the public agitator, in quieter times Carmichael confessed a fear of assassination.[45]

After three weeks abroad, Carmichael and Makeba returned to the United States on September 27 with plans to permanently move to Africa. The trip had represented a belated honeymoon and a chance for the couple to spend quality time together. After less than six months of marriage, Stokely and Miriam already faced a number of strains on their relationship. Knowledge of Carmichael's prolific love life prior to his marriage upset Makeba as did her husband's continued association with former girlfriends. Several of Carmichael's ex-girlfriends privately expressed shock and disappointment over his marriage, and one old flame from Paris came to the United States hoping to rekindle things. Political associates used to calling Carmichael at odd hours found Miriam to be "increasingly rude" and questioned whether the freewheeling activist could survive the constraints of marriage. Rumors abounded that the couple planned to break up, whispers that Stokely's public admission of Miriam's professional woes seemed to confirm. But the personal commitment between the woman nicknamed "Zenzi" and her husband, who adopted the African nickname "Shaka" after the famed Zulu warrior, remained steadfast, bound by personal love and political ambitions. For now, they both regarded their marriage as a sacred union that offered up hope and inspiration to revolutionaries struggling across the African diaspora.[46]

Although the press largely ignored his recent trip to Africa, Carmichael made a triumphant return to McGill University on October 14. There he delivered an electrifying keynote at a Black Writers' Congress, an event that announced Canada as a North American headquarters for Black Power radicalism and politicized a new generation of Afro-Canadian and Caribbean militants. One of the participants was Walter Rodney, a Guyanese historian whom Carmichael had first met at the University of Tanzania the year before and whose landmark work *How Europe Underdeveloped Africa* would be published in 1972. (After Rodney returned to Jamaica from the conference, the Jamaican government declared him persona non grata and deported him.) Fifteen hundred raucous students and activists listened as Carmichael channeled Frantz Fanon's *The Wretched of the Earth* to craft an argument that presented blacks as a colonized and exploited community whose liberation required intellectual sophistication and bold political action. "When the black man seeks to liberate himself, initially the white man reacts by being very nice, then he develops poverty programs to assist him," Carmichael said. "Later he sends agent provocateurs and later the Armed Forces." The frequent, at times furious, interruptions of applause culminated in a thirty-second standing ovation from a crowd that remained on the edge of "near pandemonium" throughout.[47]

In Mexico City, at the Olympic Games, on October 16, the Black Power salute was seen round the world. The gold and bronze medalists in the 200-meter race, Tommie Smith and John Carlos, black Americans protesting US racism, stood on the winners' platform, and as "The Star-Spangled Banner" played, they raised their black-gloved right fists and lowered their heads. On October 24, Carmichael joined former and current SNCC activists, including Rap Brown, Cleve Sellers, and former SNCC organizer Jimmy Garrett, for a celebration of John Carlos at Howard University. Carmichael and boycott organizer Harry Edwards greeted Carlos at the airport along with two hundred boisterous supporters from Howard and Federal City College, which suspended classes in Carlos' honor. Six hundred students packed Federal City College's auditorium, and two thousand attended a later rally at Howard. Wearing black gloves in tribute to Olympic sprinters he now labeled as heroes, Carmichael criticized media portrayals that called Smith and

Carlos unpatriotic. "Our heroes are not those who will bow down to white America," he said, "but those who will stand up for our people."[48]

Two weeks later, Stokely returned to the Bay Area to meet at San Francisco State on November 5 with black students. The college's racial climate reflected the organizing prowess of Jimmy Garrett, newly minted Black Panthers, and former Howard University staff now at San Francisco State. Among the latter were Carmichael's old sociology professor, Nathan Hare, who was advocating what would soon become the nation's first Black Studies program. Stokely addressed the black student body on the eve of a planned strike in support of Black Studies. Over seven hundred black students attended the evening session where Carmichael credited Hare with teaching him the proper attitude necessary for political struggle. Stokely cited the global reverberations of the clenched fists raised at the Olympics as proof that revolution required new political methods and ideas. "Our fight is a fight of this entire generation," he reminded them in a speech where the audience's cascading applause recognized the way in which Carmichael's national and international exploits indelibly shaped their own local struggles. The next day, students launched what became a 134-day strike that would result not only in the establishment of Black Studies at San Francisco State under Hare, but help legitimize the field nationally as an academic discipline. But for Nathan Hare personally, the victory was short-lived. The combination of his militancy and lack of a tenured position made him an early casualty of the wars surrounding Black Studies at universities across the nation; he was fired in early 1969.[49]

From California, Carmichael traveled to Washington to speak at Howard University's landmark conference on the future of the black university. The "Towards a Black University Conference" devoted four days to debate, discussion, and arguments over a pedagogical revolution designed to overthrow the kind of intellectual colonialism that Stokely had railed against as an undergraduate. Carmichael's advice to "quit talking and start acting" punctuated a two-hour speech that defined Black Power in dramatically international terms. Two thousand students packed Cramton Auditorium to listen to the class of 1964's most famous graduate deliver the keynote. Stokely was a grizzled veteran of American and international racial fronts at twenty-seven. In his discussion of Pan-Africanism, he acknowledged the importance of his conversations with Courtland Cox for reminding him that blacks needed an African ideology. Then he dovetailed into his typically expansive stump speech, where he lectured against the triple evils of racism, capitalism, and imperialism. He chided blacks in the audience for believing rumors that he planned to buy an expensive house. "If I had seventy thousand dollars," said Carmichael, "I'd buy me seventy thousand dollars worth of guns."[50]

The stark tone of his political rhetoric continued the next week in North Carolina during appearances at St. Augustine College and the University of North Carolina. Cleve Sellers, Willie Ricks, and Black Panther minister of culture Emory Douglass accompanied him to St. Augustine, where he warned students of a national plot to commit anti-black genocide and reminded them, to, "like good boy scouts, . . . be prepared" for an inevitably violent confrontation. At Chapel Hill, he defined the coming racial storm as a by-product of the "pitfalls of liberalism," a political ideology that remained incapable of acknowledging the depth of white racism or black anger. "Liberals want to hold hands without punishing the guilty," he said. Carmichael spent December in a blur of combative speeches amid preparations to leave the country, which he did right before the New Year.[51]

CHAPTER SIXTEEN

"The Revolution Is Not About Dying. It's About Living"

December 28, 1968–November 15, 1998

ON FEBRUARY 17, 1969, STOKELY AND MIRIAM ARRIVED IN CONAKRY. Carmichael's decision to make Guinea his new home identified Africa as the headquarters for a black revolution that to be successful required the power of nation-states behind it. He traveled to Africa as a political revolutionary in search of a movement. Banned from Trinidad and practically run out of the US, Carmichael relished the idea of living, studying, and organizing in Africa. The Tourés, President Sékou and Madame Andrée, proved gracious hosts, personally inviting Stokely and Miriam to consider Guinea their new home. But there were immediate political contradictions, perhaps none as glaring as seeking political sanctuary in a country with less political freedom than the one he had left behind. Still reeling from the shock of King's assassination and poised to break with the Black Panthers, Carmichael dived into the role of student under the awkward tutelage of Kwame Nkrumah. Nkrumah's dynamic vision of a unified Africa appealed to Carmichael's intellectual and political ambitions, although it played down the continent's unruly ethnic, religious, and regional diversity. Carmichael's support for the increasingly authoritarian Guinean president Touré provided official networks and political access but came at a heavy cost. Touré's one-party state ruthlessly dispatched enemies and imprisoned former allies, all while extolling the virtues of a revolution that had atrophied into a dictatorship. Carmichael sublimated his naturally questioning nature to his new role as a Pan-Africanist political activist. But his embrace of ideological certainty came at the expense of his identity as an intellectual maverick and political contrarian.

Stokely Carmichael's dreams of an idealized Africa often collided with the grim reality of Guinea's poverty, technological limitations, and political authoritarianism. His increasingly frequent tours of the United States served as political missions to gain new allies but also provided access to the comforts of Western living that he could not take for granted in Africa. In other words, Carmichael missed the comforts of home, which included easy access to such things as books and his favorite foods. Hidden, perhaps even from himself, in his characterization of America as a vicious and doomed land, was affection for the good parts of a country that had so indelibly shaped his own political trajectory. Carmichael explained his decision to adopt the name Kwame Ture in 1979 as a tribute to his two African mentors, Kwame Nkrumah and Sékou Touré. But it also signaled something more. The name change symbolized the evolution of Stokely Carmichael, whose combination of good looks, youth, and charisma had made him perhaps the most three-dimensional and sensitive icon of the Black Power era. Whatever doubts, insecurities, and shortcomings Carmichael freely admitted would be virtually erased by Kwame Ture, who projected superhuman confidence. Ture's defiant revolutionary proclamations replaced Carmichael's more poetic and yearningly unfulfilled descriptions of a black political transformation that would be led by sharecroppers and the urban poor. If Carmichael's past vision of a liberated future rested on the grassroots, Ture's beliefs leaned more toward the power of vanguard parties and the genius of African statesmen. Ture traveled a political journey trailblazed by early Pan-Africanists such as Edward Blyden, Alexander Crummell, and W.E.B. Du Bois, whose fiercely personal visions looked at Africa through a particular lens that inevitably shied away from the continent's at-times frustrating diversity in favor of a pre-colonial communal landscape.

Carmichael's philosophical evolution found him moving beyond the role of political and intellectual provocateur and becoming a professional activist for a revolutionary movement headquartered in one of Africa's smallest nations. The further away the possibility for a global revolution, the starker Carmichael's vision became. A hard-edged political rhetoric capable of betraying no doubts about the inevitability of the Pan-African revolution became his trademark and calling card. Political setbacks, including the death in 1984 of his benefactor and host Sékou Touré, made him a man without government patronage, as he struggled to reposition himself in post-revolutionary Guinea as an opposition leader who no longer enjoyed unfettered access to the ruling party. He remained, characteristically, more defiant than ever as the world around him underwent dramatic changes. There were other contradictions as well. Carmichael's devotion to political ideals trumped the creative and improvisational political organizing that had led to his Black Power fame in favor of a strict belief system that practically deified the deceased Nkrumah while stroking President Touré's own sizable ego. The role of Nkrumah's political emissary had seemed at once a natural extension of Carmichael's faith in Pan-African politics and a diminishment of his past role as the most bracingly independent political activist of his generation. Ideological faith seemed to cloud his once-clear political vision, and he now brooked little room for criticism of the Pan-African revolution's ultimate victory.

———————

THE INAUGURAL NOVEMBER 1969 ISSUE of *The Black Scholar* showcased Carmichael's new thinking. In "Pan-Africanism—Land and Power," he distinguished exploitation from colonization, arguing that if whites suffered from the former, only blacks experienced the latter. On this score, separate histories of subjugation required divergent liberation strategies. Only blacks and "all nonwhite peoples who have been colonized," Carmichael argued, could form alliances intent on smashing Western imperialism. He cited George Padmore, Kwame Nkrumah, and Malcolm X to support his assertion that blacks needed a political headquarters that only Africa could provide. Carmichael respectfully acknowledged Marx and Lenin "for correctly classifying" universal principles that Nkrumah's thought successfully applied to Africa's specific history. The essay introduced the idea of the All-African People's Revolutionary Party, a concept borrowed from Nkrumah that Carmichael would make his own, as a political vehicle to spread "Nkrumahism" around the world. Carmichael placed Nkrumah in a line of great men that included Mao Tsetung, Charles de Gaulle, and Winston Churchill. He compared revolution to a math problem that required careful study and political struggle and succinctly sketched the course of his activism over the next three decades. It was a direction that he would, for both better and worse, pursue with the faith of a religious convert. But it was also one with some glaring shortcomings, most notably the idea that a continent as diverse as Africa would rally around

Nkrumah's or any leader's singular vision. He now regularly consorted with African elites for whom the peasantry remained little more than a rhetorical and philosophical abstraction. Politics at the top meant access to presidents, leaders, and other dignitaries. These figures were sympathetic to the idea of a Pan-African revolution that Carmichael attempted to organize.[1]

Carmichael's speeches changed dramatically after he moved to Africa. He characterized America as an empire whose capitalist economic system needed to be destroyed. But Carmichael eschewed conventional Marxism for an interpretation of African socialism distilled by Kwame Nkrumah and politically adapted by Touré. If the old Stokely asked daringly probing and politically searching questions, Kwame Ture now supplied his own answers regarding the future of black liberation in America and around the world.

CARMICHAEL OFFICIALLY RESIGNED from the Black Panther Party on July 3, 1969, a development that sparked immediate and lifelong antagonisms between former allies. The news made the front page of *The New York Times*, which printed excerpts of a letter hand delivered to journalists by Miriam Makeba and mailed to party headquarters:

> The party has become dogmatic in its newly acquired ideology and thinks that it has the only correct position. All those who disagree with the party line, in part or completely, are lumped into the same category and labeled cultural nationalists, porkchop nationalists, reactionary pigs, etc. This may be a very convenient tactic which you choose to use; however, it is dishonest and vicious to proceed in this manner.[2]

All but one of the ex-SNCC staff who had migrated to the Panthers with Carmichael, and had helped to organize key chapters outside of Oakland, now left. The exception was field marshal D.C. Cox. Inside the party, Carmichael's supporters pushed a revolutionary Pan-Africanism that countered Eldridge Cleaver's Marxism and found a stronghold in the party's New York chapter. Ego amplified other points of disagreement, with Carmichael upset at the large number of whites attracted to the party.

THE TIMING OF CARMICHAEL'S RESIGNATION compounded the party's woes. The shooting deaths of Panthers John Huggins and Alprentice "Bunchy" Carter during a confrontation with Us members on UCLA's campus on January 17, 1969, ignited a mean season of political setbacks. The clash, fueled by FBI's Counterintelligence Program (COINTELPRO) tactics, which ratcheted up pre-existing tensions between the Panthers and Us, served as the culmination of a power struggle over control over California's Black Power Movement. The party now came under the untested leadership of David Hilliard after a process of elimination of other possible leaders: Cleaver had fled the country after jumping parole in the aftermath of the confrontation that left Bobby Hutton dead; Huey Newton was in prison, and Bobby Seale was plagued with legal troubles. Hilliard had been a boyhood friend of Newton's. The new leader's tempestuous behavior, wild and profane public speeches, and substance abuse competed with his positive efforts to streamline the party's infrastructure, weed out informants, and institutionalize surprisingly effective community programs for the poor. The Panthers responded to Carmichael's resignation with wounded scorn, characterizing their former prime minister as a lost sheep blinded by racism. "We tried to turn him around," Hilliard explained, "but he just did not come to see that you can't fight racism with racism."[3]

Algeria's Pan-African cultural festival now became the unlikely site for negotiations between Carmichael and Cleaver. Cleaver had resurfaced first in Cuba and then Algeria after fleeing America for life as a political fugitive. On July 21, 1969, President Houari Boumedienne presided over the opening of the ten-day festival, which attracted over four thousand writers, artists, dancers, and activists. The Black Panthers were among the most prominent groups at the festival, setting up a mobile station festooned with Black Power posters and organizational literature.

Upset over a resignation that he took as a personal betrayal, Cleaver reverted to prison politics, cryptically threatening Carmichael, who refused to be cowed. Carmichael offered a sanitized version of the meeting to reporters, adding that debate among militants was "healthy." The public dispute reflected deep-seated ideological divisions over the role of whites in the black freedom struggle and whether the Panthers' vision of class struggle could peacefully coexist with Carmichael's Pan-African yearnings. Privately, Stokely and Eldridge's once cordial friendship had deteriorated, and Cleaver's past admiration now turned into open contempt. In a fit of pique, he penned an outrageous open letter that accused Carmichael of fear and paranoia regarding white participation in the movement. Ironically, Cleaver's allegation about Carmichael's racial politics mimicked journalistic narratives that erroneously identified him as a conventional racial separatist whose anti-white attitudes helped to destroy SNCC. Zesty debate quickly turned into naked acrimony.[4]

Amid rumors of death threats, Carmichael met with Cleaver. Showing a reckless side that bothered many, he brought with him Miriam's fifteen-month-old grandson, Lumumba, as protection against any preemptive assaults. It was a decision that profoundly upset Miriam. "How could you?" she confronted him afterward. "I had to bring him. Who was I going to leave him with?" Carmichael protested, before Miriam's silent reply forced a confession. "All right, I knew that if I took Lumumba with me there would be second thoughts about killing me." Miriam's question of "What if there hadn't been second thoughts?" left Carmichael with no other recourse than to point to the floor at Lumumba. "Well, there's your grandson," said Stokely, reassuring himself as much as Miriam. "As you can see, he's alright." Bringing a baby to the Cleaver meeting was obviously reckless, but no act of cowardice. Carmichael's brashness at times shocked Makeba and, in this instance at least, maybe even himself.[5]

In early November, Stokely was interviewed by a London *Sunday Times* reporter. Stokely was in a playful mood, relaxing with Miriam and Lumumba on a hotel balcony in Algiers. The story featured an accompanying photo of a smiling Carmichael holding Lumumba in his arms, the backdrop of Algiers behind them. Carmichael turned wistful. He said he often thought about one of his favorite quotes, from Lewis Carroll's *Alice in Wonderland,* which he could recite verbatim:

"When I use a word," Humpty Dumpty said, in a rather scornful tone, "it means what I choose it to mean. Neither more nor less!"

"The question is," said Alice, "whether you can make words mean so many different things."

"The question is," said Humpty Dumpty, "who is to be master, that's all."[6]

Over dinner with the *Times* correspondent, Carmichael discussed his search for new political strategies. The Panthers' polemics, he said, cornered them into untenable political postures and made them vulnerable to arrest, prison, and death. "The revolution is not about dying. It's about living. There's no point in me being shut away for 10 or 15 years. What good will that do me or anyone else?"[7]

If the Panthers represented a political dead end, Carmichael remained unsure of the proper vehicle for a political revolution he still hoped to lead. "I do not know how to begin to cope with the problems" in the United States, he confessed, "so for me to stay there and to pretend that I do is for me to deceive myself and my people."[8]

Stokely recalled that disagreements over civil rights philosophy had not stopped him from attending frequent dinners at Martin Luther King's house in Atlanta. "I used to go round to Dr. King's for dinner on Sunday nearly every time I was in Atlanta. I loved Dr. King, I really did. I loved him. I would have taken a bullet for him." As he spoke, Stokely's lilting Caribbean-tinged accent gave his words a musical quality. But Cleaver proved a different character entirely. Asked by the *Sunday Times* reporter if he could remain friends with Cleaver despite political differences, Carmichael answered, "With Eldridge maybe not."

Remembrances of past conflicts shifted to a conversation about the future. Carmichael extolled Kwame Nkrumah as Africa's true leader, a statesman bold enough to encourage Pan Africanism in a continent divided by ethnic and regional differences. The romantic side of Carmichael made it all sound so exciting that the reporter briefly joined in the euphoria before stepping back and noting that most African leaders did not share Carmichael's enthusiasm for Nkrumah's leadership.[9]

IN GUINEA, the community organizer became a revolutionary ideologue. Carmichael joined Nkrumah's staff of several dozen loyalists who plotted the *Osagyefo*'s restoration to Ghana's political kingdom. Carmichael wrote political reports on Africa for Nkrumah that served as primers more for Stokely than for the *Osagyefo*. He traveled on clandestine missions on the *Osagyefo*'s behalf, and, more than once, Nkrumah upbraided him for lacking patience. "All impatience is selfishness and egotism," Nkrumah reminded him. The "old man," as Nkrumah's supporters affectionately referred to him, regarded Stokely as a work in progress, a talented but stubborn prodigy who required deft political mentoring. A born organizer, Carmichael found himself in the middle of major and minor political intrigues running through Conakry. Guinea's precarious revolution left it politically isolated and vulnerable, a situation that inspired increasingly autocratic governmental reforms. Reliance on a citizen militia, loyalty to the Democratic Party of Guinea (PDG), and a cult of personality around President Touré marked the tiny country. Carmichael threw himself into Guinea's political, social, and cultural life, although he never fully mastered French. Stokely and Miriam particularly admired Guinea's adherence to traditional African culture, and they found a secluded oasis in Dalaba, a village perched in the spectacular Fouta Djallon Mountains five hours from Conakry. They built their house in the local vein: a thatched-roofed, white-washed round house surrounded by green forests and grass. It would serve as a retreat for the couple and be one of three places where they lived in Guinea. Carmichael's social charms found fertile terrain in Guinea, and his travels on behalf of the PDG to central and remote parts of the country helped familiarize him with local customs and traditional folkways.[10]

After over a year living in Conakry and touring various countries in Africa, Carmichael and Makeba returned to the United States on March 18, 1970. The trip announced a new chapter in the development of Carmichael's persona. He wore a suit, blue shirt, and brown leather trench coat: his attentiveness to sartorial splendor reached new heights, the influence of a wife who implored him to "dress fine," advice that garnered May Charles' approval but raised the eyebrows of militants.[11]

Black Power had matured in his absence. It had carved beachheads in various cities where local issues shaped its national expression. In Durham, North Carolina, activists gathered to open Malcolm X Liberation University (MXLU). The school formed a headquarters for radical black activists in the South who were increasingly committed to Pan-Africanism. Veterans of SNCC attended, and Owusu Sadaukai, a Milwaukee native (born Howard Fuller) turned Pan-Africanist, read a message from Carmichael at MXLU's 1969 founding, who identified "sit-sins, freedom rides, freedom schools, freedom organizations, and community control" as part of the groundbreaking effort to raise black consciousness. Refugees from SNCC's dissolution found renewed political faith in Carmichael's vision of Pan-Africanism and recruited talented activists, such as Sadaukai, to the cause. MXLU would be one part of this strategy. Soon political bases in Washington popped up, and a new group, the Student Organization for Black Unity (SOBU), would build upon SNCC's legacy (and be advised by former SNCC workers) through cultural and political organizing designed to expand black America's identification with Africa.[12]

The Black Panthers remained newsworthy through debilitating confrontations with police, sensational trials, a spate of books that made them a veritable cottage industry, and community service programs the media largely ignored. While the Panthers preached an international revolution guided by Marxist-Leninist principles, black nationalists increasingly looked to Africa to help redefine black American political struggles. Pan-Africanism, which Carmichael had enthusiastically promoted with mixed results since 1968, gained support on college campuses, in local community organizations, and through the Black Arts Movement. That movement had begun at the Black Arts Repertory Theater /School organized by LeRoi Jones in Harlem in 1965. BARTS lasted only a short time, but it ignited a national movement that fused culture and politics in a quest to transform black identity and African-American politics. As dreams of guerrilla warfare faded with the declining frequency of urban rebellions, black nationalists turned to grassroots organizing.

Carmichael, looking fit and sporting a goatee, led a three-day demonstration at the United Nations in support of Angola, Rhodesia, and South Africa. His new look, most notably his beard, would prove to be a nightmare for FBI agents and informants debating whether he used a fake goatee to confuse surveillance teams.[13]

Carmichael's homecoming triggered a federal investigation. On March 24 while at his mother's home in the Bronx, he received a subpoena to appear before a special Senate subcommittee. The next day, accompanied by attorney Howard Moore, Carmichael sat mostly in silence as senators questioned him. For over two hours he invoked the Fifth Amendment more than forty times. Meanwhile, the Internal Security Subcommittee was questioning another high-profile black militant, Robert F. Williams, back from almost a decade of exile in Cuba, China, and Tanzania. Against the backdrop of the Senate Office Building, Carmichael held an unscheduled press conference on the Capitol lawn, where reporters asked him about the missing Rap Brown, still facing rioting charges in Virginia and Maryland. (Brown had vanished after SNCC workers Ralph Featherstone and William "Che" Payne were killed checking out security measures in Bel Air, Maryland, in preparation for Brown's trial. A bomb had exploded in their car. Supporters labeled their deaths an assassination, and authorities described it as a terrorist plot gone awry.) Carmichael cited the recent killing of three friends and political comrades—Black Panther leader Fred Hampton and Featherstone and Payne—as examples of coordinated political repression. "I learned from Martin Luther King," he said, "that, when repressive elements are on the move, we must not let fear immobilize us."[14]

Controversy marked Stokely's April speaking tour. In talks that switched from formal lecture to freestyle polemics, Carmichael elevated Pan-Africanism above all other revolutionary political ideologies. For much of the month, he crisscrossed the nation, visiting the Nigerian embassy in Washington, enjoying friendly jousting with TV talk show host Dick Cavett, and reuniting with activists in Boston and Chicago in a media blitz that formally reintroduced him to the American public. Quotes from *Malcolm X Speaks* now replaced ones from *The Wretched of the Earth* in his stump speech, and he patterned aspects of his organizing in Africa and efforts to build bridges in the states after Malcolm's.[15]

A series of university talks and television appearances on April 9 echoed the frenetic pace and penchant for controversy that marked his Black Power heyday. During Palestine Week at George Washington University, Carmichael denounced Israel, as Palestinian and Israeli partisans alternately cheered and booed. At Federal City College, Carmichael lectured, more coolly, on black history, guerrilla warfare, and the nature of political revolutions. Middle East politics dominated Carmichael's appearance on a local television show, where he reiterated his support for Palestine and amplified his call for blacks to recognize Africa as the missing link between them and freedom. He made a triumphant return to Howard University that evening, delivering a speech that highlighted his study with Nkrumah and fourteen months in Africa as offering startling new insights into the black freedom struggle. Carmichael's political reinvention found a receptive audience at Howard, whose tradition of enrolling international students made it a natural base for his new politics.

The overflow crowd of more than two thousand Howard students gave Miriam Makeba a standing ovation. Carmichael spent another hour after his speech receiving an enthusiastic line of supporters that lingered until past midnight. Carmichael's embrace of socialism as a tonic capable of curing Africa's myriad ills rode the wider wave of revolutionary thinking, searching for a path clear of capitalist and communist dogmas. But it bumped up against a historical tide that seemed incapable of acknowledging that Africa's diversity pre-dated its colonial past. Africa remained a continent divided as much by ethnicity, geography, culture, and language as it had been by European regimes of colonial exploitation.[16]

The April 13th telecast of David Frost's popular talk show found Carmichael playing the role of intellectual provocateur. He parried with Frost about the political effectiveness of Nkrumah and dropped a rhetorical bombshell when asked to name a great white leader. "I would think Adolf Hitler was the most—," Carmichael began, before being interrupted by a shocked audience. After the boos and hisses subsided, Carmichael continued, arguing that Hitler's talent lay in his ability to bend the world, for a time, to his own will. "When you talk about greatness, you don't put ethical or moral judgments on them. And when you talk about genius you do not put ethical or moral judgments on it. The man who created the atom bomb was a genius, even though it's used for destructive purposes—he's still a genius." With that he attempted to offer a more detailed explanation. "Adolf Hitler—I'm not putting a judgment on what he did—if you asked me for my judgment morally, I would say it was bad, what he did was wrong, was evil, etc. But I would say he was a genius, nonetheless."[17]

His effort to separate Hitler's organizational prowess from its genocidal implications worked better as an intellectual exercise than a practical public appeal. As political theater, the appearance proved a minor disaster, giving critics enduring quotes that, shorn of Carmichael's moral and ethical caveats, would be used as evidence of unbridled anti-Semitism. Critics charged that Carmichael's latest comments, coupled with harangues against the prime ministers of Trinidad and Jamaica, reflected the ravings of a frustrated activist reduced to needless provocations and guided by blood-soaked fantasies of a global revolution. The statement, outrageous and ill advised, burnished creeping suspicions that Carmichael's pro-Palestinian politics hid a barely concealed anti-Jewish bias.[18]

In short order, however, he was back on message. On April 14, the day after the Frost show, Carmichael spoke at Atlanta's Institute of the Black World, where he defended himself against lingering suspicions that he had abandoned the struggle and against FBI-fueled rumors that he secretly enjoyed a life of luxury. Hostility from SNCC and the Black Panthers hampered efforts to build a unifying political ideology, and Carmichael vowed never to return their political attacks in kind. Carmichael's sanitized version of his stint in the Panthers glossed over rugged political infighting for a narrative that stressed his personal love for Huey Newton. Carmichael bristled against charges of cowardice for abandoning the United States for Africa, asking his audience how returning home could possibly be considered self-imposed exile. He placed Martin Luther King above contemporary Black Power activists as the man who taught black people "how to confront" ancient injustices "by mobilizing the masses" in nonviolent struggle. Yet, Carmichael said, King suffered from political naïveté, foisting moral judgments on massive problems that required political solutions. Carmichael reminded his audience that SNCC, and not King and SCLC, first condemned the war in Vietnam "on a nationwide basis." It was a rhetorical salvo in a losing battle to set the historical record straight by conveying pioneer antiwar status on Black Power groups noted more for their fiery polemics than prophetic witness for peace. Carmichael closed his speech by recounting his travels over the past year through Senegal, Sierra Leone, Egypt, Tanzania, and Congo Brazzaville. He said that he had relished speaking at the University of Ibadan in Nigeria on the same platform as Malcolm X had, and he modeled his own controversial exploits after the career of Black Power's most enduring icon. He purposefully channeled Malcolm X the next week in Chicago during a taped appearance for a local television program, effortlessly quoting passages from *Malcolm X Speaks* that confirmed his own political trajectory: "It was Malcolm who began to bring our political consciousness. In this very book he says if you do not understand what is happening in the Congo then you do not understand what's happening in Mississippi. Malcolm said that because Malcolm knew where he was going and I know where he was going and I'm going with him."[19]

A series of talks in Boston reunited Carmichael with Cleve Sellers, who accompanied him to several university lectures and meetings in an effort to reinvigorate the city's Black United Front. By the end of the month, Carmichael traveled to Greensboro and Durham, North Carolina, for two days of meetings with fellow revolutionaries and some former SNCC colleagues whose tenacious organizing helped make the Tar Heel State an unlikely Pan-African beacon. Owusu Sadaukai served as the leader of this group that viewed Carmichael's international exploits as helping create domestic political space for their own activism.[20]

On May 2, just over six weeks after their well-publicized arrival, Stokely and Miriam quietly departed New York bound for Guyana. Carmichael's rhetoric of racial solidarity ran into stumbling blocks in Georgetown, Guyana, where, according to the FBI, a group of high school students walked out after he urged the Caribbean island's native-born blacks and Asians to organize separately. In parts of this address, Carmichael underestimated the Caribbean's racial diversity and imperiled his burgeoning identity as a political intellectual whose travels made him acutely aware of the international contours of black identity.[21]

Expressions of black America's domestic Pan-African solidarity reached new heights that September in Atlanta. Carmichael was scheduled to speak at the Congress of African People (CAP), but, citing a prior commitment, he sent his message of solidarity from abroad. In it, he said, "Pan-Africanism is the highest political expression of Black Power." Amiri Baraka stepped into the vacuum created by Stokely's absence and presided over the conference. CAP's success paid homage to Carmichael's belief that Africa unlocked the key to domestic freedom struggles. Black nationalists of all stripes attended, making it a practical example of the kind of politics Carmichael urged African Americans to commit themselves to. Baraka's role as the conference headliner signaled his emergence as a national political leader. Angry plays, raging poems, and caustic essays made Baraka a hero to an entire generation of young artists and writers who saw their role as political propagandists on behalf of a cultural revolution. He presided over a local political movement in Newark and was widely regarded as the symbolic figure identified with the Black Arts Movement, the cultural arm of Black Power whose impact had spread from poetry readings in coffeehouses to popular culture in music, movies, and television. While Carmichael now dismissed voting rights as the irrelevant sideshow of a decadent society, Baraka found hope in the pursuit of radical democracy, which Carmichael had revered only a few years before.[22]

IN AFRICA, Carmichael cultivated the image of a revolutionary statesman. In between speaking tours he took refuge in a simple but elegant villa whose chief attraction included its close proximity to Kwame Nkrumah, who lived three hundred yards away, and scenic views overlooking the ocean. Carmichael, who embraced Nkrumah "as a father," learned the value of patience from the elder statesman. Nkrumah reminded him that freedom was "like a boat coming to shore and my coming to shore would only get me wet, not bring the boat in faster." Carmichael said that the *Osagyefo*'s "style without vanity" and "fantastic sense of humor" helped forge a special bond between the two men that paralleled the intensity, if not the tragic arc, of Malcolm X's relationship with Elijah Muhammad. Carmichael alternated three-piece suits and Western clothes with a uniform that symbolized his commitment to guerrilla warfare in pursuit of black liberation. In Conakry, he wore the green fatigues of Guinea's militia and carried a pistol. Carmichael interrupted his voracious reading schedule to confer with the steady stream of visitors who came to meet with Nkrumah.[23]

A Portuguese-sponsored invasion in November 1970 placed Guinea on high alert and Stokely in danger. "Ready for the Revolution" signs dotted Conakry, a slogan that Carmichael would adopt as his own. President Touré, who escaped an assassination plot during the aborted invasion, successfully mobilized private citizens and the militia, in addition to military forces, to defend the nation. The combined strength of Guinean military and militia forces repelled the Portuguese invaders, but the brazen attack left Conakry tense. Tourists visiting post-invasion Conakry took note of its closed beaches, now guarded by soldiers in tents, as well as numerous roadblocks in the city's downtown where "polite young women" carrying automatic rifles vigilantly patrolled. The 11:00 P.M. curfew for non-Guineans and the conspicuous absence of the Peace Corps, kicked out for the second time since 1966, made Guinea both a welcome and precarious site of revolutionary politics. If the political scientist in Carmichael took note of the Democratic Party of Guinea's creeping authoritarianism and ideological sectarianism, the philosopher in him rationalized these circumstances as the unfortunate but necessary ingredients of nation building. Like the most radical Guineans, Carmichael proudly wore a red button adorned with Touré's face. The sight of ordinary Guineans, including the elderly, armed with guns in defense of the nation convinced Carmichael that "the African revolution would succeed." Determined to make a contribution to this endeavor, he vowed to devote his energies to "studying the African revolution through participation and observation."[24]

Carmichael returned to America in the winter and spring of 1971 still exhilarated from having witnessed Guineans repel European invaders. He sought to contrast his new identity as a Pan-African revolutionary with his recent past as a Black Power icon. In March alone, he lectured at twenty-six college campuses, churches, and community centers. Miriam Makeba remained his constant companion, and a British Broadcasting Company documentary film crew followed the couple. A politically fueled Internal Revenue

Service tax lien for over \$46,000 lent further immediacy to a fundraising tour that anticipated the publication of his first single-authored book, *Stokely Speaks: From Black Power Back to Pan-Africanism*. The detailed nature of his new stump speech, more academic lecture than crowd pleaser, at times puzzled and disappointed audiences. During a Florida trip sponsored by old friend and former SNCC activist Joe Waller, Carmichael struggled to convey his message to an audience of two thousand Florida A & M students, some of whom walked out in frustration.[25]

During visits to two Los Angeles–area colleges, Carmichael contrasted 1968 with the present, arguing that his more reflective speaking style represented a natural personal and political evolution. He compared his designation of Africa as a power base for blacks to Jews' love for Israel. Revolutionary theory, he argued, must not end with Marx and Lenin but should delve into "the roots of their theories," which he claimed, "came from communal living in Africa." This was an adaptation of Nkrumah's formulation that African socialism required the historical materialism of Marx to be combined with an appreciation of African pre-colonial collective roots.[26]

On March 18, Carmichael arrived in Jackson, Mississippi, followed by half a dozen BBC reporters and documentary film crew. They filmed speeches in Greenwood (alongside Willie Ricks) and at Tougaloo College, one of the staging grounds for the Meredith March. "The last time I was at Tougaloo was in 1966," he began. He dismissed the verbal panegyrics of the 1960s as too limited in their scope to offer blacks a viable path toward revolution:

> The whole black world today from South Africa to Nova Scotia finds itself in political chaos. Simply because we do not have a common ideology. We do not have a common ideology. If you came here tonight to hear me say how black and powerful we are, which we are, you have wasted your time. If you came here tonight to let me tell you how black and beautiful we must be, which we must be, you have wasted your time. If you came to hear me yell about right on, off the pig, kill the honky, you have wasted your time. This is past.

Instead, Carmichael proceeded to discuss the need for land as the basis for a Pan-African revolution. This need explained why he had moved to Africa, since the prospect of securing an independent land base in America would be impossible. The revolution Stokely now called for would require patience, understanding, and education.

> The major preoccupation of a revolutionary is building and creating, not destroying. Not destroying. . . . The revolutionary must destroy in order to build, but destruction is an inevitable consequence of his building. . . . Because there are two systems, and he wants to build this one. This system is in his way. This system must be destroyed, but that is not what he is concerned with. He is concerned with building because when you see so-called revolutionaries on television yelling about we are going to burn, demonstrate, and shoot, and they don't say anything else, they are not revolutionary. They are not revolutionary. Because a revolutionary must present a viable alternative to the masses.

At times, the infinite range of humanity's expression of good and evil seemed lost amid Stokely's advocacy for a "common ideology," which required blacks to abandon individual concerns in favor of a collective identity.[27]

The next day, the film crew captured historic images of Carmichael's return to Alabama. He lectured at Tuskegee before departing for an emotional visit to Lowndes County. There he reunited with his old friend John Hulett—newly elected as the first black sheriff in Lowndes County's history and one of the original defeated Black Panther Party candidates in 1966—at the Hayneville Courthouse. Then at Mount Moriah Baptist Church, where he had galvanized locals to vote for black candidates five years earlier, Carmichael delivered a passionate speech, sharing with old friends tales of the joys of living in Africa. Willie Ricks spoke about the need to build new political institutions. Carmichael introduced Bob Brown, the young Chicago organizer who had become a political surrogate and confidant, and Chico Neblett, who had transitioned seamlessly from SNCC worker and Black Panther to revolutionary Pan-Africanist. Carmichael's feelings that democratic breakthroughs in Lowndes and the rest of the nation were impossible remained unmentioned. Instead, recalling the words of Jesus ("Do not think that I came to bring peace on earth. I did not come to bring peace but a sword"), he warned, "There is bloodshed coming. We must be prepared for it."[28]

Perhaps the most important part of this visit took place away from the public spotlight at Malcolm X Liberation University in Greensboro. On

March 20 and 21, Carmichael presided at a conference of thirty key Pan-African organizers, including Cleve Sellers and Owusu Sadaukai, from around the country. Stokely outlined plans to create a Pan-African political party that he would, by the next year, publicly unveil as the All-African People's Revolutionary Party. At the conference, debates raged over race and class; organizing in Africa versus in the United States; definitions of capitalism, Marxism, and socialism; and whether the role of contemporary revolutionaries meant organizing workers or students or both. Organizational autonomy for local activists, including Carmichael supporters, loomed large. This conference revealed deeper splits and divisions that would rupture the unity that Carmichael desperately sought to organize. The depth and breadth of Carmichael's historical exploits ensured that he was respected by wide and diverse networks of activists, but their loyalty was another matter.[29]

He wrapped up this latest speaking tour with a visit to Newark, New Jersey, hosted by Amiri Baraka, whose organizing success in the US now outpaced Stokely's. Carmichael's exhausting schedule made it difficult to follow up on ambitious plans, while his itinerant and glamorous lifestyle elicited both admiration and envy among supporters. Carmichael's ability to negotiate major book contracts, his friendships with African and Caribbean leaders, and his sartorial splendor rubbed some the wrong way, as did his ambitions to consolidate various strands of a domestic Pan-African movement that predated his own Black Power advocacy. Precarious financial backing left these initiatives at the mercy of an international lecture circuit. Three days after meeting with revolutionaries in Greensboro, Stokely and Miriam jetted off to Morocco for a weeklong stay.[30]

The publication in May of *Stokely Speaks* increased Carmichael's media profile. Ethel Minor, who transitioned from SNCC to serving as Carmichael's political colleague, helped edit the book. Carmichael stood his ground after Random House editor Alice Mayhew suggested changing the book's title. Disputes with Mayhew over last-minute additions, corrections, and deletions made Carmichael welcome her replacement, his former Howard University English professor, Toni Morrison. Morrison was a master editor at America's biggest serious publishing house, and she would of course become a major novelist, winning the Nobel Prize for Literature in 1993; she was the first black woman to win a Nobel Prize. His immediate literary plans included another project (never published) more concentrated on contemporary Africa, and he implored Morrison to send him volumes of reading material, including her recently published first novel, *The Bluest Eye*, in order to "know all the trends in the Black community." Morrison forwarded the requested books to Africa and handled Stokely's more unusual requests of transferring royalties to address ongoing tax issues.[31]

Book sales confirmed the public's appetite for Carmichael's voice. Sales figures kept in line with expectations and made him a sought-after author. But with the exception of the reissue of *Black Power: The Politics of Liberation* in 1992, *Stokely Speaks* would mark Carmichael's last work with a major publisher. "I am not a good writer and I know it," he confessed to Morrison. "My books serve only as a political weapon for the period in which they are written."[32]

With regard to the impact and historical resonance of *Stokely Speaks*, Carmichael was being too modest. A collection of political speeches and essays that documented his evolution from Black Power firebrand to Pan-Africanist intellectual and professional revolutionary, *Stokely Speaks* would be embraced by Black Power–era radicals who found Carmichael's African-centered vision of a global revolution especially appealing. *Stokely Speaks* portrays Carmichael in the process of profound intellectual and political transitions, where he outlined the Third World's political and ideological importance and Africa's geographical and historical centrality to human rights struggles spanning the globe. Critics, including former SNCC colleague Julius Lester, pronounced the book a disappointment and the latest evidence that Carmichael had failed to live up to his potential as a legitimate historical successor of Malcolm X.[33]

An all-too-human event now brought Stokely to his knees. His political father, and as he saw it, the father of Pan-Africanism, Kwame Nkrumah, died on April 27, 1972, at age sixty-two. The unexpected death, from cancer, gave enhanced urgency and intensity to the anti-imperialist and Pan-African voice that Carmichael had articulated in *Stokely Speaks*. "My work here," he observed from Conakry, "has allowed me clearly to see in a scientific manner the many forces that operate against us." Weeks later, Carmichael conducted interviews at the Camayenne Hotel on the coast of Guinea. In a white open-collar casual shirt and wearing a red Sékou Touré button, Carmichael envisioned a united Africa—with one army, one leader, and one United Nations representative—that would be respected in global affairs. Memories of the Guinean people's bravery in the face of Portugal's invasion two years earlier reassured him that "the African revolution would succeed." Carmichael's belief in Africa's unification under scientific socialism followed Nkrumah's, and to a lesser extent Touré's, political thought, which defined socialism as being consistent with African communalism. He contrasted this vision with the sterile world-view of Marxist-Leninists and seemed more comfortable discussing Africa and Africans than African socialism. His professed faith in the "scientific" application of revolutionary ideas fashioned by Nkrumah manifested itself in a political zeal that paralleled the fervor of religious sects he had spent his entire life avoiding.[34]

Meanwhile, political events in the United States seemed to strengthen Carmichael's belief in, if not political leadership over, black solidarity. In March 1972, over ten thousand delegates had attended the National Black Political Assembly in Gary, Indiana, to formally announce a daring coalition of independent black political groups. Amiri Baraka once again played a central role, along with fellow conveners Gary mayor Richard Hatcher and Michigan congressman Charles Diggs, in advocating a broad-based unity among black nationalists, community organizers, intellectuals, artists, and politicians. The Gary Agenda placed black unity and self-determination at the core of a policy manifesto aimed at a refined democracy capable of renewing cities, aiding the poor, and advocating a human rights–based foreign policy.[35]

On May 13, Stokely and Miriam attended Kwame Nkrumah's funeral in Conakry. Representatives from forty countries, including many African heads of state, came to pay their respects. Sékou Touré delivered a ninety-minute eulogy praising Nkrumah's enduring revolutionary spirit. The service, which took place at Guinea's Palace of the People, brought together two thousand people, including African moderates and militants whose only point of political agreement was that Nkrumah was perhaps Africa's greatest political leader. Thoughts of Martin Luther King must have come to Carmichael as he listened to Touré's eulogy and gazed upon Nkrumah's coffin, which was draped in the red, yellow, and green colors of the Guinean flag. Seated with Makeba in a place of honor with official delegates, Carmichael mourned the loss of a political mentor whom he had come to regard as a father.[36]

In six weeks, Stokely would turn thirty-one.

IN THE UNITED STATES AT THE END OF MAY, the first African Liberation Day (ALD) festival kicked off in spectacular fashion. The ALD was directed with great success by Owusu Sadaukai. Since marching together at the United Nations immediately after Carmichael's first return from Africa, Sadaukai's profile had grown rapidly. Simultaneous demonstrations in San Francisco, Washington, Montreal, and the Caribbean islands of Grenada, Antigua, and Dominica inaugurated the May 27th celebration, and organizers dedicated the event to Nkrumah's memory. The entire affair both impressed and irked Carmichael, who viewed Sadaukai and his cohort as comparative political amateurs who owed their current leadership to his past heroics and current absence.[37]

Carmichael returned to the United States for another speaking tour in the fall, where he showcased his developing anti-imperialism. On October 17, two thousand came to Howard to hear him publicly discuss the AAPRP. The lecture's title, "Nkrumahism: The Correct Ideology," left little to the imagination, but his talk retained aspects of his vital, improvisational intelligence. He hoped that the AAPRP would become "a mass party, international in character" designed to spread Pan-Africanism and instill the particulars of Nkrumah's thought to students equipped to distinguish between late 1960s slogans and the more scientific application of revolutionary theory. Applause frequently interrupted Carmichael's ninety-minute speech, in which he railed against the scourge of drugs, the upcoming presidential election (between President Nixon and the antiwar Democrat, Senator George McGovern), and a lack of philosophical unity among the world's black population. He implored students to use their university education in service of the larger black community. "You are here because your people fought to get you here. Everything must come from the people and go back to the people."[38]

Carmichael's appearance at Howard was part of his coordinated effort to reestablish political strength in Washington. During a series of four Carmichael Seminars at Howard that October, he spoke to students about the intricacies of revolutionary theory and conducted closed-door sessions with local Washington activists. But some local leaders balked at the prospect of Carmichael's reasserted leadership and instead told journalists that his time had passed. In November, after Nixon's landslide re-election, Carmichael called for a meeting of black activists in New York to hammer out a revamped united front. Invitations went out to a cross section of African-American leaders, including Jesse Jackson (whose national profile made him Martin

Luther King's potential successor in the eyes of many), Urban League executive director Vernon Jordan, Julian Bond, and Louis Farrakhan. Whereas one
hundred leaders had responded to his Black United Front call in 1968, only
fourteen showed up now. Washington activists professed friendship toward
Carmichael but noted that America's racial landscape had changed drastically
since the late 1960s.[39]

Despite these setbacks, his very presence inspired parallel movements
for self-determination. He received a warm welcome from Native American
activists who staged a daring occupation of the Bureau of Indian Affairs in
Washington on Saturday, November 4. The occupation triggered fears of a
modern-day Wounded Knee, the nineteenth-century battle where Native
Americans were slaughtered. The charismatic leader of the American Indian Movement (AIM), Russell Means, responded to a federal request to
evict the building in uncompromising tones. "We now call this the National
Assembly. . . . It is ours. It belongs to the original sovereign peoples of this
land." Carmichael echoed his words: "The question of native Americans is
not just a question of civil rights. This land is their land. . . . we have agreed to
do whatever we can to provide help. . . . There can be no settlement until their
land is returned to them." For Carmichael, alliances with the Third World
liberation struggles began at home. Carmichael's support of AIM would
never be forgotten, especially by activist Vernon Bellecourt, who, decades
later, cited Stokely's willingness to align himself with unpopular causes as a
trademark of political courage.[40]

Stokely's return to Washington included a bittersweet reunion with his
former mentor, Julius Hobson, now stricken with spinal cancer at the age of
fifty. Carmichael joined two thousand friends and supporters to pay tribute to
Hobson at a testimonial dinner on November 14 at the Sheraton Park Hotel.

Two weeks later, Carmichael met with a woman considered the Grandmother of the civil rights movement. An educator and NAACP activist, Septima Clark had organized citizenship schools in the Deep South during the
civil rights era designed to help blacks pass voter registration tests. Born in
South Carolina in 1898 to a mother of Haitian descent, Clark mentored a
generation of civil rights activists, including Rosa Parks, whom she taught
at the legendary Highlander Folk School in Tennessee, which promoted the
outlaw philosophy of interracial democracy during the Jim Crow era. Carmichael was signing copies of *Stokely Speaks* at Washington's Martin Luther
King Memorial Library when Septima appeared. Well known among move-

ment people, she remained anonymous to the general public, her steadfast commitment to social justice destined to be recovered by historians only long after her death. Stokely cited Clark's activism in the South during the civil rights movement's heroic period as definitive proof that black women deserved equal partnership in the ongoing revolution.[41]

Carmichael's American speaking tour continued through the early part of 1973. During it he touted the AAPRP as an organizing vanguard above the polemics of the 1960s. Enthusiastically received by crowds across the nation, he nonetheless faced constant questions from sympathetic black Americans regarding his focus on Africa. Carmichael replied that he did not expect a mass exodus to Africa, but that the continent remained black people's birthright and that African Americans could practically will themselves toward a renewal through unified political organizing and collective social and economic action. He pointed to the death of Nkrumah and the recent assassination of Amilcar Cabral as spurs that would ignite further rebellion across the continent. Stokely first met Cabral, the revolutionary from Guinea-Bissau, in Conakry. They even discussed organizing a group of volunteers to fight in Portuguese Africa, but the plan went nowhere. But Cabral's untimely death, just like Nkrumah's passing, only further emboldened Stokely. Revolutionary Pan-Africanism, as defined by Nkrumah and now Carmichael, offered blueprints for salvation based on scientific principles that virtually assured victory.[42]

J. Edgar Hoover's death the previous year did not end the FBI's pursuit of Carmichael. Acting director L. Patrick Gray's annual report documented the activities of racial extremists in the United States and cited Carmichael's stinging attacks on capitalism and advocacy of socialism. *The Wall Street Journal*'s description of Stokely as an anachronistic example of the discredited 1960s mixed contemporary denunciation with palpable relief that the revolutionary panegyrics of recent years had subsided. Carmichael urged black college students, who increasingly made up his audience, to "be preoccupied with building not destroying."[43]

If Carmichael maintained his love for the controversial public statement, other parts of his persona changed dramatically. The world's best-known "Nkrumahist" admitted publicly that he had feared political assassination during the late 1960s and had not expected to survive the period's roiling turmoil. A typical speaking engagement now went on for almost three hours, included no entourage of supporters, and found him using chalk and a blackboard to explain historical and theoretical concepts that he insisted were vital to the revolution. Efforts to build a national black united front faltered amid ideological disputes and a lack of cooperation from civil rights leaders such as Roy Wilkins and Ralph Abernathy, both of whom balked at attending any meeting organized by Carmichael. The AAPRP had at times difficult relationships with fellow Pan-Africanists. Amiri Baraka, whose Congress of African People successfully established at least one version of united-front politics, now outpaced Carmichael as a domestic organizer of Pan-African revolution. Owusu Sadaukai's acceptance of financial aid from the Episcopal Church and his high-profile role in African Liberation Day celebrations soured his friendship with Carmichael.[44]

His latest speaking tour found Carmichael advocating for the release of two jailed former SNCC workers, Rap Brown and Cleve Sellers. Time apart only strengthened Carmichael and Sellers' close bond. Stokely had served as best man at Cleve's wedding the previous December. Sellers had quietly emerged as one of the AAPRP's most energetic and effective organizers. But his activism was temporarily curtailed by a one-year rioting charge stemming from the Orangeburg Massacre. Rap Brown's incarceration resulted from a shootout during an attempted robbery.[45]

Meanwhile, Miriam Makeba found herself stranded in Jamaica after a concert performance. Carmichael received permission to visit that country, which had previously banned him, to help sort out her visa problems. Michael Manley's new democratic socialist government had made Jamaica a progressive beacon in the Caribbean. A warm reception for Stokely from Manley did not extend, however, to Vincent de Roulet, the Nixon-appointed US ambassador who had initially denied Miriam a new visa. Carmichael spent his time in Jamaica giving speeches, conducting political meetings, and sightseeing. At one point, he bumped into the astonished mother of Michael Thelwell, his old comrade from NAG. Stokely literally swept her off her feet before planting a kiss that he said was from her son. Minister of State Dudley Thompson rationalized Carmichael's presence to American officials. Privately, Thompson informed Makeba that she and Stokely were "welcome in Jamaica anytime" and indeed the couple stayed at his personal residence. Thompson displayed another face to State Department officials, reassuring them that Carmichael would be under a virtual house arrest during his visit and expressing outrage when Stokely conducted an interview on Jamaican television. Carmichael's presence, according to the American Embassy, "left

a bad taste in the local mouths," leaving Jamaican officials "greatly relieved
to give back the dirty linen to America, the source from which it came."
Jamaica's daily, *The Star*, characterized Carmichael as a "non-essential im-
port," but local revolutionaries enthusiastically invited him to come back
the next year for a series of lectures. At Norman Manley Airport on March
6, he spoke to reporters before departing with Makeba. Carmichael implored Jamaican gunmen locked in internecine warfare to "stop killing each
other," chalked up his ability to visit the island as an example of the "development and unity of the black man," and dressed down De Roulet as racist and arrogant. Carmichael's description of the ambassador would prove
more than accurate. By the summer, the Manley government had reached
its limit with De Roulet's ostentatious displays of wealth, crude manner,
and habit of referring to Jamaicans as "niggers" and declared him persona
non grata, ending his four tumultuous years of service to Nixon and dis-
service to Jamaica.[46]

After seven months in the United States and Jamaica, Carmichael returned to Africa in the first week of May. He would visit a number of African
countries over the next year. By far the most controversial trip was to Uganda
at the invitation of Idi Amin. Amin's presidency had turned Uganda into
Africa's ground zero for human rights violations, and critics portrayed him
as a monster who willfully exterminated his political opponents. Supporters
touted Amin's strong support for African leaders and his anti-Zionism as
proof enough of his positive credentials. Carmichael's visit came after debate within the AAPRP, with one side arguing that his appearance in Uganda
would alienate other African countries while simultaneously providing cover
for a corrupt regime. Advocates countered that Carmichael's powers of per-
suasion might steer Amin and Uganda into more constructive engagement
with African revolutionaries, open East Africa to the AAPRP, and secure a
potential haven for political prisoners. On June 7, Stokely and Miriam arrived
at Entebbe International Airport, where they were received by an official government delegation. President Amin, who had gained a reputation as perhaps
the first black man to institutionalize racism by throwing non-Africans out
of Uganda, made Carmichael and Makeba official Ugandan citizens. Carmichael represented the "true black Africans who were kidnapped from their
motherland more than three hundred years ago," proclaimed Amin. Most of
the world despised Amin and his regime, so Makeba's performances and Carmichael's pro-Amin speeches did not make the jet-setting couple any friends

outside Uganda. Carmichael rationalized support for Amin by looking outward at the Ugandan president's critics. Amin's professed anti-imperialism and criticism of the United States and Israel trumped a more critical analysis of Ugandan politics in favor of unstinting racial loyalty. Amin successfully exploited Carmichael's racial blind spot, by touting his politics as being based on restoring African dignity.[47]

By 1973, Carmichael's African dreams encompassed the broad contours of Black Power politics. Black politicians, Black Panthers, and urban nationalists from Newark to Oakland hailed Africa as central to black liberation. Carmichael's role in leading this revolution would prove bittersweet. Having helped inspire a generation of activists through his Black Power call, Carmichael's embrace of Pan-Africanism anticipated the explosion in Africa consciousness during the early 1970s even as it forced him to navigate a minefield of personality conflicts, ideological differences, and organizational clashes. If Carmichael's political compass intermittently faltered by brokering alliances with African dictators, he continued to garner a loyal following in the States, especially among college students. At the University of Washington in Seattle in October, Carmichael lectured on Watergate, the energy crisis, and South African apartheid in wide-ranging discussions that exhibited the famous biting wit and playful humor that still left audiences energized and forced even journalists to confess a grudging admiration.[48]

Speaking tours throughout the fall left FBI agents shaking their heads at lectures that outlined the history of revolution, socialism, and capitalism while carefully avoiding what they called "violence-prone rhetoric." The quartet of agents in Phoenix who worked an eight-hour physical surveillance detail trailing Carmichael on Monday, October 22 and informants following his activities the next week in Oklahoma and Indiana all listened to a finely honed speech promoting the virtues of revolutionary Pan-Africanism, the vices of capitalism, and the potential of the AAPRP.[49]

Like Malcolm X, Carmichael maintained a punishing work schedule that frequently left him exhausted. His personal efforts to build the AAPRP proved instrumental to the group's successful, if modest, inroads among black college students. Never open to casual membership, the AAPRP instead identified and recruited the most-promising students in order to develop a new generation of organizers dedicated to Nkrumah's revolutionary vision as interpreted by Carmichael. The relatively small crowds and correspondingly modest speaking fees of his current tour proved a disappointment to

Carmichael as did the slow progress in building the party. But if the AAPRP stalled as a mass domestic political organization, it gained influential beach-heads in Washington, Chicago, New York, and other cities. The bursts of national media attention that had accompanied Stokely's initial return from Africa also waned, with journalists less interested in Carmichael speaking alongside Willie Ricks in Forkland, Alabama, about Pan-Africanism than they had been during the Meredith March. The mainstream press found revolutionary Pan-Africanism less appealing than Black Power. Nkrumah-ism proved, just as Carmichael had predicted, more difficult to co-opt than Black Power.[50]

If Pan-Africanism remained exotic in Alabama, it retained a powerful base in Washington. On May 24, 1974, Carmichael delivered an electrifying speech during the second day of Howard University's "Which Road Toward Black Liberation?" conference, organized as a vehicle for debating the fu-ture of Black Power. The conference speakers included Amiri Baraka, Owusu Sadaukai, and Muhammad Ahmad (formerly Max Stanford), the Revolution-ary Action Movement leader who advocated racial justice and class struggle based on the ideas of Robert F. Williams and Malcolm X. Recent events made the gathering especially timely as it coincided with the public unraveling of alliances forged during the National Black Political Assembly held in Gary, Indiana, in March 1972.

Dressed in the green military fatigues of the Guinean Army, Carmichael discussed the virtues of scientific socialism as the key to a global revolution. He touted Nkrumah's statesmanship in Africa as offering a deft mix of radical activity backed by painstaking planning. He acknowledged class struggle as history's motivating force but added the concept of racial solidarity to Marx-ist dialectics. Black Americans, he argued, faced an identity crisis that made them "incapable of wholeheartedly embracing African nationalism," which he called their "only just nationalism."[51]

Amiri Baraka gave a tortured speech that quoted Amilcar Cabral in vain hopes of appeasing Pan-Africanists, before moving on to a description of Lenin, the revolutionary he now claimed as his own. Owusu Sadaukai went further. His charismatic oratory reminded many of Carmichael's, and he emerged as a leader among domestic Pan-Africanists for his tireless organiz-ing and deft political skills. Sadaukai's foray into West Africa trailing guerrilla fighters several years earlier had planted the seeds for the first African Liber-ation Day. His time in Africa transformed Sadaukai, who had once cautioned his followers against reading Marx and Lenin, and he now stressed studying Marxists alongside African revolutionaries.

Sectarianism, in various forms, ruled the day. Revolutionary Pan-Africanists pursued racial equality while acknowledging capitalism's uncanny ability to shape human existence. They settled on a revisionist interpretation of class struggle that bypassed European intellectuals in favor of an indigenous African socialism. Further splits ensued based on which African revolutionary (Nkrumah, Nyerere, or Cabral) activists recognized as legitimate. Born-again Marxists preached class struggle with evangelical zeal in position papers and conference presentations that identified Marxism-Leninism as a scientific breakthrough whose inevitable victory had only momentarily been delayed. Unrepentant black nationalists warned against flirtations with white ideology and white people, preferring the comfort of purely racial appeals that, in their basest form, allowed them to oppose busing and support African regimes openly hostile to human rights. In the end, all sides would claim victory just as the wider Black Power Movement faced defeat. Political reality could be ignored inside of a cocoon.[52]

FBI agents broke through this cocoon during two interviews with Carmichael during the summer. Carmichael's willingness to be interviewed by the FBI was not unusual. Malcolm X had done the same thing, while never agreeing to be an informant or give up sensitive information.

On August 9 and September 5, 1974, Carmichael spoke to special agents on the precondition that he be allowed to tape the interviews and provide copies for the bureau at a later date. Agents grilled him about Arab terrorists, the activities of kidnapped heiress-turned-guerrilla Patty Hearst, and the inner workings of the AAPRP. Carmichael declined to offer specifics about the AAPRP, defended his recent appearance at the Organization of Arab Students' conference as part of his support for revolutionary movements, and disavowed Hearst as a "romantic" spirit of destructive revolt that set back organic revolutionary struggles. He debated with agents, who pressed him about his call to destroy capitalism, and he said that he advocated the end of an oppressive economic system and "not the destruction of America in a physical sense." Carmichael finished the interview by assuring the agents that he received no fees, money, or gratuities from any foreign governments, including Uganda. The FBI noted that Carmichael remained "cordial" throughout both interviews, an attitude that must have surprised special agents expecting the firebrand chronicled in the bureau's surveillance file.

Throughout, Carmichael repeatedly described America's political system as a "bourgeois democracy," a running fiction that the nation's citizens were increasingly aware of thanks to the disastrous Vietnam War and the Watergate scandal.[53]

Like Malcolm X during his interview with FBI agents in the 1950s, Carmichael offered no information about his political organizing. Instead he engaged in a dialogue that shielded him against charges that he was an agent of a foreign government, while simultaneously giving a human face to his revolutionary politics. "I'm only 33," he said. "But I've been out here a long time. And I know it's going to be for a much longer time." Carmichael discussed the AAPRP's slow growth and long-range outlook as part of a global revolutionary struggle that would take place over generations and inevitably result in victory. The impatient icon of the 1960s was now able to recognize that political revolution, far from the 100-yard dash he imagined in his youth, was a marathon race that required long-distance runners. The relatively modest audiences he spoke to on his most recent speaking tour reflected this pragmatism. He boasted in one speech of having AAPRP members in the United States, Canada, Africa, Central and South America, and the Caribbean, which reflected the breadth of an organization that still lacked density. The political, rather than religious, sectarianism of the AAPRP turned off potential recruits even as its detailed outlines for reading, political education, and organizing attracted smaller groups of talented and intellectually agile students and activists.[54]

Carmichael continued to regularly tour the United States during the 1970s and stoked intermittent controversy by defending African autocrats even as he denounced Zionism. When the UN General Assembly passed a resolution on November 10, 1975, determining that Zionism was a form of racism and racial discrimination, Carmichael railed against news media that erroneously equated anti-Zionism with anti-Semitism. Critics charged, however, that Carmichael's increasingly harsh denunciations crossed the line into anti-Semitism. On November 14, pro-Zionist Jewish activists brandishing a sign that read "All the World Wants the Jews Dead" picketed Carmichael's American University speech, where he backed the UN characterization of Zionism as racist. If Carmichael's speech belittled dreams of Jewish self-determination, it also questioned the legitimacy of the state of Israel on the grounds that the Bible represented an unreliable source for such a historic land claim. Israel's political isolation from large swaths of Africa and

Arab countries tied the question of Palestine to liberation struggles raging in southern Africa. Carmichael's support for Arab states and staunch anti-Zionism and the escalating assaults by pro-Zionist Jews placed him in the uncomfortable position of being in a blood feud with former friends and allies he had once considered family.[55]

The label of anti-Semite, just like the one of sexist, would prove, over time, to be an enduring one. Carmichael's denunciations of Zionism defined Jewish nationalism as an all-encompassing threat that brooked little room for nuanced debate over the ideology's strengths and shortcomings. In certain instances his blanket condemnation of the very ideal of a Jewish homeland succumbed to political blinders that he had spent much of his life fighting against. The boundless energy Carmichael exhibited in criticizing Zionism could, at times, result in rhetorical flourishes that purposely antagonized former allies. If Carmichael's defiant anti-Zionist posture placed him outside the civil rights mainstream, it earned him and the AAPRP entrée into exclusive Third World political circles that offered diplomatic access and travel privileges normally reserved for official heads of state. For Carmichael, Israel's support of the racist apartheid regime in South Africa more than justified his attack on Zionism as a tool of Western imperialism.

Carmichael's anti-Zionism and attraction to controversy garnered smaller, if still enthusiastic, crowds of college students. He remained a big draw at Howard University, whose local AAPRP chapter thrived. Eldridge Cleaver's bittersweet return from exile that same year outlined the fates of two of the most prominent Black Power icons, with the former Black Panther's newfound patriotism and conservative politics contrasting with Carmichael's steadfast revolutionary fervor. "Cleaver couldn't be a revolutionary. A revolutionary is a principled man," he explained to one reporter. During an interview with Howard University's WHUR radio station that same year, Carmichael exorcised old demons, announcing that the AAPRP valued black women as revolutionary equals in the struggle for liberation. Women, he insisted, "were stronger than men," held leading positions within the AAPRP, and formed the "backbone of our struggle." Carmichael's public discussion of black women's role in the revolution marked a subtle shift in rhetoric but proved consistent with his political beliefs and leadership style. But his political relationships with women remained fraught by virtue of Waveland, a subject that he directly addressed: "There's a little quote going around that Stokely Carmichael said that the position of the women in the movement is prone. And I did say that, I did say it. Of course I said it at a private meeting, it was a joke—and it was said in 1964. When people wanted something against me they reached back, they got that. I said O.K. you can have that one, let them have that one, I won't fight it. They need one."[56]

The world, and Carmichael, had changed dramatically since he spoke those words. His celebrity remained, but his meetings with Zambian president Kenneth Kaunda and Libyan Embassy officials in Washington no longer attracted much attention. Visits to Lowndes and Tuskegee in Alabama that November found Carmichael back in familiar surroundings but under different circumstances. Local blacks in the South responded to Carmichael's call for a Pan-African revolution more with respectful deference than with enthusiasm. His ties to Idi Amin continued to deepen, and in the summer of 1975 he attended the Organization of African Unity Conference in Kampala. That October Stokely and Miriam attended a New York reception for Amin following a speech by the Ugandan president at the UN. Carmichael's international and domestic political exploits remained of interest to the FBI, who tracked him to fundraising events, AAPRP central committee meetings, and social gatherings with friends.[57]

The FBI's continued surveillance seemed to ignore the fact that Carmichael's new political orientation lacked the influence of his Black Power heyday. Still, the bureau remained concerned with his ability to sway hearts and minds. It reported that an estimated 70,000 people had attended Carmichael's three hundred public speeches on behalf of the AAPRP, a figure high enough to warrant the bureau's official attention. Campus appearances at Cornell University and City College in 1976, on the heels of a visit to Muammar Gaddafi's Libya, briefly echoed the fiery radicalism of black students during Black Power's heyday. Similarly, an invitation by Mexican rights activist Rodolfo "Corky" González to speak in Denver recalled the heady black and brown alliances of the late 1960s. Political revolts in Angola and other parts of Africa lent immediacy to Carmichael's urgent call for Pan-African unity and revolution. A brief visit to Lowndes County in April, where Sheriff John Hulett now presided more as a political boss than a democratic leader, revealed the limits of American democracy that Carmichael had long suspected. Hulett's abandonment of independent politics in favor of building a political machine through the Democratic Party offered bittersweet lessons about the future of the type of grassroots local political movement that Carmichael championed in SNCC.[58]

Flush with plans to return to Guinea for his thirty-fifth birthday, Carmichael found time to reflect on the decade that had passed since his call for Black Power in Mississippi. Speaking tours and political work interrupted his life in the Guinean mountains with Makeba. He found himself mentioned, not always in a flattering manner, in proliferating journalistic retrospectives about the 1960s. Dueling perspectives of Carmichael emerged in the memoirs of SNCC activists. Jim Forman's pugnacious *The Making of Black Revolutionaries*, published in 1972, characterized him as a powerful if misguided and at times self-centered political talent. Cleve Sellers' lyrical *The River of No Return*, released the following year, offered a more three-dimensional portrait. The release of classified FBI documents that characterized Stokely as a potential "black messiah" hinted at the illegal counterintelligence activities directed against black radicals, with Carmichael's own file accounting for tens of thousands of pages. The "old" Stokely re-emerged that October during a press conference in Cincinnati. He announced the start of a three-week tour by calling Secretary of State Henry Kissinger a "racist pig." He said, "Capitalism is a vicious system which enslaved my people. Anyone who supports it is either a sick man or an agent of the government. I will work every second of my life to bring about this objective. I know that victory is inevitable, but I do not know when it will come."[59]

Almost eleven years after delivering his Black Power speech in Mississippi, Carmichael returned to the Magnolia State for the funeral of a dear friend. On Sunday, March 20, 1977, Carmichael joined with Julian Bond, Mary King, and John Lewis to mourn the untimely death of Fannie Lou Hamer, both a hero and casualty of America's civil rights struggle. Hamer's funeral attracted veterans of the civil rights struggle to Ruleville, Mississippi, to celebrate a life cut short by both cancer and the stress and physical toll of movement activism. Andrew Young delivered the eulogy, and other dignitaries paid tribute to Hamer's legacy of grassroots activism. Carmichael's respect and love for Hamer, something witnessed by movement activists and friends, remained a hidden feature of his legacy, as did the deference he paid to scores of anonymous black women and men in Mississippi, Alabama, and now Africa. "She represented the very best in us," said Stokely.[60]

Carmichael's AAPRP continued to celebrate African Liberation Day, drawing 10,000 to Washington in May even as former allies staged competing demonstrations, the by-product of rancorous debates during the waning days of Black Power. "I've been maintaining a low profile, but that doesn't mean I'm less active," he assured supporters.[61]

The next year, Miriam Makeba filed for divorce after ten years of marriage. Carmichael's latest extramarital affair led to the end of their marriage. By the time she discovered evidence of Carmichael sleeping with his new woman in their home in Dalaba, Miriam had seen enough. "My husband falls in love with the woman," she stoically observed in her autobiography. "This love is so great that he takes chances for it, and he does things that would seem foolish for a man who has far less intelligence than Stokely has." Despite his great love for Makeba, Carmichael proved ill suited to playing the role of husband. Reporters visiting Carmichael in Conakry found him "lying low," content to play soccer and baseball, drive Makeba's aging Volvo, and plot a global revolution that seemed, to most objective observers, a distant dream.[62]

The newly divorced Carmichael, now calling himself Kwame Ture, returned to the United States in 1979 to give the keynote address at the annual African Liberation Day festival and continue his speaking tours. The name change in honor of his two greatest political mentors reflected his political faith in Africa's restorative potential for revolutionary struggles around the world. It also reflected a break from his former, more hopeful, perspective about American democracy. Following his divorce, he traveled the world as an official Guinean ambassador privy to foreign intrigues that made the notion of an international revolution seem tantalizingly real. The Black Power lecture circuit of college campuses, cultural centers, and student unions enthusiastically welcomed him, and at least one major American city—in fact, the nation's capital—rolled out the red carpet. Washington's recent election of Marion Barry as mayor gave Ture the chance to consort with an old friend turned politician. They reminisced over picketing Jim Crow–era department stores in the capital, posed for pictures with photographers, and traded jokes about their commitment to political struggle. "Ten years ago Stokely probably would not have wanted to see the mayor," Barry joked.[63]

In the nation's capital, Marion Barry was presiding over his own version of Black Power. Former SNCC activists came along for the ride. Ivanhoe Donaldson transferred experiences as a civil rights strategist to Barry's longshot 1978 mayoral campaign, and for the next six years was the mayor's most powerful adviser. Barry placed Courtland Cox in charge of the city's minority business redevelopment agency. The Barry administration promised to prove, once and for all, that black politicians could lead a major city from the precipice of fiscal decline and urban decay to a renaissance. Friends of Barry, including Ture, knew about his wild side, and heard whispers about him dabbling in drugs and an almost obsessive pursuit of women. But many of these activists knew that if you were in a foxhole, or facing a mob of racists in the Deep South, there was no person you would want by your side more than Marion Barry. This duality caused many to deny Barry's shortcomings until it was too late. Donaldson's admission of guilt on federal corruption charges in 1985 (he would serve two years of a seven-year sentence) began a long, spectacular decline for Barry. Barry's 1989 arrest for smoking crack cocaine became a national symbol of urban corruption that was increasingly associated with black politics in the post–civil rights era.[64]

In December 1980, Stokely reunited with Jamil Al-Amin (formerly Rap Brown) for a press conference. He denounced the FBI's surveillance of black militants and traced his own marital breakup with Makeba to letters suggesting she had engaged in an extramarital affair with Sékou Touré.[65]

Such rumors undoubtedly took a personal toll on Carmichael, his marriage to Makeba, and his relationship with Touré. For Harry Belafonte, who introduced SNCC activists to Guinea in 1964 and once treated Miriam like his little sister, the rumors were part of a sad trail of wreckage left by Touré's political decline:

> I do know that by then, Sékou Touré had set aside his youthful dreams of creating a utopian socialist state and become a vengeful tyrant who tortured his real or perceived opponents. . . . Almost everyone I'd met in the country and come to regard as a friend was being branded an enemy of the state. Thousands of the country's intellectual, military, and political leaders were thrown into Camp Boiro, Guinea's gulag, many to die by torture, starvation, or firing squad. . . . Stokely and Miriam had to have known that Sékou Touré was doing this by the early 1970s, but neither ever said a public word against him.[66]

That neither Stokely nor Miriam ever spoke out publicly against Touré or his political regime does not mean that they never disagreed with the Guinean government. The couple's political access and personal security was contingent upon loyalty, which they displayed by never publicly criticizing Touré. To violate this unspoken agreement would have risked being forced to leave Guinea or, possibly, worse. On this score, Carmichael's failure to acknowledge the Guinean government's political errors and missteps, even after Touré's death, represented a moral failure as well as a political one. But for Carmichael, Sékou Touré's treatment of political enemies was no different from American political surveillance and incarceration of civil rights and Black Power activists marked as subversives. Choosing sides in a global struggle against imperialism, from this perspective, carried long-term costs that could only be judged by history.

According to Belafonte, Miriam had become, by the late 1960s, "a rebellious daughter, flaunting her brand of radical politics in my face, doing more than her share of drugs, and going from one rocky romance to the next." Belafonte judged Stokely, Miriam, and Sékou Touré to have all gotten caught up in the excesses of celebrity, power, and privilege. "One day I went to one of Miriam's concerts, and there, backstage, was Stokely, in one of the finest Nehru suits I'd ever seen. A hand-tailored Nehru suit. On one hand he sported a big jeweled ring; in the other, he held a gold-headed mahogany cane," Belafonte recalled. Part of Belafonte's criticism of Stokely stemmed from an unspoken competition between the two. The similarities between the two handsome activists of Caribbean descent did not stop with their similar radical politics, love of Africa, and courageous ability to speak truth to power. Both were also charismatic, intelligent, and politically astute. But their personal confidence and large egos could rub each other the wrong way. Both men embraced the spotlight.

When they first met in 1961, Stokely was a twenty-year-old student activist and Belafonte was the international star and movement benefactor. Stokely's ability, during the late 1960s, to take some of this spotlight away from Belafonte, along with Makeba, sparked a low-intensity conflict that was fueled as much by personal animosity as by politics. Belafonte's memory of Carmichael's expensive clothes during his time with Miriam does capture a certain moment in Stokely's life that came to an end after his divorce. In short order, the Stokely whom Miriam first met, who preferred sharecropper's overalls and straw hats to custom suits, returned.

But Carmichael would never properly confront the abuses of the Touré regime. Indeed, to do so, after he had taken Touré's surname, would be more than an admission of flawed judgment. It would be a negation of the self. For Ture, the Guinean government's mistakes paled in comparison to the global havoc wrought by American presidents. Hadn't Nixon authorized bombing campaigns in Cambodia and Vietnam that caused untold human suffering? Ronald Reagan's version of the Cold War abandoned the Carter administration's commitment to human rights in favor of muscular anti-Communist campaigns that spread chaos throughout parts of the Caribbean and Latin America, and even parts of Africa. From this perspective, Sékou Touré had nothing to apologize for if his heart remained committed to the Pan-African revolution that Nkrumah had outlined and Stokely staked his life on.[67]

In 1981, Kwame Ture married Marliatou Barre, a Guinean doctor. They had a son the next year, Boabacar "Bocar" Biro. At forty years old, he now sported flecks of gray in his hair, and a more notable accent, a combination of West Africa, Trinidad, and the American South. Ture snatched moments of domestic tranquility in between speaking to raise money and political consciousness. Despite modest success recruiting new members into the AAPRP, Ture's dreams of mobilizing a political revolution through Pan-Africanism receded against a backdrop of counter-revolution in the United States and abroad. Old political friendships found Ture speaking at the Nation of Islam's Savior's Day celebration alongside Louis Farrakhan and addressing militants in Brooklyn, who hailed him as an indefatigable political warrior.[68]

During the 1980s, Ture remained enthralled by a vision of Africa that rested more on the political imagination of a long tradition of Pan-Africanists than on the ordinary lives of Africans who cared less about ideology than survival. Ture now operated in a political reality where issues of neocolonialism, apartheid, and imperialism converged in stark ways. President Ronald Reagan and British prime minister Margaret Thatcher formed a global duo who ushered in neoliberal economic policies that placed new fiscal constraints on the Third World. The Cold War's waning days created ideological lines sharp enough to find America supporting white supremacists in South Africa as a bulwark against opposition movements suspected of being communists. Randall Robinson, who had cut his teeth in African Liberation Day celebrations during the 1970s, responded by forming TransAfrica with Harry Belafonte, the most important anti-apartheid organization of the era. Jesse Jackson, with whom Ture remained on friendly terms, became this movement's biggest mobilizer, turning the question of South Africa into a centerpiece of his foreign policy during his candidacy in the 1984 Democratic presidential primary. In a very real sense, the decade found political leaders rehearsing debates and controversies that could be traced back to the 1960s.

Revolutionary icons related to the era of African decolonization were fading fast however. Sékou Touré's death during emergency heart surgery in Cleveland on March 26, 1984, triggered domestic upheavals in Guinea that toppled the one-party state's ruling faction. Like a soldier valiantly fighting what many considered to be a forgotten war, Ture remained, according to the April 12, 1984, edition of *The New York Times,* "the unrepentant voice of the 60s." And he remained a captivating figure at forty-two, his previously unlined face showing signs of middle age and little sleep. He charmed journalists with his easy smile and self-deprecating humor, yet could instantly switch to the revolutionary ideologue. After the provisional Guinean government opened up Conakry's notorious Camp Boiro prison to illustrate to Western journalists and observers the depth of the Touré regime's mistreatment of political prisoners, Ture remained unapologetic. "In all the world's great movements from Christ's to Gandhi's, blood has had to flow," he said. "If anything, I think Sékou Touré was too soft." But the corruption in the regime to which Ture remained loyal could be seen in the incarceration and death of former Guinean ambassador Achkar Marof, who had co-hosted Stokely and Miriam's wedding reception.[69]

The death of his political patron and subsequent coup made Ture confront an existential crisis about his political future. "This was a time of deep sadness and anxiety for all my friends," he remembered. It was also a time filled with fear and introspection. He seriously contemplated leaving Guinea to ensure the safety of his wife and young son. "But the only principled decision possible for me was to stay," Ture observed in his memoir. "I wasn't about to cut and run." Carmichael dived into post-revolutionary Guinea's complex political landscape, emerging as a member of the PDG's central committee and serving as the group's liaison to the Cuban embassy. After initial hesitation, he resumed a relentless schedule of political organizing for the now dissident PDG. Ture railed against the new regime's cordial ties to France but recognized the presence of "a few competent, decent, and hardworking Europeans with some respect for Africa and Africans and a commitment to humanity." In such fleeting instances, the old Stokely Carmichael's infectious openness to political allies and unlikely coalitions resurfaced.[70]

In many ways, his Guinea was a country turned upside down. The release of political prisoners and the return of exiled citizens and figures once labeled as traitors produced a sense of vertigo that personally touched Ture on Friday, August 15, 1986. That day authorities searched his home and then escorted him to a police station in Conakry where they detained him over the weekend. Charged with plotting a coup along with other PDG members, Ture's prison cell was in fact an unoccupied office in Conakry's central police station. The timely intervention of AAPRP colleagues such as Bob Brown and civil rights leaders including Andrew Young, Jesse Jackson, and Chicago mayor Harold Washington ended Ture's forced detention after three days amid unsubstantiated rumors that the government would expel him. During a debriefing meeting with US embassy officials the day after his release, Ture seemed calm and assured enough to joke that this latest arrest was his fortieth.[71]

The next Tuesday he paid a surprise visit to the US embassy in Conakry. He thanked officials for intervening in his case and reported that he had had "no difficulties with Guinean authorities since his arrest." Ture's brief incarceration exposed him to the dangers of being part of the opposition in Guinea, a position that had landed many of Sékou Touré's enemies in jail or worse. Allegations that Ture had personally threatened the life of Minister of Planning Edouard Benjamin reached the State Department and helped fuel the government's anxiety of a possible coup. Tensions between Ture's opposition party and the new government would remain high, with each side declaring the other a brutal enemy capable of torture, death threats, and worse.[72]

Ture's precarious status in post-revolutionary Guinea found him in the familiar position of being considered a subversive dissident in his adopted land. He confronted whatever internal doubts he possessed about his place in history and culpability in the failures of Sékou Touré's government by investing himself more deeply in political activism.

In 1992, twenty-five years after its initial publication, Ture wrote a new afterword to *Black Power: The Politics of Liberation*. In it, he promoted a Pan-African revolution while analyzing race in America and around the world since the 1960s. Black Power, he wrote, had been prophetic in many ways, calling for still unimplemented political reforms. Writing two months after Los Angeles' massive riot, Ture posited an unbroken legacy of black activism that stretched back to antebellum slavery and crossed borders into Africa and faraway nations. Creative, improvisational measures advocated in 1967 now gave way to "Nkrumahism-Tureism," and the belief that his two dead mentors possessed secrets capable of changing the world.[73]

––––––––––––––

IN 1995, TURE HAD BEEN PLAGUED BY HIP AND LEG PAIN, and he finally succumbed to May Charles' insistence that he seek medical attention. A diagnosis of advanced prostate cancer in 1996 would, in Ture's recollection, "bring out the best" in former colleagues and friends, who raised funds for medical treatment in the States and abroad. Friends, supporters, and family surrounded him after his release from Columbia-Presbyterian Medical Center in New York at the end of February. The fifty-four-year-old activist, with a gray beard that matched his hair, wore a long flowing white boubou and balked at requests for interviews. Old SNCC allies called him about his health while others sent messages of concern. In the hospital, Ture and a circle of friends reminisced about political struggles fought since the 1960s. "I know," he told one reporter, "that my people love me."[74]

Old friends chipped away at the mask of the activist politician in interviews, conversations, and fetes to reclaim fleeting intimacies now buried by Ture's obsession to single-handedly ignite a political revolution. Charlie Cobb, a one-time confidant, found that, underneath his old friend's political vigilance, lay "the old loose Stokely" full of energy and eager to laugh. More often than not, however, Ture remained inside a cocoon of political certitude.[75]

The race against time included efforts, assisted by Mike Thelwell, to complete a long overdue autobiography. If Ture lived in a political reality of his own making, it was a world that grew larger as his illness progressed. Ture wanted to return to Conakry to live out his final days conducting political work. A rump group of friends and family that included Cleve Sellers convinced him that an international network of supporters would cover medical costs so as not to burden May Charles, now retired and living in Florida.[76]

Willie Ricks, from his political base in Atlanta, kept the memories of Ture's Black Power heyday alive. A fixture on the campuses of the local black colleges and universities in Atlanta, Ricks (who adopted the name Mukasa Dada) chided black students to continue to struggle for racial justice long after such rhetoric had gone out of fashion. In this he remained consistent. As a young SNCC organizer dressed in blue overalls, Ricks had chastised potential recruits about how he and his colleagues were making history instead of merely studying it. New generations of Morehouse, Spelman, and Clark Atlanta University students were introduced to the legacy of Black Power and Ture's work through Ricks' tireless activism.[77]

Ture's friendship with Louis Farrakhan made the Nation of Islam a consistent source of financial and political support, while a network of family and political supporters established the Kwame Ture Medical Fund to cover his medical expenses.

Frantic efforts for treatment took him to New York hospitals, Cuban clinics, and a holistic center in Honduras. When he traveled to Cuba in the summer of 1996, he was in good spirits, telling a reporter in Havana, "Revolution is the continual and qualitative constant change of humanity. That's all it is." Ture acknowledged racial progress since the 1960s but remained troubled by the way many blacks defined success. "The number of congress people has increased, the number of newspaper commentators, the number of basketball players," he said, grinning. "Put that in there, because they think that they got there without their people's struggles." This last statement attested to his realization that the power cords of racial unity struck during Black Power's heyday had sagged in recent decades, weighed down by a relentless search for materialism and neoliberal global politics that redefined the civil rights movement as a testament to individual achievement rather than to collective action. The nation that came closest to achieving his vision of a socialist state was Libya. "For us once Africa is united and strong, the problem will be solved because Africans will be respected wherever they are. And if they are not, they can just get up and go home." Beginning in the 1970s, Stokely maintained a close relationship with Libyan President Muammar Gaddafi.[78]

Further travels, for sentimental reasons, took him back to Guinea and then to Ghana, Egypt, and South Africa. There were other trips as well. Perhaps most notable was Ture's return to the land of his birth and early years. On June 12, 1996, Ture made his first public appearance (he had returned clandestinely before this) in Trinidad. He spoke to students at the National Heritage Library, imploring them to use books and study as tools to create a more just society. The government of Trinidad and Tobago gave Ture a $1,000 monthly allowance for medical bills, payback for having shunned a native son for decades because of his radical politics.[79]

Like Martin Luther King, Ture made a career out of a financial chastity, a choice that left him economically bereft and totally dependent upon the good will of the black community he affectionately referred to as "my people." Jesse Jackson stopped by Ture's bedside, and Louis Farrakhan kept in regular contact from Chicago. A visit by Kathleen Cleaver and her two children was followed, coincidentally, by a phone call from Eldridge Cleaver living his last year in California. Cleaver would die on May 1, 1998. Charlie Cobb reminisced with Ture about political adventures at Howard University and Mississippi. "The Stokely I remember is charismatic, full of ego and electricity—and laughter," recalled Cobb. For Cobb, the middle-aged Kwame Ture would always be Stokely Carmichael, "in blue jeans and a denim shirt leaning against a shack talking with a sharecropper."[80]

Ture's discovery that several of his SNCC comrades also suffered from cancer led him to blame his own illness on government-inspired biological warfare. Unsubstantiated theories connecting his cancer to American intelligence agencies would posthumously resurface, in the form of poignant, if fanciful, autobiographical declarations that identified a web of unsanctioned medical experiments targeting unwitting victims. Ture's claim that the CIA gave him cancer reflected the stress of over thirty years of unbroken surveillance, harassment, and investigation of both his political activities and his personal life. Over the next two years, he spent considerable time in America seeking treatment and reuniting with old friends and family. He spoke wistfully of being unable to spend time with his growing family, which now, in addition to the teenaged Bocar included a four-year-old son. But he reasoned that once they understood his political history, they would understand why "the people are more important than them."[81]

On Wednesday, April 8, 1998, hundreds of Ture's friends and colleagues gathered in Washington, DC, to pay tribute to his legacy of political activism. Memories of attending a similar event for one of his early political mentors, CORE activist Julius Hobson, over twenty-five years earlier, must have come to Ture's mind. The event was organized by Karen Spellman, a friend from Howard University associated with NAG. "It seems my whole life was there," Ture would write afterward. Close enough. Past SNCC chairmen John Lewis, Marion Barry, and Jamil Al-Amin (Rap Brown) joined Ture on a platform that included Louis Farrakhan, Amiri Baraka, and representatives from numerous organizations that had shaped his personal and political life. Friends and colleagues from Bronx Science, Howard University, NAG, the Black Panthers, SNCC, SDS, and the AAPRP coalesced, for one last time, around Kwame Ture. The somber reason for the gathering gave way to the joy of old friends whom Ture had not seen in years, sometimes decades, reuniting once more.[82]

On Friday, June 26, Ture staged a sit-in at the offices of NAACP chairman and old SNCC colleague Julian Bond after Bond had canceled a scheduled meeting with Ture and Louis Farrakhan. Despite Bond's being away from the office on vacation, Ture sat in for thirteen hours to draw attention to a vision of black unity that transcended ideological differences.[83]

Nine days after his sit-in, on Friday July 5, 1998, Ture departed New York City for the last time en route to Conakry. Jesse Jackson, in Guinea as part of his duties as the White House's special African envoy, visited him on November 12 and 13, the last Thursday and Friday he would ever see. Emaciated, with less than one hundred pounds on his once-sturdy six-foot-one-inch frame, Kwame Ture died on November 15 in Guinea, on the west coast of Africa he called home.

Kwame Ture's star-crossed relationship with the new government of Guinea made the granting of an official state funeral on Sunday, November 22, both an unanticipated honor and begrudging recognition that the former Stokely Carmichael's iconic status transcended political parties and ideological disputes. Family, political supporters, foreign diplomats, and hundreds of mourners came together that Sunday for memorial services at Conakry's Gamal Abdel Nasser University. Hundreds of people, including diplomats from Cuba and Libya, gathered at an outdoor pavilion while Ture's coffin rested on a table. Speakers combined political rhetoric with personal memories that recalled Ture's sensitivity, infectious humor, and political commitment. May Charles led a contingent of relatives that included Ture's four sisters and his second ex-wife, Marliatou Barre. His seventeen-year-old son Bocar said that his father would be "very happy" to be laid to rest in Guinea. John Lewis, now a Georgia congressman, sent a public statement of grief over his one-time adversary's death: "I am deeply saddened by the death of Stokely Carmichael. He spent his lifetime committed to the principles of freedom and racial equality for people of African descent around the world. He never wavered. He never yielded to popular criticism."[84]

A wide range of family, friends, and colleagues traveled to Conakry to pay their respects. AAPRP organizers, government officials, and representatives from Libya, Cuba, Trinidad and Tobago, Palestine, and the Nation of Islam came. Guinea's foreign minister, Lamine Camara, read a message from President Lansana Conte. "All Africa mourns our brother, a son who chose to return to his roots." Camara's personal journey from a seven-year stay in Camp Boiro prison to foreign minister attending the funeral of one of Sékou Touré's staunchest allies illustrated the ironies of Guinean politics. The Cuban ambassador praised Ture's support for "real democracy" while the Palestinian representative noted the poetic symmetry of the funeral coinciding with the twenty-eighth anniversary of Guinea's victory over Portuguese-sponsored invaders, a historic event Ture always recalled with great satisfaction. Sinn

Féin sent a letter of support praising Ture's solidarity with political dissidents in Ireland, while one observer noted that media coverage proved "that the capitalists can only recognize him as a great man after his death."[85]

Bob Brown, perhaps Ture's closest political ally over the past quarter-century, recalled him as a tireless worker who, until his last days, struggled to promote the political revolution he remained defiantly committed to. A sixty-car procession escorted Ture to his final resting place, Cameroun Cemetery. Three framed pictures of Kwame Ture and Presidents Kwame Nkrumah and Sékou Touré adorned the flower-covered casket. Buried in a public cemetery that housed Christians and Muslims, Ture's final resting place would be in Cameroun's left side among Muslims.

Epilogue:
From Stokely Carmichael to Kwame Ture

IN THE 1960S, STOKELY CARMICHAEL TRANSFORMED AMERICAN DEMOCRACY and race relations. In doing so he achieved a level of political notoriety that rivaled, indeed at times surpassed, that of Malcolm X. Poised between Malcolm's sword and Martin's shield, Carmichael deployed both in an effort to reimagine America's purpose, destiny, and soul.

His political activism during the decade offered a genealogy of black political activism and its local, national, and global character. Carmichael's exodus to Africa and subsequent travails enlarged the scope of his political ambitions even as it diminished the memory of youthful exploits. His activism helped to shape the political outlook of an entire generation. Carmichael's student organizing at Howard University anticipated the creation of black student unions and the rise of Black Studies programs, and he counted himself as one of the earliest members of SNCC and a veteran Freedom Rider. Carmichael's unique persona allowed him to wear business suits, leather jackets, dashikis, Nehru jackets, and sharecropper's overalls with an unadorned grace and dignity that made him a global icon: a rock star whose political speeches proved no less popular than a musical performance. Carmichael's good looks, brash intelligence, and bold politics created a brand-new version of radical style and culture in late 1960s America.

Stokely Carmichael's political and historical legacy, as well as his contemporary relevance, remains overshadowed by the ritualized commemorations and national celebrations associated with the civil rights movement's heroic period. His central role in reshaping domestic race relations and reimagining American democracy is overwhelmed by his volatile public image and fiery polemics. This is as unfortunate as it is historically shortsighted. Carmichael is best recognized as the activist who unleashed Black Power upon an unsuspecting nation. The physical contrast between Carmichael and Martin Luther King, one short and stout, the other long and lean, mirrors the popular perception regarding civil rights and Black Power. These movements came out of a historic moment of racial crisis, one filled with undreamed-of possibilities, when blacks found themselves excluded from American prosperity even after helping secure world peace in the Second World War. Southern civil rights activists reached back to the social justice advocated by black militants during the Depression era, although they scaled back its radical social-democratic politics. Black Power activists promoted racial unity, self-determination, and internationalism in a quest to right ancient historical wrongs. Despite robust debate over tactics and strategies, activists from one camp switched to the other, and certain organizations and individuals simultaneously straddled both approaches. Both movements dreamed of fundamentally altering American democratic institutions but settled for exposing rough truths and hard lessons of social change, racial justice, and economic equality. In doing so, they helped to forever transform race in America.

Of all of Carmichael's personas—Black Power icon, civil rights organizer, Black Panther, revolutionary Pan-Africanist—perhaps the least recognized is that of public intellectual. It was a role in which he thrived, while also consciously fulfilling his youthful dreams of becoming a college professor. Life experiences, as much as books, marked his political education. Trinidad, the Bronx, Harlem, Mississippi, Alabama, Cuba, and Conakry are some of the geographical landscapes that shaped him, just as May Charles and Adolphus, Martin and Malcolm, Fannie Lou Hamer and Ella Baker offer glimpses of his role models. Whether vowing to end the Vietnam War as a young organizer or railing against the evils of social injustice in middle age, Carmichael embraced the identity of teacher. His audience changed over time, however, as did he, with his earlier more flexible and humorous lectures giving way to a more strident and less equivocal posture. The crowds that gathered in rapt attention to his Black Power iconography were larger than for his subsequent evolutions, but he remained steadfast in his belief that political education would lead to transformations in consciousness, identity, and values necessary to achieve revolutionary change.

Carmichael's political exodus to Africa afforded him the political maturity denied Malcolm X and Martin Luther King. Time, however, came at a high cost, removing him from domestic racial struggles and curtailing his political influence. He refused to characterize his departure as self-imposed exile, contending that he had merely returned home. There were also self-inflicted wounds. Carmichael's All-African People's Revolutionary Party failed to convince large numbers of the viability of his Pan-African dreams. Raucous debate over the black revolution's correct ideology redirected vital energy away from organizing and toward sectarian political struggles that seemed far removed from the lives of ordinary black people. Carmichael's increasingly rigid application of Kwame Nkrumah's political thought offered audiences the unappealing prospect of replacing one kind of orthodoxy (capitalism) with a new one (socialism).

His support of the increasingly paranoid and erratic Sékou Touré proved tragic. Touré's youthful dreams attracted a host of glamorous supporters at the dawn of Guinea's revolution. Over time, Guinea's bright dreams turned dark, marked by Touré's growing political isolation and the brutal incarceration of former allies. Kwame Ture, the loyal political ally of the Guinean president and its ruling political party, remained publicly silent about the revolution's decay and the government's corresponding descent into authoritarianism. This inability to confront the depredations of the governments of Guinea and other African nations with the same moral power and force that he deployed against Jim Crow in the 1960s allowed him, up until his death, to align himself with a host of authoritarian figures that the young Stokely Carmichael would have shunned. But this evolution did not take place in a vacuum. The American government's illegal surveillance and harassment of Carmichael, which continued long after his Black Power heyday, changed him. This illegal use of power, which stretched from the White House to national and international intelligence agencies to local police departments, helped to shape Carmichael's increasingly jaundiced view of American democracy. He came to view America as a hopelessly corrupt empire even as he turned a blind eye to the contradictions of the postcolonial African state and the larger Third World.

If Stokely's call for "Black Power" in Mississippi remains the most iconic part of his legacy, multiple dimensions of his activism helped to transform American democracy in the 1960s. His willingness, indeed eagerness, to risk physical danger for freedom's cause earned him a well-deserved reputation for courage and fearlessness. Carmichael's activism changed the aesthetics of the black freedom struggle in ways that still reverberate around the world. Through speeches, books, and interviews, Carmichael transformed the discourse on race, war, and democracy in a manner that influenced Martin Luther King. Carmichael, at his critically improvisational best, reimagined democracy's political, geographical, and economic frontiers. And he did so with style. Following Malcolm X and Martin Luther King, he turned the quest for black freedom and citizenship into a performance that enthralled and inspired supporters.

Carmichael's most enduring identity is that of an organizer. As a teenaged activist in Harlem, Freedom Rider in Mississippi, Howard University student, and fomenter of insurrection from Alabama to Africa, Carmichael transformed local, national, and global race relations. More than any other activist of his generation, Carmichael shaped the contours of civil rights and Black Power activism through participation in sit-ins, Freedom Rides, independent political organizing, and antiwar protests. From the Mississippi Delta and Lowndes County to the gritty streets of Harlem and Oakland out to the international cities of Havana, Conakry, Paris, and Dar es Salaam, Carmichael utilized his uncanny gifts to form coalitions of the powerless to combat racial and economic oppression. He tapped into what Martin Luther King memorably called "the great wells of democracy" through organizing black sharecroppers in the Deep South and urban militants in northern ghettoes. He imagined the Mississippi Delta as the birthplace of a new America and placed more faith in ordinary people than in political leaders or politicians. For Carmichael, America's racial underclass represented democracy's last hope.

Carmichael's style and tactics stoked controversy within the black movement, with many disapproving of the harsh tenor of his anti-American jeremiad and his call for black political self-determination. Activists split over Carmichael's bold approach and confrontational tactics. His unabashed criticism of white liberals and Zionism alienated old friends and former colleagues. Yet Carmichael's outspoken antiwar rhetoric anticipated, and helped to spur, a national change of heart regarding Vietnam. He unapologetically attacked the war as an example of American ideological hubris and imperial ambition. Carmichael's beliefs anticipated and emboldened both King and Muhammad Ali, the duo most commonly associated with anti–Vietnam War protest. His antiwar posture placed him on the cutting edge of a global revolutionary politics that linked domestic Jim Crow to anti-colonial insurgencies sweeping the world. It also identified Black Power as a complex human rights movement that viewed revolution, violence, and urgent means as a sword against racism, war, and poverty. Human rights activism remained at the core of his political life even as his ideological positions changed over time.

Carmichael's first international tour introduced him to the world stage and the process that would transform him into Kwame Ture, Pan-Africanist revolutionary. Politically, trips to Cuba, Algeria, Vietnam, and Guinea thrust him into the high altitude of anti-colonial struggles, a world that muffled his more poetic side. As Kwame Ture, his radicalism appeared largely anachronistic in a post–civil rights global landscape where former militants reinvented themselves as political reformers, entrepreneurs, and elected officials. Long after Black Power's heyday, Ture insisted that America, far from being a purveyor of freedom and democracy, was in fact an empire.

During the last two years of Martin Luther King's life, Carmichael dominated national and international politics, occupying the role of King's chief political counterpart. Whereas King and Malcolm X met only once in passing, Stokely and Martin developed a warm friendship that took shape on the civil rights movement's front lines. King recognized Carmichael as a radical warrior for democracy even as he disagreed with his talk of self-defense and confrontation. Carmichael, in turn, respected King as an authentic political leader and uncanny mobilizer whose rapport with ordinary black folk remained unparalleled. In a very real sense, Malcolm X, Stokely Carmichael, and Martin Luther King form a largely unacknowledged trio whose revolutionary politics dominated the world stage during the 1960s.

Stokely Carmichael's iconography remains both earthier and less appreciated than that of his two closest historical counterparts. Of the three, only he would live to see the age of forty. His time as a civil rights militant turned Black Power revolutionary established the stellar credentials that burnished his iconography even after his celebrity diminished. Carmichael's rare combination of personal authenticity and political sincerity made him a historically transcendent figure. Beyond the public image of the indefatigable political warrior lay a flesh-and-blood human being, one whose political career exacted a substantial personal cost in the form of two failed marriages, time away from his two sons, and the failure to receive routine medical care that might have saved his life.

Carmichael's greatest legacy on the national and international stage remains his role as a political educator. In thousands of speeches, interviews, and lectures, he preached forgotten lessons about political self-determination, cultural dignity, and racial solidarity. His elevation of black sharecroppers in

Mississippi and Alabama challenged contemporary notions of citizenship, just as his unabashed embrace of Africa redefined racial and ethnic boundaries. His gift for fashioning a coherent intellectual vision out of disparate political and cultural traditions made him, like the jazz musicians he admired, a master of improvisation who found no contradiction in his ability to draw lessons from Malcolm X, Fannie Lou Hamer, Martin Luther King, Ella Baker, Fidel Castro, and Kwame Nkrumah.

Carmichael forever changed the course of American history thirteen days before turning twenty-five. His Black Power cry altered national race relations in a manner that still confounds and stirred controversy within the black movement for its blunt language and threats of violence. Carmichael's inescapable message—that black citizenship required unprecedented levels of political self-determination—continues to both resonate and haunt contemporary American society. Stokely's words echoed throughout the nation with reverberations that would soon reach the far corners of the world. During the first half of the 1960s, Carmichael expansively reimagined the outer limits of American democracy, finding comfort in the idea that black sharecroppers in rural Mississippi and Alabama might one day control their own destiny. According to Carmichael, genuine democracy in parts of America sometimes required guns as defense against racial terror that local authorities denied and the federal government ignored. His vision of democracy sought to turn abstract notions of freedom and citizenship into reality through the collective action of poor, unlettered, and forgotten people. On this score, Carmichael's political strategy during the first half of the 1960s dovetailed with Martin Luther King even if his tactics differed. He fashioned a sophisticated understanding of the connection between race, democracy, and war that made him the nation's most outspoken antiwar activist and the FBI's most sought-after dissident. In doing so, Carmichael transformed national race relations by consciously connecting Black Power to Vietnam. He framed America's involvement in colonial wars as a betrayal of its democratic traditions while simultaneously upholding black sharecroppers as democracy's best hope and final opportunity.

Carmichael's democratic vision receded as the decade progressed, worn down by white backlash and mesmerized by a global political vision that combined revolutionary Pan-Africanism with Third World anti-imperialism. The world stage offered him confirmation that politics contained unimaginable layers, and he quickly established an alliance with Kwame Nkrumah and Sékou Touré in hopes of utilizing Africa to further the political revolution he helped to ignite as a college student. As Kwame Ture, he argued that blacks around the world were Africans who shunned their ancestral homeland at the expense of establishing a powerful collective identity. In this way, he saw himself as completing the political circle of radical Pan-African political engagement begun by Malcolm X. Ture's bold vision of black nationalism, which evolved into full-throated faith in Pan-Africanism, ran past Malcolm's. Malcolm died seeing himself as a black man attempting to escape America's searing racial wilderness. Ture, until his last breath, identified himself as an African.

Blessed with the gift of a greater longevity that eluded both King and Malcolm, he became a professional revolutionary, outspoken anti-imperialist, and jet-setting Pan-Africanist. This last identity received a warm welcome from hard-core black militants and true believers, and skeptical, even dismissive, treatment from critics. Intelligence agencies hedged their bets by continuing surveillance and gloating that Ture's latest incarnation failed to attract a large following. The claustrophobic environs of sectarian politics changed Ture and blunted his political effectiveness. The man who once freely admitted to doubts and confusion about the direction of black politics in the late 1960s embraced Nkrumahism-Tureism as a political cure to Africa's ills despite mounting evidence to the contrary. Political faith, however, carried a high cost. His vision of an idealized Africa, bound by a unifying culture, ideology, and economic system, seemed to at times veer toward magical thinking. Ture's past success in shaping history through acts of sheer will and extraordinary political organizing convinced him that the black community remained destined for a rendezvous with victory, even if it was one that he would not live to see.

Kwame Ture's unapologetic articulation of Pan-African revolution continued unabated into the 1980s as America made a wrenching transition from the Great Society's hopeful politics to the more austere Reagan era. The political space that, for a time, allowed revolutionaries such as Martin Luther King, Malcolm X, and a young Stokely Carmichael to thrive no longer existed. Ture's unwavering belief in revolutionary politics became regarded in the post–civil rights era as a kind of affliction. Barack Obama's inability to comprehend the full meaning behind Ture's anti-imperialism while he was a student at Columbia in the early 1980s reflects a generational transition that Carmichael helped to spur. Ture defiantly proclaimed the inevitability of a worldwide socialist revolution even as a majority of the most well-known civil rights activists of his generation pragmatically adapted to new political realities, realities that Obama would soon embrace as a national politician and the nation's first black president.

Ture's legacy remains central to understanding a historical epoch with which our collective memory has yet to make peace. Ture's journey from civil rights militant and Black Power icon to the revolutionary socialist who unfurled the Pan-African banner high enough for much of the world to see indelibly changed the black freedom struggle. He leaves behind a complex legacy, one marked by historic successes, glaring errors of judgment, and both large and small political failures. If Ture's once clear-eyed organizing vision faltered over misplaced faith in flawed politicians, he remained an indefatigable warrior for political and social justice. Just as the dogged pursuit of radical democracy marked his early civil rights activism, dreams of global political transformation would inspire the professional organizer he became.

Ture's revolutionary politics took shape against the backdrop of a domestic war for America's very soul. The question, asked by one SNCC activist, whether Mississippi would become part of America or the nation would turn into the Magnolia State remained unanswered long after the 1960s. Ture's embrace of black nationalism and revolutionary Pan-Africanism was at least partially shaped by the stubborn adherence to white supremacy that claimed the lives of fellow activists and poised him, more than once, on the verge of a nervous breakdown. In the face of increased resistance to the very idea of black equality and robust democracy, Ture abandoned his use of tactical nonviolence in favor of a political struggle he remained determine to wage from Africa and the larger Third World.

In the 1960s, Ture's critics openly advocated abandoning constitutional principles to arrest him. The FBI, White House, and Justice Department used their vast resources to illegally surveil, harass, and curtail his political activism. Intelligence agencies innovated measures on Ture that they later used against the Black Panthers. Even after departing the United States for Africa, he remained under the watchful eye of national and international intelligence agencies. *The Saturday Evening Post*'s proudly racist declaration that all white Americans were Mississippians after the Meredith March signaled to Ture, and many in his generation, that civil rights activism had exposed a deeper wellspring of hatred and inequality than previously imagined. Whereas Ture had once seen democracy as capacious enough to quell the evils of Jim Crow, by the late 1960s his gnawing skepticism turned into open apostasy. Having lost faith in the democratic institutions that promised to end ancient racial injustices, Ture found renewed purpose in the political environs traveled by African and Third World revolutionaries even as he remained indebted to Martin Luther King for inspiring him to face racial terror without fear.

Between 1966 and 1968, Ture became a more vilified figure in the United States than Malcolm X had been. Presidential candidates accused him of treason, politicians called for his deportation and arrest, and the Justice Department seriously considered charging him with sedition. Ture's notoriety thrust him into the ages as a revolutionary icon. If his creative versatility, intellectual dexterity, and deft ability to travel in multiple worlds marked his youthful activism, a belief in the higher purpose of the African Revolution guided his final three decades.

His final political evolution displayed flashes of youthful energy tempered by hard-earned political maturity. The boldest political activist of his generation gave way to the most stubborn. A belief in the power of self-determination in the face of long odds marked the arc of his life's activism, and traces of poetry could still be found in his most vociferous exhortations. When he was a young man struggling for an expansive vision of citizenship and democracy, Ture's activism defied conventional wisdom and embraced the seemingly quixotic belief that Jim Crow might be toppled and democracy flourish in parts of America where it had never existed. Considering Ture's historic success in bringing about new worlds in the American South and new realities domestically and internationally, it's not surprising that he believed that ultimate victory, while delayed, could never be denied. During his last, turbulent years, Ture increasingly defined politics as another form of combat, war by other means. His lifetime offered potent examples that underdogs could defeat Goliaths. Ture remained both an organizer and an itinerant activist who dedicated his life to combating social and political injustices long past their expiration dates in the American and global imagination. In so doing, Kwame Ture displayed the kind of revolutionary spirit that would have made the young Stokely Carmichael proud.

Acknowledgments

My journey into the life of Stokely Carmichael/Kwame Ture started in earnest a decade ago as I completed my first book on the history of the Black Power Movement. During the course of that time, my life has undergone sometimes dramatic and sometimes subtle changes. What has remained constant is the generosity of friends, the love of my family, and the graciousness of a wide and international network of professional colleagues, archivists, and activists who aided in the book's completion.

A resident fellowship at Harvard University's Charles Warren Center allowed me valuable time and space to conduct research around the center's theme of "Race and Law in the Making of the Long Civil Rights Movement." Evelyn Brooks Higginbotham, one of the Warren Center's co-conveners that year, has been unbelievably generous in both her personal friendship and professional support of my work. Ken Mack's quiet determination to mine undiscovered historical territory helped to set the perfect tone for what was an important year of research and writing.

My students and colleagues at the University of Rhode Island, Stony Brook University, and Brandeis were extraordinarily patient with me as I rattled on about Stokely Carmichael's significance.

Joining the faculty of Tufts University in 2009 proved to be especially beneficial to this biography's completion. I would like to thank all of my colleagues in the history department for their support and interest in my work. Thanks to Virginia Drachman, Alisha Rankin, Elizabeth Foster, Howard Malchow, Ben Carp, David Ekladh, Beatrice Manz, Ina Baghdiantz McCabe, Reed Ueda, Steve Marrone, Gary Leupp, Kris Manjapra, Hugh Roberts, Peter Winn, Ayesha Jalal, Christopher Schmidt-Nowara, Jeanne Penvenne, David Proctor, Man Xu, Leila Fawaz, and Dan Mulholland. Annette Lazzara Aloise, our department administrator, is brilliant at her job and a wonderful person as well. Jamshed Bharucha, the former provost and now president of Cooper Union, provided enthusiastic support for my work. Tufts University president Anthony Monaco, provost David Harris, and dean of the School of Arts and

Sciences Joanne Berger-Sweeney have been steadfast in supporting the creation of the Center for the Study of Race and Democracy, a research center that is the by-product of an interest in race and democracy that my research on Stokely Carmichael further amplified.

Liz has been a friend from my first day on campus and for that I am grateful. Dennis Rasmussen, Emily Wiemers, Stephan Pennington, and Dai Ellis all expressed interest about this book project and have listened to its progression in various stages.

Thanks to all of the activists, scholars, writers, former colleagues, and friends of Stokely Carmichael/Kwame Ture who agreed to be interviewed by me. Thanks to the numerous archives, listed in the bibliography, which were indispensible to this book's completion. Ian Greaves provided important research assistance during earlier stages of this project. Theresa Sullivan, Nina Bernstein, and Benji Cohen have been invaluable to completing this biography.

Ambre Ivol invited me to the Université de Nantes in France to speak about my research on Stokely, and Hélène de Lantec-Lowery organized a lecture at the Université Sorbonne Nouvelle. Both talks were stimulating and provided me the opportunity to do research on Stokely's time in Paris and meet with wonderful new colleagues.

The late Columbia University historian Manning Marable was completing his major biography of Malcolm X while I was working on this book. Manning's death represents a great loss for scholar-activists devoted to researching and writing about the history of black radicalism. When I was a young graduate student, Manning's work inspired me, and he generously supported my work and aspirations as a junior scholar even as he battled a debilitating illness. Walter Hill and Ronald Walters left us too soon, but I'm grateful for their support and mentorship.

Robin D.G. Kelley's groundbreaking scholarship continues to serve as a source of inspiration. Gerald Horne was kind enough to pause from his prodigious scholarship on black internationalism to provide words of encouragement and to carefully read an entire manuscript on short notice. Herb Boyd's comments were brilliantly instructive and insightful. Numerous colleagues helped to make this work better in ways both large and small. On this score thanks go to Jeremi Suri, Tom Sugrue, Obery Hendricks, Farah Jasmine Griffin, Sandy Darity, Jeanne Theoharis, Ira Katznelson, Darlene Clark Hine, Nell Irvin Painter, Peter Levy, Barbara Ransby, Ibram X.

Xendi, Martha Biondi, David Levering Lewis, Taylor Branch, Robert Caro, Nico Slate, Donna Murch, Zachery Williams, Dayo Gore, Kent Germany, Johanna Fernandez, Robyn Spencer, Russell Rickford, Premilla Nadasen, James Jennings, Gene Jarrett, Linda Heywood, John Thornton, Kenneth Kusmer, Bettye Collier-Thomas, William Julius Wilson, Lawrence Bobo, Clarence Lang, Tommie Shelby, Komozi Woodard, Eddie Glaude, Khalil Gibran Muhammad, Michael Thelwell, Bill Strickland, Ernie Allen, Lawrence Jackson, Dwayne Mack, Derek Musgrove, Scot Brown, Jeff Ogbar, Hasan Jeffries, Sharon Harley, Lewis Gordon, Jane Gordon, David Oshinsky, Angela Aards, Michael Ralph, Waldo Martin, Michelle Alexander, and Cornel West.

Yohuru Williams has been a great friend and brother for fifteen years. Rhonda Y. Williams continues to be an exemplar of the best tradition of merging scholarship with community building. Matthew Whitaker, Jeremy Levitt, Ricky Jones, and Jelani Cobb are terrific scholars and just plain good people. Olufemi Vaughan is that rare combination of brilliant scholar, inspiring teacher, and wonderful human being. Thanks to Rosemary, Ayo, Olu, and Moni for their support over the years.

During the 2012–13 academic year I had the good fortune to be a Caperton Fellow at Harvard University's Hutchins Center. Henry Louis "Skip" Gates Jr., the director of the institute, has been generous and kind in his support of my work. Skip served as the consummate host, interlocutor, and orchestrator of a series of dazzling events that were never less than intellectually stimulating and effervescent. The Hutchins Center staff was always gracious and helpful, led by the amazing executive director Abby Wolf. Thanks to Krishna Lewis, Sara Bruya, Alvin Benjamin Carter III, Vera Grant, Amy Gosdanian, Justin Sneyd, and Matt Weinberg.

Diane McWhorter, Fred Opie, Patrick Douthit (AKA 9th Wonder), Ed Pavlic, Patricia Sullivan, Charles Van Onselen, Nigel Hatton, Celia Cussen, Patricia Hills, Tahir Hemphill, Juliet Hooker, and Marial Iglesias Utset made my time at the Du Bois Institute memorable and special. Vince Brown and Laurence Ralph have been like brothers as I completed this book. John Stauffer has been a great friend and colleague.

Gloria Loomis, my literary agent, has been a great champion of my work from the instant we first met, and I remain grateful. Sonia Sanchez, professor, human rights activist, and Black Arts icon, continues to inspire my scholarship and study of the social movements of the past and present.

Lara Heimert, the publisher of Basic Books, has been patient, supportive, and enthusiastic about this project from the start. Norman MacAfee's sharp eye for detail and love of words made the editorial process enjoyable. I could not have had a better editorial team, and for that I am grateful.

Many lifelong friends have lived with this project. Darryl Toler, Larry Hughes, Derrick Myers, Rodney Leon, Sal and Jess Mena, Chris and Ina Pisani, Mark Barnes, Mike and Natalie Williams all provided support over the years. Thanks as well to Patrick, Jalane, Alexis, and Francisco.

Many thanks to Goran Olsson, the director of "The Black Power Mixtape," for his hospitality during a research trip to Stockholm. To my brother Kerith, my sister-in-law Dawn, and niece Caitlin, your love, enthusiasm, and generosity are so appreciated. Thank you. This and every book I've written has been made possible thanks to the unconditional love and inspiration of my mother, Germaine Joseph. I could not have completed this book without my extended family. Tane Lowe is brilliantly curious about so many things, including history. Geoff and Liz Domenico always made me feel welcome in their home. A special thanks to Liz for her terrific home cooking on holidays and regular days. Alex, Adryon, and Andrew were good listeners as I discussed this project endlessly. I'm profoundly fortunate to have Astrid Domenico in my life. Astrid has been the best partner and friend one could hope for. She's served as a critic, sounding board, support system, and reality check all in one. Throughout, her enthusiasm never wavered. Astrid shaped this book in ways that go beyond words.

Notes

Preface

1. Charlie Cobb poem quoted in *The New York Times*, April 25, 1969, p. 94. Peniel E. Joseph, *Waiting 'Til the Midnight Hour: A Narrative History of Black Power in America* (New York: Henry Holt, paperback, 2007), pp. 149–73.

2. Mumia Abu-Jamal, "Foreword," *Stokely Speaks: From Black Power to Pan-Africanism* (1971; Chicago: Lawrence Hill Books, 2007), p. vii.

3. Stokely Carmichael with Ekwueme Michael Thelwell, *Ready for Revolution: The Life and Struggles of Stokely Carmichael (Kwame Ture)* (New York: Scribner, 2003), p. 759.

4. John Edgar Wideman, "Introduction," Carmichael with Thelwell, *Ready for Revolution*, p. 9.

Prologue

1. Taylor Branch, *At Canaan's Edge: America in the King Years, 1965–1968* (New York: Simon & Schuster, 2006), p. 486.

2. *Barack Obama, Dreams from My Father: A Story of Race and Inheritance* (New York: Crown, 2004), p. 140.

Chapter One: The Chocolate Fred Astaire

1. FBIKT 100–446080–1975, "Stokely Carmichael," September 17, 1968, p. 4.

2. Carmichael with Thelwell, *Ready for Revolution*, p. 34.

3. Ibid., pp. 29–31.

4. Ibid., p. 37.

5. May Charles Carmichael quoted in Göran Hugo Olsson, *The Black Power Mixtape 1967–1975* (IFC Films, 2011). FBIKT 100–446080–27, "Stokely Carmichael," September 26, 1966, p. 1; *The Black Power Mixtape*.

6. FBIKT 100–446080–23, "Airtel to Director Hoover," September 22, 1966, p. 1. Mabel Carmichael quoted in *The Black Power Mixtape. London Observer Review*, July 23, 1967, p. 17.

7. Carmichael with Thelwell, *Ready for Revolution*, pp. 50–57, 58, 49.

8. Ibid., p. 64. FBIKT 100–446080–24, "Stokely Carmichael: Airtel to Director Hoover from WFO SAC," September 22, 1966, pp. 1–2.

9. Isabel Wilkerson, "Soul Survivor: From Stokely Carmichael to Kwame Ture, Still Ready for Revolution," *Essence*, May 1998, p. 184.

10. Carmichael with Thelwell, *Ready for Revolution*, pp. 66–74. Also see Simeon Wright with Herb Boyd, *Simeon's Story: An Eyewitness Account of the Kidnapping of Emmett Till* (Chicago: Chicago Review Press, 2010).

11. *London Observer Review*, July 23, 1967, p. 17; Mayble Craig Interview, pp. 2–3.

12. Carmichael with Thelwell, *Ready for Revolution*, pp. 106–107.

13. Robert Penn Warren Interview with Stokely Carmichael, 1964, Robert Penn Warren Papers, pp. 7–8, Folder 3628, Typescripts of interviews: Stokely Carmichael. Beinecke Library, Yale University.

14. Carmichael with Thelwell, *Ready for Revolution*, pp. 92–93, 94.

15. Ibid., pp. 92–93.

16. John D'Emilio, *Lost Prophet: The Life and Times of Bayard Rustin* (New York: The Free Press, 2003), pp. 66–67. Devon W. Carbado and Donald Weise, eds., *Time on Two Crosses: The Collected Writings of Bayard Rustin* (San Francisco: Cleis Press, 2003), pp. x–xx. Jervis Anderson, *Bayard Rustin: Troubles I've Seen* (New York: Harper Collins, 1997), pp. 187–196.

17. Carmichael with Thelwell, *Ready for Revolution*, p. 95.

18. Miriam Makeba, *Makeba: My Story* (New York: New American Library, 1987), pp. 89–99; Carmichael with Thelwell, *Ready for Revolution*, pp. 651–652.

19. Makeba, *Makeba*, pp. 81–88. Anderson, *Bayard Rustin*, pp. 95–99.

20. Odd Arne Westad, *The Global Cold War: Third World Interventions and the Making of Our Times* (Cambridge: Cambridge University Press, 2008), pp. 89–90.

21. Milton Viorst, *Fire in the Streets: America in the 1960s* (New York: Simon & Schuster, 1979), p. 350. Carmichael with Thelwell, *Ready for Revolution*, p. 93; Peniel Joseph, *Waiting 'Til the Midnight Hour* (New York: Henry Holt, 2006), p. 20.

22. Carmichael with Thelwell, *Ready for Revolution*, pp. 100–105.

23. Peggy Trotter Dammond Preacely, "It Was Simply in My Blood," in Faith S. Holsaert, Martha Prescod Norman Noonan, Judy Richardson, Betty Garman Robinson, Jean Smith Young, and Dorothy M. Zellner, eds., *Hands on the Freedom Plow: Personal Accounts by Women in SNCC* (Urbana: University of Illinois Press, 2010), pp. 165–166. Robert Penn Warren Carmichael Interview, pp. 15–16. Robert Penn Warren, *Who Speaks for the Negro?* (New York: Random House, 1965), p. 392.

24. Robert Penn Warren Carmichael Interview, p. 22; Grace Elizabeth Hale, *A Nation of Outsiders: How the White Middle Class Fell in Love with Rebellion in Postwar America* (New York: Oxford University Press, 2011). Gordon Parks, "Whip of Black Power," *Life,* May 19, 1967, p. 79. Robert Penn Warren, Carmichael Interview, pp. 18–20.

Chapter Two: Howard and NAG

1. William H. Chafe, *Civilities and Civil Rights: Greensboro, North Carolina, and the Black Struggle for Freedom* (New York: Oxford University Press, 1981), pp. 71–101; Clayborne Carson, *In Struggle: SNCC and the Black Awakening of the 1960s* (Cambridge, MA: Harvard University Press, 1981), pp. 9–11.

2. *New York Times*, March 6, 1960, p. 45.

3. Ibid., March 17, p. 1. Taylor Branch, *Parting the Waters: America in the King Years, 1954–1963* (New York: Touchstone, 1988), p. 314.

4. Carmichael with Thelwell, *Ready for Revolution*, pp. 139–140; Lerone Bennett, "Stokely Carmichael: Architect of Black Power," SNCC Pamphlet. Reprinted from *Ebony,* July 1966 profile, p. 6. Stokely Carmichael–Lorna D. Smith papers, Stanford University (hereafter SCLDS).

5. Branch, *Parting the Waters*, pp. 272–284. See also Wesley Hogan, *Many Minds, One Heart: SNCC's Dream for a New America* (Chapel Hill: University of North Carolina Press, 2009). *New York Times Sunday Magazine*, May 1, 1960, p. 11, and *New York Times*, May 30, 1960, p. 9.

6. Barbara Ransby, *Ella Baker and the Black Freedom Movement: A Radical Democratic Vision* (Chapel Hill: University of North Carolina Press, 2003), p. 240, pp. 13–63. Jeanne Theoharis, *The Rebellious Life of Mrs. Rosa Parks* (Boston: Beacon Press, 2013), pp. 25–26.

7. Ransby, *Ella Baker and the Black Freedom Movement*, pp. 290–291.

8. Ibid.

9. Branch, *Parting the Waters*, pp. 290–293; Carson, *In Struggle*, pp. 23–25; Carmichael with Thelwell, *Ready for Revolution*, pp. 140–141. *New York Times*, April 18, 1960, p. 21; Branch, *Parting the Waters*, pp. 291–292.

10. Andrew B. Lewis, *The Shadows of Youth: The Remarkable Journey of the Civil Rights Generation* (New York: Hill and Wang, 2009), pp. 79–80. Tom Hayden Interview.

11. Following the HUAC hearings in the nation's capital, Stokely went to Virginia and joined his first sit-in. Robert Penn Warren Carmichael Interview, pp. 14–15.

12. Ibid., p. 26.

13. Carmichael with Thelwell, *Ready for Revolution*, pp. 113, 132.

14. Milton Viorst, "Howard University: Campus and Cause," *Harper's Magazine*, November 1961, p. 59.

15. Carmichael with Thelwell, *Ready for Revolution*, p. 114.

16. Ibid., pp. 120, 115–116.

17. *The Hilltop*, November 3, 1961, pp. 1–2.

18. Carmichael with Thelwell, *Ready for Revolution*, pp. 133–135; Ekwueme Michael Thelwell, "The Professor and the Activists: A Memoir of Sterling Brown," *Massachusetts Review*, vol. 40, no. 4, Winter 1999/2000, pp. 617–638; excerpts reprinted in *After Winter: The Art and Life of Sterling A. Brown*, eds., John Edgar Tidwell and Steven C. Tracy (New York: Oxford University Press, 2009), p. 257 and John Edgar Tidwell, "Clarifying Philosophy: Sterling A. Brown and the Nonviolent Action Group," in *After Winter*, pp. 384–385; Lawrence Jackson, *The Indignant Generation: A Narrative History of African American Writers and Critics, 1934–1960* (Princeton: Princeton University Press, 2011), pp. 36–41.

19. Carmichael with Thelwell, *Ready for Revolution*, pp. 127–131.

20. Ibid., p. 136. Ed Brown Interview, pp. 1–5. Thelwell Interview, 12–16–1999, pp. 1–4; Carmichael with Thelwell, *Ready for Revolution*, p. 160. Thelwell Interview, 11–16–2002, pp. 2–3; Thelwell, "The Professor and the Activists," p. 624.

21. Courtland Cox Interview, 08–19–08, pp. 7–8.

22. Carmichael with Thelwell, *Ready for Revolution*, pp. 136–145.

23. Devon W. Carbado and Donald Weise, eds., *Time on Two Crosses: The Collected Writings of Bayard Rustin* (San Francisco: Cleis Press, 2003), p. 10.

24. Ibid., p. 124.

25. D'Emilio, *Lost Prophet*, pp. 296–301, 323–325.

26. Branch, *Parting the Waters*, p. 418; Nick Bryant, *The Bystander: John F. Kennedy and the Struggle for Black Equality* (New York: Basic Books, 2006), pp. 263–264; Diane McWhorter, *Carry Me Home: Birmingham, Alabama: The Climactic Battle of the Civil Rights Revolution* (New York: Simon and Schuster, 2013).

27. Bryant, *The Bystander*, pp. 263–266.

28. Carmichael with Thelwell, *Ready for Revolution*, pp. 188–189 Robert Penn Warren Carmichael Interview, p. 27.

29. Carmichael with Thelwell, *Ready for Revolution*, p. 189; Robert Penn Warren Carmichael Interview, p. 28.

30. Carmichael with Thelwell, *Ready for Revolution*, p. 192; Stokely Carmichael Interview, May 5, 1986, p. 2: Manuscript, Archives, and Rare Book Library, Emory University: hereafter cited as EU; Robert Penn Warren Carmichael Interview, p. 29.

31. Joan Trumpauer Mulholland, "Diary of a Freedom Rider," in Holsaert et al., eds., *Hands on the Freedom Plow*, pp. 67–70. "Breach of Peace: Portraits of the 1961 Mississippi Freedom Riders," http://breachofpeace.com/blog/?p=278. Stokely Carmichael Interview, May 5, 1986, p. 3, EU. Carmichael with Thelwell, *Ready for Revolution*, pp. 193, 195–198. Holsaert et al., eds., *Hands on the Freedom Plow*, p. 73.

32. Parks, "Whip of Black Power," p. 79; Carmichael with Thelwell, *Ready for Revolution*, pp. 247; Joseph, *Waiting 'Til the Midnight Hour*, pp. 124–127.

33. Bill Mahoney, "Sadism in a Southern Prison," *The Hilltop*, October 27, 1961, pp. 2, 6; Branch, *Parting the Waters*, p. 483; Lewis, *The Shadows of Youth*, pp. 102–103; John Lewis with Michael D'Orso, *Walking with the Wind: A Memoir of the Movement* (New York: Simon & Schuster, 1998), p. 171. Carmichael with Thelwell, *Ready for Revolution*, p. 203. James Farmer, *Lay Bare the Heart: An Autobiography of the Civil Rights Movement* (New York: Arbor House, 1985), p. 23.

34. Carmichael with Thelwell, *Ready for Revolution*, pp. 202–204; David Oshinsky, *Worse Than Slavery: Parchman Farm and the Ordeal of Jim Crow Justice* (New York: Simon and Schuster, 1997), pp. 235–236.

35. Farmer, *Lay Bare the Heart*, pp. 23–25.

36. Carmichael with Thelwell, *Ready for Revolution*, pp. 208, 210. Lewis, *Walking with the Wind*, p. 173.

Chapter Three: Finding a Way in New Worlds

1. All quotes from this paragraph, Carmichael with Thelwell, *Ready for Revolution*, pp. 210–211.

2. Robert Penn Warren Carmichael Interview, pp. 36–38.

3. Carmichael with Thelwell, *Ready for Revolution*, p. 214. Makeba, *Makeba*, p. 81. Carmichael with Thelwell, *Ready for Revolution*, pp. 213–15.

4. Carmichael with Thelwell, *Ready for Revolution*, pp. 152–153, 217, 223.

5. Winston A. Grady-Willis, *Challenging U.S. Apartheid: Atlanta and Black Struggles for Human Rights, 1960–1977* (Durham: Duke University Press, 2006), pp. 4–6; Lewis, *The Shadows of Youth*, pp. 75–77.

6. Cynthia Griggs Fleming, *Soon We Will Not Cry: The Liberation of Ruby Doris Smith Robinson* (Lanham: Rowman & Littlefield, 1998), pp. 1–100.

7. Branch, *Parting the Waters*.

8. Carmichael with Thelwell, *Ready for Revolution*, pp. 241–242; FBIKT-100–446080–2X, "Stokely Carmichael," July 13, 1966, p. 1. See also Stokely Carmichael to Wyatt Walker, October 22, 1961, pp. 1–2, SCLC, part 2, Reel 4, frame 42.

9. *The Hilltop*, October 6, 1961, p. 2. Stokely Carmichael, "We've Got Red Blood . . . and Heart," *The Hilltop*, October 6, 1961, p. 4.

10. Charlie Cobb Interview, December 17, 2002, pp. 1–10.

11. Ibid., p. 6.

12. Joseph, *Waiting 'Til the Midnight Hour*, pp. 15–18; Peniel Joseph, *Dark Days, Bright Nights: From Black Power to Barack Obama* (New York: Basic Books, 2010), pp. 35–38; Manning Marable, *Malcolm X: A Life of Reinvention* (New York: Viking, 2011).

13. Stokely Carmichael Interview, November 7, 1988, p. 5. Southern Regional Council (SRC), "Will the Circle Be Unbroken?" Jervis Anderson, *Bayard Rustin: Troubles I've Seen* (New York: Harper Collins, 1997), p. 237; Marable, *Malcolm X*, pp. 185–186.

14. *The Hilltop*, October 27, 1961, p. 6. Anderson, *Bayard Rustin*, pp. 236–237.

15. Carmichael with Thelwell, *Ready for Revolution*, pp. 260–261. *The Hilltop*, November 10, 1961, pp. 4, 3.

16. *Baltimore Afro-American*, November 11, 1961, p. 8. Stokely Carmichael Interview, November 7, 1988, p. 4. SRC, "Will the Circle Be Unbroken?"

17. Carmichael with Thelwell, *Ready for Revolution*, p. 259. *The Chicago Defender*, November 11, 1961, p. 8. *The Hilltop*, November 10, 1961, p. 2.

18. Cox Interview, p. 6.

19. The major protest was called off after the Maryland Commission of Interracial Problems and Relations announced that almost three-dozen eating establishments would serve blacks starting on November 22. *The Hilltop*, November 17, 1961, p. 4.

20. *The Chicago Defender*, October 14, 1961, p. 2.

21. *The New York Times*, October 21, 1961, p. 24. Cleveland Sellers with Robert Terrell, *The River of No Return: The Autobiography of a Black Militant and the Life and Death of SNCC* (Jackson: University of Mississippi Press, 1990), pp. 52–53.

22. Carmichael with Thelwell, *Ready for Revolution*, pp. 242–243; *The Hilltop*, December 1, 1961, pp. 3–4.

Chapter Four: "The Movement Was My Fate"

1. All quotes in paragraph, Carmichael with Thelwell, *Ready for Revolution*, p. 246.

2. Ibid., pp. 246–249. *The Hilltop*, March 23, 1962, pp. 1, 3; *Baltimore Afro-American*, March 24, 1962, p. 1.

3. Stokely Carmichael, "We Shall Not Be Moved," *The Hilltop*, March 23, 1962, pp. 2–3.

4. *The Hilltop*, May 18, 1962, p. 2.

5. FBIKT 100–446080–2X, "Stokely Carmichael," July 13, 1966, p. 278. Carmichael with Thelwell, *Ready for Revolution*, p. 310. Stokely lauded Moses as the man who "taught me a lot of philosophy" that went beyond purely intellectual pursuits. Carmichael with Thelwell, *Ready for Revolution*, p. 311; Bob Moses Interview, pp. 5–6.

6. Cobb Interview Part 1, pp. 15–18. Carmichael with Thelwell, *Ready for Revolution*, pp. 278–280.

7. Carmichael with Thelwell, *Ready for Revolution*, p. 281.

8. Ibid., p. 283.

9. John Dittmer, *Local People: The Struggle for Civil Rights in Mississippi* (Champaign: University of Illinois Press, 1995), p. 127. Carmichael with Thelwell, *Ready for Revolution*, p. 283.

10. Charles Payne, *I've Got the Light of Freedom: The Organizing Tradition and the Mississippi Freedom Struggle* (Berkeley: University of California Press, 1995), pp. 127–131.

11. Dittmer, *Local People*, pp. 134–136; J. Todd Moye, *Let the People Decide: Black Freedom and White Resistance Movements in Sunflower County, Mississippi, 1945–1986* (Chapel Hill: University of North Carolina Press, 2004).

12. Carmichael with Thelwell, *Ready for Revolution*, pp. 277–286.

13. Cleve Sellers Interview, 12–14–09, pp. 6–7. Sellers, *The River of No Return*, pp. 57–61.

14. Sellers Interview; Faith S. Holsaert, "Resistance U," in Holsaert et al., eds., *Hands on the Freedom Plow*, p. 184.

15. *The Hilltop*, February 22, 1963, pp. 1–2, 5.

16. All quotes in this paragraph are from ibid., March 8, 1963, p. 4 and March 16, 1963, pp. 1–2.

17. Ibid., March 22, 1963, pp. 1, 6.

18. The student council officially endorsed NAG's application for recognition that spring. See ibid., March 16, 1963, p. 1 and April 1, 1963, p. 1.

19. Thomas J. Sugrue, *Sweet Land of Liberty: The Forgotten Struggle for Civil Rights in the North* (New York: Random House, 2008), pp. 290–296.

20. Ibid., p. 338. Sharon Harley, "The Chronicle of a Death Foretold: Gloria Richardson, the Cambridge Movement, and the Radical Black Activist Tradition," in Bettye Collier-Thomas and V. P. Franklin, eds., *Sisters in the Struggle: African American Women in the Civil Rights–Black Power Movement* (New York: New York University Press, 2001). Peter B. Levy, *Civil War on Race Street: The Civil Rights Movement in Cambridge, Maryland* (Gainesville: University of Florida Press, 2003), pp. 87–88, 104. Lewis, *Walking with the Wind*, pp. 212–213.

21. For the group of Howard University students affiliated with SNCC, Cambridge represented "NAG's local Mississippi." Carmichael with Thelwell, *Ready for Revolution*, p. 336. Warren, *Who Speaks for the Negro?*, p. 402.

22. Branch, *Parting the Waters*, p. 822. Bryant, *The Bystander*, pp. 422–424, 425; http://www.americanrhetoric.com/speeches/jfkcivilrights.htm (accessed July 9, 2010). JFK Speech, June 11, 1963, YouTube (accessed July 8, 2010).

23. Carmichael with Thelwell, *Ready for Revolution*, pp. 330, 323.

24. Dittmer, *Local People*, pp. 174, 200; Payne, *I've Got the Light of Freedom*, p. 295; William Chafe, *Never Stop Running: Allard Lowenstein and the Struggle to Save American Liberalism* (New York: Basic Books, 1995); Hogan, *Many Minds, One Heart*, p. 146. Clayborne Carson, *Martin's Dream: My Journey and the Legacy of Martin Luther King Jr.* (New York: Palgrave Macmillan, 2013).

25. Hogan, *Many Minds, One Heart*, pp. 133–134, 144.

26. *New York Times*, June 11, 1963, p. 19; Branch, *Parting the Waters*, pp. 818–820.

27. All quotes in paragraph are from Carmichael with Thelwell, *Ready for Revolution*, pp. 320–321.

28. Stokely Carmichael, "Shotguns in Mississippi," *The Hilltop*, September 20, 1963, pp. 3, 5.

29. Payne, *I've Got the Light of Freedom*, p. 291; Dittmer, *Local People*, p. 200. Branch, *Pillar of Fire*, pp. 128–129; Carmichael with Thelwell, *Ready for Revolution*, p. 337. Carmichael, "Shotguns in Mississippi," p. 5.

30. Carmichael with Thelwell, *Ready for Revolution*, pp. 312–313.

31. Branch, *Parting the Waters*, p. 874; *Boston Globe*, August 18, 1963, p. 8.

32. Henry Hampton and Steve Fayer, *Voices of Freedom: An Oral History of the Civil Rights Movement from the 1950s Through the 1980s* (New York: Bantam reissue, 1991), p. 164. Branch, *Parting the Waters*, pp. 876–877.

33. *New York Times*, August 29, 1963, p. 21.

34. Lewis, *Walking with the Wind*, p. 224.

35. *New York Times*, August 29, 1963, p. 21.

36. Ibid.

37. http://www.usconstitution.net/dream.html; Branch, *Parting the Waters*, pp. 882–883.

Chapter Five: The Local Organizer

1. *Baltimore Afro-American*, September 7, 1963, p. 7.

2. *The Hilltop*, November 15, 1963, pp. 1, 4.

3. *The Washington Post*, November 7, 1963, p. D23.

4. *The Hilltop*, November 15, 1963, p. 1; November 22, 1963, p. 2; November 8, 1963, p. 2.

5. Carson, *In Struggle*, pp. 104–105.

6. *New York Times*, November 29, 1963, p. 25. Carmichael with Thelwell, *Ready for Revolution*, p. 328; Peniel E. Joseph, "Kennedy's Finest Moment," *New York Times*, June 11, 2013, p. A21.

7. *Washington Post*, November 30, 1963, p. A4. *New York Times*, November 30, 1963, p. 8.

8. *New York Times*, December 1, 1963, p. 50; *Washington Post*, December 1, 1963, p. A9.

9. Sellers, *The River of No Return*, p. 69; Joseph, *Waiting Til' the Midnight Hour*, pp. 88–89. Carmichael, *Ready for Revolution*, pp. 340–344.

10. Mary Aickin Rothschild, *A Case of Black and White: Northern Volunteers and the Southern Freedom Summers, 1964–1965* (Westport, CT: Greenwood Press, 1982), pp. 56–57; Branch, *Pillar of Fire*, p. 353. Carmichael with Thelwell, *Ready for Revolution*, p. 383.

11. WATS Report, June 24, 1964, SNCC Papers, Reel 15, frames 334, 335, 337, 339.

12. Stokely Carmichael Affidavit, June 25, 1964, SNCC Papers Reel 63, frame 400. Branch, *Pillar of Fire*, p. 372; SNCC WATS Report, June 26, 1964, Reel 15, frame 350.

13. Carmichael with Thelwell, *Ready for Revolution*, pp. 377–380; WATS Report, June 29, 1964, Reel 15, frame 392.

14. Bob Zellner with Constance Curry, *The Wrong Side of Murder Creek: A White Southerner in the Freedom Movement* (Montgomery, AL: New South Books, 2008), p. 262. Mary King, *Freedom Song: A Personal History of the 1960s Civil Rights Movement* (New York: William Morrow, 1988), pp. 98–99; Carmichael with Thelwell, *Ready for Revolution*, pp. 377–378.

15. Stokely Carmichael Interview, May 5, 1986, pp. 12–15.

16. Sally Belfrage, *Freedom Summer* (Charlottesville: University of Virginia Press, 1990), pp. 39–40.

17. "Memorandum from Charlie Cobb Re: Summer Freedom Schools in Mississippi," January 14, 1964, p. 2. SNCC Papers, Reel 63, frame 456. "What is Good English: A Class by Stokely Carmichael," February–March 1965. Notes by Jane Stembridge. SNCC Papers, Reel 63, frame 403.

18. "What is Good English: A Class by Stokely Carmichael," February–March 1965. Notes by Jane Stembridge. SNCC Papers, Reel 63, frame 403, p. 41.

19. Ibid., p. 55.

20. *The Saturday Evening Post*, July 25–August 1, 1964, SNCCP, Reel 20, frame 291. Elizabeth Martínez, *Letters from Mississippi* (Brookline, MA: Zephyr Press, 2002), pp. 207, 39.

21. Martínez, *Letters from Mississippi*, p. 185.

22. Branch, *At Canaan's Edge*, pp. 408–409; Michael Beschloss, ed., *Taking Charge: The Johnson White House Tapes, 1963–1964* (New York: Touchstone Books, 1998), pp. 459–462.

23. Wilkerson, "Soul Survivor," p. 112.

24. WATS Report, August 4, 1964, SNCC Papers, Reel 15, frames 797 and 799. WATS Report, August 4, 1964, SNCCP, Reel 57, frame 166; Len Holt, *The Summer That Didn't End* (New York; Da Capo Press, 1992), p. 230.

25. Holt, *The Summer That Didn't End*, pp. 182–183.

26. Ibid., p. 45. Belfrage, *Freedom Summer*, p. 183.

Chapter Six: A Struggle for Democracy

1. Branch, *Pillar of Fire*, pp. 456–460; King, *Freedom Song*, pp. 343–345.

2. *Washington Post*, August 26, 1964, p. A2.

3. Forman, *The Making of Black Revolutionaries*, pp. 391–393.

4. Carmichael with Thelwell, *Ready for Revolution*, pp. 409–410. Stokely Carmichael Interview, May 5, 1986, p. 27. EU.

5. Carmichael with Thelwell, *Ready for Revolution*, p. 415.

6. SNCC Press Release, August 29, 1964, JFP, Box 37, "Greenwood," Folder.

7. Fleming, *Soon We Will Not Cry*, pp. 143–150.

8. *Chicago Daily Defender*, October 6, 1964, p. 4. *Chicago Tribune*, October 4, 1964. MDAH SCR#2-150-1-7-2-1-1; *Chicago Daily Defender*, September 23, 1964, p. 2.

9. *Chicago Tribune*, October 4, 1964. MDAH SCR#2-150-1-7-2-1-1; *Chicago Daily Defender*, September 23, 1964, p. 2.

10. Carson, *In Struggle*, pp. 147–148; Fleming, *Soon We Will Not Cry*, pp. 100–141.

11. King, *Freedom Song*, p. 452. Jean Smith Young, "Do Whatever You Are Big Enough to Do," p. 249 and Martha Prescod Norman Noonan, "Captured by the Movement," p. 500 in *Hands on the Freedom Plow*. Casey Hayden, "In the Attics of My Mind," in *Hands on the Freedom Plow*, p. 385.

12. Cleveland Sellers to Jim Forman, November 22, 1964, pp. 1–2. JFP, Box 17, "Nov. 64 Corr." LOC.

13. Ruby Doris Smith to Jim Forman, March 5, 1964, pp. 1–2. JFP, Box 17, "Nov. 64 Corr." LOC.

14. WATS Reports, September 26 and December 9, 1964, SNCC Papers, Reel 15, frames 861 and 966. Stokely Carmichael Interview, May 5, 1986, pp. 30–31. EU.

15. Branch, *At Canaan's Edge*, p. 55; Fay Bellamy Powell, "Playtime Is Over," in *Hands on the Freedom Plow*, pp. 477–478. Jack Rabin Photo Collection, "March 9, 1965 Symbolic March Across Pettus Bridge," Penn State University.

16. Branch, *At Canaan's Edge*, pp. 109–110.

17. Ibid., pp. 112–114.

18. FBI SAC Atlanta Report, February 4, 1966, p. 24; Branch, *At Canaan's Edge*, pp. 130–132. King regarded Forman as a "revolutionary" intent on rejecting the compromises necessary to produce social transformation. FBI SAC Atlanta Report, February 4, 1966, pp. 26–27.

19. Stokely Carmichael interview with Clayborne Carson, October 18, 1977, p. 5. CA. All quotes from paragraph, Stokely Carmichael interview, May 5, 1986, p. 36. EU. Stokely Carmichael interview with Clayborne Carson, February 15, 1973, p. 2. Carson Archives.

20. Stokely Carmichael interview, May 5, 1986, p. 39. EU; David Levering Lewis, *W.E.B. Du Bois: Biography of a Race, 1868–1919* (New York: Henry Holt, 1994), pp. 354–356. Carmichael with Thelwell, *Ready for Revolution*, p. 455.

21. Carmichael with Thelwell, *Ready for Revolution*, pp. 191–192.

22. "Riding in the Car from Atlanta to Tuskegee on February 19, 1966," Transcribed April 1966, pp. 1–2, SNCCP, Reel 38, frame 1168; Carmichael with Thelwell, *Ready for Revolution*, pp. 459–460. Hasan Kwame Jeffries, *Bloody Lowndes: Civil Rights and Black Power in Alabama's Black Belt* (New York: New York University Press, 2009), p. 65.

23. Carmichael Interview, November 7, 1988, CR 1032, pp. 1–9; CR 1033, p. 4. SRC, "Will the Circle Be Unbroken?"

Chapter Seven: Lowndes County: New Directions

1. *The Movement*, June 4, 1966, p. 4; Jeffries, *Bloody Lowndes*, p. 71.

2. Jeffries, *Bloody Lowndes*, pp. 66–67. In a July WATS report, Carmichael described Fort Deposit as a town overrun by Klan violence and "intimidation" that featured cross burnings and the brutal beating of a local activist's son-in-law. "WATS Report," July 12, 1965, SNCC Papers, Reel 15, frame 264.

3. WATS Report, August 9, 1965, SNCCP, Reel 16, frame 589; Charles Eagles, *Outside Agitator: Jon Daniels and the Civil Rights Movement in Alabama* (Chapel Hill: University of North Carolina Press, 1993), p. 167; Branch, *At Canaan's Edge*, p. 279. Eagles, *Outside Agitator*, pp. 167–168.

4. WATS Report, August 13, 1965, SNCCP Reel 16, frame 491; Eagles, *Outside Agitator*, pp. 163–64. Branch, *Pillar of Fire*, pp. 290–91.

5. WATS Report, August 14, 1965, SNCCP, Reel 16, frame 489; Eagles, *Outside Agitator*, p. 171. "Alabama Bonding Company," August 20, 1965, SNCC Papers, Reel 38, frame 1163; Carmichael with Thelwell, *Ready for Revolution*, p. 467.

6. WATS Report, August 14–15, 1965, SNCCP, Reel 16, frames 489–490. WATS report, August 15, 1965, p. 2, SNCCP, Reel 16, frame, 625. Eagles, *Outside Agitator*, p. 175.

7. Carmichael interview, CR1034, pp. 1–2. SRC. Branch, *At Canaan's Edge*, p. 313. WATS Report, August 20, 1965, SNCCP, Reel 16, frame 638. "Statement Issued by the Selma Office of SNCC," August 21, 1965. SNCCP, Reel 16, frame 620.

8. Eagles, *Outside Agitator*, p. 181. Carmichael interview, CR 1034, p. 1. Cleveland Sellers interview, December 2009.

9. Carmichael with Thelwell, *Ready for Revolution*, p. 470. Eagles, *Outside Agitator*, pp. 182–183. *Los Angeles Times*, July 3, 1966, p. B2.

10. Branch, *At Canaan's Edge*, pp. 315–317, p. 279. "Stokely Carmichael Memo," September 2, 1965, SNCCP Reel 16, frame 661.

11. *New York Times*, December 10, 1965, p. 37. *The Student Voice*, December 20, 1965, p. 1; Dorothy M. Zellner, "My Real Vocation," in *Hands on the Freedom Plow*, p. 324.

12. *The Movement*, March 1966, p. 1. Stokely Carmichael interview with Clayborne Carson, February 15, 1973, p. 7.

13. *New York Times*, January 5, 1966, p. 1. Branch, *At Canaan's Edge*, p. 404, 406. James Forman, *The Making of Black Revolutionaries* (Seattle: University of Washington Press, 1997), p. 445.

14. *New Journal and Guide*, January 15, 1966, p. A7.

15. Carson, *In Struggle*, pp. 187–188. Branch, *At Canaan's Edge*, p. 411; *New York Times*, January 7, 1966, p. 2.

16. Branch, *At Canaan's Edge*, p. 411–412; Carson, *In Struggle*, p. 189.

17. All quotes from Stokely Carmichael, "Who Is Qualified?," *The New Republic*, January 8, 1966, p. 22.

18. All quotes from Ibid.

19. Jeffries, *Bloody Lowndes*, pp. 29, 157.

20. Ibid., p. 162.

21. All quotes from *New York Times*, April 20, 1966, p. 27.

22. Ibid., April 21, 1966, p. 38.

23. *New York Times*, April 30, 1966, pp. 1, 14; *Los Angeles Times*, April 30, 1966, p. 14; Branch, *At Canaan's Edge*, p. 460.

24. Branch, *At Canaan's Edge*, p. 463. Carmichael with Thelwell *Ready for Revolution*, p. 471.

25. Jeffries, *Bloody Lowndes*, p. 183. John Benson, "Interview with New SNCC Chairman," *The Militant*, May 23, 1966. Stokely Carmichael Schomburg Clipping File.

Chapter Eight: The Meredith March

1. Lewis, *Walking with the Wind*, p. 364. Carson, *In Struggle*, pp. 196–199; Lewis, *Walking with the Wind*, pp. 365, 366–373. Harry Belafonte fundraising letter, July 11, 1966, p. 2. SCLC Papers, Pt1, R15, 187.

2. *The Washington Post*, June 8, 1966, p. 12. James Lawson interview by Eric Etheridge, "How Stokely Carmichael Betrayed the Movement," http://breachofpeace.com/blog/?p=278.

3. *Los Angeles Times*, May 25, 1966, p. 16, and May 24, 1966, p. 16; Joseph, *Waiting 'Til the Midnight Hour*, p. 131.

4. *New York Times*, May 22, 1966. JFP, Box 24, "Black Power Clippings," LOC. *Time*, May 27, 1966, p. 22.

5. *Newsweek*, May 30, 1966. JFP, Box 24, "Black Power Clippings," LOC. *Boston Globe*, May 25, 1966, p. 27. *The New Republic*, June 4, 1966. JFP, Box 24, "Black Power Clippings," LOC. *New York Post*, June 4, 1966. JFP, Box 24, "Black Power Clippings," LOC.

6. Carmichael interview, CR 1037, p. 7; Carmichael interview, CR 1036, p. 2.

7. SCR-1-103-0-6-1-1-1, June 9, 1966, p. 2.

8. *Clarion-Ledger*, June 8, 1966, p. 7. *New York Times*, June 8, 1966, pp. 1, 26; *Chicago Daily Defender*, June 8, 1966, p. 1.

9. *Boston Globe*, June 8, 1966, p. 2. *New York Post*, June 8, 1966. JFP, Box 24, "Black Power Clippings," LOC; *Baltimore Afro-American*, June 18, 1966, p. 13. Carmichael with Thelwell, *Ready for Revolution*, p. 503; *Jackson Daily News*, June 8, 1966, p. 14.

10. *New York Post,* June 8, 1966. JFP, Box 24, "Black Power Clippings," LOC; *Chicago Daily News,* June 8, 1966, CSTSCC.

11. Branch, *At Canaan's Edge,* p. 477; *New York Times,* June 8, 1966, p. 26. *New York Times,* June 8, 1966, p. 26. *Chicago Tribune,* June 8, 1966, p. 1.

12. For Wilkins article on SNCC, see *Los Angeles Times,* June 6, 1966, p. A5. For Carmichael and Wilkins meeting, see Joseph, *Waiting 'Til the Midnight Hour,* pp. 135–136; Carmichael with Thelwell, *Ready for Revolution,* pp. 494–500.

13. Meeting of June 13, 1966, p. 21, Reel 12, frame 707. David J. Garrow, *Bearing the Cross: Martin Luther King, Jr. and the Southern Christian Leadership Conference* (New York: Morrow, 1987), p. 478.

14. *Clarion-Ledger,* June 9, pp. 1, 16; and "Manifesto of the Meredith Mississippi March," 1966, SCLC, Pt 3, Reel 4, frame 157. *Boston Globe,* June 9, 1966, p. 3.

15. "Manifesto of the Meredith Mississippi Freedom March," June 9, 1966, p. 2. SCR 1–67–4-130–1-1–1; *Jackson Daily News,* June 10, 1966, p. 10.

16. *Washington Post,* June 11, 1966, p. 1. *Clarion-Ledger,* June 11, 1966, p. 1. *Los Angeles Times,* June 11, 1966, pp. 5, F1; *New York Times,* June 12, 1966, pp. 1, 82.

17. *New York Times,* June 13, 1966, p. 32. "March to Jackson, Mississippi," June 13, 1966, p. 2.

18. Meeting of June 13, 1966, p. 3. SNCCP, Reel 12, frame 698.

19. Sellers, *The River of No Return,* p. 164.

20. *Time,* June 24, 1966, p. 31. *New York Times,* June 15, 1966, p. 26.

21. *Clarion-Ledger,* June 15, 1966, pp. 1, 16; *Jackson Daily News,* June 15, 1966, pp. 1, 16; Garrow, *Bearing the Cross,* p. 480; *New York Times,* June 14, 1966, pp. 1, 26. *New York Times,* June 16, 1966, p. 35; Joseph, *Waiting 'Til the Midnight Hour,* p. 140. *Clarion-Ledger,* June 16, 1966, p. 18.

22. Lorna Smith to Stokely Carmichael, August 1966, p. 1, SNCCP, Reel 2.

23. Lorna Smith to Stokely Carmichael, August 1966, p. 1 and May 22, 1966, pp. 1–2, SNCCP, Reel 2. Lorna Smith to Stokely Carmichael, May 24, 1966, p. 1, SNCCP, Reel 2. Lorna Smith to *Newsweek* Editors, May 24, 1966, SNCCP, Reel 2.

24. Stokely Carmichael to Lorna Smith, June 15, 1966, p. 1, SCLDSC.

25. *New York Times,* June 17, 1966, p. 33.

26. Ibid., June 18, 1966, p. 20.

27. *Los Angeles Times,* June 15, 1966, p. 16. *Clarion-Ledger,* June 17, 1966, p. 2.

28. *New York Times,* June 17, 1966, pp. 1, 33; *Clarion-Ledger,* June 17, 1966, pp. 1, 16; *Los Angeles Times,* June 17, 1966, p. 2.

29. *Boston Globe,* June 17, 1966, p. 18.

30. *New York Times,* June 17, 1966, p. 33. *Chicago Tribune,* June 17, 1966, p. A6.

31. Carmichael with Thelwell, *Ready for Revolution,* pp. 528, 504. Carmichael interview, CR 1037, pp. 3–6; *Jackson Daily News,* June 17, 1966, pp. 1, 10, 17; *Clarion-Ledger,* June 17, 1966, pp. 1, 16.

32. Carmichael interview, CR 1037, p. 8. *Clarion-Ledger,* June 18, 1966, p. 1; *Chicago Tribune,* June 18, 1966, p. A6. *Los Angeles Times,* June 19, 1966, p. J4.

33. *New York Times,* June 18, 1966, p. 20. *Baltimore Afro-American,* June 25, 1966, p. 2.

34. Joseph, *Waiting 'Til the Midnight Hour,* pp. 143–144; *Chicago Sun-Times,* June 20, 1966. CSTSCC. Stokely Carmichael to William Worthy, June 23, 1966. SNCCP, Reel 2. Joseph, *Waiting 'Til the Midnight Hour,* p. 144; *Boston Globe,* June 20, 1966, p. 3. *Philadelphia Tribune,* June 25, 1966, p. 28; *Face the Nation,* June 19, 1966, Transcript, p. 8. SNCCP, Reel 2, frame 58. *Face the Nation,* June 19, 1966, Transcript, pp. 9–27. SNCCP, Reel 2, frame 58; *I.F. Stone's Weekly,* June 6, 1966, p. 3. SCLDS; Robert Lewis Shelton, "The Real Stokely Carmichael," SR, July 9, 1966. SCLDS.

35. *Boston Globe,* June 19, 1966, pp. 30–31; *Los Angeles Times,* June 19, 1966, p. J4.

36. *Jet*, June 23, 1966, p. 20.

37. "Selected Racial Developments: Continuation of the March from Memphis, Tennessee, to Jackson, Mississippi," LBJ Papers, June 22, 1966, pp. 2–3; *New York Times*, June 23, 1966, p. 22. *New York Times*, June 22, 1966, p. 25. "Selected Racial Developments," June 22, 1966, p. 1.

38. "Eyes on the Prize II: The Time Has Come, 1964–1966;" *New York Times*, June 24, 1966, p. 20; Branch, *At Canaan's Edge*, p. 490.

39. *New York Times*, June 24, 1966, p. 1. *Los Angeles Times*, June 24, 1966, pp. 1, 13: "CBS News Special Report: The Meredith March in Mississippi," June 26, 1966; "Selected Racial Developments," June 24, 1966, pp. 1–2. Carmichael with Thelwell, *Ready for Revolution*, p. 508.

40. *Chicago Tribune*, June 24, 1966, p. 1. *New York Times*, June 24, 1966, p. 20.

41. *New York Times*, June 25, 1966, p. 15; *Boston Globe*, June 25, 1966, p. 2; *Clarion-Ledger*, June 25, 1966, p. 1.

42. "Selected Racial Developments," June 27, 1966, pp. 1–2; *New York Times*, June 27, 1966, p. 29. *Washington Post*, June 27, 1966, pp. 1, 10; *New York Times*, June 27, 1966, p. 29.

43. *Washington Post*, June 27, 1966, p. 1. *Chicago Daily Defender*, June 27, 1966, p. 1; *Chicago Sun-Times*, June 23, 1966. CSTSCC.

44. The broadcast traced the chronology of significant events during the march. An early press conference of march leaders provided the stark image of Carmichael in a crisp white shirt with short sleeves outlining a militant call to action and characterizing Lyndon Johnson's promises as empty since words "could not stop bullets." "CBS News Special Report: The March in Mississippi," Museum of Radio, Film, and Television Archives, New York City.

45. Ibid.

46. *New York Times*, June 27, 1966, p. 29; *Clarion-Ledger*, June 27, 1966, pp. 1, 14; *Jackson Daily News*, June 27, 1966, pp. 1, 16.

47. *Los Angeles Times*, June 27, 1966, p. 6. Lorna Smith to Stokely Carmichael, August 1966, p. 3. SNCCP, Reel 2.

48. Branch, *At Canaan's Edge*, p. 493. *Los Angeles Times*, June 27, 1966, p. 6. *Baltimore Afro-American*, July 9, 1966, p. 14. *Los Angeles Times*, June 27, 1966, p. 13; *New York Times*, June 27, 1966, p. 29.

49. *Washington Post,* June 28, 1966, p. A6.

Chapter Nine: The Magnificent Barbarian

1. Lerone Bennett Jr., "Stokely Carmichael: Architect of Black Power," *Ebony*, July 1966; SNCC reprint of *Ebony* article, pp. 1–3. Ibid., pp. 4–6.

2. Branch, *At Canaan's Edge*, p. 496. *Los Angeles Times*, July 3, 1966, p. B5.

3. *Los Angeles Times*, June 28, 1966, p. 19 and June 29, 1966, p. 4.

4. "Keynote Address of Roy Wilkins, July 5, 1966," p. 2. NAACP Papers, Group IV, A-3. LOC. See also Kevin Boyle, *Arc of Justice: A Saga of Race, Civil Rights, and Murder in the Jazz Age* (New York: Henry Holt, 2004). *Los Angeles Sentinel*, July 7, 1966, p. A1.

5. John T. Woolley and Gerhard Peters, *The American Presidency Project* [online]. Santa Barbara, CA. Available from: http://www.presidency.ucsb.edu/ws/?pid=27705.

6. "Black Power: The Widening Dialogue," *New South*, Summer, 1966, p. 68; *Los Angeles Times*, July 3, 1966, pp. B1–2. All quotes in paragraph, *Philadelphia Tribune*, July 19, 1966, pp. 1–2.

7. *Chicago Defender*, July 30, 1966, p. 1; *Chicago Tribune*, July 28, 1966, p. 14; *New Journal and Guide*, July 30, 1966, p. A1; *Washington Post*, July 28, 1966, p. A9.

8. Quotes in this paragraph from *Chicago Sun-Times*, July 24, 1966, pp. 1, 4 and July 29, 1966, p. 4. CSTSCC.

9. *Chicago Daily News*, July 29, 1966; *Chicago Sun Times*, July 29, 1966. CSTSCC.

10. *Boston Globe*, August 1, 1966, p. 5; *Baltimore Afro-American*, August 13, 1966, p. 14; Joseph, *Waiting 'Til the Midnight Hour*, pp. 153–154.

11. *Los Angeles Times*, August 4, 1966, p. 11; *Chicago Tribune*, August 4, 1966, p. B12; *Chicago Tribune*, August 3, 1966, p. A2.

12. Carson, *In Struggle*, p. 227. *New York Times*, August 5, 1966, p. 10; Joseph, *Waiting 'Til the Midnight Hour*, p. 157; see also *U.S. News and World Report*, August 15, 1966, p. 12, which reprinted excerpts from the *Times* stories as the "Inside Story of 'Black Power' and Stokely Carmichael."

13. Lyndon Johnson and Joseph Beirne, Track 3, 10581, August 5, 1966. LBJ Library and Museum, WH6608.07.

14. *Washington Post*, August 7, 1966, p. A3. *Los Angeles Times*, August 9, 1966, p. A4; *Call and Post*, August 13, 1966, p. 1; "Stokely Carmichael," FBI Report, November 4, 1966, p. 24 in NAACD (Kerner Commission), report 023, LBJ Papers.

15. *Muhammad Speaks*, August 12, 1966, p. 4; August 19, 1966, pp. 3–4; August 26, 1966, p. 13; Joseph, *Waiting 'Til the Midnight Hour*, pp. 154–155. See also FBIKT 100–446080-3X, "Stokely Carmichael: Racial Matter," July 29, 1966, pp. 1–4; FBIKT 100–446080-NR, "Nation of Islam," August 15, 1966, p. 1; Carmichael with Thelwell, *Ready for Revolution*, p. 523.

16. *Newsweek*, August 8, 1966, p. 54; *Christian Science Monitor*, September 22, 1966. SCLDSC.

17. Joseph, *Waiting 'Til the Midnight Hour*, p. 155; FBIKT 100–446080, "Mendel Rivers to Nicholas Katzenbach," August 10, 1966, p. 1. FBI agents supplemented their growing dossier with background interviews that detailed his first several arrests for civil rights activity and confidential sources from Bronx Science who identified Carmichael as part of a cohort of students "devoted to left-wing activities" while in high school. FBIKT 100–446080-NR, "Stokely Carmichael," August 10, 1966, p. 1; FBIKT 100–446080-5, "Stokely Carmichael," August 12, 1966, p. 1.

18. *The Bay State Banner*, August 27, 1966, p. 1; *Muhammad Speaks*, September 2, 1966, p. 5. Stokely Carmichael at open meeting, Harvard University, August 1966. UCD 443A/45. Wisconsin State Historical Society (hereafter WSHS). "Communist Infiltration of SNCC," October 26, 1966, p. 23. SNCC FBI Reports File #1. Federal Records, NACCD (Kerner Commission) Box E19. LBJ Library. "Carmichael on 'Black Power,'" *Harvard Crimson*, August 23, 1966, thecrimson.com; *Boston Globe*, August 19, 1966, p. 2; Stokely Carmichael at open meeting, Harvard University, August 1966. UCD 443A/45. WSHS.

19. "SNCC–Stokely Carmichael," August 24, 1966, p. 2. Taylor Branch Collection, UNC–Chapel Hill (LBJ Office Files, Office Files of Mildred Stegall, SNCC-Stokely Carmichael, August–December 1966). *Boston Globe*, August 21, 1966, p. 80.

20. FBIKT 100–446080-NR, "Airtel, Boston SAC to FBI Director," September 9, 1966, p. 5. FBIKT 100–446080-15, "Stokely Carmichael," September 13, 1966, p. 1; FBIKT 100–446080-10, Memorandum, New York SAC to FBI Director, September 1, 1966, p. 1. *Muhammad Speaks*, September 2, 1966, p. 5. *Bay State Banner*, August 27, 1966, p. 1.

21. Joseph, *Waiting 'Til the Midnight Hour*, p. 15.

22. All quotes are from *Newark Evening News*, August 26, 1966. MDAH, 1–92–0–74–1–1–1. Sovereignty Commission Files.

23. Forman, *The Making of Black Revolutionaries*, p. 457.

24. "Report of the Communications Section of the Atlanta Office," August 1, 1966, pp. 1–3. SNCCP, Reel 16.

25. Carson, *In Struggle*, pp. 229–235; Sellers, *The River of No Return*, pp. 183–184; FBIKT 100–446080-NR, "SNCC: Stokely Carmichael," August 26, 1966, p. 1; Alice Moore to Stokely Carmichael, August 10, 1966. SNCCP, Reel 2; August 29, 1966, Book Contract, Special Manuscript Collection, Random House, Columbia University.

26. *Stokely Carmichael v. Ivan Allen, Jr.*, p. 4, December 13, 1966, Atlanta, GA, Records of *The Southern Courier*, Box 43, f1. Tuskegee University Archives.

27. *Atlanta Constitution*, September 7, 1966, pp. 1, 12; *Chicago Tribune*, September 7, 1966, pp. 1, 7; *Los Angeles Times*, September 7, 1966, pp. 1, 13; *New York Times*, September 7, 1966, pp. 1, 38 and September 9, 1966, pp. 1, 30 and September 11, 1966, p. 2E; Carson, *In Struggle*, pp. 225–226, 239; Joseph, *Waiting 'Til the Midnight Hour*, pp. 159–160; Branch, *At Canaan's Edge*, pp. 524–526; *Chicago Sun-Times*, October 2, 1966. CSTSCC. *Carmichael v. Allen*, pp. 6–7.

28. *Boston Globe*, September 8, 1966, p. 14; *Chicago Tribune*, September 10, 1966, p. 3; *Atlanta Constitution*, September 8, 1966, pp. 1, 7. *Atlanta Constitution*, September 9, 1966, pp. 1, 6.

29. *Atlanta Constitution*, September 9, 1966, pp. 1, 6. *Nashville Tennessean*, September 9, 1966, p. 10. *The Movement*, December 1966, p. 10.

30. Tomiko Brown-Nagin, *Courage to Dissent: Atlanta and the Long History of the Civil Rights Movement* (New York: Oxford University Press, 2011), pp. 285–290.

31. *Time*, September 16, 1966. SCLDSC; Brown-Nagin, *Courage to Dissent*, pp. 285–290. Ralph McGill, "Story of a Man and of SNCC" and "The Story of Two 'Snicks,'" *Atlanta Constitution*, September 8 and 9, 1966, p. 1; "Why Did Snick Turn to Hate?," *Boston Globe*, September 8, 1966, p. 14 and "This New Snick Is a Travesty," *Boston Globe*, September 10, 1966, p. 6; Howard Zinn et al., "In Defense of SNCC," *Boston Globe*, September 15, 1966, p. 22; *Atlanta Constitution*, September 10, 1966, p. 8; *New York Times*, September 10, 1966, p. 1. See also *Boston Globe*, September 17, 1966, p. 6; *U.S. News and World Report*, September 19, 1966, p. 36. Howard Zinn, "Changing People: Negro Civil Rights and the Colleges," *Black and White in American Culture: An Anthology of the Massachusetts Review* (Amherst: University of Massachusetts Press, 1971), p. 66.

32. *Boston Globe*, October 2, 1966, pp. 7, 6.

33. Ibid., September 12, 1966, p. 1; *Los Angeles Times*, September 11, 1966, p. F4; *Chicago Daily Defender*, September 14, 1966, p. 12; *New York Times*, September 21, 1966, p. 33; *New Journal and Guide*, September 24, 1966, p. 20; *Chicago Daily News*, October 5, 1966. CSTSCC. All quotes in this paragraph, *Nashville Tennessean*, September 10, 1966, p. 7; *New Journal and Guide*, September 17, 1966, pp. 1–2; Carson, *In Struggle*, p. 239. *Washington Post*, September 11, 1966, pp. 1, 8.

34. FBIKT 100–446080-NR, Martin Luther King–Stanley Levison Telephone Surveillance, September 10, 1966, pp. 1–2; FBIKT 100–446080-NR, "SNCC: Stokely Carmichael," September 21, 1966, pp. 1–2. FBIKT 100–446080-NR, New York SAC to FBI Director, September 23, 1966, pp. 1–3; FBIKT 100–446080-NR, Airtel, FBI Director to WFO SAC, September 22, 1966, pp. 1–2.

35. *Saturday Evening Post*, September 10, 1966, p. 88.

36. Stokely Carmichael, "A Letter from Jail," *Sunday Ramparts*, October 2, 1966, p. 7.

37. *Los Angeles Times*, September 17, 1966, p. 14; *Chicago Tribune*, September 17, 1966, p. 5; *Chicago Daily Defender*, September 19, 1966, p. 8; Branch, *At Canaan's Edge*, p. 532; FBIKT 100–446080-NR, "Stokely Carmichael," November 4, 1966, pp. 11, 18, LBJL.

38. *Los Angeles Times*, September 16, 1966, p. 16. *Pittsburgh Courier*, October 15, 1966, p. 8B. *New Journal and Guide*, September 17, 1966, p. 12. Joseph, *Waiting 'Til the Midnight Hour*, p. 166. *Boston Globe*, September 18, 1966, p. 4; *Chicago Tribune*, September 19, 1966, p. C19. *Chicago Defender*, October 1, 1966, p. 10.

Chapter Ten: "A New Society Must Be Born"

1. *Baltimore Afro-American*, October 8, 1966, pp. 1–2.

2. Stokely Carmichael, "What We Want," *New York Review of Books*, September 22, 1966.

3. All quotes in paragraph from "CBS Reports: Black Power, White Backlash," September 27, 1966, pp. 1, 6. LBJ. CBS Special Report, "Black Power, White Backlash," September 27, 1966. Museum of Radio, Film, and Television Archive, New York City; *New York Times*, September 27, 1966, pp. 75, 7.

4. "CBS Reports: Black Power, White Backlash," p. 10.

5. FBIKT 100–446080-NR, "Martin Luther King, Jr, Stokely Carmichael," October 4, 1966, pp. 1–4 and October 3, 1966, pp. 1–2.

6. *Michigan Chronicle*, October 8, 1966, p. 7.

7. FBIKT 100–446080-39, "Stokely Carmichael," Airtel, October 19, 1966, pp. 1–2; *Boston Globe*, October 12, 1966, pp. 1, 3 and October 14, 1966, pp. 1, 3; *Washington Post*, October 15, 1966, p. 6; *Chicago Defender*, October 15, 1966, p. 3; FBIKT 100–446080-35, "Stokely Carmichael," UPI press release, October 11, 1966, pp. 1–5; Branch, *At Canaan's Edge*, pp. 538–540.

8. *Los Angeles Times*, October 16, 1966, p. F4 and October 19, 1966, p. 25; *Chicago Tribune*, October 22, 1966, p. 10.

9. All quotes from Minutes of Central Committee Meeting October 23, 1966, pp. 6–10, SNCCP, Reel 16.

10. Carson, *In Struggle*, p. 230; Branch, *At Canaan's Edge*, p. 545.

11. Carson, *In Struggle*, pp. 232–235; Joseph, *Waiting 'Til the Midnight Hour*, pp. 155–164. Minutes of Central Committee Meeting October 23, 1966, pp. 6–10, SNCCP, Reel 16.

12. All quotes from FBIKT 100–446080-NR, "Meeting with Acting AG Clark," October 27, 1966, pp. 1–5.

13. Ibid.

14. All quotes from FBIKT 100–446080-51, "Stokely Carmichael: Internal Security," October 28, 1966, pp. 1–2; FBIKT 100–446080-NR, Teletype, Director Hoover from New York SAC, October 27, 1966, p. 1; *New York Times*, October 29, 1966, pp. 1, 9; *Washington Post*, October 29, 1966, p. 3; *Chicago Tribune*, October 28, 1966, pp. 1, 8; *Chicago Tribune*, October 29, 1966, pp. 1–2; *Los Angeles Times*, October 28, 1966, p. 31; Joseph, *Waiting 'Til the Midnight Hour*, p. 167; *Los Angeles Times*, October 30, 1966, p. 15.

15. FBIKT 100–446080-NR, "Stokely Carmichael–Selective Service Act," September 19, 1966, p. 1 and FBIKT 100–446080-NR, Correspondence to Marvin Watson, September 22, 1966, pp. 1–2.

16. Joshua Bloom and Waldo E. Martin, Jr., *Black Against Empire: The History and Politics of the Black Panther Party* (Berkeley: University of California Press, 2013), pp. 128–130. Bloom and Martin correctly highlight Carmichael's importance to the New Left's antiwar activism, especially this particular Berkeley speech. I go further however and argue that Stokely Carmichael represented the nation's most important antiwar protester from the Meredith March until MLK's much publicized opposition in April 1967. Carmichael popularized the "Hell No, We Won't Go!" chant to black and white college students and explicitly linked Vietnam, Black Power, and anti-imperialism before the Black Panthers. Moreover, Carmichael's notoriety was instrumental in mainstreaming the Free Huey Movement and the Black Panther Party. In short, Carmichael's rhetoric and politics proved the most generative for radicals who were part of the antiwar, Black Power, New Left, Pan-Africanist, and Third World anti-imperialist movements. For Carmichael in Haight-Ashbury, see Clayborne Carson, *Martin's Dream: My Journey and the Legacy of Martin Luther King, Jr.* (New York: Palgrave Macmillan, 2013), p. 45.

17. *Los Angeles Times*, October 30, 1966, pp. C1, B.

18. *Chicago Tribune*, October 30, 1966, p. 3; *Chicago Daily Defender*, October 31, 1966, p. 4; *Berkeley Daily Gazette*, October 31, 1966, pp. 1, 3.

19. FBIKT 100–446080-395, "Airtel FBI Director to San Francisco SAC," July 13, 1967, p. 7.

20. Stokely Carmichael, "Speech at University of California, Berkeley, October 29, 1966," Catherine Ellis and Stephen Drury Smith, eds., *Say It Plain: A Century of Great African American Speeches* (New York: New Press, 2005), p. 57.

21. *Los Angeles Times*, October 30, 1966, p. C1; *New York Times*, October 30, 1966, p. 62. *Chicago Tribune*, October 30, 1966, p. 3. Carmichael, *Stokely Speaks*, pp. 54, 58. "Speech by Stokely Carmichael at the Greek Theater, University of California, Berkeley, on the Occasion of 'Black Power' Day," October 29, 1966, pp. 3, 9. FBIKT 100–446080–395, July 13, 1967.

22. *Los Angeles Times*, October 31, 1966, p. 3; Joseph, *Waiting 'Til the Midnight Hour*, p. 168. *Chicago Tribune*, October 31, 1966, p. 14. *Washington Post, Times Herald*, November 1, 1966, p. A2; *Los Angeles Times*, November 1, 1966, p. 22. *New Journal and Guide*, November 5, 1966, p. 1.

23. Stokely Carmichael to Alice Moore, September 19, 1966. SNCCP, Reel 2. *New York Times*, November 6, 1966, p. 28.

24. *Yale Daily News*, November 21, 1966, p. 8.

25. *The Movement*, December 1966, p. 8. Stokely Carmichael and Charles V. Hamilton, *Black Power: The Politics of Liberation* (New York: Random House, 1967), p. 115. *The Movement*, December 1966, p. 9. See also *National Guardian*, November 5, 1966, p 9 for pre-election coverage of Lowndes by the radical press. *The Movement*, December 1966, p. 8; see also, Branch, *At Canaan's Edge*, p. 548.

26. Joseph, *Waiting 'Til the Midnight Hour*, p. 170.

27. Harry Golden, "Black Power Brought Out White Backlash," *Chicago Defender*, December 17, 1966, p. 12. Joseph, *Waiting 'Til the Midnight Hour*, pp. 170–171; *New Journal and Guide*, November 5, 1966, p. 11; *Los Angeles Times*, November 6, 1966, p. D4; *Boston Globe*, November 18, 1966, p. 13; *Los Angeles Times*, November 21, 1966, p. 5.

28. FBIKT 100–446080–99X, Memorandum, November 17, 1966, p. 1; David Corcoran to Roy Wilkins, December 13, 1966, NAACP, Reel V.

29. *Yale Daily News*, November 16, 1966, pp. 1, 6.

30. *San Francisco Chronicle*, November 19, 1966, p. 2; FBIKT 100–446080–92, "Stokely Carmichael," November 28, 1966, p. 4; *San Francisco Chronicle*, November 19, 1966, p. 2. Donna Jean Murch, *Living for the City: Migration, Education, and the Rise of the Black Panther Party in Oakland, California* (Chapel Hill: University of North Carolina Press, 2010).

31. Carmichael with Thelwell, *Ready for Revolution*, pp. 475–476.

32. *The Movement*, December 1966, pp. 3, 5; FBIKT 100–446080–98, Teletype, November 25, 1966, pp. 1–2.

33. *Los Angeles Times*, November 27, 1966, p. B; *Boston Globe*, November 27, 1966, p. 44; *Chicago Tribune*, November 27, 1966, p. D33; *Los Angeles Sentinel*, December 1, 1966, pp. 1, 5; *Los Angeles Free Press*, December 2, 1966, pp. 5, 8; Joseph, *Waiting 'Til the Midnight Hour*, p. 171.

34. Forman, *The Making of Black Revolutionaries*, p. 479.

35. Carson, *In Struggle*, pp. 240–241; Forman, *The Making of Black Revolutionaries*, p. 479. Judy Richardson, "My Enduring 'Circle of Trust,'" in *Hands on the Freedom Plow*, p. 365.

36. FBIKT 100–446080–95, Memorandum, December 6, 1966, p. 1. Parks, "Whip of Black Power," p. 78; FBIKT 100–446080, "Stokely Carmichael," November 16, 1967, p. 8. Carmichael, Stokely, Box E7, LBJ Library.

37. All quotes from Bayard Rustin to Rabbi Everett Gendler, November 11, 1966, in Michael G. Long, ed., *I Must Resist: Bayard Rustin's Life in Letters* (San Francisco: City Lights, 2012), p. 323.

38. Bayard Rustin to Stokely Carmichael, July 27, 1966; Stokely Carmichael to Bayard Rustin, August 2, 1966. SNCCP. Reel 2.

39. Quotes from FBIKT 100–446080–100, "Stokely Carmichael," December 19, 1966, pp. 1–4.

40. Ibid.; *Chicago Tribune,* December 14, 1966, p. C9; *New York Times,* December 15, 1966, p. 34.

41. *Washington Post,* December 19, 1966, p. 10.

42. *New York Times,* December 18, 1966, p. BR8; *Washington Post,* December 21, 1966, p. C21.

43. *Village Voice,* December 29, 1966, Vol. XII, No. 11, http://blogs.villagevoice.com/runnin scared/archives/2010/01/clip_job_stokel_1.php (accessed September 10, 2010); *New York Amsterdam News,* December 17, 1966, p. 22.

Chapter Eleven: "Hell No, We Won't Go!"

1. Joseph, *Waiting 'Til the Midnight Hour; New York Times,* January 19, 1967, p. 38; *The Movement,* February 1967, pp. 196–197. Clay Carson Archives King Center, Stanford University (hereafter CAKC). *The Afro-American,* January 28, 1967, p. 18; *National Guardian,* February 18, 1967, p. 6; FBIKT 100–446080–1133, "Stokely Carmichael," 1968.

2. *Washington Post,* January 11, 1967, p. 8.

3. *Boston Globe,* January 11, 1967, p. 61.

4. *New York Times,* January 11, 1967, p. 20.

5. Ibid., January 16, 1967, p. 22; FBIKT 100–446080–106, "Stokely Carmichael," January 13, 1966, p. 1; FBIKT 100–446080-NR, Memorandum, January 25, 1967, p. 2; FBIKT 100–446080–108, "Stokely Carmichael," January 18, 1967, pp. 1–2; FBIKT 100–447080-NR, "Stokely Carmichael," January 13, 1967, pp. 1–3. After his two speaking engagements in Chicago, Carmichael relaxed at a West Side lounge until 2 A.M. FBIKT 100–446080-NR, "Stokely Carmichael," January 13, 1967, p. 5.

6. Quotes from Stokely Carmichael to Central Committee, Memo, Subject: D.C. Office, January 19, 1967; Stokely Carmichael to Central Committee, Memo, Subject: Los Angeles Office, January 19, 1967; Stokely Carmichael to Central Committee, Memo, Subject: San Francisco Office, January 19, 1967; Central Committee Decisions, January 20–23, 1967, p. 2; SNCCP, Reel 16.

7. The best study of Douglass as a self-made man is found in John Stauffer, *Giants: The Parallel Lives of Frederick Douglass and Abraham Lincoln* (New York: Twelve, 2008). Carmichael, *Stokely Speaks,* pp. 66–67, 76; *Chicago Daily Defender,* January 18, 1967, p. 5; *Los Angeles Times,* January 17, 1967, p. 10.

8. Ransby, *Ella Baker and the Black Freedom Movement,* p. 355. *Chicago Tribune,* January 26, 1967, p. 7; *Boston Globe,* January 26, 1967, p. 10; FBIKT 100–446080-NR, "Communist Infiltration of SNCC," January 27, 1967, pp. 1–4. FBIKT 100–446080-NR, "Communist Infiltration of SNCC," June 12, 1967, p. 15. SNCC FBI Reports File #2. Federal Records, NACCD (Kerner Commission) Box E19. LBJ Library. FBIKT 100–446080-NR, "Communist Infiltration of SNCC," January 25, 1967, pp. 1–4. FBIKT 100–446080-NR, "Foreign Broadcast Information Service Daily report," January 26, 1967, p. 4.

9. FBIKT 100–446080-NR, "Communist Infiltration of SNCC," June 12, 1967, p. 16. SNCC FBI Reports File #2; FBIKT 100–446080-NR, "Communist Infiltration of SNCC," January 27, 1967, pp. 3–4; FBIKT 100–446080-NR, "Communist Infiltration of SNCC," January 27, 1967, p. 2; *New York Amsterdam News,* February 4, 1967, p. 2.

10. *Los Angeles Times,* January 30, 1967, pp. 3, 24. *The Movement,* February 1967, p. 205. CAKC.

11. Quotes from *Los Angeles Times,* February 5, 1967, pp. DB, 14 and January 30, 1967, p. 3; *Berkeley Barb,* February 10, 1967, p. 3.

12. Stokely Carmichael to James Baldwin, January 24, 1967; Stokely Carmichael to Gwendolyn Biggs, January 10, 1967; Stokely Carmichael to Kathi Simmons, January 23, 1967. SNCCP, Reel 2. Stokely Carmichael to Gloria Madden, January 24, 1967, p. 1.

13. Stokely Carmichael to Pernicia Morris, January 28, 1967; Stokely Carmichael to Lynn McKinley, January 28, 1967; Stokely Carmichael to Sandra Williams, January 30, 1967; Stokely Carmichael to Carol Matthews, January 30, 1967. SNCCP, Reel 2. Stokely Carmichael to Gloria Madden, February 4, 1967. SNCCP, Reel 2. Lorna Smith to Stokely Carmichael, January 20, 1967. Stokely Carmichael to Lorna Smith, January 28, 1967. SNCCP, Reel 2.

14. Joseph, *Waiting 'Til the Midnight Hour.*

15. Eldridge Cleaver, "My Father and Stokely Carmichael," *Ramparts*, April 1967, pp. 10–14. FBIKT 100–446080–141, "Airtel from San Francisco SA to FBI Director," February 28, 1967.

16. FBIKT 100–446080–no serial, "Stokely Carmichael," February 20, 1967, p. 1; *Washington Post*, February 18, 1967, p. 2. FBIKT 100–446080–131, "Stokely Carmichael; Student Non Violent Coordinating Committee (SNCC)," February 28, 1967, pp. 1–2; *New Journal and Guide*, February 25, 1967, p. 1; *San Francisco Chronicle*, February 18, 1967, p. 26. FBIKT 100–446080–119, "Stokely Carmichael—Teletype," February 16, 1967, pp. 1 2; FBIKT 100–446080–120, "Stokely Carmichael—Teletype," February 18, 1967, pp. 1–3; FBIKT 100–446080–121, "Stokely Carmichael—Airtel," February 21, 1967, pp. 1–2 and pp. 1–6; *Los Angeles Times*, February 16, 1967, p. A8.

17. "Stokely Comes to McGill," *Sanity*, May 11, 1967, p. 2; C.L.R. James, "Black Power: Its Past, Today, and the Way Ahead," pp. 1–3. Speech Delivered by C.L.R. James, August 1967. FBIKT 100–446080–301, *Montreal Gazette*, February 25, 1967; C.L.R. James, "Black Power: Its Past, Today, and the Way Ahead," August 1967. Speech Delivered in London. SCLDSC.

18. FBIKT 100–446080–127, "Teletype," March 3, 1967; *New Pittsburgh Courier*, March 11, 1967, pp. 1, 3, 5.

19. *New York Times*, March 3, 1967, pp. 1, 21.

20. Central Committee Meeting, March 4, 1967, pp. 1–32. SNCCP, Reel 16.

21. Quotes from Central Committee Meeting, March 4, 1967, pp. 41–43.

22. FBIKT 100–446080–no serial, "Student Non Violent Coordinating Committee: Stokely Carmichael," March 17, 1967, pp. 1–2.

23. Branch, *At Canaan's Edge*, pp. 593, 603. King had come out against the war as early as 1965 but was quickly pressured into silence. SNCC subsequently became one of the war's leading critics and from June 1966 to April 1967, Carmichael emerged as the black freedom struggle's most vocal antiwar critic. See Branch, *At Canaan's Edge*, pp. 254–255, 308–309, 591–597; Joseph, *Waiting 'Til the Midnight Hour*, pp. 179–183. *Chicago Tribune*, April 6, 1967, p. 20.

24. FBIKT 100–446080–550, "Stokely Carmichael Speech Delivered at Tennessee A & I State University on April 7, 1967," September 11, 1967, p. 3.

25. Ibid.

26. Quotes from ibid., pp. 1–6; *New York Amsterdam News*, April 15, 1967, pp. 1, 15. *New Journal and Guide*, April 22, 1967, p. 9. Kathleen Cleaver, ed., *Target Zero: A Life in Writing by Eldridge Cleaver* (New York: Palgrave Macmillan, 2006), p. 74.

27. Jennifer Hendricks, "Stokely Carmichael and the 1967 IMPACT Symposium: Black Power, White Fear, and the Conservative South," *Tennessee Historical Quarterly*, vol. 63, no. 4, p. 295. FBIKT 100–446080–250, "Airtel from Knoxville SAC to FBI Director," June 1, 1967; Branch, *At Canaan's Edge*, p. 608; Joseph, *Waiting 'Til the Midnight Hour*, p. 178; *New York Times*, April 9, 1967, pp. 1, 55.

28. *New York Times*, April 10, 1967, pp. 1, 19. *Washington Post*, April 10, 1967, p. 3. *Nashville Forum*, April 1967, Metro Nashville Archives, Metro Government Audio Tape, Record Group 312 (312–500). *New York Times*, April 11, 1967, p. 46.

29. *Boston Globe*, April 13, 1967, p. 2; *Chicago Tribune*, April 11, 1967, p. 12; FBIKT 100–446080-NR, Memorandum, April 20, 1967, p. 1; FBIKT 100–446080-NR, "Spring Mobilization Committee to End the War in Vietnam," April 8, 1967, pp. 1–3.

30. *New York Times*, April 15, 1967, p. 3; Branch, *At Canaan's Edge*, pp. 599–60.

31. Quotes from Stokely Carmichael, "Spring Mobilization to End the War in Vietnam," April 15, 1967, pp. 1–2. SCLDSC.

32. Joseph, *Waiting 'Til the Midnight Hour*, pp. 180–181.

33. Quotes from Stokely Carmichael, "Spring Mobilization to End the War in Vietnam," April 15, 1967, p. 2. SCLDSC.

34. Stokely Carmichael to Lorna Smith, May 2, 1967. SCLDSC.

35. Branch, *At Canaan's Edge*, p. 600. FBIKT 100–446080-NR, "Stokely Carmichael," November 16, 1967, p. 24. Carmichael, Stokely. Box E7. LBJ Library.

36. Parks, "Whip of Black Power," p. 82.

37. Ibid., pp. 78, 82.

38. Quotes from Carmichael with Thelwell, *Ready for Revolution*, pp. 514–515; FBIKT 100–446080-NR, "SNCC: Stokely Carmichael," May 5, 1967, pp. 1–3; FBIKT-100–446080–489, "Stokely Carmichael: Prosecutive Summary," August 12, 1967, p. 239.

39. Branch, *At Canaan's Edge*, p. 604. *New York Times*, April 30, 1967, pp. 1, 10; Branch, *At Canaan's Edge*, p. 604.

40. Branch, *At Canaan's Edge*, pp. 605–606; FBIKT 100–446080-no serial, "Stokely Carmichael," May 5, 1967, p. 2; FBIKT 100–446080–666, Airtel from Director Hoover to Atlanta SAC, November 17, 1967, which notes that Assistant Attorney General Walter Yeagley requested that agents "obtain the names of these 16 individuals, the city where they refused induction, and what action was instituted against them for their refusal." *Los Angeles Times*, May 2, 1967, p. 9.

41. Stokely Carmichael, "Report from the Chairman," May 5, 1967, pp. 1–6. SNCC Papers, Box 7, "May 1967 Staff Meeting" folder. King Center Archives.

42. *Los Angeles Times*, May 6, 1967, p. 4. *New York Times*, May 6, 1967, pp. 1, 6.

43. *New York Times*, May 13, 1967, p. 20; *Washington Post*, May 13, 1967, p. 4; *Chicago Tribune*, May 13, 1967, p. 6; *Los Angeles Times*, May 13, 1967, p. 14.

44. *The Southern Courier*, May 20–21/1967, 2–150–2–6–1–1–1.

45. FBIKT 100–446080–240, Memorandum, "Stokely Carmichael: Director's Testimony Before House Appropriations Subcommittee February 16, 1967," May 17, 1967, p.1; FBIKT 100–446080–240X, "Proposed Appearance of Stokely Carmichael, Grand Rapids, Michigan, May 17, 1967," May 18, 1967, p. 1; FBIKT 100–446080–205, "SNCC: Stokely Carmichael," May 17, 1967, p. 2. Bureau files reported Carmichael asserting that Hoover was in his "dotage and should retire." FBIKT 100–446080–213, "Proposed Appearance of Stokely Carmichael, Grand Rapids, Michigan, May 17, 1967," pp. 1–2. One angry citizen wrote the FBI director pledging support and alleging that, according to news accounts, Carmichael had referred to the director as "J. Edgar Notetaker." See FBIKT 100–446080–214 Teletype, May 17, 1967, p. 1; FBIKT 100–446080–215, Correspondence to FBI director, May 18, 1967, p. 1. In Grand Rapids, Cleve Sellers gave a brief speech before Carmichael, discussing his decision to resist the draft. See FBIKT 100–446080–486, "Stokely Carmichael," July 24, 1967, pp. 1–4; FBIKT "SNCC: Stokely Carmichael," May 29, 1967, p. 1. TBC. FBIKT 100–446080–344, "Stokely Carmichael," June 20, 1967, 1.

46. *Chicago Daily Defender*, May 17, 1967, p. 10; FBIKT 100–446080–209, Airtel, Detroit SAC to FBI Director, May 15, 1967, pp. 1–4; FBIKT 100–446080–210, Teletype, FBI Detroit to Director Hoover, May 16, 1967, pp. 1–4; FBIKT 100–446080–240x, "Proposed Appearance of Stokely Carmichael, Grand Rapids, Michigan, May 17, 1967," May 18, 1967, pp. 1–9; FBIKT 100–446080–228, Unidentified newspaper clipping, May 8, 1967.

47. *Washington Post*, May 19, 1967, p. 4; Bernard Weinraub, "The Brilliancy of Black," *Esquire*, January 1967, p. 134; MSC, May 18, 1967, 3–11–0–29–10–1–1.

48. *The Movement*, July 1967. SCLDS.

49. Sol Stern, "The Call of the Panthers," *New York Times Magazine*, August 6, 1967.

50. FBIKT 100–446080-NR, Correspondence to Mildred Stegall, May 23, 1967; Joseph, *Waiting 'Til the Midnight Hour*, p. 182; *Muhammad Speaks*, May 26, 1967, p. 24.

51. District Court of Alabama, 1968, *Houser v. Hill*, 278 F. Supp. 920, pp. 15, 23. FBIKT 100–446080–324, "After Civil Rights—Black Power," June 13, 1967, pp. 1–6 and FBIKT 100–446080–327, Memorandum, "NBC News Special: June 11, 1967," June 12, 1967, p. 1; FBIKT 100–446080–292, "Stokely Carmichael," June 12, 1967, pp. 1–4; *New York Times*, June 12, 1967, p. 91; *Boston Globe*, June 13, 1967, p. 39; http://www.nbcuniversalarchives.com/nbcuni /clip/51A06589_s01.do (accessed August 6, 2013).

52. FBIKT 100–446080–292, "Stokely Carmichael," June 12, 1967, pp. 1–4. FBIKT 100–446080–286, Teletype, "Stokely Carmichael," pp. 1–2; FBIKT 100–446080–289, "Memorandum—Stokely Carmichael," June 12, 1967; FBIKT 100–446080–290, "Memorandum—Stokely Carmichael," June 12, 1967, pp. 1–2; *Los Angeles Times*, June 12, 1966, p. 16; *Washington Post*, June 13, 1967, p. 3; *New York Times*, June 14, 1967, p. 31. *The Movement*, July 1967, p. 259. CAKC; FBIKT 100–446080-A, *Birmingham Post-Herald*, June 12, 1967, p. 1; FBIKT 100–446080–299, "Teletype," June 12, 1967; *New York Times*, June 14, 1967; FBIKT 100–446080–323, "Stokely Carmichael: Coordinating Council for Black Power," July 13, 1967, p. 1. See also, Sellers with Terrell, *The River of No Return*, pp. 197–199.

53. FBIKT 100–446080-NR, *Tampa Times*, June 13, 1967, p. 14; *Chicago Daily Defender*, June 15, 1967, p. 2. *Boston Globe*, June 16, 1967, p. 11; *Los Angeles Times*, June 22, 1966, p. 4.

54. *Boston Globe*, July 27, 1967, p. 52 and August 22, 1967, p. 22.

55. FBIKT 100–446080-NR, Deke DeLoach to Clyde Tolson, July 10, 1967, pp. 1–4; FBIKT 100–446080–249, Memorandum, May 23, 1967, p. 1; FBIKT 100–446080-NR, Correspondence to Mildred Stegall, May 24, 1967, pp. 1–2. Front-page headlines in *The Wall Street Journal* sounded a public warning over Carmichael's threat to return to Washington for activities almost preordained as violent. SNCC's summer campaign to eradicate "votelessness, police brutality, the racist war in Vietnam, starvation diets and racist courts" struck the *Journal* as a blunt call for subversion. They cited black local leaders (including former SNCC activist Marion Barry) as more credible advocates for the city's indigenous population, dismissing Carmichael as a rabble-rousing carpetbagger while ignoring his roots in the community and his status as one of Howard University's most famous alumni. SNCC's new chairman inspired fevered interest from journalists and the FBI. Informants detailed Rap Brown's Houston lecture on rioting, which allegedly discussed effective ways to damage urban areas despite the presence of National Guard. At a June 22nd press conference, Brown ratcheted up the race-war talk, suggesting that "If America chooses to play the Nazi, black people don't choose to play the Jews." Brown's penchant for outrageous comments that laced predictions of guerrilla warfare with pungent humor made him Carmichael's contemporary in the ability to outrage white Americans, if not inspire black militants. Joseph, *Waiting 'Til the Midnight Hour*; FBIKT 100–446080-NR, "Student Nonviolent Coordinating Committee: Stokely Carmichael," June 27, 1967, pp. 1–4.

Chapter Twelve: The World Stage: London, Cuba, and Vietnam

1. Angela Davis, *Angela Davis: An Autobiography* (1974; New York: International Publishers, 1988), p. 150. FBIKT 100–446080-no serial, *Observer Review*, July 23, 1967.

2. *Boston Globe*, July 16, 1967, p. 14.

3. Carmichael with Thelwell, *Ready for Revolution*, pp. 573–577. Kalbir Shukra, *The Changing Pattern of Black Politics in Britain* (London: Pluto Press, 1998), pp. 24–25, 30–31.

4. Carmichael with Thelwell, *Ready for Revolution*, p. 576; Ware Interview, pp. 36–43; *Observer Review*, July 23, 1967, p. 17; *London Times*, July 25, 1967, p. 2.

5. *Stokely Speaks*, p. 78.

6. Ibid., p. 80, 81.

7. Ibid., p. 91.

8. Carmichael with Thelwell, *Ready for Revolution*, p. 580; Tariq Ali, *Street-Fighting Years: An Autobiography of the Sixties* (London: Verso, 2005), pp. 198–199. Quotes from Stokely Carmichael, Dialectics of Liberation Panel, July 1967. 1CDR0002893; 1CDR0002893_BD02 [1]. Mp3; 1CDR)))2894_BD01[1].Mp3; 1CDR0002894_BD02[1]. Stokely Carmichael Recordings, British Library.

9. *Berkeley Barb*, September 1–7, 1967, p. 5. *London Tribune*, July 28, 1967, p. 7. *The Observer Review*, July 23, 1967, p. 17; *Washington Post*, July 25, 1967, p. 3.

10. FBIKT 100–446080–521, Foreign Broadcast Information Service, Special Memorandum, "Reportage and Comment on Stokely Carmichael's Activities and Statements Abroad," p. 24; *London Times*, July 25, 1967, p. 2; *Boston Globe*, July 24, 1967, p. 14; *Washington Post*, July 27, 1967, p. 7.

11. Joseph, *Waiting 'Til the Midnight Hour*, pp. 186–187.

12. *New York Times*, July 26, 1967, p. 22; *New Journal and Guide*, July 29, 1967, p. B4. FBIKT 100–446080-no serial, "Cuban Clandestine Operation in the United States," Memorandum, July 26, 1967; FBIKT 100–446080–521, "Reportage and Comment on Stokely Carmichael's Activities and Statements Abroad," August 9, 1967, p. 1; Ware interview, p. 46.

13. FBIKT 100–446080–521, "Reportage and Comment on Stokely Carmichael's Activities and Statements Abroad," pp. 32, 49; *The Militant*, August 21, 1967, pp. 24–32, Stokely Carmichael Clippings. Schomburg Center.

14. Ware interview, p. 48. FBIKT 100–446080–521, "Reportage and Comment on Stokely Carmichael's Activities and Statements Abroad," p. 23; Ware interview, p. 48. Elizabeth Martínez interview, March 6, 2009, pp. 12–13; Carmichael with Thelwell, *Ready for Revolution*, p. 583; Ware interview, pp. 49–50. FBIKT 100–446080–521, "Reportage and Comment on Stokely Carmichael's Activities and Statements Abroad," August 9, 1967, p. 40; *New York Times*, July 27, 1967, pp. 1–11.

15. FBIKT 100–446080–410, "Stokely Carmichael," July 28, 1967, p. 1. FBIKT 100–446080–616, *Christian Science Monitor*, July 28, 1967.

16. "July 26, 1967: Castro Adds the US to His Revolutionary List," pp. 1–3. US Dept. of State, File No: POL 23–8; 4/1/67, Box: 2605; FBIKT 100–446080–521, "Reportage and Comment on Stokely Carmichael's Activities and Statements Abroad," p. 2; *New York Times*, July 26, 1967, p. 38; *Christian Science Monitor*, July 1967, SCLDSC.

17. FBIKT 100–446080–448, "Stokely Carmichael," August 4, 1967, pp. 1–2; FBIKT 100–446080–521, "Reportage and Comment on Stokely Carmichael's Activities and Statements Abroad," August 9, 1967, pp. 38–39. FBIKT 100–446080-not recorded, Memorandum, August 4, 1967; Carmichael interview with Clayborne Carson, October 18, 1977, p. 13.

18. FBIKT 100–446080–466, "Snick—Castro's Arm in U.S.," *Omaha World Herald*, August 6, 1967. *Boston Globe*, July 29, 1967, p. 7.

19. Correspondence between Nicholas Katzenbach and Dr. James H. Mendel, July 26 and September 12, 1967; Tom Adams to Dean Rusk, August 14, 1967; Winthrop Brown to Tom Adams, August 22, 1967; Dixon Donnelly to Frank R. Chase, August 31, 1967; Dixon Donnelly to C.N. Woodruff, August 31, 1967; RG 59, GRDS, SC, 1/1/67, Box 234. Winthrop G. Brown to Lurleen Wallace, August 11, 1967, pp. 1–2; RG 59, GRDS, SC, 1/1/67, Box 234.

20. *Los Angeles Times*, July 30, 1967, p. F4; *Los Angeles Times*, August 3, 1967, pp. 1, 8. *Boston Globe*, July 29, 1967, p. 5. For discussion of Reagan quote see *Washington Post*, July

28, 1967, p. 17 and *Boston Globe*, July 29, 1967, p. 5. Detroit's Police Chief Ray Giradin, while conceding that Stokely Carmichael's speeches inflamed local militants, denied that the riot had been the product of an organized conspiracy. See *New York Times*, July 28, 1967, p. 10. *Baltimore Afro-American*, July 29, 1967, p. 15. *New York Times*, July 30, 1967, p. 141. FBIKT 100–446080–498, Memorandum, "Stokely Carmichael, Sedition," To Clyde Tolson from Deke DeLoach, August 7, 1967, p. 1.

21. Carmichael with Thelwell, *Ready for Revolution*, pp. 583–584.

22. *Boston Globe*, July 31, 1967, pp. 1, 5; *Los Angeles Times*, July 31, 1967, pp. 1, 6; *Chicago Tribune*, August 1, 1967, p. 6; *Los Angeles Times*, August 1, 1967, p. 14.

23. FBIKT 100–446080–521, "Reportage and Comment on Stokely Carmichael's Activities and Statements Abroad," pp. 7, 12, 49; *The Movement*, September 1967, p. 280.

24. FBIKT 100–446080–686, "Stokely Carmichael," Airtel, November 9, 1967, pp. 1–5. James Reston, "Havana: Stokely Carmichael's Game," *New York Times*, August 2, 1967, p. 36; Ware interview, pp. 51–52 ; Carmichael with Thelwell, *Ready for Revolution*, pp. 588–589; see also James Reston, "Havana: The American Negro and Communist Strategy," *New York Times*, July 28, 1967, p. 23 and "Havana: Castro's Achievements and Contradictions," *New York Times*, July 30, 1967, p. 140.

25. *Washington Post*, August 2, 1967, pp. 1, 14; *Chicago Tribune*, August 2, 1967, p. 8; *Boston Globe*, August 2, 1967, p. 46. See also *Chicago Tribune* editorial "If It Isn't Sedition, What Is It?," August 5, 1967, p. 8; Richard Helms to President Johnson, Memorandum, August 8, 1967, p. 1. LBJL, Case # 91–33, Document #108A.

26. "Reportage and Comment on Stokely Carmichael's Activities and Statements Abroad," August 10 to October 5, 1967, pp. 16–25, 27. State Department. LBJL.

27. FBIKT 100–446080–NR, "Stokely Carmichael: Foreign Broadcast Information Service Reports, July–December 1967," January 22, 1968, pp. 4–8.

28. Carmichael, *Stokely Speaks*, p. 104.

29. Ibid., pp. 101–110.

30. "Speech of the U.S. Representative, Stokely Carmichael, at the First Conference of Latin American Solidarity (OLAS) July 31–August 10, 1967," FBIKT 100–446080–675, pp. 2–3.

31. *Los Angeles Times*, August 11, 1967, p. 23; *National Guardian*, September 9, 1967, p. 3; *Chicago Tribune*, August 12, 1967, p. 6. *Los Angeles Times*, August 13, 1967, p. E3.

32. "Reportage and Comment on Stokely Carmichael's Activities and Statements Abroad," August 10 to October 5, 1967, p. 28; *Washington Post*, August 12, 1967, p. 4; *Chicago Daily Defender*, August 15, 1967, p. 2.

33. Carmichael with Thelwell, *Ready for Revolution*, pp. 594–595.

34. Stokely Carmichael Interviewed by David Du Bois in Cairo, Week of September 19, 1967, p. 3. Schlesinger Library, Radcliffe Institute, Harvard University. "Reportage and Comment on Stokely Carmichael's Activities and Statements Abroad," August 10 to October 5, 1967, p. 48; *New York Times*, September 1, 1967, p. 18; *Washington Post*, September 1, 1967, p. 14; "Reportage and Comment on Stokely Carmichael's Activities and Statements Abroad," October 6 to December 12, 1967, p. 8.

35. Carmichael with Thelwell, *Ready for Revolution*, p. 600. "Reportage and Comment on Stokely Carmichael's Activities and Statements Abroad," August 10 to October 5, 1967, pp. 43; *Washington Post*, August 10, 1967, p. 22; *New York Times*, August 11, 1967, p. 3; *Los Angeles Sentinel*, August 24, 1967, p. 2; *Baltimore Afro-American*, August 26, 1967, pp. 1–2; Carmichael with Thelwell, *Ready for Revolution*, pp. 600–601. "Reportage and Comment on Stokely Carmichael's Activities and Statements Abroad," August 10 to October 5, 1967, p. 49.

36. *Chicago Sun Times*, September 5, 1967; *Chicago Daily News*, September 5, 1967; CSTA. *New Journal and Guide*, September 9, 1967, p. 1.

Chapter Thirteen: The World Stage: Africa

1. "Visit of Stokely Carmichael to Algeria," September 21, 1967. CIA-FOIA, Case No. E)-1998–00458; Dept. of State Airgram, October 2, 1967, pp. 1–2. POL 23–8; August 1, 1967, Box 2605. American Embassy Algiers to Secretary of State, September 6, 1967, pp. 1–2, RG 59, GRDS, SC, 1/1/67, Box 234. Quotes from "Stokely Carmichael," September 7, 1967, pp. 1–2. RG 59, GRDS, SC, 1/1/67, Box 234.

2. *The Egyptian Gazette*, September 8, 1967, p. 2.

3. Quote from "Stokely Carmichael Interview in *Révolution Africaine*," September 11, 1967, pp. 1–2; "Stokely Carmichael in Algeria," September 11, 1967, pp. 1–2. RG 59/GRDS, FN: SC, 1/1/67, Box 234. "Reportage and Comment on Stokely Carmichael's Activities and Statements Abroad," August 10 to October 5, 1967, p. 57; "Stokely Carmichael," Telegram, September 7, 1967, p. 1 and American Embassy Algiers to Secretary of State, Telegram, September 8, 1967, p. 1, RG 59, GRDS, SC, 1/1/67, Box 234; "Stokely Carmichael Interview in *Révolution Africaine*" September 11, 1967, pp. 1–2; "Stokely Carmichael in Algeria," September 11, 1967, pp. 1–2. RG 59/GRDS, FN: SC, 1/1/67, Box 234.

4. *Los Angeles Times*, September 9, 1967, p. 9; *Washington Post*, September 9, 1967, p. 6. "Stokely Carmichael," September 11, 1967, SD Airgram, RG 59, GRDS, SC, 1/1/67, Box 234. "Reportage and Comment on Stokely Carmichael's Activities and Statements Abroad," August 10 to October 5, 1967, pp. 57, 62–63. "A Visit to Oran: IV. Thoughts on Stokely Carmichael," October 2, 1967, pp. 1–2, SD Airgram, RG 59, GRDS, SC, 1/1/67, Box 234.

5. "Stokely Carmichael Interview in *Révolution Africaine*," September 11, 1967, pp. 1–2; RG59/GRDS, FN: SC, 1/1/67, Box 234. *The Egyptian Gazette*, September 12, 1967, pp. 1, 3 and September 13, 1967, p. 2.

6. "Stokely Carmichael in Algeria," September 18, 1967, pp. 1–2. RG59/GRDS, FN: Carmichael, Stokely, 1/1/67, Box: 234. American Embassy Algiers to Secretary of State, September 14, 1967, pp. 1–2. RG 59, GRDS, SC, 1/1/67, Box 234. *Philadelphia Tribune*, September 12, 1967, p. 1.

7. "Stokely Carmichael in Algeria," September 18, 1967, pp. 1–2. RG59/GRDS, FN: Carmichael, Stokely, 1/1/67, Box: 234; "Reportage and Comment on Stokely Carmichael's Activities and Statements Abroad," August 10 to October 5, 1967, pp. 61–62; *National Guardian*, September 16, 1967, p. 8.

8. "Stokely Wasn't All That Great," October 2, 1967, pp. 1–2. RG 59, GRDS, SC, 1/1/67, Box 234.

9. *Boston Globe*, August 16, 1966, p. 14; *New York Times*, August 15, 1967, pp. 1, 16. "Reportage and Comment on Stokely Carmichael's Activities and Statements Abroad," August 10 to October 5, 1967, p. 55. "Complete Transcript of a Taped Interview with Mr. Stokely Carmichael Made in Cairo the Week of September 19, 1967," pp. 1–8. Shirley Graham Du Bois Papers, Schlesinger Library, Radcliffe Institute. Harvard University; Joseph, *Waiting 'Til the Midnight Hour*, pp. 194–195.

10. Carmichael with Thelwell, *Ready for Revolution*, p. 605. "Reportage and Comment on Stokely Carmichael's Activities and Statements Abroad," August 10 to October 5, 1967, p. 77. Carmichael and Du Bois Transcript, p. 8; *Egyptian Gazette*, September 18, 1967, p. 3.

11. "Reportage and Comment on Stokely Carmichael's Activities and Statements Abroad," August 10 to October 5, 1967, pp. 79, 83–84; *Chicago Daily Defender*, September 25, 1967, p. 4; *Washington Post*, September 24, 1967, p. B2; Carmichael, *Ready for Revolution*, pp. 606, 608–609; *The Egyptian Gazette*, September 24, 1967, p. 2. *The Egyptian Gazette*, September 28, 1967, p. 2.

12. Carmichael with Thelwell, *Ready for Revolution*, p. 614.

13. Marable, *Malcolm X*, pp. 384–385.

14. Miriam Makeba with James Hall, *My Story* (New York: New American Library, 1987), p. 109.

15. Ibid., pp. 142–147.

16. Carmichael with Thelwell, *Ready for Revolution*, pp. 617–620; Makeba, *Makeba*, pp. 147–153, 109.

17. Carmichael with Thelwell, *Ready for Revolution*, pp. 622, 614–15.

18. "Stokely Carmichael," Telegram, September 28, 1967, pp. 1–2, RG 59, GRSD, SC, 1/1/67, Box 234.

19. "Stokely Carmichael Visit to Guinea," October 16, 1967, pp. 1–2; Carmichael with Thelwell, *Ready for Revolution*, p. 603.

20. "Reportage and Comment on Stokely Carmichael's Activities and Statements Abroad," August 10 to October 5, 1967, p. 86.

21. Fleming, *Soon We Will Not Cry*, pp. 1–12.

22. "Reportage and Comment on Stokely Carmichael's Activities and Statements Abroad," October 6 to December 12, 1967, p. 5.

23. Ibid., pp. 6–7; Carmichael with Thelwell, *Ready for Revolution*, p. 632; *Chicago Daily Defender*, October 25, 1967, p. 2.

24. "Stokely Carmichael in Tanzania Backwash and Backlash," December 15, 1967, p. 1. RG 59, GRDS, SC, 1/1/67, Box 234.

25. Quotes from "Stokely Carmichael," November 1, 1967, pp. 1–4, RG 59/GRDS, FN: Carmichael, Stokely, 1/1/67, Box: 234; FBIKT 100–446080–1012, "Stokely Carmichael," January 19, 1968, Transcript of November 1967 interview by Tom Looker, p. 1.

26. *The Nationalist*, November 4, 1967, p.1; Carmichael with Thelwell, *Ready for Revolution*, p. 638; Makeba, *Makeba*, pp. 148–149.

27. "ANC on Stokely Carmichael," November 27, 1967, pp. 1–3, RG59/GRDS, FN: Carmichael, Stokely, 1/1/67, Box: 234. DS Telegram, November 23, 1967, RG59 GRSD, FN: Carmichael, Stokely, 1/1/67, Box: 234; *Chicago Tribune*, November 5, 1967, p. 12; *Washington Post*, November 5, 1967, p. 28; *New York Times*, November 5, 1967, p. 24. See also *New York Amsterdam News*, November 25, 1967, p. 2.

28. "Stokely Carmichael in Tanzania: Backwash and Backlash," December 15, 1967, pp. 1–8. RG 59, GRDS, SC, 1/1/67, Box: 234; "ANC on Stokely Carmichael," November 27, 1967, pp. 1–3, RG 59, GRDS, SC, 1.1.67, Box 234. *Baltimore Afro-American*, December 2, 1967, p. 1; FBIKT 100–446080–1012, "Stokely Carmichael," January 19, 1968, Transcript of November 1967 interview by Tom Looker, p. 2.

29. FBIKT 100–446080–1038, United States Information Agency, "Stokely Carmichael," January 23, 1968, pp. 1–5; FBIKT 100–446080–1038, "Stokely Carmichael: Talk at Kivukoni College, November 6, 1967," January 23, 1968, pp. 1–8; Carmichael with Thelwell, *Ready for Revolution*, pp. 635–638; "Stokely Irks African Rebel Leaders," *New York Post*, November 20, 1967; "Reportage and Comment on Stokely Carmichael's Activities and Statements Abroad," October 6 to December 12, 1967, p. 18.

30. "Reportage and Comment on Stokely Carmichael's Activities and Statements Abroad," October 6 to December 12, 1967, p. 18; *Washington Post*, November 28, 1967, p. 10; FBIKT 100–446080–877, FBI Director to SAC Atlanta, Airtel, December 28, 1967.

31. FBIKT 100–446080–NR, Telegram, American Embassy London, November 29, 1967; *International Herald Tribune*, November 30, 1967, p. 3.

32. "Reportage and Comment on Stokely Carmichael's Activities and Statements Abroad," October 6 to December 12, 1967, p. 20; *International Herald Tribune*, December 1, 1967, p. 3. FBIKT 100–446080–NR, American Embassy Oslo to United States Information Office, Washington, DC, December 1, 1967, pp. 1–2.

33. State Dept. Telegram, November 28, 1967, p. 1; State Dept. Telegram, November 30, 1967, pp. 1–2; State Dept. Telegram, November 30, 1967, pp. 1–2; State Dept. Telegram, December 5, 1967, pp. 1–2, RG 59/GRDS, FN: Carmichael, Stokely, 1/1/67, Box 234; FBIKT 100–446080–998, "Sojourn in Paris of the Colored American Extremist Leader Stokely Carmichael," December 11, 1967, p. 1; *International Herald Tribune*, December 6, 1967, p. 1.

34. *New York Times*, December 7, 1967, p. 2; FBIKT 100–446080–758, "Stokely Carmichael," Memorandum, December 5, 1967. *New York Times*, February 10, 1965, p. 3; *Chicago Defender*, December 9, 1967, p. 3; *The Chicago Daily Defender*, December 7, 1967, p. 19 and *New York Times*, December 7, 1967; FBIKT 100–446080–1012, *The Sunday San Francisco Chronicle & Examiner*, December 10, 1967, p. 6; *New York Times*, December 6, 1967, p. 3; *International Herald Tribune*, December 6, 1967, p. 1. Various accounts state that Carmichael's time in quarantine was between twelve and seventeen hours; FBIKT 100–446080–NR, "French Bar Carmichael At Airport," *International Herald Tribune*, December 6, 1967; FBIKT 100–446080–740, FBI New York to Director Hoover, Teletype, December 6, 1967. Based on accounts from FBI, newspaper sources, and French intelligence, Carmichael arrived at Orly Airport at 7:40 P.M. on December 5 and departed at 3:00 P.M. the next day, making seventeen hours the most accurate assessment of his time in quarantine.

35. After his ordeal at Orly Stokely thanked the French police for their hospitality when they returned his stamped passport on Wednesday afternoon. FBIKT 100–446080–NR, "Carmichael at Paris Rally As French Reverse Stand," *International Herald Tribune*, December 7, 1967, pp. 1–2; *International Herald Tribune*, December 6 and 7, 1967.

36. *San Francisco Sunday Examiner & Chronicle*, December 10, 1967, p. 6.

37. *Greensboro Daily News*, December 7, 1967. SCLDS; *New York Times*, December 7, 1967, p. 2; *Chicago Tribune*, December 7, 1967, p. 7; *U.S. News & World Report*, December 15, 1967, p. 28.

38. FBIKT 100–446080–1042, "Stokely Carmichael: Sedition," February 1, 1968, pp. 23–24; FBIKT 100–446080–779, Paris Legat to Director Hoover, Airtel, December 12, 1967, "Translation from French: An Address by Mr. Stokely Carmichael at a Meeting Held December 6, 1967, at 'La Mutualité' House." FBIKT 100–446080–812, "CBS Evening News with Walter Cronkite (Excerpt)," December 7, 1967, p. 1.

39. FBIKT 100–446080–NR, *International Herald Tribune*, December 7, 1967, pp. 1–2.

40. FBIKT 100–446080–998, "Sojourn in Paris of the Colored American Extremist Leader Stokely Carmichael," December 11, 1967, p. 3.

41. Dick Perrin with Tim McCarthy, *GI Resister* (Victoria, Canada: Trafford Press, 2002), pp. 74–80; *New York Times*, December 10, 1967, p. 6; *Boston Globe*, December 10, 1967, p. 93; FBIKT 100–446080–813, "Stokely Carmichael," December 11, 1967, pp. 1–4; FBIKT 100–446080–824, "Carmichael Loses Passport," *Washington Daily News*, December 12, 1967, p. 49; *Boston Globe*, December 12, 1967, p. 17; *Chicago Daily Defender*, December 12, 1967, p. 20; *Chicago Tribune*, December 12, 1967, p. B9; *New York Times*, December 12, 1967, p. 15; *Washington Post*, December 12, 1967, p. 1. See also editorials, "Call Carmichael's Bluff," *Chicago Tribune*, December 13, 1967, p. 22 and "Carmichael Returns," *Chicago Daily Defender*, December 18, 1967, p. 13. *Chicago Tribune*, December 13, 1967, p. 22; *Chicago Daily Defender*, December 18, 1967, p. 13; *Washington Post*, December 18, 1967, p. 20.

42. Joseph, *Waiting 'Til the Midnight Hour*, p. 204; *New York Times*, December 12, 1967, p. 14 and December 17, 1967, p. 188; FBIKT 100–446080–744, "Stokely Carmichael," December 12, 1967; FBIKT 100–446080–765, "Stokely Carmichael," December 11, 1967; *Chicago Daily Defender*, December 12, 1967, pp. 1, 3. Carmichael with Thelwell, *Ready for Revolution*, p. 639. *New York Times*, October 8, 1967, p. 28; *Baltimore Afro-American*, October 14, 1967, p. 1.

43. FBIKT 100–446080–824, "Carmichael Loses Passport," *Washington Daily News*, December 12, 1967, p. 49; FBIKT 100–446080–844, Copy of Stokely Carmichael Passport, issued

January 26, 1967; *Chicago Daily Defender*, December 12, 1967, pp. 1, 3; *New York Times*, December 12, 1967, p. 14; *Los Angeles Times*, December 12, 1967, pp. 1, 9 and December 17, 1967, p. L4; *Washington Post*, December 12, 1967, pp. 1, 4; *New York Amsterdam News*, December 16, 1967, pp. 1, 44. FBIKT 100–446080–777, "Stokely Carmichael," December 11, 1967; FBIKT 100–446080–919, "Stokely Carmichael," December 28, 1967, p. 1. FBIKT 100–446080–NR, "Carmichael's Mother Lives in Fear," *Barbados Advocate*, December 14, 1967.

44. *New York Times*, October 10, 1967, p. 47. Enterprising staff members attempted to turn Carmichael's strategic silence into financial profit. Desperate for money, SNCC representatives approached news media with an offer to sell an exclusive Carmichael interview for $70,000 only to be rebuffed. FBIKT 100–446080–882, "Stokely Carmichael," Teletype, December 28, 1967, p. 1; FBIKT 100–446080–900, "Stokely Carmichael," Memorandum, December 29, 1967.

45. *Los Angeles Times*, December 3, 1967, p. D21 and December 17, 1967, p. L3; *Washington Post*, December 3, 1967, p. K6.

Chapter Fourteen: Black Panther

1. Bloom and Martin, *Black Against Empire*, p. 101.

2. *Chicago Defender*, October 7, 1967, p. 1; *New York Times*, January 22, 1968, p. 18.

3. Christopher Lasch, "The Trouble with Black Power: A Special Supplement," *The New York Review of Books*, February 29, 1968. Albert Murray, "The Illusive Black Image," *Chicago Sun-Times*, November 26, 1967, pp. 4, 10. Joseph, *Waiting 'Til the Midnight Hour*, p. 200; *New York Times*, December 10, 1967, pp. 3, 66; *San Francisco Examiner-Chronicle*, November 19, 1967; *Chicago Daily News*, October 21, 1967. CST.

4. "Possible Criminal Prosecution of Stokely Carmichael," December 20, 1967, pp. 1–6. RG 59/State Dept. Records, Carmichael, Stokely, 1/1,67, Box: 234; Leonard Meeker to Walter Yeagley, December 29, 1967, and Walter Yeagley to Leonard Meeker, December 20, 1967, RG 59, GRDS, SC, 1/1/67.

5. FBIKT 100–446080–881, NY FBI to Director and Atlanta, Teletype, December 28, 1967, p. 1; FBIKT 100–446080–883, Domestic Intelligence Division to FBI Director, Teletype, December 31, 1967; *New York Times*, December 30, 1967, p. 21; *Chicago Daily Defender*, January 2, 1968, p. 8.

6. FBIKT 100–446080–1047, "Stokely Carmichael," January 23, 1968, pp. 7–8. *Washington Post*, January 10, 1968, pp. 1, 12. FBIKT 100–446080–1818, "Stokely Carmichael: Washington Field Office Report," July 30, 1968, p. P.

7. FBIKT 100–446080–970, Washington SAC to FBI Director, Teletype, January 15, 1968, pp. 1–3. *Washington Post*, January 18, 1968, pp. 1, 7. *New York Times*, January 18, 1968, p. 29; Robert C. Maynard, "Negro Coalition Leadership Rift Brews," *Washington Post*, January 13, 1968, p. B3; "Clerics denounce Negro Coalition Led by Carmichael," *Washington Post*, January 14, 1968, p. C3 and "Carmichael in Church Plays It Like Pro," *Washington Post*, January 15, 1968, p. B1; *Chicago Daily Defender*, January 15, 1968, p. 8; FBIKT 100–446080–946, "Stokely Carmichael," January 10, 1968, pp. 1–2.

8. *Chicago Daily Defender*, January 27, 1968, p. 4; *Los Angeles Sentinel*, January 25, 1968, p. D1. FBIKT 100–446080–987, NY FBI to FBI Director, Teletype, January 20, 1968; FBIKT 100–446080–988, WFO SAC to FBI Director, Teletype, January 20, 1968; FBIKT 100–446080–989X, WFO SAC to FBI Director, Teletype, January 21, 1968; Robert C. Maynard, "Carmichael Enigma: What Are His Aims?," *Washington Post*, January 21, 1968, pp. 1, 10; *New York Times*, January 29, 1968, p. 40.

9. FBIKT 100–446080–1167, Memorandum, Stokely Carmichael, February 27, 1968, pp. 1–2; Bobby Seale, *Seize the Time* (New York, Random House, 1970). pp. 214–218.

10. FBIKT 100–446080-NR, "Washington Spring Project," February 6, 1968, p. 2; FBIKT 100–446080-NR, "Washington Spring Project," February 7, 1968, pp. 1–3.

11. FBIKT 100–446080-1096, "Stokely Carmichael," February 5, 1968, p. 2; FBIKT 100–446080-NR, "Washington Spring Project: Racial Matters," January 31, 1968, p. 1. Ethel Payne, "King, Stokely Join in Capitol Camp-In," *Chicago Defender*, January 30, 1968. Carmichael with Thelwell, *Ready for Revolution*, pp. 648–650; FBIKT 100–446080, "Stokely Carmichael," pp. 77–78; *Muhammad Speaks*, February 23, 1968, p. 22; *Chicago Daily Defender*, February 5, 1968, p. 6; *Baltimore Afro-American*, February 17, 1968, p. 4; *Washington Post*, February 11, 1968, p. D1; *New York Times*, February 11, 1968, p. E4.

12. Carmichael with Thelwell, *Ready for Revolution*, pp. 647–648; Branch, *At Canaan's Edge*, pp. 689–690; *Baltimore-Washington Afro-American*, February 10, 1968, p. 1. Garrow, *Bearing the Cross*, pp. 584–585. FBIKT 100–446080-NR, "Washington Spring Project: Racial Matters," February 9, 1968, pp. 1–3; FBIKT 100–446080-1104, WFO SAC to FBI Director, Teletype, February 7, 1968, pp. 1–3.

13. *New Pittsburgh Courier*, February 17, 1968, pp, 1, 4; Branch, *At Canaan's Edge*, pp. 691–692.

14. Joseph, *Waiting 'Til the Midnight Hour*. FBIKT 100–446080-1237, "Stokely Carmichael," March 6, 1968, p. 1. FBIKT 100–446080-1397, "Stokely Carmichael," April 11, 1968, p. 2.

15. Ethel Minor Interview, pp. 1–12. Carmichael and Hamilton, *Black Power*, p. 179.

16. Newton, *Revolutionary Suicide*, p. 209. *Call and Post*, February 17, 1968, p. 5B; *Oakland Tribune*, February 17, 1968; *Berkeley Gazette*, February 17, 1968. Stanford University, Green Library, Newton Foundation Papers (hereafter, NFP).

17. Carson, *In Struggle*, pp. 277–286.

18. Forman, *The Making of Black Revolutionaries*, pp. 518–21.

19. See Joseph, *Waiting 'Til the Midnight Hour*; Clayborne Carson, *In Struggle*; *National Guardian*, February 24, 1968, p. 6. Joseph, *Waiting 'Til the Midnight Hour*, pp. 224–226.

20. Carmichael, *Stokely Speaks*, pp. 121–122.

21. Quotes from FBIKT 100–446080-1397, "Stokely Carmichael," April 11, 1968, pp. 4–21.

22. Carmichael with Thelwell, *Ready for Revolution*, pp. 115–118.

23. *Oakland Tribune*, February 19, 1968. NFP. Carson, *In Struggle*, p. 281; Scot Brown, *Fighting for US: Maulana Karenga, the US Organization, and Black Cultural Nationalism* (New York: New York University Press, 2003), pp. 82–93.

24. FBIKT 100–446080-1209, "Stokely Carmichael, Black Congress Sponsored Rally for Defense of Huey P. Newton, Los Angeles Sports Arena, February 18, 1968," March 5, 1968.

25. Ibid., p. 58; *Chicago Sun-Times*, February 18, 1968. CSTA. FBIKT 100–446080-1209, "Stokely Carmichael, Black Congress Sponsored Rally for Defense of Huey P. Newton, Los Angeles Sports Arena, February 18, 1968," March 5, 1968, pp. 71–72, 72–73.

26. Joseph, *Waiting 'Til the Midnight Hour*, pp. 218–219; Brown, *Fighting for US*, pp. 94–95.

27. Minor Interview, p. 43; Carson, *In Struggle*, p. 283.

28. FBIKT 100–446080-1245, "Stokely Carmichael," March 13, 1968, pp. 1–8; FBIKT 100–446080-1274, "Stokely Carmichael," Transcript of Morehouse Speech, March 14, 1968, pp. 1–25. FBIKT 100–446080-1193, Teletype, "Stokely Carmichael," February 28, 1968, p. 1.

29. Herb Boyd, *Baldwin's Harlem* (New York: Atria Books, 2008). Joseph, *Waiting 'Til the Midnight Hour*. All Baldwin quotes in this and the next paragraph: James Baldwin, "From Dreams of Love to Dreams of Terror," *Los Angeles Free Press*, Feb. 23–29, 1968, pp. 1, 3; *Los Angeles Times*, July 7, 1968, p. 23; "Baldwin Batting for Carmichael," *Washington Post*, March 3, 1968, p. B2.

30. FBIKT 100–446080-1235, "Stokely Carmichael," March 12, 1968, pp. 1–4; FBIKT 100–446080-1213, "Stokely Carmichael," Teletype, March 10, 1968, pp. 1–2; FBIKT 100–446080-

1311, "Stokely Carmichael," March 19, 1968, pp. 1–2; FBIKT 100–446080–1279, "Stokely Carmichael," March 14, 1968, pp. 1–2; FBIKT 100–446080–1212, "Stokely Carmichael," Teletype, March 11, 1968, pp. 1–2; FBIKT 100–446080–1276, "Stokely Carmichael," March 13, 1968, pp. 1–4. Condoleezza Rice, *Extraordinary, Ordinary People: A Memoir of Family* (New York: Crown, 2010), pp. 117–119, 136–137. Officials at Miles College in Alabama reportedly initially refused to let Carmichael speak at the school during his tour of Alabama but relented. FBIKT 100–446080–1244, "Stokely Carmichael," Teletype, March 13, 1968, p. 1 and FBIKT 100–446080–1285, "Stokely Carmichael," March 18, 1968, pp. 1–2.

31. FBIKT 100–446080–1321, "Stokely Carmichael," March 19, 1968, pp. 1–5. Carmichael with Thelwell, *Ready for Revolution*, p. 655; *Boston Globe*, March 15, 1968, p. 2; *Washington Post*, March 16, 1968, p. 3; *New York Times*, March 16, 1968, p. 34; *Chicago Daily Defender*, March 18, 1968, p. 19; *Call and Post*, March 23, 1968, p. 10C. *Chicago Daily Defender*, March 21, 1968, p. 10. Makeba, *Makeba*, p. 162.

32. FBIKT 100–446080–1308, "Stokely Carmichael," March 18, 1968, pp. 1–4; FBIKT 100–446080–NR, "Possible Racial Violence Major Urban Areas: Washington, D.C.," March 20, 1968, pp. 1–6; FBIKT 100–446080–1251, "Stokely Carmichael," Teletype, March 17, 1968, pp. 1–2.

33. LeRoi Jones, *Home: Social Essays* (1966; Hopewell, NJ: Ecco Press, 1998), p. 85.

34. *Philadelphia Tribune*, March 23, 1968, p. 1; Quotes from FBIKT 100–446080–1441, "Stokely Carmichael," April 18, 1968, p. 9; FBIKT 100–446080–1357, "Stokely Carmichael," March 27, 1968, p. 4.

35. FBIKT 100–446080–1382, "Stokely Carmichael," April 1, 1968, pp. 1–5; FBIKT 100–446080–1337, "Stokely Carmichael," March 25, 1968, pp. 1–2.

36. *Chicago Daily Defender*, April 4, 1968, p. 10; *Baltimore Afro-American*, April 6, 1968, p. 10; Clay Risen, *A Nation on Fire: America in the Wake of the King Assassination* (Hoboken: John Wiley & Sons, 2009), p. 47; FBIKT 100–446080–NR, "Stokely Carmichael: Inciting to Riot," April 30, 1968, pp. 60–61, 66–67; FBIKT 100–446080–1357, "Stokely Carmichael," March 27, 1968, p. 7; FBIKT 100–446080–1613, "Stokely Carmichael," May 23, 1968, pp. 1–17.

Chapter Fifteen: The Prime Minister of Afro-America

1. James M. Washington, ed., *A Testament of Hope: The Essential Writings and Speeches of Martin Luther King, Jr.* (New York: Harper Collins, 1991), p. 286.

2. FBIKT 100–446080–1474, "Stokely Carmichael," April 23, 1968, pp. 1–2; FBIKT 100–446080–1389, "Stokely Carmichael: Inciting to Riot," April 8, 1968, p. 1. FBIKT 100–446080–1389, "Stokely Carmichael: Inciting to Riot," April 8, 1968, pp. 15–18.

3. FBIKT 100–446080–1389, "Stokely Carmichael: Inciting to Riot," April 8, 1968; Cara Skubel, "The Shaw Community: The Impact of the Civil Rights Movement, as told by Mrs. Virginia Ali, Owner of Ben's Chili Bowl," February 9, 2004, pp. 21–23. Oral History.

4. *Boston Globe*, April 5, 1968, p. 14; Risen, *A Nation On Fire*, pp. 54–58, 63; *Wall Street Journal*, April 8, 1968, p. 25; FBIKT 100–446080–NR, "Stokely Carmichael: Inciting to Riot," April 30, 1968, p. 99.

5. Sellers with Terrell, *The River of No Return*, pp. 229–233; Risen, *A Nation on Fire*, p. 67. *Chicago Daily Defender*, April 6, 1968, p. 2; *New York Times*, April 5, 1968, pp. 1, 26.

6. Lewis, *The Shadows of Youth*, p. 227.

7. Norman MacAfee, *The Gospel According to RFK: Why It Matters Now* (New York: Basic Books, 2008), pp. 97–98; Thurston Clarke, *The Last Campaign: Robert F. Kennedy and 82 Days That Inspired America* (New York: Henry Holt, 2008), pp. 95–96.

8. *Boston Globe*, April 6, 1968, p. 9; *Chicago Tribune*, April 6, 1968, pp. N1, 8. *Washington Post*, April 6, 1968, p. 16; *Chicago Daily Defender*, April 8, 1968, p. 17; FBIKT 100–446080–1389,

"Stokely Carmichael: Inciting to Riot," April 8, 1968, pp. 29–30. *Wall Street Journal*, April 8, 1968, p. 25.

9. *Washington Post*, April 6, 1968, p. A16 in FBIKT 100–446080–1403, p. 102.

10. Ibid.

11. Risen, *A Nation on Fire*, pp. 88–91; *New York Times*, April 6, 1968, p. 23.

12. FBIKT 100–446080–1818, "Stokely Carmichael," pp. 116–131; *Boston Globe*, April 6, 1968, p. 5; FBIKT 100–446080-NR, "Stokely Carmichael," MLK Assassination Summary, pp. 122–141; Risen, *A Nation on Fire*, pp. 101–102; FBIKT 100–446080–1439, "Stokely Carmichael," April 6, 1968, pp. 1–2. *New York Times*, April 7, 1968, p. 62; FBIKT 100–446080-NR, "Cuban Propaganda Activities," April 18, 1968, pp. 1–2.

13. *New York Times*, April 6, 1968, pp. 1, 22; FBIKT 100–446080-NR, "Stokely Carmichael," MLK Assassination Summary, April 1968, p. 70; *Washington Post*, April 7, 1968, p. B6 and April 8, 1968, pp. 11, 16.

14. *New York Times*, April 6, 1968, p. 38.

15. *Chicago Tribune*, April 6, 1968, p. N2.

16. *Philadelphia Evening Bulletin*, April 9, 1968. Temple University Urban Archives, hereafter cited as PEBUA. See also *New York Post*, April 7, 1968. FBI director J. Edgar Hoover publicly claimed a connection between Black Power and communists, who found Black Power–inspired urban and racial unrest useful for their overall political agenda. See *U.S. News & World Report*, January 15, 1968, p. 14. *San Jose Mercury,* April 9 and April 15, 1968. SCLDS. *San Jose Mercury*, July 3, 1968. SCLDS.

17. *Washington Post*, April 7, 1968, pp. B1, 3, 14; *New York Times*, April 8, 1968, p. 35; *Boston Globe*, April 8, 1968, p. 3; *New York Times,* April 14, 1968, p. E2.

18. *Washington Post*, April 8, 1968, pp. 1, 9, B1, B3; Risen, *A Nation on Fire*, pp. 183–186; *New York Times*, April 10, 1968, p. 35. FBIKT-100–446080–1380, "Stokely Carmichael," Teletype, April 7, 1968; FBIKT 100–446080–1389, "Stokely Carmichael: Inciting to Riot," April 8, 1968, pp. 39, 203–209.

19. *Chicago Tribune*, April 9, 1968, p. 1; *New York Times*, April 9, 1968, p. 37; *Washington Post*, April 12, 1968, p. B1; FBIKT 100–446080-NR, Memo, Fred Vinson to FBI Director, April 12, 1968, pp. 1–2.

20. *New York Times*, April 10, 1968, p. 33. Washington, ed., *The Essential Writings and Speeches of Martin Luther King, Jr.,* p. 267. *San Francisco Chronicle*, April 19, 1968. SCLDS; Carmichael with Thelwell, *Ready for Revolution*, p. 659; *Los Angeles Times*, April 10, 1968, pp. 1–2, 20; *Washington Post*, April 10, 1968, pp. 1, 11.

21. Michael K. Honey, *Going Down Jericho Road: The Memphis Strike, Martin Luther King's Last Campaign* (New York: W.W. Norton, 2008), p. 482.

22. Risen, *A Nation on Fire*, pp. 212–213. *Washington Post*, April 10, 1968, p. 1; *Boston Globe*, April 10, 1968, p. 13; *Chicago Daily Defender*, April 10, 1968, p. 3; *Chicago Tribune*, April 10, 1968, pp. 1–2; *New York Times*, April 10, 1968, pp. 1, 34; *New York Amsterdam News*, April 13, 1968, pp. 1, 49; FBIKT 100–446080–1371, "Stokely Carmichael," Teletype, April 10, 1968, pp. 1–2.

23. *Washington Post*, April 12, 1968, p. 23; Risen, *A Nation on Fire*, pp. 219–224; *New York Times*, April 12, 1968, p. 20; *Baltimore Afro-American*, April 13, 1968, pp. 1, 15; FBIKT 100–446080-NR, Memo, From Baltimore SAC to FBI Director, April 17, 1968, pp. 1–3.

24. Ransby, *Ella Baker and the Black Freedom Movement*, pp. 310, 350–351.

25. FBIKT 100–446080–1535, "Stokely Carmichael," April 29, 1968, pp. 1–3; FBIKT 100–446080–1593, "Stokely Carmichael," May 14, 1968, p. 2; *Boston Globe*, April 27, 1968, p. 2; *Chicago Daily Defender*, April 27, 1968, p. W2; *Los Angeles Times*, April 27, 1968, p. 1; *Washington Post*, April 27, 1968, pp. 1, 4; *New York Amsterdam News*, May 11, 1968, p. 32; Stefan Bradley, *Harlem vs. Columbia University: Black Student Power in the Late 1960s* (Urbana: University of Illinois Press, 2009).

26. *Baltimore Afro-American*, May 4, 1968, p. 14 and May 11, 1968, p. 21; *Washington Post*, December 14, 1968, p. C9.

27. FBIKT 100–446080–1703, "Stokely Carmichael," June 11, 1968, pp. 1–2; *New York Times*, May 18, 1968, p. 27.

28. Quotes from "Stokely Takes a Bride," *Ebony*, July 1968, pp. 137–142.

29. Ibid. *Washington Afro-American* in FBIKT 100–446080, May 21, 1968, pp. 185–188; see also, *The Oregonian*, May 20, 1968, and *Sepia*, July 1968. SCLDS.

30. FBIKT 100–446080-NR, "Stokely Carmichael–Counterintelligence Program," July 9, 1968, pp. 1–2.

31. *Call and Post*, June 15, 1968, p. 4B. Hubert Humphrey characterized media coverage of "the emotional appeals of the Stokely Carmichaels and other agitators" as tantamount to "throwing gasoline on the flames" of racial discontent. *New York Times*, June 18, 1968, p. 29; *Chicago Tribune*, June 13, 1968, p. 24; *Call and Post*, June 15, 1968, p. 4B; *Washington Post*, June 17, 1968, p. D11; *New York Amsterdam News*, June 15, 1968, p. 3; *New York Times*, June 25, 1968, p. 83; FBIKT 100–446080-NR, Airtel, Cleveland SAC to Director Hoover, June 20, 1968.

32. FBIKT 100–446080–1720, "Stokely Carmichael," Teletype, WFO SAC to Director and NY SAC, June 19, 1968; Carmichael with Thelwell, *Ready for Revolution*, p. 673.

33. *New York Times*, July 8, 1968, pp. 1, 23; *Los Angeles Times*, July 8, 1968, p. 4; *New York Amsterdam News*, July 20, 1968, p. 27; *New Pittsburgh Courier*, July 20, 1968, p. 5; *Chicago Daily Defender*, July 18, 1968, p. 16. Firing Line # 60, "Protest in Vietnam," William F. Buckley and Benjamin Spock, June 26, 1967, p. 7, Hoover Institute, Stanford University; *Boston Globe*, August 4, 1968, pp. 7.

34. Joseph, *Waiting 'Til the Midnight Hour*, pp. 232–233. See also *International Herald Tribune*, July 13–14, 1968. SCLDS.

35. FBIKT 100–446080–1842, "Stokely Carmichael," July 29, 1968, pp. 1–5; FBIKT 100–446080-NR, Signed Passport Affidavit, July 17, 1968; *Chicago Tribune*, July 27, 1968, p. N5; FBIKT 100–446080–1858, "Stokely Carmichael," Teletype, July 28, 1968, pp. 1–2; FBIKT 100–446080-NR, "Stokely Carmichael: Mobile, Alabama," September 9, 1968, pp. 34–50.

36. *New York Amsterdam News*, July 27, 1968, p. 16; Carmichael with Thelwell, *Ready for Revolution*, p. 702.

37. *New York Times*, August 9, 1968, p. 28; *Washington Post*, August 9, 1968, p. 3; *Boston Globe*, August 10, 1968, p. 2.

38. *Call and Post*, September 14, 1968, p. 6B.

39. Gerald C. Fraser, "SNCC Breaks Ties with Stokely Carmichael," *New York Times*, August 23, 1968, p. 45; "Carmichael's View," *New York Times*, August 23, 1968, p. 45; *Chicago Tribune*, August 23, 1968, p. 14; *Washington Post*, August 23, 1968, pp. 1, 23. *San Jose Mercury*, August 23, 1968. SCLDS. Carson, *In Struggle*, p. 283; Touré interview with Carson, May 4, 1983. Joseph, *Waiting 'Til the Midnight Hour*.

40. FBIKT 100–446080, COINTELPRO (Stokely Carmichael), July 9, 1968, pp. 1–2. FBI plans also included a bogus invitation to Carmichael to travel to China on a thirty-four-day tour to be underwritten by the Chinese government. See FBIKT 100–446080-Not Recorded, August 22, 1968, pp. 1–3. See also "Wedding Mansion For Carmichaels?" *U.S. News & World Report*, June 10, 1968, p. 14. *Washington Post*, August 24, 1968, p. D10; Carson, *In Struggle*, pp. 291–292; Bloom and Martin, *Black Against Empire*, pp. 123–124.

41. FBIKT 100–446080-Not Recorded, "Re Trial Huey P. Newton, Minister of Defense, Black Panther Party," p. 2; *Philadelphia Tribune*, August 31, 1968, p. 31. *Berkeley Barb*, 2–8, 1968, pp. 7, 17.

42. FBIKT 100–446080-Not Recorded, "Stokely Carmichael: Racial Matters," August 23, 1968, pp. 1–28.

43. *National Guardian*, August 31, 1968, p. 5. FBISNCC 100–439190 (Boston), "Student Non-Violent Coordinating Committee," July 22, 1968, pp. 1–18. See also, Kwame Ture interview

with Clayborne Carson, May 4, 1983. Carson Archives King Center, Stanford University; FBIKT 100–446080–1975, "Stokely Carmichael," September 17, 1968, p. 38.

44. FBIKT 100–446080–1929, Teletype, September 6, 1968, pp. 1–2; Jules Milne, ed., *Kwame Nkrumah: The Conakry Years: His Life and Letters* (London: Panaf Books, 1990), pp. 260–262. FBIKT 100–446080–NR, Stokely Carmichael Press Conference, Dakar, Senegal, September 1968, Department of State Telegram. Milne, *Kwame Nkrumah*, p. 261.

45. FBIKT 100–446080–1915, *Rocky Mountain News*, August 22, 1968, p. 70; Airtel, Denver SAC to FBI Director, August 22, 1968, pp. 1–3.

46. FBIKT 100–446080–1975, "Stokely Carmichael," September 17, 1968, pp. 226, 260–263.

47. FBIKT 100–446080–2201, "Stokely Carmichael," January 13, 1969 (Transcript of October 14, 1968, Black Writers Congress Speech), pp. 1–35.

48. *Baltimore Afro-American*, October 26, 1968, p. 31.

49. Diran Karaguezian, *Blow It Up!: The Black Student Revolt at San Francisco State College and the Emergence of Dr. Hayakawa* (Boston: Gambit, 1971), pp. 95–103.

50. *New York Times*, November 15, 1968, p. 34. FBIKT 100–446080–2089, "Stokely Carmichael," November 20, 1968, Transcript of Carmichael's Howard Speech, pp. 1–24.

51. FBIKT 100–446080–2112, Newspaper clipping, November 22, 1968; FBIKT 100–446080–2183, "Stokely Carmichael: Racial Matters–Black Panther Party," January 3, 1969, p. 2. FBIKT 100–446080–1975, "Stokely Carmichael," September 17, 1968, pp. 136–147; FBIKT 100–446080–2100, Teletype, "Stokely Carmichael," November 22, 1968; FBIKT 100–446080–2139, *Durham Morning Herald*, November 22, 1968, p. 8C. The State Department had returned his passport months earlier after he agreed to stay out of banned countries so he could honeymoon overseas. See *San Francisco Chronicle*, July 26, 1968, and *The Oregonian*, August 7, 1968. SCLDS.

Chapter Sixteen: "The Revolution Is Not About Dying. It's About Living"

1. Stokely Carmichael, "Pan-Africanism—Land and Power," *The Black Scholar* (originally published, November 1969, vol. 1, no. 1, pp. 36–43), vol. 27, nos. 3/4 Fall/Winter 1997, pp. 58–64.

2. *New York Times*, July 4, 1969, p. 25.

3. *San Francisco Chronicle*, July 5, 1969. SCLDS.

4. Carson interview with Carmichael, 1983; *Los Angeles Times*, July 22, 1969, p. 8. *New York Times*, July 25, 1969, p. 16; *New York Times*, July 26, 1969, p. 9; *New York Times*, August 18, 1969, p. 30; *Philadelphia Tribune*, August 23, 1969, p. 4; *Call and Post*, August 23, 1969, p. 7; Joseph, *Waiting 'Til the Midnight Hour*.

5. Makeba, *My Story*, p. 173.

6. *The Sunday Times* (London), November 3, 1969, p. 28.

7. Ibid.

8. Ibid., pp. 28–29, 31.

9. *New York Times*, July 26, 1969, p. 9; *Chicago Tribune*, July 31, 1969, p. N12; *Boston Globe*, July 31, 1969, p. 16.

10. Carmichael with Thelwell, *Ready for Revolution*, pp. 691, 704.

11. Makeba, *Makeba*, p. 156.

12. Carmichael, *Stokely Speaks*, pp. 185–182; Joseph, *Waiting 'Til the Midnight Hour*.

13. FBIKT 100–446080–2615, "Stokely Carmichael," Airtel, April 22, 1970, pp. 1–2.

14. *Greensboro Daily News*, March 20 and 25, 1970; *San Francisco Chronicle*, March 26, 1970; *Washington Post*, March 26, 1970, p. 6. SCLDS; *Chicago Tribune*, March 26, 1970, p. J14; *New York Times*, March 26, 1970, p. 51; *Los Angeles Times*, March 26, 1970, p. 27; *Baltimore Afro-American*, April 4, 1970, p. 1; Joseph, *Waiting 'Til the Midnight Hour*, p. 258.

15. See for example his April 11, 1970, speech in Baltimore. FBIKT 100–446080–2672, "Stokely Carmichael," June 11, 1970, p. 8.

16. FBIKT 100–446080–2503, "Stokely Carmichael: Racial Matters," April 10, 1970, pp. 1–2; FBIKT 100–446080–2512, "Stokely Carmichael," April 10, 1970, p. 1; FBIKT 100–446080–2530, "Stokely Carmichael," Teletype, April 10, 1970, pp. 1–3 *Washington Post*, April 10, 1970, p. B5; FBIKT 100–446080–2626, "Stokely Carmichael," May 12, 1970 (Transcript of Howard Speech), pp. 6–43.

17. *New York Times*, April 14, 1970, p. 51.

18. *Philadelphia Tribune*, April 18, 1970, p. 9. *New York Times*, April 14, 1970, p. 51; *Greensboro Daily News*, October 4, 1970. SCLDS.

19. *New York Times*, April 21, 1970; *Newsweek*, April 27, 1970; *Greensboro Daily News*, April 27, 1970. SCLDS. Carmichael, *Stokely Speaks*, pp. 186–190, 205–220. *Chicago Daily Defender*, April 21, 1970, pp. 3, 20; FBIKT 100–446080–2622, "Stokely Carmichael," April 29, 1970, pp. 10–45; FBIKT 100–446080–2675, "Stokely Carmichael," May 19, 1970, p. 7.

20. FBIKT 100–446080–2655, "Stokely Carmichael," April 27, 1970, pp. 1–8; FBIKT 100–446080–2665, "Stokely Carmichael," May 4, 1970, pp. 1–33.

21. FBIKT 100–446080–2604, "Stokely Carmichael," Teletype, May 2, 1970; *Washington Post*, May 6, 1970, p. B9; *Chicago Tribune*, May 6, 1970, p. 1.

22. Stokely Carmichael, "To the Brothers and Sisters of the Congress of African Peoples," August 17, 1970, Conakry, Guinea. SCLDS. Komozi Woodard, *A Nation Within a Nation* (Chapel Hill: University of North Carolina Press, 1999).

23. *New York Times*, April 14, 1996, p. E9. "Interview With Stokely Carmichael," *Afriscope*, July 1972, p. 33. SCLD. *New York Times*, February 6, 1971, p. 11.

24. *New York Times*, November 6, 1971, p. 8; *Washington Post*, June 18, 1972, p. L4; *Los Angeles Times*, July 6, 1972, p. D5.

25. FBIKT 100–446080–2883, "Stokely Carmichael: Racial Matters," March 25, 1971, pp. 1–2; FBIKT 100–446080–NR, "Domestic Intelligence Division," March 24, 1971. FBIKT 100–446080–2888, "Stokely Carmichael," March 22, 1971, pp. 1–30.

26. *Los Angeles Sentinel*, March 18, 1971, pp. 1, 12; FBIKT 100–446080–2951, "Stokely Carmichael," May 10, 1971, pp. 1–3.

27. FBIKT 100–446080–2917, "Stokely Carmichael," March 26, 1971, pp. 1, 23.

28. FBIKT 100–446080–2926, "Stokely Carmichael," April 5, 1971, pp. 1–12; FBIKT 100–446080–2880, "Stokely Carmichael," Teletype, March 20, 1971, pp. 1–3.

29. FBIKT 100–446080–NR, "Stokely Carmichael," March 30, 1971, pp. 1–4; FBIKT 100–446080–2938, "Stokely Carmichael: Racial Matters," April 8, 1971, pp. 1–36.

30. FBIKT 100–446080–2881, "Stokely Carmichael," Teletype, March 24, 1971, pp. 1–3; FBIKT 100–446080–2882, "Stokely Carmichael," Teletype, March 25, 1971, pp. 1–2; FBIKT 100–446080–2865, "Stokely Carmichael," Teletype, March 24, 1971, pp. 1–3; FBIKT 100–446080–NR, "Stokely Carmichael," March 23, 1971, pp. 1–3.

31. Stokely Carmichael to Toni Morrison, October 5, 1971; Stokely Carmichael to Toni Morrison, November 15 and December 15, 1971, March 16 and April 9, 1972; Toni Morrison to Stokely Carmichael, September 21, 1971. RHC, RBMLCU.

32. Stokely Carmichael to Toni Morrison, October 5, 1971. See also Stokely Carmichael to Toni Morrison, November 15 and December 15, 1971, March 16 and April 9, 1972; Toni Morrison to Stokely Carmichael, September 21, 1971; Stokely Carmichael to Alice Mayhew, November 26, 1970, November 26, 1970, February 1, April 12, and May 12, 1971. RHC, RBMLCU.

33. *New York Times*, May 16, 1971, pp. BR4, 22. See also "Carmichael's 'Molotov Cocktail,'" *Evening Star*, August 9, 1971, p. 23 in FBIKT 100–446080–NR, "Stokely Carmichael," September 16, 1971, p. 54.

34. Stokely Carmichael, "A Message From Stokely Carmichael In Guinea," *Black World*, July 1972, p. 25, SCLDS. *Oregonian*, June 16, 1972. SCLDS. *Afriscope*, July 1972. SCLDS.

35. Joseph, *Waiting 'Til the Midnight Hour*; Woodard, *A Nation Within a Nation*.

36. *New York Times*, May 14, 1972, p. 8.

37. FBIKT 100–446080–3152, "Stokely Carmichael," December 22, 1972, pp. 1–7.

38. *Baltimore Afro-American*, October 1972; *Washington Post*, October 13, 1972. SCLDS; *Washington Post*, October 18, 1972, p. 39; FBIKT 100–446080–3083, "Stokely Carmichael," October 30, 1972, p. 15.

39. *Washington Post*, October 25, 1972; *Washington Evening Star*, October 31, 1972; "Statement by Stokely Carmichael on Harambee Controversy," October 24, 1972. SCLDS; FBIKT 100–446080–3069, "Stokely Carmichael," Teletype, October 13, 1972, pp. 1–4; FBIKT 100–446080–3070, "Stokely Carmichael," Teletype, October 15, 1972, pp. 1–2; FBIKT 100–446080–3103, "Stokely Carmichael," November 8, 1972, pp. 19–21, *Howard Hilltop*, October 20, 1972. *Memphis Commercial Appeal*, November 16, 1972; *Los Angeles Times*, November 24, 1972.

40. *Washington Post*, November 5, 1972, pp. A1, A10.

41. *San Jose Mercury News*, December 3, 1972. SCLDS; *Washington Post*, November 5, 1972, p. 10; *New York Times*, November 14, 1972, p. 22; *Washington Post*, November 15, 1972, pp. D1, 3; *New York Times*, November 16, 1972, p. 54; *Washington Post*, November 23, 1972, B1–2; FBIKT 100–446080–3190, "Stokely Carmichael," February 14, 1973, pp. 4–5; Theoharis, *The Rebellious Life of Mrs. Rosa Parks*, pp. 38–42. Katherine Charron has written the definitive account of Clark's life: *Freedom's Teacher: The Life of Septima Clark* (Chapel Hill: University of North Carolina Press, 2009).

42. *San Francisco Chronicle*, January 27, 1973; *San Jose Mercury*, February 14, 1973. SCLDS. *San Jose News*, February 22, 1973. SCLDS.

43. *New York Times*, January 26, 1973, p. 77. *Chicago Daily Defender*, January 30, 1970, p. 2; *Call and Post*, February 10, 1972, p. 5.

44. *Boston Globe*, February 13, 1973, p. 3.

45. *Baltimore Afro-American*, March 10, 1973, p. 6; *Chicago Daily Defender*, January 1973, p. 2; *New York Times*, April 1, 1973, p. 6E.

46. FBIKT 100–446080–NR, "Stokely Carmichael," Teletype, March 6, 1973, pp. 1–2. "Mr. Carmichael," *The Star*, March 19, 1973, p. 6. SCLDS. *The Daily Gleaner*, March 15, 1973, in FBIKT 100–446080–3255: "Our Man in Kingston," *Time*, August 6, 1973.

47. FBIKT 100–446080–3324, "Stokely Carmichael," Teletype, May 6, 1973; FBIKT 100–446080–3288, "Stokely Carmichael," Teletype, April 17, 1973, pp. 1–5. *Voice of Uganda*, June 7, 18, and 19, 1973, p. 6. SCLDS; FBIKT 100–446080–3343, "Stokely Carmichael Given Ugandan Citizenship," State Department File, June 19, 1973, pp. 1–3.

48. *Seattle Post-Intelligencer*, October 4, 1973; *University of Washington Daily*, October 5, 1973. SCLDS.

49. FBIKT 100–446080–3523, "Stokely Carmichael," Teletype, October 29, 1973, p. 2. FBIKT 100–446080–3520, "Stokely Carmichael," October 23, 1973; FBIKT 100–446080–3532, "Stokely Carmichael," Teletype, October 25, 1973, pp. 1–3; FBIKT 100–446080–3517, "Stokely Carmichael," Teletype, October 29, 1973, pp. 1–4.

50. FBIKT 100–446080–3661, "Visit of Stokely Carmichael," March 1, 1974, pp. 1–2; FBIKT 100–446080–NR, "Stokely Carmichael," March 24, 1974; FBIKT 100–446080–3709, "Stokely Carmichael," Teletype, May 5, 1974, pp. 1–2.

51. FBIKT 100–446080–3661, "Visit of Stokely Carmichael," March 1, 1974, pp. 1–2; FBIKT 100–446080–NR, "Stokely Carmichael," March 24, 1974; FBIKT 100–446080–3709, "Stokely Carmichael," Teletype, May 5, 1974, pp. 1–2.

52. Joseph, *Waiting 'Til the Midnight Hour*, pp. 288–295; Woodard, *A Nation Within a Nation*; Haki Madhubuti, *Enemies: The Clash of Races* (Chicago: Third World Press, 1978);

Adolph Reed, *Stirrings in the Jug: Black Politics in the Post-Segregation Era* (Minneapolis: University of Minnesota Press, 1999) and ed., *Race, Politics, and Culture: Critical Essays on the Radicalism of the 1960s* (New York: Greenwood Press, 1986); Cedric Johnson, *From Revolutionaries to Race Leaders* (Minneapolis: University of Minnesota Press, 2007).

53. FBIKT 100–446080–3854, "Stokely Carmichael," October 7, 1974, p. 17, Transcript of September 5, 1974, interview. FBIKT 100–446080–3842, "Stokely Carmichael," Teletype, September 5, 1974, pp. 1–5. FBIKT 100–446080–3854, "Stokely Carmichael," October 7, 1974, p. 17, Transcript of September 5, 1974, interview.

54. Quotes from FBIKT 100–446080–3854, "Stokely Carmichael," October 7, 1974, p. 22; Transcript of September 5, 1974, interview; Marable, *Malcolm X*, pp. 111–112. FBIKT 100–446080–3924, "Stokely Carmichael," December 3, 1974, p. 2; FBIKT 100–446080–NR, "Stokely Carmichael," November 12, 1974, pp. 1–10.

55. *Bay State Banner*, March 3, 1977, pp. 1, 11; *Tri-State Defender*, March 19, 1977, p. 1. SCLDS; FBIKT 100–446080–4078, "Stokely Carmichael," November 7, 1975, pp. 1–6; FBIKT 100–446080–4082, "Stokely Carmichael," Teletype, November 15, 1975, pp. 1–3; FBIKT 100–446080–4091, "Stokely Carmichael," January 27, 1976.

56. *Washington Post*, February 24, 1975, p. C1; *Los Angeles Times*, May 17, 1976, p. F6; Joseph, *Waiting 'Til the Midnight Hour*. FBIKT 100–446080–4057, "Stokely Carmichael," June 2, 1975, Transcript of WHUR Interview Broadcast on May 5–7, 1975, p. 20.

57. FBIKT 100–446080–4054, "Stokely Carmichael," July 18, 1975, pp. 1–13; FBIKT 100–446080–4083, "Stokely Carmichael," Teletype, November 25, 1975, pp. 1–2; FBIKT 100–446080–4084, "Stokely Carmichael," November 14, 1975, pp. 1–2; FBIKT 100–446080–4091, "Stokely Carmichael," January 27, 1976, pp. 1–6; FBIKT 100–446080–4103, "Stokely Carmichael," Teletype, March 15, 1976, pp. 1–2.

58. FBIKT 100–446080–4202, "Stokely Carmichael: All-African People's Revolutionary Party (AAPRP)," July 29, 1976, p. 15. FBIKT 100–446080–4177, "Stokely Carmichael," May 21, 1976, pp. 1–2; Jeffries, *Bloody Lowndes*, pp. 244–245.

59. *New York Amsterdam News*, May 1, 1976, p. 8; *Los Angeles Times*, May 4, 1976, p. 7 and May 17, 1976, pp. F1, 5, 6; FBIKT 100–0446080–4091, "Stokely Carmichael," January 27, 1976, p. 16; FBIKT 100–446080–4114, "Stokely Carmichael," April 1, 1976, pp. 1–4. *New York Times*, October 7, 1976, p. 17; *Los Angeles Sentinel*, October 14, 1976, p. 3.

60. *Washington Post*, March 21, 1977, p. 2; *New York Amsterdam News*, March 26, 1977, p. B6.

61. *Bay State Banner*, July 7, 1977, p. 1. SCLDS; *Philadelphia Tribune*, May 3, 1977, p. 10; *Washington Post*, May 29, 1977, p. 53.

62. Makeba, *Makeba*, p. 204. *Washington Post*, May 14, 1978, pp. B1, 7; *Philadelphia Tribune*, March 21, 1978, p. 1; *Los Angeles Times*, December 27, 1978, p. B2; *Washington Post*, December 28, 1978, p. 20.

63. *Washington Post*, January 25, 1979, p. C9.

64. Harry S. Jaffe and Tom Sherwood, *Dream City: Race, Power, and the Decline of Washington, D.C.* (New York: Simon & Schuster, 1994), pp. 125–268.

65. *New York Amsterdam News*, December 20, 1980, p. 4; Carmichael with Thelwell, *Ready for Revolution*, pp. 673–674.

66. Harry Belafonte, *My Song: A Memoir* (New York: Alfred A. Knopf, 2011), p. 341.

67. Ibid., p. 340.

68. Carmichael with Thelwell, *Ready for Revolution*, p. 712. *Philadelphia Tribune*, March 6, 1984, p. 2; *New York Amsterdam News*, November 6, 1982, p. 32.

69. *New York Times*, April 12, 1984, p. 4.

70. Carmichael with Thelwell, *Ready for Revolution*, pp. 720, 721.

71. "Arrest: Case of Kwame Shaka Ture AKA Stokely Carmichael," August 19, 1986, pp. 1–2, State Dept. Records, Case: 200701907.

72. "Arrest: Case of Kwame Shaka Ture AKA Stokely Carmichael," August 1986, State Department Records, Case ID: 200701907 and "Arrest and Release of Kwame Shaka Ture AKA Stokely Carmichael," August 1986, pp. 1–3. Carmichael with Thelwell, *Ready for Revolution*, pp. 724–727; *Chicago Tribune*, August 18, 1986, p. 6; *New York Times*, August 19, 1986, p. 11; *Chicago Tribune*, August 20, 1986, p. 6; "Arrest: Case of Kwame Shaka Ture AKA Stokely Carmichael," August 1986, State Department Records, Case ID: 200701907 and "Arrest and Release of Kwame Shaka Ture AKA Stokely Carmichael," August 1986, pp. 1–3.

73. Kwame Ture and Charles Hamilton, *Black Power: The Politics of Liberation* (New York: Vintage, 1992), pp. 187–199.

74. *New York Times*, March 1, 1996, p. B4; *New York Amsterdam News*, March 9, 1996, p. 3.

75. Charlie Cobb, "Revolution: From Stokely Carmichael to Kwame Ture," *The Black Scholar*, vol. 27, no. 3–4 (Fall/Winter 1997), p. 33.

76. Ibid., pp. 728–746.

77. Holsaert et al., eds., *Hands on the Freedom Plow*, p. 15.

78. *New York Beacon*, July 3, 1996, p. 9. *Michigan Citizen*, June 29, 1996, p. A1.

79. Carmichael with Thelwell, *Ready for Revolution*, pp. 764–767. *New York Amsterdam News*, August 17, 1996, p. 24.

80. Carmichael with Thelwell, *Ready for Revolution*, p. 738. Cobb, "Revolution: From Stokely Carmichael to Kwame Ture," p. 33.

81. Carmichael with Thelwell, *Ready for Revolution*, pp. 752–756. Wilkerson, "Soul Survivor," p. 184.

82. Carmichael with Thelwell, *Ready for Revolution*, pp. 777–778; *Jacksonville Free Press*, April 29, 1998, p. 2; *Washington Informer*, April 22, 1998, p. 16.

83. *New York Voice, Inc., Harlem U.S.A.*, July 15, 1998, p. 9.

84. *The Los Angeles Sentinel*, November 26, 1998, p. A1.

85. American Embassy Conakry to Secretary of State, "Death Comes for the Arch-Activist: Stokely Carmichael/Kwame Ture Eulogized and Laid to Rest in Guinea," November 1998, pp. 1–6, State Department Records, Case: 200701907; "State Funeral for Kwame Ture," November 20, 1998.

Sources and Bibliography

Libraries and Collections Consulted

FRANCE
  National Library of France (BN F)
  New York Herald Tribune Archives
  Le Monde Archives
  Voix Ouvrière Files
  Personal Archives of Daniel Guérin, BDIC

SWEDEN
  Swedish Television Archives

UNITED KINGDOM
  British Library
  Daily Express Archive
  Stokely Carmichael Recordings, Compact Disk Collections
  North Kensington Community Archive

UNITED STATES

ATHENS, GEORGIA
  Walter J. Brown Media Archives & Peabody Awards Collection, University of Georgia, Athens, Georgia: WHWH, Princeton, New Jersey, "The Mississippi Negro"

ATLANTA, GEORGIA
  Auburn Avenue Research Library on African-American Culture and History,
  Atlanta–Fulton Public Library
  Andrew Young Papers

Annie McPheeters Papers
Atlanta University Research Center
Emory University Manuscript, Archives, and Rare Book Library
The King Center for Nonviolent Social Change and Archives
Ben Brown Papers
Civil Rights Film Collection
Civil Rights Oral History Collection
Charlotte News Archive
James Forman Collection
Julian Bond Papers
National Lawyers Guild Records
Papers of the Congress of Racial Equality
Papers of Fred W. Shuttlesworth
Papers of Martin Luther King Jr.
Records of the Mississippi Freedom Democratic Party
Records of the United States National Student Association Southern
    Project
Septima P. Clark Papers
Southern Christian Leadership Conference Records

AUSTIN, TEXAS
Lyndon B. Johnson Library and Museum
Lyndon B. Johnson Papers
Kerner Commission
Federal Records
Recordings of Telephone Conversations and Meetings WH6607.02,
    July 15, 1966
Recordings of Telephone Conversations and Meetings WH6607.03,
    July 22–26, 1966
Recordings of Telephone Conversations and Meetings WH6608.08,
    August 5, 1966

BOSTON, MASSACHUSETTS
John F. Kennedy Presidential Library and Museum
Berl I. Bernhard Personal Papers
John F. Kennedy Presidential Papers
Lee C. White Papers
Robert F. Kennedy Papers

CAMBRIDGE, MASSACHUSETTS
Schlesinger Library, Radcliffe Institute for Advanced Study, Harvard
University

CHAPEL HILL, NORTH CAROLINA
Interview with Septima Poinsette Clark, July 30, 1976, Southern Oral
History Program Collection, University Library, University of North
Carolina at Chapel Hill
The University of North Carolina at Chapel Hill
Taylor Branch Collection in the Southern Historical Collection, Manu-
scripts Department, Wilson Library

CHARLOTTESVILLE, VIRGINIA
University of Virginia, Harry F. Byrd Jr. Papers

CHICAGO, ILLINOIS
Chicago History Museum
The Studs Terkel/WMFT Archives
Department of Rights and Reproductions, Recordings T1860 A, T1860
B, and T1860 C
Chicago State University Archives
University of Illinois–Chicago, Special Collections–Daley Library: Student
Nonviolent Coordinating Committee Collection
Underground Newspaper Collection, Center for Research Libraries at
the Chicago Public Library

EVANSTON, ILLINOIS
The Melville J. Herskovits Library of African Studies, Northwestern
University

GREENSBORO, NORTH CAROLINA
University of North Carolina at Greensboro, Benjamin Smith
Papers

HATTIESBURG, MISSISSIPPI
The University of Southern Mississippi

Hayneville, Alabama
Hayneville Public Library

Jackson, Mississippi
Tougaloo College Civil Rights Collections, Mississippi Department of
    Archives and History
Aaron Henry Papers, 1953–1997
Fannie Lou Townsend Hamer Collection, 1964–2001
Joan Harris Trumpauer Civil Rights Scrapbooks, 1961–1964
Joyce Ann Ladner Collections, 1931–2003
Mississippi Freedom Democratic Party Collection, ca. 1963–1971
Jackson State University
Mississippi Sovereignty Commission, Mississippi Department of Ar-
    chives and History

Los Angeles, California
Los Angeles Public Library
Los Angeles Times (Microfilm)
Black Panther Party Collection
KPFA, Pacifica Radio Archives
University of California, Los Angeles
Special Collections, Charles E. Young Library

Madison, Wisconsin
Wisconsin Historical Society Archives
Carl and Anne Braden Papers
Michael Lipsky and David J. Olsen Papers
Stokely Carmichael at Open Meeting (1966), Harvard University,
    Cambridge, MA
Stokely Carmichael Speech, Unitarian Universality Fellowship, Colum-
    bus, OH

Medford, Massachusetts
Tufts University Digital Collections and Archives

Memphis, Tennessee
Mississippi Valley Collection, University of Memphis, University
    Library

MONTGOMERY, ALABAMA
Alabama State University
Mobile Register, Alabama Department of Archives and History

NASHVILLE, TENNESSEE
Metro Nashville Archives
Vanderbilt University Archives

NEW HAVEN, CONNECTICUT
Robert Penn Warren Papers, Beinecke Rare Book and Manuscript
Library, Yale University
Afro-American Cultural Center at Yale, Yale University

NEW YORK CITY
Random House Papers, Columbia University Rare Book & Manuscript
Library
Schomburg Center for Research in Black Culture, New York Public Library
American Society of African Culture Papers
August Meier Papers
Black Panther Party—FBI File
Catherine Clarke Papers
Ella Baker Papers
IFCO Papers
Institute for the Black World Papers
James Baldwin Papers
John Henrik Clarke Papers
Julian Mayfield Papers
Larry Neal Papers
Lorraine Hansberry Papers
The Militant
National Alliance Against Racist and Political Repression Papers
Otis Turner Papers
Preston Wilcox Papers
Robert S. Browne Papers
St. Claire Drake Papers
Museum of Radio, Film, and Television Archives
Carmichael–Sally Belfrage Correspondence, Tamiment Library, Elmer
Bobst Library at New York University

OXFORD, MISSISSIPPI
The Center for the Study of Southern Culture, University of Mississippi

PALO ALTO, CALIFORNIA
Stanford University
Carmichael and Ginsburg Dialectics of Liberation Confab
Clayborne Carson Collection, Martin Luther King, Jr. Center
New Left Collection, Hoover Institute
Stokely Carmichael–Lorna D. Smith Collection (SCLDS), Green Library
Newton Foundation Papers (NFP), Green Library

PRINCETON, NEW JERSEY
Collections of the Seeley G. Mudd Manuscript Library, Princeton
    University
ACLU Records
WHWH Records
Stokely Carmichael v. City of Selma
"The Future Looks Black: A Report on the Debate Between Stokely
    Carmichael and Bayard Rustin"

PROVIDENCE, RHODE ISLAND
Brown University
The John Hay Library
Hall-Hoag Collection

RALEIGH, NORTH CAROLINA
North Carolina State University Archives Photograph Collection

SAN FRANCISCO, CALIFORNIA
San Francisco State University: Bay Area Television Archives

ST. LOUIS, MISSOURI
Ernest Calloway Papers, Western Historical Manuscript Collection,
    University
of Missouri–St. Louis

STATE COLLEGE, PENNSYLVANIA
Jack Rabin Photo Collection, Penn State University

Syracuse, New York
    Charles Brooks Papers, Syracuse University

Tuskegee, Alabama
    Tuskegee University Archives and Museums
    Records of the *Southern Courier*
    Stokely Carmichael v. Ivan Allen Jr.

Washington, DC
    Justice Department
    Library of Congress
    Congress of Racial Equality Papers
    James Forman Papers
    National Association for the Advancement of Colored People Papers
    Southern Christian Leadership Conference Papers
    National Archives
    RG 59/General Records of the Department of State, Central Foreign
        Policy Files, 1967–1969, Political & Defense, File No. POL 23–8;
        1/1/68, Box: 2606
    Havana Domestic Radio/TV Service (CMQ TV). Statement from Stokely
        Carmichael from the Havana Libre Hotel. "(His Voice, Recorded and
        Filmed)," August 2, 1967
    Howard University, Ralph J. Bunche Oral History Collection, Moorland–
        Spingarn Research Center
    Recordings of Telephone Conversations and Meetings WH6612.15, De-
        cember 31, 1966
    University of Texas, Gloria Anzaldúa Papers, 1942–2004

FBI Files

    FBIKT   File No. 100–446080 (Kwame Ture/Stokely Carmichael)

    FBIBN   File No. 100–448006 (Black Nationalist–Hate Groups)
    FBIEC   File No. 100-HQ-447251 (Eldridge Cleaver)
    FBIHPN   File No. 92-HQ-13682/14778 (Huey Percy Newton)
    FBISPAC   File No. 157-HQ-24813 (Sixth Pan-African Congress, Tan-
        zania, 1974)
    FBISNCC   File No. 100–147963 (Student Non-Violent Coordinating
        Committee)

FBIRFK File No. 77–51387 (Robert F. Kennedy)
FBIBNPC File No. 157–5215 (Black National Political Convention, 1972)
FBIALSC File No. 157–25073 (African Liberation Support Committee)
FBIMX File No. 100–399321 (Malcolm X)

Films and Television

CBS Reports: "Black Power, White Backlash," September 27, 1966
CBS News Special Report: "The March in Mississippi," June 26, 1966
NBC News Special: "After Civil Rights—Black Power," June 13, 1967
The Black Power Mixtape, 2011
Eyes on the Prize, PBS, 1987, 1990

Recordings

David Eaton Show, 1968
Department of Rights and Reproductions, Recording T1860 A-C
Eldridge Cleaver FBI Recordings
Havana Domestic Radio/TV Service (CMQ TV). Statement from Stokely Carmichael from the Havana Libre Hotel. "(His Voice, Recorded and Filmed)," August 2, 1967
International Dialectics of Liberation Congress, London, July 27, 1967, Beats 39, no. 7, Rare Book Collection, University of North Carolina at Chapel Hill
Kwame Ture, SNCC Press Conference, April 5, 1968
Public Meeting and Discussion [at the Dialectics of Liberation Congress], London, July 1967, Beats 39, no. 13, Rare Book Collection, University of North Carolina at Chapel Hill
Public Meeting and Discussion [at the International Dialectics of Liberation Congress], London, July 27, 1967, Beats 39, no. 14, Rare Book Collection, University of North Carolina at Chapel Hill
Recordings of Conversations and Meetings WH6607.02, July 15, 1966, WH6607.03, July 22–26, 1966, WH6608.08, August 5, 1966, WH6612.15, December 31, 1966
Stokely Carmichael at Open Meeting (1966), Harvard University, Cambridge, MA

Stokely Carmichael Speech, Unitarian Universality Fellowship, Columbus, OH

WHWH, Princeton, New Jersey, "The Mississippi Negro"

Pacifica Radio Archive, KPFA, Los Angeles

PRA No. BB0720: Stokely Carmichael Interview, February 5, 1966

PRA No. BB1709: Stokely Carmichael Berkeley Black Power Speech, 1966

PRA No. BB4532: Stokely Carmichael and H. Rap Brown, February 21, 1968

PRA No. BB4525: Black Power Rally, February 27, 1968

PRA No. BB3142: Salute to Ella Baker, April 24, 1968

PRA No. BB1781: Stokely Carmichael, August 25, 1968

PRA No. BC0153: Stokely Carmichael at Whittier College, 1971

PRA No. BC2142: Stokely Carmichael On *Nommo*, February 22, 1975

PRA No. AZ0478: Kwame Ture at Berkeley, May 5, 1980

Newspapers/Magazines/Journals

Africa and the World

African World (SOBU newsletter)

Afriscope (Paris)

American Bar Association Journal

Atlanta Constitution

Atlanta Daily World

The Atlantic

Baltimore Afro-American

The Bay State Banner

Berkeley Barb

Berkeley Daily Gazette

Black Politics (Berkeley, California)

Black Scholar

Black World (*Negro Digest*)

Boston Globe

The Call and Post (Cleveland, Ohio)

Chicago American

Chicago Daily News

Chicago Defender

Chicago Sun-Times

Chicago Tribune

The Christian Science Monitor

Clarion-Ledger (Jackson, Mississippi)

Dallas Times Herald

Durham Morning Herald

Ebony

The Egyptian Gazette

El-Moudjahid (Algeria)

Esquire

Essence

Freedomways

Greensboro Daily News

Greensboro Daily Times

Greensboro Record

Harper's Magazine

Harvard Crimson

Hawaii Military Press

The Hilltop (Howard University)

Honolulu Advertiser

I.F. Stone's Weekly

International Herald Tribune

Jackson Daily News

Jacksonville Free Press

Jet

Jeune Afrique (Paris, France)

Journal Herald (Dayton, Ohio)

Le Monde

Liberator

London Observer

London Observer Review

London Tribune

Los Angeles Free Press

Los Angeles Herald-Examiner

Los Angeles Sentinel

Los Angeles Times

The Massachusetts Review

Match (Paris, France)

Memphis Commercial Appeal

Michigan Chronicle

Michigan Citizen

The Militant

Mississippi Independent Community Newspaper

Mobile Register

Montreal Gazette

The Movement (SNCC newspaper)

Muhammad Speaks

Nashville Banner

Nashville Tennessean

National Guardian

The Nationalist (Tanzania)

Negro Digest (Chicago)

New Haven Register

New Journal and Guide (Norfolk, Virginia)

New Pittsburgh Courier

The New Republic

New South

Newsweek

New York Amsterdam News

New York Beacon

New York Daily News

New York Herald Tribune

New York Post

The New York Review of Books

The New York Times

The New York Times Magazine

Oakland Tribune

Omaha World Herald

The Oregonian

Palo Alto Times

Peace and Freedom News (California)

Philadelphia Evening Bulletin
Philadelphia Tribune
Pittsburgh Courier
Ramparts
Rocky Mountain News (Denver, Colorado)
San Francisco Chronicle
San Francisco Examiner-Chronicle
San Jose Mercury News
The Saturday Evening Post
Seattle Post-Intelligencer
Sepia (Fort Worth, Texas)
Southern Courier (Montgomery, Alabama)
The Star (Jamaica)
St. Louis Post-Dispatch
The Student Voice (SNCC newspaper)
The Sunday Times (London)

Tampa Times
Tennessee Historical Quarterly
Time
The Times (London)
The Times of India
Tri-State Defender (Memphis, Tennessee)
Tufts Daily
Tufts Observer
University of Washington Daily
U.S. News and World Report
Village Voice
Voice of Uganda
The Wall Street Journal
Washington Afro-American
Washington Evening Star
Washington Informer
The Washington Post
Yale Daily News

Stokely Carmichael Interviews

Stokely Carmichael Interviewed by Terrance Cannon, February 5, 1966, Pacifica Radio Archives, North Hollywood, California

Stokely Carmichael Interview in *Révolution Africaine*, September 11, 1967, National Archives, Washington, DC

Stokely Carmichael Interview by David Du Bois, September 19, 1967, Schlesinger Library, Radcliffe Institute, Harvard University, Cambridge, Massachusetts

Stokely Carmichael Interview, May 5, 1986, Manuscript, Archives, and Rare Book Library, Emory University, Atlanta, Georgia

Stokely Carmichael Interview, November 7, 1988, Southern Regional Council, Atlanta, Georgia

Stokely Carmichael Interview by Clayborne Carson, 1973, Stanford University, Palo Alto, California

Oral Histories and Interviews

Baraka, Amiri. Telephone interview. Newark, New Jersey. February 3, 2000. Audiotape. Telephone interview. Newark, New Jersey. July 7, 2004. Audiotape.

Brook, Owen. Telephone interview. October 13, 2010. Audiotape.

Brown, Bob. Telephone interview. October 15, 2010. Audiotape.

Brown, Ed. Telephone interview. January 9, 2010. Audiotape.

Cannon, Terry. Telephone interview. Two interviews, no date. Audiotape.

Carson, Clayborne. Telephone interview. September 16, 2010. Audiotape.

Cleaver, Kathleen. Telephone interview. December 18, 2003. Audiotape.

Cobb, Charlie. Telephone interview. Stony Brook, New York. December 17, 2002. Audiotape. Telephone interview. Stony Brook, New York. December 20, 2002. Audiotape.

Cox, Courtland. Telephone interview. August 19, 2008. Audiotape.

Curry, Connie. Telephone interview. October 15, 2010. Audiotape.

Donaldson, Ivanhoe. Telephone interview. October 8, 2010. Audiotape.

Fuller, Howard. Telephone interview. November 19, 2002. Audiotape. Telephone interview. July 1, 2003. Audiotape.

Garrett, James. Telephone interview. March 19, 2003. Audiotape. Telephone interview. April 2, 2003. Audiotape. Telephone interview. April 4, 2003. Audiotape. Telephone interview. April 27, 2003. Audiotape. Telephone interview. May 14, 2003. Audiotape. Oakland, California. June 6, 2004. Audiotape.

Gavin, Joanne. Telephone interview. July 14, 2009. Audiotape.

Gregory, Robin. Audiotape. Telephone interview. December 13, 2009. Audiotape.

Guyot, Lawrence. Telephone interview. February 6, 2010. Audiotape.

Holt, Thomas. Telephone interview. July 20, 2010. Audiotape.

Hutchings, Phil. Telephone interview. September 8, 2010. Audiotape.

Jenkins, Timothy. Telephone interview. August 31, 2010. Audiotape.

Karro, Betty-Chia. Telephone interview. January 1, 2010. Audiotape.

King, Mary. Telephone interview. November 30, 2008. Audiotape.

Martínez, Elizabeth. Telephone interview. March 6, 2009. Audiotape.

Minor, Ethel. Telephone interview. November 21, 2010. Audiotape.

Moses, Robert. Telephone interview. August 10, 2009. Audiotape.

Muhammad, Curtis. Telephone interview. October 14, 2010. Audiotape.

Mulholland, Joan. Telephone interview. February 5, 2010. Audiotape.

Patel, Penny. Telephone interview. June 15, 2010. Audiotape.

Richardson, Judy. Telephone interview. Stony Brook, New York. April 19, 2003. Audiotape.

Sales, Ruby. Telephone interview. July 3, 2009. Audiotape.

Sanchez, Sonia. Telephone interview. Stony Brook, New York. December 12, 2002. Audiotape. Telephone interview. Stony Brook, New York. December 13–18, 2002. Audiotape. Telephone interview. Stony Brook, New York. January 28, 2003. Audiotape. Telephone interview. Stony Brook, New York. August 25, 2003. Audiotape.

Sellers, Cleveland. Telephone interview. Stony Brook, New York. March 27, 2003. Audiotape. Telephone interview. December 21, 2009. Audiotape. Telephone interview. December 30, 2009. Audiotape.

Stoller, Nancy. Telephone interview. May 5, 2011. Audiotape.

Thelwell, Mike. Telephone interview. Amherst, Massachusetts. December 16, 1999. Audiotape Telephone interview. November 16, 2002. Audiotape. Telephone interview. August 24, 2010. Audiotape.

Thomas, Hank. Telephone interview. October 16, 2010. Audiotape.

Tillinghast, Muriel. Telephone interview. July 13, 2009. Audiotape.

Ware, George. Telephone interview. August 19, 2009. Audiotape.

Wilkins, Roger. Telephone interview. June 30, 2008. Audiotape.

Zinn, Howard. Telephone interview. July 27, 2009. Audiotape.

Select Books

Adamolekun, 'Ladipo. *Sékou Touré's Guinea: An Experiment in Nation Building*. London: Methuen, 1976.

Ali, Tariq. *Street-Fighting Years: An Autobiography of the Sixties*. London: Verso, 2005.

Anderson, Jervis. *Bayard Rustin: Troubles I've Seen*. New York: Harper Collins, 1997.

Baldwin, James. *The Fire Next Time*. New York: Dell Books, 1964.

————. *No Name in the Street*. New York: Dell Books, 1972.

Baraka, Amiri. *African Congress: A Documentary of the First Modern Pan-African Congress*. New York: William Morrow, 1972.

_____. *The Autobiography of LeRoi Jones.* New York: Lawrence Hill Books, 1997.

Bass, Amy. *Not the Triumph but the Struggle: The 1968 Olympics and the Making of the Black Athlete.* Minneapolis: University of Minnesota Press, 2002.

Belfrage, Sally. *Freedom Summer.* Charlottesville: University of Virginia Press, 1990.

Biondi, Martha. *To Stand and Fight: The Struggle for Civil Rights in Postwar New York City.* Cambridge, MA: Harvard University Press, 2003.

Blake, John. *Children of the Movement.* Chicago: Lawrence Hill Books, 2004.

Bloom, Josh, and Waldo E. Martin Jr. *Black Against Empire: The History and Politics of the Black Panther Party.* Berkeley: University of California Press, 2013.

Boyle, Kevin. *Arc of Justice: A Saga of Race, Civil Rights, and Murder in the Jazz Age.* New York: Henry Holt, 2004.

Branch, Taylor. *Parting the Waters: America in the King Years, 1954–1963.* New York, Touchstone, 1988.

_____. *Pillar of Fire: America in the King Years, 1963–1965.* New York: Simon & Schuster, 1998.

_____. *At Canaan's Edge: America in the King Years, 1965–1968.* New York: Simon & Schuster, 2006.

Brown, Scot. *Fighting for US: Maulana Karenga, the US Organization, and Black Cultural Nationalism.* New York: New York University Press, 2003.

Brown-Nagin, Tomiko. *Courage to Dissent: Atlanta and the Long History of the Civil Rights Movement.* New York: Oxford University Press, 2011.

Carmichael, Stokely. *Stokely Speaks: Black Power Back to Pan-Africanism.* New York: Vintage Books, 1971.

_____, and Charles V. Hamilton. *Black Power: The Politics of Liberation.* New York: Random House, 1967.

_____, with Michael Thelwell. *Ready for Revolution: The Life and Struggles of Stokely Carmichael (Kwame Ture).* New York: Scribner, 2003.

Carson, Clayborne. *In Struggle: SNCC and the Black Awakening of the 1960s.* Cambridge, MA: Harvard University Press, 1981.

_____. *Martin's Dream: My Journey and the Legacy of Martin Luther King Jr.* New York: Palgrave Macmillan, 2013.

Chafe, William. *Civilities and Civil Rights: Greensboro, North Carolina, and the Black Struggle for Freedom.* New York: Oxford University Press, 1981.

_____. *Never Stop Running: Allard Lowenstein and the Struggle to Save American Liberalism.* New York: Basic Books, 1995.

Cleaver, Kathleen, ed. *Target Zero: A Life in Writing by Eldridge Cleaver.* New York: Palgrave Macmillan, 2006.

D'Emilio, John. *Lost Prophet: The Life and Times of Bayard Rustin.* New York: Free Press, 2003.

Diamond, Andrew J. *Mean Streets: Chicago Youths and the Everyday Struggle for Empowerment in the Multiracial City, 1908–1969.* Berkeley: University of California Press, 2009.

Dittmer, John. *Local People: The Struggle for Civil Rights in Mississippi.* Champaign: University of Illinois Press, 1995.

Eagles, Charles. *Outside Agitator: Jon Daniels and the Civil Rights Movement in Alabama.* Chapel Hill: University of North Carolina Press, 1993.

Farmer, James. *Lay Bare the Heart: An Autobiography of the Civil Rights Movement.* New York: Arbor House, 1985.

Forman, James. *The Making of Black Revolutionaries.* Seattle: University of Washington Press, 1997.

Garrow, David J. *Bearing the Cross: Martin Luther King, Jr. and the Southern Christian Leadership Conference.* New York: Morrow, 1987.

Hampton, Henry, and Steve Fayer. *Voices of Freedom: An Oral History of the Civil Rights Movement from the 1950s Through the 1980s.* New York: Bantam reissue, 1991.

Hayden, Tom. *Reunion: A Memoir.* New York: Random House, 1988.

Jeffries, Hasan Kwame. *Bloody Lowndes: Civil Rights and Black Power in Alabama's Black Belt.* New York: New York University Press, 2009.

_____, ed. *The Black Power Movement: Rethinking the Civil Rights–Black Power Era.* New York: Routledge, 2006.

_____. *Waiting 'Til the Midnight Hour: A Narrative History of Black Power in America.* New York: Henry Holt and Company, 2006.

Joseph, Peniel E. *Dark Days, Bright Nights: From Black Power to Barack Obama.* New York: Basic Books, 2010.

Kelley, Robin. *Race Rebels: Culture, Politics, and the Black Working Class.* New York: The Free Press, 1994.

Kerner Commission. *Report of the National Advisory Commission on Civil Disorders.* New York: Bantam Books, 1968.

King, Martin Luther. *Where Do We Go from Here: Chaos or Community?* New York: Penguin Books, 1968.

King, Mary. *Freedom Song: A Personal History of the 1960s Civil Rights Movement.* New York: William Morrow, 1988.

Kurlansky, Mark. *1968: The Year that Rocked the World.* New York: Ballantine Books, 2004.

Lee, Chana Kai. *For Freedom's Sake: The Life of Fannie Lou Hamer.* Urbana: University of Illinois Press, 1999.

Lewis, Andrew B. *The Shadows of Youth: The Remarkable Journey of the Civil Rights Generation.* New York: Hill and Wang, 2009.

Lewis, David Levering. *W.E.B. Du Bois: The Fight for Equality and the American Century, 1919–1963.* New York: Henry Holt, 2000.

Lewis, John, with Michael D'Orso. *Walking with the Wind: A Memoir of the Movement.* New York: Simon & Schuster, 1998.

Marable, Manning. *Malcolm X: A Life of Reinvention.* New York: Viking, 2011.

Murch, Donna Jean. *Living for the City: Migration, Education, and the Rise of the Black Panther Party in Oakland, California.* Chapel Hill: University of North Carolina Press, 2010.

Newton, Huey P. *Revolutionary Suicide.* New York: Ballantine Books, 1974.

Oshinsky, David. *Worse Than Slavery: Parchman Farm and the Ordeal of Jim Crow Justice.* New York: Simon & Schuster, 1997.

Payne, Charles. *I've Got the Light of Freedom: The Organizing Tradition and the Mississippi Freedom Struggle.* Berkeley: University of California Press, 1995.

Ransby, Barbara. *Ella Baker and the Black Freedom Movement: A Radical Democratic Vision.* Chapel Hill: University of North Carolina Press, 2003.

Rhodes, Jane. *Framing the Panthers: The Spectacular Rise of a Black Power Icon.* New York: New Press, 2007.

Risen, Clay. *A Nation on Fire: America in the Wake of the King Assassination.* Hoboken: John Wiley & Sons, 2009.

_____. *Mobilizing the Masses: Gender, Ethnicity, and Class in the Nationalist Movement in Guinea, 1939–1957*. Portsmouth: Heinemann, 2005.

Schmidt, Elizabeth. *Cold War and Decolonization in Guinea, 1946–1958*. Athens: Ohio University Press, 2007.

Self, Robert. *American Babylon: Race and the Struggle for Postwar Oakland*. Princeton: Princeton University Press, 2003.

Sellers, Cleveland, with Robert Terrell. *The River of No Return: The Autobiography of a Black Militant and the Life and Death of SNCC*. Jackson: University of Mississippi Press, 1990.

Shukra, Kalbir. *The Changing Pattern of Black Politics in Britain*. London: Pluto Press, 1998.

Stauffer, John. *Giants: The Parallel Lives of Frederick Douglass and Abraham Lincoln*. New York: Twelve, 2008.

Sugrue, Thomas. *Sweet Land of Liberty: The Forgotten Struggle for Civil Rights in the North*. New York: Random House, 2008.

Theoharis, Jeanne. *The Rebellious Life of Mrs. Rosa Parks*. Boston: Beacon Press, 2013.

Tyson, Timothy B. *Radio Free Dixie: Robert F. Williams and the Roots of Black Power*. Chapel Hill: University of North Carolina Press, 1999.

Valk, Anne M. *Radical Sisters: Second-Wave Feminism and Black Liberation in Washington, D.C.* Chicago: University of Illinois Press, 2008.

Viorst, Milton. *Fire in the Streets: America in the 1960s*. New York: Simon & Schuster, 1979.

Woodard, Komozi. *A Nation Within a Nation*. Chapel Hill: University of North Carolina Press, 1999.

Zellner, Bob, with Constance Curry. *The Wrong Side of Murder Creek: A White Southerner in the Freedom Movement*. Montgomery: New South Books, 2008.

Zinn, Howard. "Changing People: Negro Civil Rights and the Colleges." *Black and White in American Culture: An Anthology from the Massachusetts Review*. Amherst: University of Massachusetts Press, 1971.

Stokely Carmichael–Authored Articles

Carmichael, Stokely. "We've Got Red Blood . . . and Heart." *The Hilltop*. October 6, 1961.

Carmichael, Stokely. "Shotguns in Mississippi." *The Hilltop*. September 20, 1963.

Carmichael, Stokely. "Demonstrators State Their Position on Rally; Ask Policy Clarification." *The Hilltop*. March 23, 1962.

Carmichael, Stokely. "We Shall Overcome." *The Hilltop*. December 14, 1962.

Carmichael, Stokely. "Who Is Qualified?" *The New Republic*. January 8, 1966.

Carmichael, Stokely. "A Letter From Jail." *The Sunday Ramparts*. October 2, 1966.

Carmichael, Stokely. "What We Want." *The New York Review of Books*. September 22, 1966.

Carmichael, Stokely. "Toward Black Liberation." *The Massachusetts Review*. vol. 7, no. 4, Autumn 1966.

Index